THE BEAUTY OF
CLOSED DOORS

How Detours, Delays, and Dead Ends Reveal the Purpose Behind Life's Interruptions

DUNAMIS DUPLESSIS

Editing, design, and distribution by Bublish

ISBN: 979-8899890-45-1 (eBook)
ISBN: 979-8899890-47-5 (paperback)
ISBN: 979-8899890-46-8 (hardcover)

TABLE OF CONTENTS

DEDICATION

To my father, Donald L. Duplessis, and my mother, Evelyn Duplessis, whose guidance and love as pastors, leaders, mentors, church planters, teachers, and community builders have profoundly shaped my life. Your unwavering dedication to our family and your relentless pursuit of serving others have instilled in me the values of hard work, integrity, and compassion. You have shown me the importance of faith and resilience in the face of challenges, and your example continues to inspire me every day. Your ability to balance family, ministry, and community outreach has left an indelible mark on my heart and mind, teaching me that true leadership is rooted in service and love.

My brother, Dan Duplessis, a beacon of strength and guidance, stands as an exemplar of dedication and love in his roles as a father, military leader, and mentor to both his family and peers. Dan, your unwavering commitment to your responsibilities and your selfless service to others reflect the highest ideals of integrity and courage. Your story, marked by acts of valor and deep compassion, is one I eagerly await in published form, ripe for the season it is meant to blossom. Your influence has been a guiding light in my own journey, showing me the power of perseverance and the importance of leading with both heart and mind.

Josh, your resilience in the face of trials, obstacles, and adversities over the last five years is nothing short of inspiring. Your journey speaks volumes of your strength, and I stand with you, knowing the tapestry God is weaving within you is far from complete. Your ability to rise above challenges and your unwavering faith in the midst of hardship have been a testament to your inner strength and character. Your story is a powerful reminder that every setback is a setup for a greater comeback, and I am proud to walk alongside you as you continue to grow and achieve.

Denisha Duplessis, my beloved wife, you are the prism through which the true spectrum of love is revealed. Your influence has deepened my capacity for romance, vision, self-belief, and the ability to perceive beyond the immediate, drawing me closer to the grand design of our lives together. Your unwavering support, your patience, and your love have been my anchor through life's storms. My love for you is boundless, a testament to the divine timing that brought us together. You have shown me the beauty of partnership, the strength found in unity, and the joy that comes from sharing a life built on mutual respect and unconditional love.

To Denise and Trinity, know that Papi's heart beats with love for you both. To Devin, Reggie, and all who played a part in the proposal on Prayer Mountain, my gratitude is immense. The journey from purchasing the engagement ring to the proposal was a chapter in our lives I will forever cherish. This book is a lifelong dedication to anyone who has endured seasons of repeatedly closed doors for the wrong reasons. I dedicate this work to every father who was discouraged, never overcoming the missed opportunities that failed to manifest into tangible freedom and fulfillment. It is also for the single mother who, post-divorce, felt that her status, age, and financial hardships would forever close doors to new relationships. I extend this dedication to every leader, author, parent, government worker, engineer, designer, professional athlete, lawyer, doctor, senator, teacher, dentist, nurse, investor, actor, singer, artist, active-duty soldier, and veteran who has experienced the true pain and frustration of what a real closed door feels like. This book aims to change the common perceptions of closed doors. Here, I seek to transform the notion of a closed door, imbuing it with value, purpose, strategy, and opportunity. In Chapter 2, I dismantle the typical association of closed doors with failure. This book will revolutionize your perspective on people, positions, businesses, cultures, and backgrounds. It delves into what truly happens when you explore what lies beyond those closed doors. Peace, joy, and privacy—all these await behind the closed door, along with the space to strategize your next move. As you navigate life, try not to focus solely on the "goal." Instead, concentrate on the system behind that goal. The true advantage lies in this system—the way your strategy functions and the value it brings to those around you.

*

Special Thanks:

This book was brought to life through the editorial expertise of Tracey L. Smith, whose keen eye, dedication, and attention to detail helped shape every chapter with excellence. I'm truly grateful for her work and her heart for helping authors—both local and global—share their stories with the world.

INTRODUCTION

There's no better way to start this book than by recognizing that a closed door was actually a blessing in disguise. Consider all the doors that have closed in your life for the right reasons. Take, for example, the door that closed on a broken marriage, a necessary end to prevent physical abuse and potentially save a life. Closed doors speak volumes on many levels. The inspiration for the title of this book came from a TikTok post that shifted my perspective. In that post, I remarked, "Most people get excited about an open door; it's easy to be fascinated by what's immediately in front of us. But the truth is, you need to be thanking God for the closed door."

My background is in full-time ministry as a pastor and influencer, but I intentionally did not want this book to be overtly churchy or biblical because I aimed to step out of my usual comfort zone. One of my all-time favorite quotes, which always gives me goosebumps, is from Bruce Lee. He said with great conviction, "Be like water making its way through cracks. Do not be assertive, but adjust to the object, and you shall find a way around or through it. If nothing within you stays rigid, outward things will disclose themselves. Empty your mind, be formless, shapeless, like water. If you put water into a cup, it becomes the cup; you put water into a bottle, and it becomes the bottle; you put it in a teapot, it becomes the teapot. Now, water can flow or it can crash. Be water, my friend." This profound insight was a significant inspiration for this book.

I began to envision myself as soda in a glass bottle, tightly capped. The closed cap represents the closed doors in my life that have made me stronger and infused my content with potency. The glass bottle symbolizes the transparency I strive for despite the obstacles and external factors beyond my control. The soda represents the necessity to shake things up internally to deliver the value of this book to millions around the world who feel the same way I do about closed doors.

Closed doors often lead to frustration because they make us feel helpless, overlooked, hurt, and undervalued when things don't go as planned. So, what do you do when life continually presents the same closed door, leaving you numb and irritated with life itself? This book aims to unpack the benefits and solutions that emerge when doors close.

The answer lies not in the obstacles themselves, but in how we respond to them. This book is an invitation to view each closed door, not as a blockade, but as a redirection—a chance to pivot towards something even greater. It's about learning to see every closure as an opportunity to reflect, reassess, and reinvent oneself. Here, you will find the tools and insights necessary to transform these challenging moments into catalysts for personal growth and innovation. We will explore the concept of resilience, the art of bouncing back stronger than ever after a setback. We'll discover how resilience isn't inherent, but cultivated through experiences and mindful reflection. We'll delve into strategies that help turn closed doors into open windows, letting in fresh air and new perspectives.

Moreover, this journey through closed doors will teach us about patience and timing. Often, what seems to be a denial is simply a delay—a necessary pause that ensures we are better prepared when we step through the next door than we ever could have imagined. We will learn to recognize the signs that guide us toward our true paths, understanding that sometimes the best route is the one we hadn't initially considered.

Each chapter of this book is designed to equip you with the mindset to embrace closed doors with courage and optimism. You will not only understand the 'why' behind the closed doors you've encountered, but also how to harness the hidden potential they hold. You will see how these experiences have shaped you into a more resilient, insightful, and compassionate individual. Prepare to journey through stories of those who have turned their deepest disappointments into their greatest victories. Their experiences are woven with practical advice and actionable steps that you can apply to your own situations, ensuring that the next time a door closes, you'll be ready to find the open window waiting just around the corner. So, let us begin by stepping back from the closed doors and viewing them from a new vantage point. Let's learn, grow, and open ourselves to the infinite possibilities that await when we choose to see every end as a new beginning.

As we stand on the brink of embarking on this transformative journey together, it's crucial to shift our perspective. What often appears as a setback or closed door is not merely a hindrance, but a directive pointing us toward new, unexplored paths. This book is crafted to change the way we perceive these apparent endings, revealing them as opportunities for new beginnings and exciting adventures. In this introduction, we prepare to rethink our approach to life's challenges, viewing them not as barriers, but as invitations to explore, learn, and grow.

Embracing resilience and proactive exploration is key to navigating life's unexpected turns. Here, I will lay out a blueprint of practical strategies and actionable steps, designed to arm you with the tools necessary for turning adversities into advantages. By reflecting on each challenge as a learning opportunity, we can enrich our experiences, gaining insight and fortitude for whatever lies ahead. Flexibility allows us to pivot when necessary and approach problems with innovative solutions, while strengthening our networks opens doors that once seemed invisible.

Staying proactive and maintaining a positive outlook are vital, as they catalyze opportunities and foster an environment where creativity thrives. This introduction sets the stage for the chapters to follow, each delving deeper into the art of transforming closed doors into gateways of possibility. Let's step back, reassess, and learn to embrace the infinite possibilities that await when we choose to see every end as a new beginning. As you turn these pages, prepare to unlock the doors to your potential, finding open windows where walls once seemed to stand. Together, we'll discover how each closed door can lead to a garden of opportunities, encouraging us to continually seek, learn, and grow.

CHAPTER 1

EVERY CLOSED DOOR IS NOT FAILURE

Growing up as a young adult in the military at age 19, I often found myself wrestling with frustration each time I faced the same closed door. The truth was, I was grappling with self-esteem issues; I was stubborn and impatient with both myself and others. I thought I was a thug, yet I didn't have a clue about street life and certainly wasn't raised in the hood to prove any street credibility. My fellow soldiers would often tease me, saying, "Bro, you ain't no thug; you're a church boy." They picked up on my mannerisms, how I spoke, and how I tried to mask feelings that bled into other emotions I was attempting to hide. In reality, I was a living, breathing closed door that they had no clue about. I never spoke about my pain or discussed things that made me vulnerable; I was always trying to be someone else, and not myself. Back then, I viewed every closed door as personal failure.

Over the years, I matured and found myself, yet I continued to associate closed doors with failure. When discussing closed doors with others, they would often echo the same sentiment, expressing their own feelings of disappointment by saying things like, "Yeah man, I feel your pain. I went through the same thing. That closed door was crazy, and I'm still suffering from PTSD and bipolar issues, bro." What am I trying to say? After years and years of setbacks and missing the mark, I realized that every closed door is shaped by our perception of it. If you view it as a huge loss with no solution, that's exactly what it becomes—a loss that leads to depression, poverty, and uncertainty. I want to delve deeper into this concept to transform how you approach, view, and navigate closed doors. Keep in mind, closed doors don't have to be seen as failures. Here are three key insights to help you shift your perspective:

1. **Closed Doors Give You Time to Heal:** After experiencing the pain and wounds of closed doors, it's important to step back and think about what "actually" happened, as you enter healing and recovery mode. Never cover deep wounds with band aids that barely cover the surface. Consider how a surgeon operates: First, he ensures that his trusted team is with him—individuals who are trained and qualified to assist across multiple levels of surgery. The surgeon also needs the right tools and equipment to complete the procedure. Just as a surgeon requires tools and a team, we too need people in our circle who can add value and purpose to the process behind closed doors. The surgery doesn't begin until the surgeon closes the door. This is the beauty of closed doors.

2. **Closed Doors Make You Ask Questions:** As you ponder the questions to ask yourself behind closed doors, devise a game plan to understand why the failure happened. What could I

have done differently? Was it the environment I was in? Was it something I ate that made me lazy and complacent? Remember this principle: The questions you never ask yourself could be the answers that help you find yourself.

3. **Closed Doors Redirect Your Path:** Often, the closure of one door, though initially perceived as a setback, is actually steering you toward a new and better direction. This redirection can sometimes be subtle and may not become apparent until much later. It's important to recognize that what seems like a denial of one opportunity actually preserves your energy for opportunities more suited to your growth and ultimate success. Behind every closed door lies the potential for a new beginning, a different path that might lead you closer to where you truly belong. Embrace the redirection with an open mind and consider the new doors that may open as a result. This shift in perspective can transform a perceived failure into a launching pad for a journey that aligns more closely with your strengths and passions. By understanding that closed doors are not necessarily failures, but opportunities for healing, self-reflection, and redirection, you can begin to view each closure, not as a barrier, but as a necessary step toward greater personal and professional development. These principles are not just about coping with loss or failure; they're about actively reshaping the way we approach life's inevitable challenges.

"The questions you never ask yourself could be the barrier that prevents you from finding yourself."

This realization brings a significant change in how we approach life's challenges. Instead of dwelling on the loss and the pain, we can begin to look for the hidden opportunities and lessons each closed door might be presenting us. Closed doors force us out of our comfort zones, pushing us to explore new avenues and undertake new endeavors that we wouldn't have considered otherwise. This can lead to personal growth, as we acquire new skills and gain new experiences. It's in these moments, when we're thrust into the unknown, that we often discover more about our capabilities, our desires, and our true potential.

Sometimes, a closed door serves as a critical stop sign, urging us to reassess our paths and refine our goals. It forces us to pause and reflect on our current trajectory and to consider whether our actions and strategies align with our long-term objectives. This reflection can lead to a clearer understanding of what we truly want, and what we need to do to achieve it. It may prompt us to make necessary adjustments to our plans, ensuring that our efforts are more focused and aligned with our desired outcomes.

Embracing these insights can dramatically alter our experience of life's inevitable closures. Instead of perceiving each closed door as a personal failure, we can choose to see it as a catalyst for introspection, innovation, and improvement. This mindset shift is about actively leveraging every situation to propel ourselves forward. As we navigate through these closed doors, we become more resilient, purpose-driven, and aligned with our true selves and our ultimate life goals.

*

After leaving the military in May 2002, I recognized another significant closed door that ultimately became a victory in itself. When the planes struck the World Trade Center towers in September 2001, I was still in the military, serving in the 82nd Airborne Division, 2nd Battalion, 504th Infantry Regiment. As a frontline soldier, I was positioned to be among the first deployed overseas, likely to be caught in direct combat. I remember the moment clearly: I was training in the field when my staff sergeant received a radio call from the company commander. The message was urgent: everyone needed to head back to the quarters immediately. Two planes had hit the towers, the Capitol was reported hit and in flames, and our nation was at code red. We were told to stay alert and be ready to deploy at any moment. I had no clue what was fully happening until we returned to the barracks and turned on the TV. The images were horrifying. People were jumping from the towers because the flames were overwhelming them on the 50th floor, and they couldn't take the elevators or the stairs due to the extensive damage and destruction. At that moment, consumed by fear and uncertainty, I began to pray, asking God to spare my life.

As the military went into high alert, I was confronted with the possibility of a "stop-loss" order, which could extend my service indefinitely due to the wartime needs. Facing the prospect of unexpected and prolonged deployment, I felt a deep urgency to reassess my future. After much prayer and reflection behind closed doors, I made a decision that would change the course of my life. I wrote a letter to the general, formally requesting to leave the military with an honorable discharge on my scheduled date. In the letter, I expressed my desire to go to college and pursue a new profession, hoping for a chance to build a different life.

"Some closed doors aren't just endings;
they are protections against paths that might have led to harm."

The waiting period that followed was tense and filled with uncertainty, but eventually, I received a response. My request was granted, and I was released with an honorable discharge in May 2002, as initially planned. This moment of closure was a bureaucratic formality—it was the best closed-door moment I needed. It allowed me to exit from a situation that almost took my life in a time of war. This closed door from the military marked the end of my time in uniform, but opened up a new chapter where I could pursue further education and a new career. It was a profound reminder that some closed doors aren't just endings; they are protections against paths that might have led to harm. Instead, they guide us toward new beginnings that align better with our life's purpose and potential. This experience underscored the power of closed doors to direct us toward safer, more fulfilling paths when we have the courage to approach them with faith and proactive determination.

*

AUTHOR OF HARRY POTTER —STORY OF CLOSED DOORS

J.K. Rowling's journey to becoming a bestselling author is a quintessential example of how career rejections can inadvertently guide one toward greater achievements. Before Rowling became a household name, she faced an uphill battle, receiving numerous rejections from publishers for her manuscript of "Harry Potter and the Philosopher's Stone." Each rejection could have been a point to give up, to close the book on her dreams, but instead, they served as crucial moments of resilience. Rowling, a then-struggling single mother, living on welfare, did not let the closed doors deter her spirit or ambition. With each rejection, she only grew more determined. The repeated setbacks helped her refine her pitches and enhance her manuscript, each iteration bringing her story closer to the magic that would eventually captivate a global audience.

The persistence paid off when Bloomsbury, a relatively small publisher in the UK, decided to take a chance on Rowling's work. This decision came partly due to the encouragement of the Bloomsbury CEO's young daughter, who, after reading the manuscript, eagerly demanded the next chapters. This pivotal moment was not just about finding a publisher willing to print her book; it was about finding the right partnership that believed in the potential of her story as much as she did.

The release of "Harry Potter and the Philosopher's Stone" marked a turning point in Rowling's career and in the literary world. The book, and its subsequent series, not only broke sales records but also rejuvenated interest in reading among the youth, sparking a cultural phenomenon with a lasting impact on all ages across the globe. Rowling's initial rejections taught her the importance of resilience, a lesson she often shares in talks to inspire others. Her experience underscores that closed doors in one's career are not merely setbacks but are instead opportunities to persevere and pivot one's approach. In Rowling's case, the closed doors led her to innovate, not only in her writing, but also in how she dealt with the publishing industry.

Her journey from rejection to success is a powerful reminder that entrepreneurship often requires one to face closed doors head-on, equipped with the courage to persevere and innovate. Rowling's story exemplifies how embracing the challenges of entrepreneurship, maintaining faith in one's vision, and harnessing the feedback from each rejection can open doors to unimaginable opportunities. In the world of entrepreneurship, rejections are not the end of the road, but signposts guiding the way to potentially greater paths not yet explored.

Rowling's experience also highlights the importance of resilience and adaptability in the face of closed doors. When faced with numerous rejections, she did not give up on her dream of becoming a published author. Instead, she used each rejection as an opportunity to refine her craft, improve her manuscript, and find the right publisher who believed in her work. This resilience and willingness to learn from setbacks are essential qualities for any entrepreneur looking to turn closed doors into stepping stones toward success.

*

NFL HALL-OF-FAMER STEVE YOUNG'S STORY

This next example further underscores the significance of transferable skills in overcoming what initially appears to be a career-ending closed door. Steve Young's transition from the NFL to broadcasting is particularly inspiring because it illustrates how abilities honed in one area can seamlessly translate to success in another. His story is a powerful testament to the utility of maintaining a broad skillset and the importance of adaptability. What makes Steve Young's story so compelling is the fact that he didn't allow desperation to drive his career decisions post injury. Instead, he leveraged his extensive knowledge of football, his on-field leadership skills, and his mental acuity to carve out a new niche in sports broadcasting.

He approached this transition with the same strategic mindset that made him a legendary quarterback, ensuring that he wasn't just finding a job, but was crafting a role that fit his skills and passions. The beauty of this transition was also in how Young approached his new career. He wasn't pushy or desperate; he knew his value and understood that his background as an NFL player provided a unique perspective that major sports networks valued. This confidence allowed him to enter broadcasting in a way that felt natural and well-suited to his talents, rather than as a second choice.

This scenario highlights a crucial lesson: the more gifted and versatile you are, the more options you have at your disposal. However, with more options comes the need for greater discernment. It's essential to surround yourself with people who are solution-oriented, those who can help navigate through these choices and support your growth, rather than complicate your path. As Young demonstrated, navigating career transitions successfully often depends on having a strong support network—people who bolster your strengths and encourage your best, rather than those who might lead you astray.

Let Steve Young's story serve as a reminder of the power of skill transferability following a closed door prompted by an injury. His ability to adapt and apply his talents in new ways not only shows resilience but also offers a roadmap for anyone facing similar crossroads. It teaches us that skills are never wasted; they can be redirected to open new doors, create new opportunities, and lead to new successes. In facing closed doors, we are not just confronting the end of one path, but the potential beginning of another—possibly more aligned with our evolving interests and capabilities. This perspective is vital for anyone navigating the uncertain waters of career change, especially those induced by unforeseen circumstances.

When an unexpected injury curtailed the professional football career of Steve Young, it might have seemed like the end of his dreams. Young, a driven and talented athlete, had dedicated the majority of his life to reaching the pinnacle of sports achievement. However, this significant setback, a closed door to what he had always known, led him to channel his determination and leadership into entirely new arenas. Transitioning from the football field to the courtroom and the broadcasting studio, Steve Young didn't simply replace one career with another; he used the skills he had honed as an athlete—leadership, quick thinking, and strategic analysis—in his new roles. His journey underscores how skills developed in one context can be incredibly valuable in another, often in ways not immediately apparent.

> *"Skills are often transferable and setbacks can redirect us to opportunities we might never have considered."*

As a quarterback, Young was celebrated for his ability to read the play and make split-second decisions under pressure. These abilities translated well into his legal career, where analysis, strategy, and quick thinking are paramount. His ability to communicate effectively, a necessity on the football field, also served him exceptionally well in broadcasting. Here, his insights and clear articulation made complex plays and strategies accessible to fans and viewers, enhancing their understanding and enjoyment of the game. Moreover, Young's public persona as a former professional athlete helped him to establish credibility and a unique niche in the broadcasting world. His firsthand experience brought authenticity and depth to his commentary, drawing in viewers who appreciated the perspective of someone who had performed at the highest levels of the sport.

However, the transition wasn't just about transferring skills. It was about personal growth and adaptation. Young's story is a powerful example of how facing a closed door can encourage an individual to look inward and rediscover themselves. It highlights the importance of adaptability, an essential trait for anyone who must navigate career changes or unexpected life shifts. For many, an injury that ends an athletic career might signify the end of their world as they know it. For Steve Young, however, it marked the beginning of new ventures that would not only make use of his existing talents but also push him to develop new ones. His ability to pivot from professional sports to law and broadcasting illustrates the broad potential for reinvention and shows that a closed door in one part of your life can open a corridor of multiple doors leading to diverse opportunities.

This narrative teaches us that our skills are often transferable and that setbacks can redirect us to opportunities we might never have considered. It encourages us to remain open to new paths that emerge from closed doors, and to continue pursuing excellence, no matter the arena. For those facing their own closed doors, Young's journey is a reminder that, with the right mindset, the end of one thing can indeed be the fruitful beginning of another.

*

ACADEMIC REJECTION FOSTERING NEW OPPORTUNITIES

In the world of success stories, few are as compelling as Warren Buffett's. Often, we admire the finished portrait of a billionaire's life, rich in wealth, influence, and prestige without appreciating the complex tapestry of challenges and setbacks that were instrumental in crafting such a masterpiece. Warren Buffett's journey, marked notably by an early academic rejection, unveils not just a path to financial success but a narrative rich with lessons on resilience and adaptability.

This story begins with a moment of significant disappointment: Buffett's rejection from Harvard Business School. For many, such a rejection from a prestigious institution could spell the end of their dreams, but for Buffett, it opened another door—one that would lead him to Columbia Business School and to Benjamin Graham, the father of value investing. Graham's philosophy of searching for undervalued stocks, ready to be bought at a bargain price, would deeply influence Buffett's approach to investments, embedding a strategy of long-term value that would define his career. The serendipitous meeting with Graham was more than fortuitous; it was transformative. It provided Buffett not only with a solid foundation of the principles of investing but also shaped his future business decisions profoundly. Such mentorship, grounded in practical experience and aligned with Buffett's intrinsic investment inclinations, might not have been as impactful had he been accepted at Harvard.

Buffett's reaction to his Harvard rejection exemplifies a vital lesson: that a closed door is not an endpoint, but a redirection—a shift toward opportunities potentially more aligned with one's skills and deeper aspirations. His time at Columbia opened up avenues that a more conventional path might never have offered, enabling hands-on learning and direct mentorship that proved invaluable. Moreover, Buffett's journey underscores the importance of remaining adaptable and open to the unexpected. Instead of dwelling on the disappointment of a rejection, he embraced the new opportunities that unfolded, which were replete with distinctive learning experiences that ultimately shaped his legendary career.

As we explore Warren Buffett's early challenges, we are reminded of the broader truth that each rejection, each closed door we encounter, harbors the potential for significant opportunity. For those prepared to look beyond immediate setbacks and adapt to new paths, these moments of redirection can become pivotal turning points leading to remarkable success. Buffett's story is not merely about achieving financial greatness; it is a narrative about the power of resilience and the importance of an open mind, teaching us that the most profound achievements often follow in the wake of what initially appeared to be insurmountable obstacles.

Reflecting on Warren Buffett's educational journey offers profound insights into how closed doors, such as his rejection from Harvard Business School, can lead to transformative opportunities. This example provides a powerful framework for understanding and embracing closed doors in our own lives.

Quotes for Reflection:

- "The most important thing to do if you find yourself in a hole is to stop digging." This wisdom is particularly relevant when facing closed doors. Instead of persisting down a path that isn't yielding results, it's often wiser to reassess and explore alternative routes.

- "In the business world, the rearview mirror is always clearer than the windshield." This quote highlights the clarity that often comes with hindsight. Closed doors might seem discouraging in the moment, but they often make more sense in hindsight, revealing they were guiding us toward better paths.

Strategies Inspired by Buffett's Closed Door Experience:

- Evaluate the Learning Potential, Not Just the Prestige: Buffett's redirection from Harvard to Columbia allowed him to meet Benjamin Graham, who profoundly influenced his investment strategy. This teaches us to look beyond the surface prestige of opportunities and evaluate the actual learning potential they hold.

- Actively Seek and Value Mentorship: The mentorship Buffett received from Graham at Columbia was pivotal. When one door closes, it's an opportune time to seek guidance from those more experienced. Mentors can offer not only knowledge but also alternative perspectives that can open new doors.

Relatable Tips:

- **View Each Closed Door as a Redirection:** Like Buffett's Harvard rejection, every closed door redirects you to potentially greater opportunities tailored to your growth and success. Recognizing this can transform disappointment into proactive exploration.

- **Embrace Alternative Paths with Openness:** Buffett's unconventional route to success illustrates the benefits of being open to paths outside the norm. What might initially seem like a setback could lead to uncharted territories ripe with opportunities.

- **Leverage Setbacks as Learning Experiences:** Every setback or closed door comes with lessons. Embracing these lessons helps refine your strategies and approaches, much like how Buffett honed his investment philosophy.

- **Persistence in the Face of Rejection:** Persistence is crucial. Continuing to pursue your goals despite rejections can lead you to the right opportunities, much like how Buffett's continued pursuit of education led him to his mentor.

Warren Buffett's story of facing a closed door with his Harvard rejection and finding a monumental opportunity at Columbia is a testament to the power of perspective. It shows us that closed doors aren't just endings but are protective redirects guiding us toward where we need to be, not necessarily where we thought we wanted to go. His journey underscores the importance of resilience, adaptability, and the willingness to embrace the unknown, turning what could be seen as failures into foundations for future success.

SHOW CANCELLATIONS LED TO NEW CREATIVE VENTURES

When we think about the entertainment industry, the highs are often as public as the lows, and when shows are canceled, it often results in casts and crews abruptly losing their jobs. The story of Donald Glover is a vivid illustration of how, despite such setbacks, creative talent can pivot and thrive, leading to even greater achievements.

Donald Glover, known widely for his role on the popular television show *Community*, faced such a moment when the show was unexpectedly canceled due to various complications, including creative disagreements and declining viewership. However, Glover didn't let this setback dampen his spirit or halt his creative output. Instead, he redirected his energies toward his music career under the moniker Childish Gambino.

The transition wasn't simple or immediate. Glover had to navigate the music industry, a different beast altogether, applying the same creativity and hard work that he had devoted to his acting. The payoff was spectacular. Glover's musical talents, combined with his unique voice and innovative style, led to the creation of hits like "Redbone" and "This is America," the latter of which earned him multiple Grammy Awards, including Record of the Year—a rare achievement for any artist, let alone one transitioning from another entertainment medium.

For fans of beloved shows like *Martin, The Fresh Prince of Bel-Air, The Cosby Show, Family Matters,* and *Full House,* the idea of these series ending was a disappointing reality. Each show brought laughter, lessons, and a sense of identity to their viewers. When they ended, it wasn't just the storyline that was missed, it was the weekly presence of beloved characters and the communal experience these shows provided. However, taking a leaf from Glover's book, we see that the end of one creative venture can be the beginning of another. Stars from these shows have often found new paths following their show's conclusion. For instance, Will Smith from *The Fresh Prince of Bel-Air* moved into a highly successful film career, becoming one of Hollywood's most beloved actors. Others, like Jaleel White from *Family Matters,* continued to work in television and explore new creative opportunities.

Donald Glover's journey from a canceled TV show to winning Grammys is more than an inspiring comeback; it serves as a testament to the power of resilience and the importance of not being defined by a single narrative or career path. It encourages artists and professionals, in all fields, to consider how skills from one area can translate into another, and how 'closed doors' may indeed lead to grand entrances on entirely new stages. This perspective helps us understand that while the cancellation of a favorite show is disappointing, it doesn't spell the end for the talent involved. Rather, it sets the stage for the next act, potentially brighter than the last.

Donald Glover is a multifaceted artist whose talents span acting, music, writing, and directing. Here are five interesting facts about him that not only illuminate his diverse capabilities, but also relate closely to his journey through the entertainment industry's unpredictable twists and turns:

FIVE THINGS PEOPLE MIGHT NOT KNOW ABOUT DONALD GLOVER

1. Early Writing Role on *30 Rock*:

Fact: Before he became known for his role on *Community* or his music career as Childish Gambino, Donald Glover was a writer for the popular NBC comedy series *30 Rock.*

Relation to Story: Glover's early experience as a writer on *30 Rock* honed his scriptwriting and comedic skills, which he later applied to his own projects like *Atlanta.* This background in a major network comedy underscores his versatility, and creative foundation, setting the stage for his multifaceted career.

2. NYU Residence Hall Named After Him:

Fact: In a testament to his impact on pop culture and his alma mater, an NYU residence hall was named after Donald Glover.

Relation to Story: This honor reflects Glover's significant influence and the inspiration he provides to current students, demonstrating how his journey through various entertainment mediums continues to inspire and shape future generations.

3. Grammy Awards for Different Genres:

Fact: Donald Glover has won Grammy Awards in multiple music genres, including Best Traditional R&B Performance for "Redbone," and Best Music Video for "This Is America."

Relation to Story: Glover's success in different music genres showcases his ability to cross creative boundaries and excel, highlighting his adaptability—a key factor in his ability to pivot successfully from acting to music following the cancellation of *Community*.

4. Voice Actor in Disney's "The Lion King":

Fact: Glover voiced the character Simba in the 2019 remake of Disney's "The Lion King."

Relation to Story: His role in such a high-profile film not only showcases his range as an actor, but also illustrates his appeal across different audiences and media, proving that his creative talents extend beyond television and music into major cinematic projects.

5. Directorial Pursuits:

> **Fact:** Beyond acting and music, Glover has directed several episodes of his critically acclaimed television series *Atlanta,* for which he has also received numerous awards.

> **Relation to Story:** His role as a director on *Atlanta* demonstrates his leadership and vision in bringing complex narratives to life, further illustrating how he turned the closed door of one TV show's cancellation into an opportunity to lead and innovate in another.

Each of these facts about Donald Glover not only enriches our understanding of his artistic versatility but also underscores how his early experiences and talents have interwoven to support his career's evolution. From writing for television, to making music, and directing, Glover has consistently used setbacks as springboards for further success, making him a true renaissance man in the modern entertainment landscape.

*

QUENTIN TARANTINO'S REJECTION FROM FILM SCHOOL SPARKED AN ICONIC FILMMAKING CAREER

Quentin Tarantino's origin story within the film world serves as a striking example of how early rejections can redirect creative advantages toward monumental achievements. Quentin Tarantino, now a seminal figure in modern cinema, faced his share of closed doors early on ... one of the most notable being his rejection from acting school. Far from deterring him, this setback became the impetus for him to delve into filmmaking on his own terms. Instead of treading the conventional path through film school, Tarantino turned to writing and directing, areas where he could exercise full creative control over his work.

This transition wasn't without its challenges. Tarantino had to navigate the complex dynamics of the film industry, which demanded not only creative talent but also a knack for storytelling that could captivate both audiences and critics alike. His perseverance paid off spectacularly with the release of groundbreaking films like "Pulp Fiction" and "Kill Bill," which not only earned critical acclaim, but also redefined genre filmmaking, cementing his reputation as an industry innovator.

This story resonates with the journeys of many other artists who have experienced the unexpected conclusion of beloved television projects like *Friends* and *Seinfeld*. These endings left not only the casts, but also legions of fans facing a significant sense of loss. Yet, beyond their entertainment value, these shows served as crucial incubators for talent, providing cast members with significant opportunities to develop their skills and carve out unique artistic identities. Each episode offered a new chance to refine their craft in front of a national audience, setting the stage for future endeavors in the broader world of entertainment.

Quentin Tarantino's journey from a would-be actor to a master filmmaker underscores the power of resilience and the necessity of adapting one's skills to new opportunities. His story is a testament to the idea that the end of one chapter can set the stage for the next, often leading to greater successes. It teaches us that in the world of creative endeavors, closed doors are not just endings but are also beginnings— opportunities to reinvent oneself and to impact the world in new and exciting ways. This perspective is vital for anyone in the arts, reminding us that when one door closes, sometimes, if we're prepared to seize the moment, it leads to grander stages and even brighter spotlights.

Over the years, again and again, I've found myself facing the discouraging force of "closed doors"—those missed opportunities that seemed to spell failure. Each time, part of me would wrestle with doubt, wondering, "Why can't I get through this? I know I'm better than this." Have you ever reached into the depths of your spirit, speaking to the innermost part of yourself, affirming, "I'm better than this"? This isn't just self-assurance; it's a profound declaration of your resilience and capability, a recognition that, despite setbacks, you possess the strength to exceed your own expectations. Every great comeback story is underscored by this sentiment. It's the resilient heartbeat at the core of every tale of overcoming adversity. The truth is, you are equipped—more than capable—to redefine the narrative that those closed doors seem to suggest. You can transform them from apparent endings into exciting beginnings. What was labeled as a limitation can become a launchpad for innovation and exploration.

When you face these challenges, it's not just about finding a way to open the door; it's about understanding why it was closed and how you can use this moment as a pivotal point for growth. It's about not just stepping through to the other side but also leaving a marked trail for others to follow. Each closed door is an invitation to step up and out into a realm where you redefine possibilities—not just for yourself, but for all who watch and learn from your journey. Reflect on these closed doors, and rather than seeing them as barriers, view them as a call to elevate your perspective and to harness your abilities for greater endeavors. Embrace the adversity, for within it lies the strength you need to forge ahead. Rally with determination, armed with the knowledge that you are *indeed* better than this, capable of turning every setback into a setup for a remarkable revival.

So, the next time you encounter a closed door, take a moment to affirm your worth and capability. Let each "I'm better than this" resonate as a powerful affirmation of your potential. Remember, what awaits beyond each closed door is not just a continuation of your journey but a testament to your unyielding spirit and relentless pursuit of excellence. Stand tall and push forward, for you have everything it takes to redefine the landscape of your life and leave an indelible mark on the world.

*

HOWARD SHULTZ, CEO OF STARBUCKS: FAILED BUSINESSES LED TO A REVOLUTIONARY COFFEE CHAIN

For all the coffee lovers and Starbucks fans, Howard Schultz's journey encapsulates a powerful narrative about overcoming obstacles and transforming failures into stepping stones for success. Before Starbucks became a synonym for coffee culture around the globe, Howard Schultz faced multiple challenges and even failures in his initial business ventures. His first coffee-related business did not meet the expectations he had envisioned, leading him to reassess his approach to coffee and retail. These early failures were not mere setbacks; they were instrumental in shaping his understanding of the coffee shop model and customer engagement.

Schultz's persistence is a testament to his belief in the potential of his idea. Each closed door led him to refine his business model, focusing more on the ambiance and customer experience than just the coffee itself. This shift in focus was pivotal. When he introduced the concept of Starbucks as a "third place" between home and work—a place where people could enjoy coffee in a comfortable, inviting environment—he revolutionized the coffee shop model.

This transformation wasn't just about rebranding coffee sales; it was about creating an experience. Schultz's vision extended beyond the beverage to crafting an atmosphere that appealed to the senses and cultivated community. This strategy, born from the lessons of past failures, catapulted Starbucks into an unprecedented realm of success.

For business owners currently facing their own "slow seasons," Schultz's story offers a blueprint for resilience and innovation. It teaches the importance of:

1. Adapting and refining your vision based on feedback and setbacks.

2. Understanding the broader potential of your business to provide an experience, not just a product.

3. Staying committed to your core values while being flexible in how you achieve your goals.

4. Building a brand that connects with customers on multiple levels.

Embracing the philosophy that every closed door can lead to greater opportunities, just as it did for Schultz, can transform periods of stagnation into moments of strategic reevaluation and growth. The key lies in viewing each challenge, not as a definitive stop, but as a detour directing you toward a more successful path. By staying resilient, continuously learning, and adapting, business owners can navigate their ventures through turbulent times and emerge stronger, much like Schultz did with Starbucks. Howard Schultz's story is not just a testament to entrepreneurial resilience but also one of personal triumph over challenging circumstances. His journey from a humble background to the pinnacle of global business success is marked by numerous obstacles that shaped his character and defined his leadership style.

EARLY LIFE AND FAMILY CHALLENGES

Howard Schultz grew up in the Canarsie Bayview Houses of Brooklyn, New York, a public housing project that was fraught with the challenges typical of lower-income neighborhoods. His father, a truck driver and later a factory worker, often struggled with unstable employment and poor working conditions. This instability was compounded when his father broke his ankle at work and lost his job due to the injury, leaving the family without income or health insurance. This early experience with financial insecurity and lack of worker protection profoundly impacted Schultz. It instilled in him a strong desire, not only to achieve financial stability, but also to build a company that treated its employees with respect and dignity. This resolve would later become a cornerstone of Starbucks' corporate ethos.

EDUCATIONAL PURSUITS

Schultz was the first in his family to go to college, attending Northern Michigan University on a football scholarship. However, his athletic career did not pan out as expected, and he found himself navigating academia without the sports accolade he had relied on. This shift forced him to refocus his energies and redefine his identity beyond being an athlete. His time at university, while challenging, helped broaden his horizons and solidify his aspirations to pursue a career in business.

EARLY CAREER AND VISION FOR STARBUCKS

After college, Schultz worked for Xerox, where he honed his skills in sales and marketing. However, it was during a visit to a small coffee bean store called Starbucks, in Seattle, that Schultz's vision for his future began to take shape. Intrigued by the quality and community potential of coffee, he saw an opportunity to transform the coffee drinking experience in America. However, convincing the original owners of Starbucks to adopt his idea for coffee houses was no easy feat. They were reluctant to shift their business model from selling coffee beans and equipment to brewing and serving drinks. Schultz's vision faced significant resistance, prompting him to leave Starbucks and start his own coffee shop, Il Giornale, which successfully implemented his ideas.

RE-ACQUISITION OF STARBUCKS AND GLOBAL EXPANSION

Schultz's success with Il Giornale led to an opportunity to purchase Starbucks, which had only a few stores at the time. After acquiring

Starbucks, he implemented his vision on a larger scale, but not without facing new challenges. The aggressive expansion strategy came with financial risks, and maintaining the quality and culture of Starbucks as it grew presented continuous hurdles.

PERSONAL PHILOSOPHY AND CORPORATE RESPONSIBILITY

Schultz's leadership has always been driven by a commitment to corporate social responsibility, a value stemming from his early experiences with poverty and his father's struggles. Under his guidance, Starbucks was one of the first American companies to provide comprehensive health care to both full-time and part-time employees. He also initiated a program to offer stock options to employees, including baristas, helping them to share in the company's success.

Howard Schultz's journey through numerous personal and professional challenges underlines the power of vision, resilience, and ethical leadership. His story is a reminder that one's background does not define one's future, and that with determination and a commitment to core values, it is possible to overcome great obstacles and profoundly impact the world.

Howard Schultz, through his transformative leadership at Starbucks, has shared numerous insights that resonate with entrepreneurs, leaders, and anyone looking to make a meaningful impact in their field.

Here are five powerful quotes from Schultz that encapsulate his philosophy and can inspire your business practices, sharpen your niche, and shape your character:

1. On Passion and Perseverance:

Quote: "When you're surrounded by people who share a passionate commitment around a common purpose, anything is possible."

Application: This quote emphasizes the importance of building a team that is not only skilled but also passionately committed to the company's mission. For business owners, fostering an environment where employees feel part of a purpose-driven team can lead to incredible achievements.

2. On the Importance of Values:

Quote: "If people believe they share values with a company, they will stay loyal to the brand."

Application: Schultz highlights the critical role that shared values play in customer loyalty. For businesses, this underscores the necessity of articulating clear, strong values that resonate with their target audience, reinforcing the brand's identity and enhancing customer engagement.

3. On Facing Challenges:

Quote: "In times of adversity and change, we really discover who we are and what we're made of."

Application: This quote is particularly relevant for startups and entrepreneurs navigating the often-turbulent waters of business. It serves as a reminder that challenges are not just obstacles but opportunities to learn, grow, and reaffirm the core strengths of your business and team.

4. On Responsibility and Leadership:

Quote: "The companies that are lasting are those that are authentic."

Application: Schultz stresses the importance of authenticity in a business's longevity. This means being transparent with your customers and true to your brand, which builds trust and establishes a sustainable connection with your market.

5. On Innovation and Growth:

Quote: "Dream more than others think practical. Expect more than others think possible."

Application: Encouraging a culture of dreaming big and setting high expectations can drive a business to innovate and push beyond conventional boundaries. This mindset is crucial for businesses looking to differentiate themselves in competitive markets, or those seeking to redefine their sectors. Each of these quotes from Howard Schultz not only reflect his successful approach at Starbucks but also offers universal lessons that can help refine your business strategy, enhance your engagement with customers and employees, and foster a resilient and innovative company culture.

Each of these stories—from J.K. Rowling's initial rejections, Steve Young's career transition, Warren Buffett's redirection from Harvard, Donald Glover's shift from television to music, to Howard Schultz's evolution from a barista to a global business leader—collectively weave a narrative of hope. They teach us that behind every closed door lies a universe of potential new doors waiting to be opened.

Each narrative brings to light how closed doors are not the endpoints of our journeys but pivotal moments that open us to new beginnings. Rowling's persistence in the face of rejection led to the creation of a beloved literary world. Young's ability to pivot his career path post-injury highlights the value of adaptability and resilience. Buffett's embrace of an unexpected educational path shows the importance of being open to alternative routes that may lead to greater opportunities. Glover's artistic reinvention from actor to Grammy-winning musician underlines the power of leveraging one's diverse talents. Schultz's transformation of a small coffee shop into a global empire exemplifies the impact of visionary leadership and ethical business practices.

As we reflect on these lessons, let us carry forward the understanding that our responses to closed doors define our paths. Adversity is not merely an obstacle but a gateway to deeper insights and greater achievements. These stories inspire us to view our own closed doors as opportunities to innovate, grow, and ultimately succeed in ways we might never have imagined before. As you move to the next chapter, remember that the true test is not how we avoid failure, but how we rise after we fall. The beauty of closed doors lies in the ability to challenge us, to make us question our methods and motives, and to push us toward paths that we might not have considered but that lead us to our greatest successes and most profound growth.

Let the resilience of Rowling, the adaptability of Young, the foresight of Buffett, the creativity of Glover, and the visionary leadership of Schultz, remind you that every closed door holds the seed of something potentially groundbreaking. Embrace these moments of closure, not as finalities, but as the beginnings of new adventures that await just on the other side. Reflect on the spaces between what we once wanted, and where we are directed to go next. These spaces, filled with potential and possibility, invite us to explore, to dream bigger, and to redefine what success means to us personally. They encourage us to think outside conventional frameworks and push the boundaries of what we believe is achievable.

Moreover, consider the role of community and support in navigating closed doors. Just as Howard Schultz envisioned Starbucks as a "third place" between home and work for customers, our own networks of peers, mentors, and supporters act as critical sanctuaries where we can find encouragement and guidance. These relationships are vital, providing us with different perspectives and helping us to see beyond the immediate disappointment of closed doors to the potential that lies ahead. As you continue your journey, take with you the lessons from those who have turned their closed doors into open avenues of opportunity. Let their stories remind you that every setback is laden with the seeds of a major breakthrough. It is through our most challenging times that we often gain the clarity and strength needed to succeed. So, as you turn the page on each closed door, remember that what lies ahead could be more exciting and fulfilling than anything you've left behind. Remain open, curious, and proactive. Seek out new opportunities with enthusiasm and the fearless spirit of a pathfinder. With each step forward, you are building a story of resilience and success that is uniquely yours—a story that might one day inspire others to see the beauty in their own closed doors.

CHAPTER 2

CLOSED DOORS ARE ROSES IN DIGUISE

In 2008, as the world stood on the edge of financial chaos, I found myself in Brooklyn, New York, grappling with a job market that seemed to swallow opportunities whole. My gig, as a security officer at Chase Bank, suddenly vanished; and the side job I had as a bouncer dried up just as quickly, leaving me with a mere $900 and a need to seriously rethink my next steps. The fleeting idea of diving into modeling just wasn't cutting it anymore. At this pivotal moment, I reached out to my father, a man whose wisdom had always been my compass. Living in Japan as a clergyman and missionary after his retirement from the Navy, he offered me advice that would change my course: "Buy a ticket to Narita Airport. Come to Japan and see if you can get a work visa to teach English."

This wasn't just about finding another job—it was about completely reshaping my life. So, with his guidance ringing in my ears, I moved fast. Within two weeks, I wrapped up my life in Brooklyn, bought a one-way ticket, and boarded a plane to Japan. I wasn't running away from unemployment; I was stepping into a new chapter in a land that held promise and familiarity. Switching from the fast-paced hustle of New York to the structured rhythm of Tokyo was both a relief and a thrill. Teaching English wasn't just a paycheck—it was a way to reconnect with a culture I respected deeply, and gave me the stability to rebuild and grow. This chapter was more than just a career shift; it was a transformative experience that showed me the power of turning a closed door into a gateway of opportunity.

Looking back, Dulce Ruby's words capture the essence of what I went through: "A rose does not lose sleep over the dead leaves it sheds, it blooms anew. Just like the rose, we must shed our past over and over until we bloom again." That move to Japan was my way of shedding old leaves—letting go of what was familiar and secure to embrace something uncertain, yet full of potential. The whole experience taught me a profound lesson about closed doors: they're not just endings. They're often new beginnings in disguise, waiting for us to step through and find the beauty on the other side. My journey from Brooklyn to Tokyo proved that setbacks are sometimes just hidden passages to growth and renewal.

This chapter of my life, much like a rose, was about embracing the cycles of growth, letting go, and blooming anew. Each challenge, every closed door, was part of that cycle—reminding me that with resilience, hope, and a willingness to embrace change, we can always find the roses hidden in the rough.

FAILURE WAS NOT AN OPTION

After I ended the call with my father, I began planning ahead, making calls, and researching the best English teaching companies in Japan. I was determined not only to get hired but also to secure a legal work status in Japan. Growing up, my dependency was largely on military access and benefits afforded by my parents' status. As I navigated these steps, I could see the rose slowly emerging from the concrete cracks—as opportunities began to open up. It felt as though every door that closed in New York was paving the way to an open door in Japan that was meant for me. Before leaving, I would often look at myself in the mirror and affirm with four life-changing words: "You got this, bro." This self-encouragement, looking into my own reflection, gave me a level of push and drive that's hard to express in words. It's like staring into a mirror that reflects not just your image but the potential and possibilities that lie ahead. It amplifies your resolve and solidifies your commitment to forge ahead despite the uncertainties.

The flight from New York to Japan was 12 hours. By the time I disembarked, I was drained, craving real food, and antsy after being confined to the plane for so long. Despite having watched enough movies and slept for about six hours, the flight's duration weighed heavily on me. However, the friendly and welcoming demeanor of the flight attendants made the journey more bearable. As I stepped off the plane at Narita Airport, I felt exhilarated to be back in Japan—the place I last visited in 2002 for my brother Dan's graduation. Now, I was here to make my own mark, to immerse myself in the real world of Japanese business. Understanding the strict immigration laws, I was aware that as an American, my association with the military provided a slight advantage due to the high standards of order and accountability expected.

After collecting my belongings, my first stop was at a Japanese restaurant in the airport. Even though I knew the best ramen chefs were in Shibuya, Yokohama, and Shinjuku, airport ramen still rated an impressive 8 out of 10 in my book. This meal was not just about satiating hunger; it was symbolic of me indulging in the familiar comforts of a culture I deeply respected. Living in Japan as an African American was a unique experience. On the train, people often waved, smiled, and sometimes even approached me to strike up a conversation. It made me feel like a celebrity—this acknowledgment and curiosity from the locals were both endearing and uplifting.

As I recount these experiences through the lens of turning closed doors into opportunities, I hope to convey a unique perspective on how *what initially* appears as a setback can lead to enriching and life-altering experiences. Here's a powerful thought from an unknown writer:

> *"When the door closes, don't stare at it for too long; instead, look for the windows that have been opened for you."*

This quote reminds us not to dwell on the past, or on what could have been. Instead, it encourages us to seek new paths—side doors, back doors, and windows of opportunity—that prevent us from wasting time and allow us to move forward boldly into spaces where we are meant to thrive.

NAVIGATING LANGUAGE AND LIFE AS AN ENGLISH INSTRUCTOR IN JAPAN

Returning to Japan as an English instructor brought with it a deeper integration into Japanese society, significantly facilitated by my fluency in Japanese. My foundational language skills were shaped early in life during my time at Saint Maur's, a Catholic international school in Yokohama. The immersive educational environment there (at Saint Maur's) was crucial in introducing me to the Japanese language through interactive methods like flashcards, which displayed words in romaji, English, and Hiragana. At Saint Maur's, my initial exposure to Japanese included basic vocabulary—fruits, vegetables, objects, and essential grammatical structures like nouns, adjectives, and full sentences. The flashcards were particularly effective, offering a visual and textual representation of words in both romaji and Hiragana. For example, tomato was presented as "Tomaato," orange as "Orenji," and French fries as "Furaido potato." This early education was pivotal in setting the foundation for my language skills, also including the introduction to the Japanese vowels—A, I, U, E, O—and the entire Hiragana alphabet.

THE COMPLEXITIES OF A NEW LANGUAGE

As my understanding of Japanese deepened, I encountered the complexities of Kanji, which represents one of the more challenging aspects of mastering the language. Kanji characters, derived from Chinese, are used in combination with Hiragana and Katakana in written Japanese, each character representing a word or concept. The intensity of learning Kanji, with its thousands of characters and multiple readings, was a significant leap from the simpler structures of Hiragana. Being fluent allowed me to navigate daily life and work responsibilities with greater ease. However, it was the practical use of the language that truly tested and honed my skills. Learning to catch trains and navigating the extensive, and sometimes bewildering, public transit system in Japan became daily lessons in language and cultural understanding. Getting lost in translation, quite literally while using the trains, turned into invaluable learning experiences. Each mishap on the train prompted me to research and recall the necessary Japanese words to resolve the situation, reinforcing my language skills through real-world application. This hands-on approach not only improved my linguistic ability but also deepened my connection to the places and people around me.

My ability to speak and understand Japanese transformed my experience as an expatriate into one of profound local engagement. It allowed for richer interactions with my students, deeper conversations with colleagues, and a more nuanced appreciation of the cultural subtleties that define Japanese society. Fluency in the language opened up doors that went beyond professional opportunities; it facilitated a genuine immersion into the lifestyle, traditions, and social nuances of Japan. This integration through language was emblematic of the broader theme of finding opportunity in every challenge—each closed door leading to new pathways of growth and understanding. In this context, every linguistic hurdle overcome, and every train successfully navigated, were not just personal victories but steps toward a larger journey of cultural and personal discovery in Japan.

EMBRACING THE LANGUAGE OF CLOSED DOORS: STRATEGIES FOR NAVIGATING UNCERTAINTY

Just as learning a new language in a foreign country at an early age equipped me to better understand and integrate into a new culture, understanding the language of closed doors is crucial for navigating life's unpredictable challenges. As I embarked on my journey with the English-teaching company Interac in 2009, I recognized the importance of having a backup plan—my "just-in-case" strategy—especially when job and opportunity landscapes appeared precarious.

THE THREE-POINT METHOD FOR NAVIGATING CLOSED DOORS

When faced with potential or actual closed doors, I developed and relied on a three-point method to ensure I continued to move forward, undeterred by setbacks or slow progress. This method is not just about coping, but about actively turning situations to your advantage, finding the hidden opportunities behind each closed door.

1. **Be Consistent in the Right Environment of the Closed Door:** Consistency in your efforts is key, particularly in environments that seem challenging or unyielding. By consistently showing up and offering value, you position yourself as an indispensable asset rather than a liability. This consistency needs to be strategic and aligned with the needs and goals of the environment you're in—whether it's a company, a community, or a new market.

2. **Don't Assume They Will Say No:** A common trap many fall into is preemptively assuming rejection or failure. This mindset can prevent you from taking the very actions that could lead to success. Instead, adopt a mindset of possibility—ask questions, make the proposal, take the chance. You might be surprised by the willingness of others to open doors you thought were firmly shut. This point emphasizes the importance of initiative and courage in testing the waters, even when the outcome is uncertain.

3. **Give Them a Reason to Call You Back:** In every interaction or opportunity, aim to leave a memorable impression that makes potential employers or partners see you as a valuable investment. Whether it's through the skills you demonstrate, the ideas you bring to the table, or the enthusiasm you show for the project, make sure they have a compelling reason to keep you in mind. Like photography, where negatives are developed into beautiful images, use your initial rejections or setbacks as a foundation for future success.

APPLYING THE METHOD

In my case, while waiting for confirmation from Interac, I didn't sit by idly. Instead, I actively sought other opportunities, knowing that my value does not diminish with rejection. I continued to hone my skills, expand my network, and learn from each experience. This proactive approach not only prepared me for potential closed doors but also enhanced my readiness when new doors opened.

This three-point method helped me navigate the uncertainties of working abroad and reinforced the idea that closed doors aren't just endings—they are detours leading us to potentially greater paths. Each closed door tested my resolve and forced me to adapt and innovate, ultimately teaching me valuable lessons about persistence, perspective, and personal growth. In summary, understanding the language of closed doors involves more than enduring rejection; it's about actively engaging with our circumstances, learning from them, and turning apparent setbacks into setups for future success. As we navigate our paths, let us remember that behind every closed door lies a myriad of possibilities waiting to be discovered.

Engaging with these closed doors involved a deep dive into self-awareness and an openness to evolving my strategies in response to new challenges. This process was not just about overcoming obstacles but about transforming them into stepping stones for further achievements. It taught me the importance of flexibility—of being able to pivot and recalibrate my approach when the first, or even second strategies did not pan out as expected.

Understanding the language of closed doors involves more than enduring rejection; it's about actively engaging with our circumstances, learning from them, and turning apparent setbacks into setups for future success. It's about seeing each closed door as an opportunity to explore alternate routes and uncover opportunities that we might not have considered otherwise. As we navigate our paths, let us remember that behind every closed door lies a myriad of possibilities waiting to be discovered. These are not just mere openings; they are invitations to new beginnings, urging us to broaden our horizons and embrace the unknown with optimism and courage.

As we continue on our journeys, the key is to maintain a proactive stance, anticipating and preparing for the challenges that lie ahead. By doing so, we ensure that we are not just reactive to our circumstances but are continuously shaping and directing the course of our lives. This proactive approach not only empowers us to handle current challenges but also equips us to leverage future opportunities, ensuring that each step we take is one closer to our ultimate goals.

This three-point method has significantly enhanced the way I approach daily life, particularly when encountering the inevitable closed doors that often appear as rejections. By implementing these strategies, I've transformed what might traditionally be seen as setbacks into valuable opportunities for personal and professional growth. This shift in perspective has not only allowed me to handle challenges more effectively but has also enabled me to recognize the potential advantages hidden behind each closed door. Understanding and utilizing this method has taught me to embrace rejection as a catalyst for development, prompting me to explore alternative paths that may not have been apparent initially. Each rejection is now viewed as a critical evaluation point, where I can assess and adjust my strategies, refine my goals, and better align my actions with my long-term objectives. This proactive engagement with challenges ensures that I am continuously learning and growing, turning potential negatives into positives that contribute to my overarching ambitions.

*

EDUCATION BEYOND THE CLASSROOM: LIFE LESSONS FROM TEACHING IN JAPAN

After securing my work visa to teach English in Japan, the classroom quickly became a place of profound cultural exchange—not just for my students, but for me as well. From the very first day, I was introduced to an unexpected depth of cultural awareness among the students. They were surprisingly knowledgeable about various aspects of Black culture, hip-hop music, fashion, and sports, demonstrating the global reach and influence of these cultural spheres. It was fascinating to see how the world I grew up in had made such an impact halfway across the globe. One particularly memorable encounter occurred on my first day. A Japanese student, full of curiosity, asked me in Japanese if I was related to Michelle Obama or if she was a close friend of mine. His question, inspired by the global impact of Obama's presidency in 2008, was a poignant reminder of how deeply American culture had permeated the world. Rather than brush off his curiosity, I seized the moment, asking if he wanted to learn more about Michelle Obama and the culture of Chicago. His eager response and attentive listening were a testament to the genuine interest, and eagerness to learn that characterized many of my students.

This interaction marked the beginning of what I now call "Education Beyond the Classroom." My role extended beyond teaching English; it became about fostering cultural understanding and breaking down stereotypes. I realized that in this cross-cultural setting, I had the unique opportunity to introduce my students to perspectives they might never have encountered otherwise. I learned to tailor my lessons into "bite-size pieces" to ensure the information was accessible and engaging for students of varying comprehension levels, while also making the learning process enjoyable.

During my time teaching approximately 1,500 students weekly, I observed that learning extends far beyond the classroom walls. Life itself offered lessons—some involving subtle rejections and challenges outside of teaching. There were moments when the workload felt overwhelming, and the temptation to quit loomed large. However, the need to provide my students with the attention they deserved kept me going, driven by a determination not to waste the opportunity that the "closed door" in New York had ultimately presented.

The experience of working in Japan taught me that education occurs on multiple levels during everyday interactions and experiences—some of which may initially appear as closed doors. These are not just obstacles, but opportunities for growth, learning, and new perspectives. I came to see that what might initially seem like a setback could actually be a setup for discovering new potential. The beauty and the rose still exist within each closed door; it's just a matter of perspective and perseverance. In this journey, I learned that resilience is key. Challenges that seemed daunting at first became stepping stones for personal and professional growth. Teaching in Japan allowed me to contribute to the education of others while also enriching my life in ways I hadn't anticipated. Each experience became a teacher, imparting lessons that would guide me through life's complex, often unpredictable journey. The process of navigating these challenges reaffirmed the importance of embracing change and viewing every closed door as an invitation to explore new possibilities.

EVERY ROSE HAS ITS THORNS: THE FIVE LEVELS OF POSITIVE AND NEGATIVE THORNS

In life, as in gardening, not every rose is without its thorns. While working day after day in Japan, I began to understand more deeply how these thorns can metaphorically represent the dual nature of experiences—both positive and negative. Here, I explore the five levels of how thorns can work in your favor or against the mission, providing a nuanced perspective on handling challenges.

LEVEL 1: PROTECTION VS. ISOLATION

Positive Effects: Thorns protect the rose from herbivores and other threats, serving as a natural defense mechanism. In life, personal boundaries or defensive mechanisms can protect us from being taken advantage of or harmed.

In nature, thorns are vital for the protection of roses. They serve as a robust defense mechanism against herbivores who might damage the plant as they attempt to eat the leaves and blossoms. This natural protection allows roses to survive and thrive, undisturbed by the threats around them. Similarly, thorns also serve as a reminder to handle the rose with caution, care and respect, thus preserving its beauty and integrity. Drawing a parallel to human experiences, personal boundaries act much like these thorns. They safeguard our emotional and psychological well-being by setting clear limits on what is acceptable behavior from others and what is not. These boundaries are crucial in preventing exploitation, as they define our limits and protect our time, energy, and personal space from being misused.

Personal boundaries also foster mutual respect. They communicate our values, expectations, and the way we wish to be treated, encouraging others to interact with us respectfully. Moreover, these boundaries are a key component of our identity—they reflect our beliefs, principles, and past experiences, shaping how we engage with the world. Effectively setting boundaries promotes emotional health by helping us distinguish our emotions from the actions of others, maintaining emotional stability even in challenging situations. This clarity reduces stress and enhances our overall well-being. Furthermore, while it might seem that setting boundaries could distance us from others, it actually leads to healthier and more genuine connections. By clearly communicating our boundaries, we invite others to understand us better and interact in more thoughtful, intentional ways.

Thus, like the protective thorns of a rose, personal boundaries enable us to cultivate a safe personal space where we can grow and flourish. They ensure that our personal "gardens" are well-maintained and vibrant, allowing for relationships and personal well-being to thrive. Embracing the concept of thorns as protective, not only empowers us to take control of our interactions but also encourages a more respectful and mindful approach to personal connections, fostering an environment where genuine growth and development are possible.

Negative Effects: However, too many thorns can lead to isolation. Overly rigid boundaries can prevent meaningful connections and opportunities for growth, leaving us isolated in our own gardens.

While thorns are essential for the protection and survival of roses, shielding them from external threats, they can also have a less desirable effect when they become too prevalent. In the case of roses, an overabundance of thorns can make the plant less accessible, deterring not only potential threats but also beneficial interactions, such as pollination by bees. Similarly, in our personal lives, setting overly rigid boundaries can lead to isolation and hinder our ability to form meaningful connections. When we construct too many barriers around ourselves, we risk shutting out more than just potential harms—we might also block opportunities for personal growth, new experiences, and the deep, enriching relationships that contribute to a fulfilling life. These boundaries, while intended to protect us, can keep others at such a distance that they inhibit the mutual exchange of ideas, feelings, and support that is crucial for personal and professional development.

For instance, if someone insists on extremely strict boundaries regarding their time and space, they might miss out on spontaneous interactions and serendipitous moments that could lead to important insights or new friendships. In professional settings, being overly guarded can prevent the kind of collaborative spirit that fosters innovation and teamwork. Moreover, when we isolate ourselves with rigid boundaries, we may find ourselves alone in our own 'gardens,' safe but stagnant, without the new challenges and stimuli that help us grow and evolve. This isolation can lead to a lack of diverse perspectives and experiences, which are often the catalysts for personal development and deeper understanding of the world around us.

Thus, while it's important to maintain boundaries for our well-being, it's equally vital to ensure they are flexible enough to allow for healthy interactions and growth. Balancing protection with openness is key to thriving personally and professionally, just as a rose thrives with the right balance of defense and exposure to the elements. It's about finding that middle ground where we keep the thorns sufficient to protect ourselves, but not so many that we end up isolated and disconnected from the vibrant life around us.

Finding this middle ground requires introspection and adjustment, a continuous process where we evaluate and recalibrate our boundaries based on our experiences and changing circumstances. It's a dynamic balance, much like the natural ebb and flow of life itself. By being attuned to our needs and the feedback from our environment, we can ensure that our thorns—our protective measures—do not overshadow our need for human connection and new experiences. This approach not only enhances our ability to respond to life's challenges but also enriches our interactions and deepens our connections, allowing us to engage fully with the world in a meaningful and fulfilling way.

LEVEL 2: RESILIENCE VS. RIGIDITY

Positive Effects: Thorns symbolize the resilience needed to survive and thrive in harsh environments. They remind us of the importance of resilience in the face of adversity, helping us to endure and adapt.

The concept of resilience as a thorn really resonates with me because it served as my defense mechanism against the challenges of adapting to a new environment. Stepping out of my comfort zone was no small feat, and honestly, half the battle was against my own doubts and fears. There were times I would look in the mirror and give myself a pep talk, acknowledging that this resilience was my thorn. It was what I needed to keep pushing forward, not just to survive but to truly thrive in an unfamiliar setting. Every new classroom and school I adapted to also taught me the value of rigidity, not in terms of inflexibility but as a necessary structure. Establishing a consistent routine was crucial. Just like a rose uses its thorns to maintain structure and ward off threats, I used my preparedness and established routines to create a stable and effective learning environment for my students and myself. This wasn't about being strict, it was about finding a rhythm that worked—where my preparations met the dynamic needs of each location.

This balance between resilience and rigidity was essential. My resilience helped me persevere through personal and professional upheavals, ensuring that I could face each day with renewed vigor. Meanwhile, the rigidity in my preparations provided a dependable framework that allowed me to navigate the complexities of teaching in diverse settings. Together, they helped me not only to manage but excel, turning each new challenge into an opportunity for growth. So, in this dance between being flexible and maintaining necessary boundaries, I found my footing. Each day was a testament to the power of resilience and the importance of a solid structure, allowing me to thrive in every new environment and turn potential setbacks into stepping stones.

Embracing the 'thorn of resilience' has taught me that true strength is not just about withstanding adversity but also about transforming it into a catalyst for growth and learning. At the same time, the 'rigidity' in my routines has underscored the importance of having a reliable system in place, one that supports consistency and excellence regardless of external changes. As I continue on this journey, these lessons remain with me, enriching my understanding and approach to new challenges. They remind me that every closed door, every thorn along the way, holds a lesson in disguise, teaching me that with the right mindset and strategies, I can uncover the rose—full of potential and beauty—waiting to bloom from within each challenge. The thorns of resilience not only guard but guide, pushing me toward opportunities to learn and expand beyond my perceived limits. As I navigate through life's complexities, I am continually reminded that every challenge, every moment of discomfort, is an invitation to grow. It encourages me to remain open to new possibilities and to welcome change with a proactive and prepared mindset. Through this, I have learned that the most formidable barriers often hide the most significant opportunities for personal evolution and success. Each thorn, each closed door, enriches my journey, imbuing it with depth and meaning, transforming potential setbacks into the seeds of future triumphs.

Negative Effects: On the flip side, thorns can also represent rigidity. Being too set in our ways or too tough can hinder our ability to adapt to new circumstances or to learn from new experiences.

As I settled into the rhythm of teaching English day by day, I encountered the complexities of what I like to refer to as the "flip side of thorns"—the rigidity of sticking too firmly to my own ways and being overly tough in my mindset to the point where I struggled to fully embrace and adapt to the experiences before me. This rigidity not only influenced how I approached my role, but also shaped my interactions within the educational environment, particularly in dealing with both students and fellow teachers. The notion of "being frustrated behind the defense" emerged as a significant challenge. This defense wasn't merely about protecting myself; it also involved the barriers I unconsciously erected that prevented me from engaging more openly with my colleagues. Often, I didn't discuss my struggles or share my experiences with other teachers, which might have eased my integration and adaptation process. In the teachers' lounge or during staff meetings, while ensuring that everything was ready for my classes, I sometimes felt a sense of isolation, compounded by my own defenses that kept others at arm's length.

Similarly, in the classroom, my initial rigidity reflected on my face and perhaps made me seem unapproachable or overly stern to the students. This was especially evident during the early days when I noticed a lack of appreciation on the students' faces—a defensive response on their part to my demeanor. This mutual guardedness was a learning curve for both me and my students. It was a defense mechanism from their end too, perhaps unsure how to respond to my teaching style or personality. However, as time progressed—over six months to a year—I began to soften these defenses. I learned to mesh better with the program and to align more naturally with my students' and colleagues' expectations and needs. This process was transformative, not just in my professional role but also in my personal growth. I began to understand the importance of flexibility, of lowering one's guard, and of being open to the cultural and interpersonal nuances that define a shared educational experience.

Gradually, I realized that adapting requires making changes to fit in and evolving in response to one's environment to foster genuine understanding and cooperation. By embracing this approach, I was able to break down the barriers that my "thorns" had created, leading to richer, more fulfilling interactions, and a deeper appreciation of the diverse community around me. This journey of adaptation taught me valuable lessons about the balance between being resilient and remaining receptive to new experiences, ultimately enhancing my effectiveness as an educator and enriching my experience abroad.

Metaphorical rigidity in our personal or professional lives manifests as an unwillingness to adapt, making us resistant to change and closed off to new ideas or practices that could potentially enhance our experiences or lead to significant breakthroughs. When we are overly rigid, we risk missing out on valuable learning opportunities and the chance to innovate. Just as a rosebush, overgrown with thorns, might restrict the very pollinators it needs to reproduce, too much rigidity can isolate us from beneficial collaborations and exchanges. It creates barriers not just against potential threats but also against beneficial influences that necessitate a certain level of vulnerability and openness.

LEVEL 3: PERSISTENCE VS. RESISTANCE

Positive Effects: The presence of thorns can encourage persistence; they are part of the plant's strategy to survive and flourish despite challenges. This level teaches us the value of persistence in achieving our goals despite obstacles.

The value of persistence was a cornerstone of my ability to fulfill my teaching contract in Japan. Understanding my purpose (my "why") and devising a personal strategy that included leveraging my own metaphorical thorns were key to navigating the complexities of living and working in a different culture. As I persisted, I noticed a shift in the classroom dynamics: the more open and engaged my students became, the more intriguing and effective the lessons were. To foster this engagement, I incorporated interactive techniques such as icebreakers into the lessons. For example, I would hold a ball in one hand and shout out a color, then instruct the students to name a new color I had taught them. After naming the color, they would throw the ball to another student, who would then have to continue with another color. To keep the activity dynamic and challenging, I would introduce new colors and objects, adding layers of complexity and fun to the learning process. This not only helped to break down initial barriers but also encouraged active participation and reinforced the vocabulary in a memorable and enjoyable way.

DEFINING PERSISTENCE IN THE CONTEXT OF CLOSED DOORS AND THORNS

Persistence, in this context, is the continuous effort to overcome challenges and obstacles while striving to achieve one's goals, despite setbacks or hardships. In the metaphor of roses and thorns, persistence is like the life force of the rose, pushing it to grow and bloom, even among thorns that might hinder its progress. Thorns, while protective, can also represent the hardships and challenges that one might face along the path to achieving personal and professional goals.

In the environment of a classroom in Japan, persistence was my thorn in a positive sense—it shielded me from the discouragement that can come with cultural and linguistic barriers, allowing me to continuously refine my strategies and improve my interactions with students. This persistence was crucial, not only for personal growth, but also for fostering a learning environment where students felt encouraged to take risks and engage openly.

Persistence in the face of closed doors means not giving up when initial attempts are met with resistance or failure. It involves maintaining a focus on long-term goals and using the lessons learned from each setback to fortify oneself against future challenges. Just as a rose uses its thorns to protect itself from external threats while continuing to grow and bloom, employing persistence allows us to navigate through our challenges, using them as opportunities to strengthen our resolve and advance our capabilities.

Negative Effects: Conversely, thorns can manifest as resistance to necessary change. Sometimes, what once protected us can become a barrier to our development, making it hard to move forward and embrace necessary transformations.

Understanding the nuances of resistance was a pivotal aspect of my journey while teaching in Japan. Initially, my inclination was to resist rest and keep pushing through despite the signs of burnout, believing this relentless drive was necessary for success. However, this approach soon proved to be unsustainable. Recognizing the need to balance work and life, I made the difficult decision to curtail social outings during weekdays, allowing me to focus more on my well-being and effectiveness as a teacher. This balance became particularly important when I secured my first apartment in Japan, a tranquil place located just outside the military base, near a golf course. The peace and solitude of my new home provided a stark contrast to my earlier lifestyle and offered me the space to reflect on my journey. It was here that I truly began to understand the concept of productive resistance—the idea that resisting certain habits or inclinations can actually propel us forward, rather than hold us back.

THE NEGATIVE SIDE OF THORNS: WHEN RESISTANCE HINDERS GROWTH

Thorns, while primarily defensive, can also symbolize the resistance we exhibit against changes necessary for our growth and adaptation. In my case, the initial resistance to slowing down and integrating rest was a thorn that needed to be carefully managed. What once served as a protective mechanism—my relentless drive and energy—had become a barrier, preventing me from embracing the transformations required to succeed in a new cultural and professional landscape. This kind of resistance can be subtle, yet profoundly impactful. It often stems from a place of fear or comfort with the status quo. Just as thorns can prevent a rose from being handled too roughly, our personal thorns can keep us within a safe, familiar boundary, staving off the discomfort that often accompanies growth and change. However, without confronting these thorns, without allowing ourselves to face and embrace these necessary changes, we risk stagnation.

In reflecting on how far I had come, I realized the power of the right kind of resistance—resisting the urge to stay in constant motion, resisting the fear of missing out, and instead, embracing the resistance that leads to rest and rejuvenation. This was not merely about resisting change but about redirecting my energies in more sustainable, constructive ways. Thus, managing resistance effectively requires us to discern when our defenses are serving us, and when they are hindering us. By recognizing when to let down our guard and when to fortify it, we can navigate our personal and professional lives with greater wisdom and balance. This discernment is crucial in turning potential setbacks into stepping stones and in ensuring that our thorns protect without limiting our potential to grow and thrive in new environments.

LEVEL 4: GRIT VS. HARM

Embracing and cultivating grit is an essential strategy for navigating the complexities of major life transitions, like moving from New York to Japan. As you reflect on the different layers of grit and how they can be applied, it's important to recognize how each type supports your journey in unique ways. Let's break down how these aspects of grit played a pivotal role in my transition and how you might leverage them in your own pursuits:

UNDERSTANDING AND APPLYING THE LAYERS OF GRIT

1. **Courage Grit:** This form of grit was crucial as I stepped into the unknown, leaving behind the familiarity of New York for Japan. Courage grit meant facing the fear of cultural missteps and language barriers head-on. Embracing this grit involves acknowledging fears but choosing to move forward despite them, a lesson valuable for anyone facing daunting new challenges.

2. **Perseverance Grit:** The daily grind of adapting to a new educational system and lifestyle required perseverance grit. This is about staying the course even when the initial excitement wanes and you're faced with the daily realities of hard work. For anyone in transition, perseverance grit means pushing through fatigue and discouragement, keeping your ultimate goals in sight.

3. **Adaptability Grit:** Living in a different culture tested my ability to adapt. This type of grit involves thinking on your

feet and being willing to adjust tactics without changing your vision. Whether it's navigating a new city, or adjusting to local customs, adaptability grit allows you to find creative solutions to unexpected challenges.

4. **Purpose Grit:** My "why" for moving to Japan was clear—to grow professionally and personally. Purpose grit keeps you aligned with your core reasons for your goals, providing a compass when distractions or temptations arise. It's about remembering why you started when things get tough and using that motivation to keep pushing forward.

5. **Resilience Grit:** Finally, resilience grit has been vital in bouncing back from setbacks, whether they were misunderstandings due to language barriers, or challenges in classroom management. This grit ensures that each setback is a springboard for growth rather than a reason to give up. It's about recovering quickly from disappointments and using the experience to fortify yourself for the next challenge.

CULTIVATING GRIT IN YOUR JOURNEY

To cultivate these types of grit, begin by clarifying your "why." Understand the deep-seated reasons behind your actions—this will be your guiding light through challenges. Break down your larger goals into smaller, manageable tasks and celebrate each achievement, no matter how minor it seems. Surround yourself with a support network that uplifts and motivates you, and actively seek resources that fuel your journey. Moreover, approach setbacks as learning opportunities. Every mistake, every misstep, is a chance to refine your strategies and strengthen your resolve. Regularly step out of your comfort zone—this is where true growth happens. Be patient and compassionate with yourself, recognizing that progress is rarely linear. In essence, grit is more than just persistence; it's a multifaceted strength that, when nurtured, can help you navigate life's transitions and achieve your dreams. It requires a balanced approach, blending fierce determination with an openness to learn and adapt. With grit as your companion, you're well-equipped to face whatever comes your way, continuously striving toward your aspirations with confidence and resilience.

NO HARM, NO DAMAGE

Discussing the topic of harm in Japan certainly presents a unique perspective, given the contrast between my experiences growing up on a military base and my later experiences living in Japan. While the base had its share of youthful drama and skirmishes, reflective of a diverse military community with many students from backgrounds like California's West Coast, Japan itself presented a starkly different environment. In Japan, the societal commitment to peace and protection is evident at every level. Public disturbances are uncommon, and the cultural emphasis on maintaining harmony extends to every aspect of life. The legal and community standards that discourage disruptive behavior are strictly enforced. For instance, even minor public altercations, or something as seemingly innocuous as raising one's voice can lead to police intervention. Authorities take these measures to prevent any potential escalation, reflecting the high value placed on public order and individual safety.

This approach to community safety and personal responsibility was vividly illustrated by an incident that happened to me while riding the train back home after school. Unbeknownst to me, a hole in my pocket had caused my wallet to fall onto the seat as I stood to exit at my stop. What happened next left a profound impression on me about the character of everyday life in Japan. A fellow passenger, a lady who had noticed the fallen wallet, called out to me repeatedly, chasing me down to return it. In her haste to ensure I didn't lose something valuable; she even sacrificed her convenience by getting off at a stop that wasn't hers.

This experience underscored not just the societal norms of honesty and responsibility, but also the personal integrity that is deeply woven into Japanese culture. Such actions are common in Japan, where people often go out of their way to assist others, even if it means incurring a personal inconvenience. This lady's selfless act was a powerful demonstration of the communal ethic that underpins Japanese society, where looking out for one another, especially in preventing harm or loss, is a shared responsibility.

I frequently share this story when asked about safety in Japan because it highlights *not just* the absence of physical harm or theft, but the proactive steps taken by individuals to care for one another in everyday situations. It's a testament to a culture that prizes safety and civility, making Japan one of the safest countries in the world. This incident not only reinforced my feelings of security but also deepened my appreciation for the social fabric that makes living in Japan uniquely reassuring. This act of kindness was not just an isolated event but a reflection of the broader societal norms in Japan, where such civic mindedness is routine. The profound respect for personal property and an ingrained sense of duty to one's community are characteristics that permeate through all layers of Japanese society. This culture of mutual respect and proactive assistance significantly contributes to the low crime rates and high safety standards that Japan is known for globally.

Living in Japan, these experiences became daily affirmations of the country's collective commitment to harmony and security. They not only foster a sense of safety but also encourage reciprocal respect among residents. This environment allowed me to navigate my daily life with an ease and assurance that was very different from my earlier experiences on the military base. There, while camaraderie was strong, the undercurrents of youthful recklessness could sometimes disrupt the sense of community. Moreover, the difference in cultural dynamics between Japan and the military base highlighted the impact of environmental and cultural influences on behavior and social interaction. In Japan, the emphasis on social etiquette, the importance of group harmony over individual expression, and the inherent expectation of looking out for each other help to mitigate conflicts before they escalate. This proactive approach to social harmony ensures that even potential misunderstandings or minor conflicts are managed with a level of civility and respect that is rare.

This ethos extends beyond just preventing harm; it builds a foundation of trust and cooperation that enhances community life. The reassurance that comes from knowing your neighbors and even strangers will act in the community's best interest, creates a welcoming and secure atmosphere. It encourages not just expatriates like me, but also tourists and new residents to engage with the community more openly and confidently. Reflecting on these experiences, I realize how much they shaped my understanding of societal structures and their impact on individual and collective well-being. The contrast between my upbringing on a military base and my life in Japan enriched my appreciation for different ways of life and reinforced the value of cultural understanding and adaptability. These lessons continue to influence how I approach new environments and challenges, always mindful of the balance between personal freedom and communal responsibility.

LEVEL 5: WARNING VS. WELCOMING

Throughout my teaching journey in Japan, from 2010 to 2013, I gained a multitude of perspectives that deeply influenced my approach to life and work. As I navigated this new lifestyle, it became clear that the balance between giving my all in the classroom and maintaining my health was crucial. Life's subtle warnings—like feeling overwhelmed or under the weather—reminded me to keep this balance, illustrating that life can indeed offer warnings and welcomes simultaneously. The teaching contracts were financially rewarding and provided a stable income, but they also came with their own set of challenges. One significant concern was the transient nature of my work visa status, which tied directly to my employment. This reality served as a constant reminder—the thorn's warning—of the temporary security provided by my current situation and the necessity of planning for the future. This warning was not just about financial preparedness but also about ensuring continuity in my professional and personal life, post-contract.

THE DUAL NATURE OF THORNS: WARNINGS AND WELCOMES

Thorns, by their very nature, serve as a protective warning. In my case, they symbolized the need to remain vigilant and proactive about my career trajectory and visa status. These warnings are vital as they compel us to prepare for what lies ahead, ensuring that we respect and protect our future through careful planning and thoughtful decision-making. Just as thorns protect a rose from unwarranted contact, these cautionary signs in life help us safeguard our well-being and future prospects.

However, these same protective warnings can sometimes create barriers that are perceived as unwelcoming. In the context of my professional life, the end of a contract and the uncertainty of visa renewal could seem daunting and unwelcoming, potentially deterring me from fully engaging with community or long-term projects. This aspect of the thorn could be isolating, as it might discourage forming deeper relationships or taking on commitments that extend beyond the visa's duration. My determination to save and plan for a return to the states, post-recession, reflects both the warning and the welcoming nature of my experience.

The recession I witnessed in 2008 was a stark reminder of economic vulnerabilities, thus reinforcing the need for a solid backup plan. This foresight was instrumental in navigating the uncertainties of working abroad and planning for a stable transition back home. Understanding and appreciating the dual nature of warnings—both as protective advisories and potential barriers—has been essential. It taught me to approach each situation with caution, yet optimism, respecting the protective measures while remaining open to the opportunities they guard. This delicate balance between heeding warnings and embracing welcomes has been a critical component of my journey, allowing me to navigate the complexities of working internationally with resilience and foresight.

*

EMBRACING THE LESSONS OF CLOSED DOORS AS ROSES IN DISGUISE

In this pivotal chapter, we navigated through a transformative journey that began with a significant career setback in New York and transitioned to a life-altering opportunity in Japan. This narrative serves as a profound testament to the potential for professional growth and personal enlightenment that can emerge from the shadows of closed doors. We explored the essential nature of boundaries that, much like the thorns on a rose, serve to protect us. These boundaries are crucial for safeguarding our emotional and psychological health, preventing us from falling prey to situations that might otherwise harm us. While protection is vital, an excess of it can lead to isolation. This section delved into how overly rigid boundaries might limit our growth and restrict our ability to form meaningful connections. It's a delicate balance between safeguarding oneself and remaining open to new experiences and relationships.

STRATEGIES IMPLEMENTED:

1. PERSISTENCE IN THE FACE OF OBSTACLES

Persistence in the face of obstacles was a cornerstone of my journey in Japan, essential for navigating the cultural and linguistic barriers that initially seemed daunting. Each day presented challenges, from grasping the complexities of the Japanese language, to adapting to a different educational system, and understanding nuanced social etiquette.

However, viewing each hurdle as a learning opportunity allowed for smoother adaptation and eventual thriving in a new environment. To maintain this persistence, I set small, achievable goals that made the overall process of acclimatization less intimidating and more manageable. Celebrating these small victories provided continuous motivation and a sense of accomplishment that fueled further efforts. Engaging with local resources, such as language exchange meetups and professional development workshops, was invaluable. These resources not only offered support but also helped diminish feelings of isolation by connecting me with others facing similar challenges.

Additionally, I adopted a practice of regular reflection, assessing both successes and setbacks. This reflective practice encouraged a mindset of continuous improvement and resilience, enabling me to refine my teaching methods and social interactions continuously. By embracing each challenge as an opportunity for growth, the transition not only became manageable, but also a profoundly enriching experience that underscored the importance of persistence in achieving professional success and personal fulfillment in a foreign cultural context.

2. ADAPTING TO NEW CULTURES

Adapting to new cultures is an essential skill, particularly when life takes you across borders for work, study, or personal growth. My early experiences living in Japan as a child provided me with a foundational understanding of the culture, which greatly benefited me when I returned as an adult. This prior exposure eased the initial shock and sped up my acclimatization, demonstrating how past experiences can serve as a roadmap for navigating current challenges. Understanding and leveraging previous experiences can ease transitions and boost confidence during new interactions, helping anticipate and grasp cultural nuances that might otherwise be overlooked. Diving deep into the local lifestyle through engagement with the community, participation in traditional events, and sampling of local cuisine allows for a rapid connection and a genuine understanding of cultural subtleties.

Maintaining openness and flexibility is crucial, as cultural norms can vary greatly from those you are accustomed to. Approaching these differences with openness, rather than resistance, facilitates smoother adaptation and enriches the experience. It's important to seek understanding rather than making assumptions when faced with unfamiliar customs or behaviors. This approach fosters respect and minimizes misunderstandings. Using language as a bridge is vital. Investing time to learn the local language, even basic phrases, not only facilitates communication but also deepens cultural understanding, showing respect for the culture, and significantly enhancing daily interactions.

By embracing these strategies, you can transform the challenge of adapting to a new culture into opportunities for substantial personal growth and broader global awareness. Each step not only enhances adaptability, but also enriches your life, providing a wider perspective and deeper empathy for people from all walks of life. This chapter has explored the concept of closed doors as hidden opportunities, encouraging us to perceive every challenge as a potential gateway to new beginnings and richer experiences.

This perspective on closed doors as opportunities encourages us to explore and utilize every encounter as a pivotal learning moment, turning what could be seen as setbacks into stepping stones for growth and success. Embracing each challenge that comes with moving across cultural borders, not only tests our resilience, but also broadens our understanding of the world, making us more rounded and insightful individuals. The journey through adapting to a new culture is not just about surviving—but thriving—finding joy in the discoveries, and satisfaction in overcoming the challenges. The nuances of cultural adaptation, from understanding social cues to appreciating local humor and participating in community life, are intricate dances that enrich our lives and deepen our connections with others.

It teaches us that flexibility and openness are not merely about accommodating differences, but about embracing a way of life that continuously evolves our worldview. In this context, closed doors do not signify the end but mark the beginning of new explorations and adventures. They compel us to look beyond the immediate and familiar, pushing us toward unforeseen paths that might hold the key to our personal and professional fulfillment. Each closed door, each cultural challenge, reshapes our character, molds our perceptions, and refines our approaches to life's complexities.

As we move forward, let us carry these lessons with us, using them as tools to navigate, not only new cultures, but any of life's uncertain terrains. Let the knowledge that each closed door can open to a garden of possibilities fuel our journey, encouraging us to continually seek, learn, and grow. This way, we can truly understand that every experience—no matter how daunting—holds the potential to teach us, shape us, and ultimately lead us to our own unique rose gardens, disguised previously as insurmountable walls.

3. BALANCING PROTECTION WITH OPENNESS

Balancing protection with openness was a critical strategy in my transition to working legally in Japan. Previously, my life was cushioned by the familiarities of military resources and the moral framework instilled by a family-centric, church-going upbringing. This background had shaped a version of myself accustomed to a structured support system, making the shift to navigating the complex legal and cultural landscapes of Japan a profound challenge. In this new chapter, I had to recalibrate my approach. The necessity to protect myself—legally and professionally—while remaining open to the unfamiliar workings of a foreign bureaucratic system was paramount. This meant diligently understanding and adhering to the stringent requirements of a work visa while embracing the subtle cultural nuances that defined my daily interactions and professional engagements.

This dual approach of safeguarding my interests while remaining receptive to new methods and ideas was not just about ensuring compliance but about thriving within a system vastly different from what I was accustomed to. It involved a delicate dance between maintaining enough of my core values to feel secure, while being flexible enough to adopt new practices and perspectives that were essential for success in my new environment. By strategically navigating these challenges, I was able to protect myself from potential pitfalls without closing off valuable opportunities for growth and integration. This balance allowed me to leverage my background as a strength, using it to build bridges rather than barriers, and ultimately enriching my experience abroad. This strategic openness has not only facilitated smoother transitions; but it has also fostered a deeper understanding and appreciation of the diversity and complexity of life, transforming what could have been mere survival into a richer, more fulfilling journey of personal and professional growth.

4. ADAPTING TO REAL CHANGE

Change, indeed, can be a complex and unpredictable force. Some people change out of necessity, others from a desire for improvement, and some because they find themselves unable to persist in a stagnating situation. The presence of four distinct seasons each year allows for continuous renewal and growth in nature, a phenomenon that mirrors the personal transformations we undergo. My move to Japan was a significant shift—a change driven not just by circumstance, but by a conscious choice to embrace growth outside my comfort zone. As an adult, independent and prepared to face whatever came my way, this transition represented more than just a physical relocation. It was a spiritual and emotional journey, a step toward the life I believed was destined for me. Japan wasn't just a change of scenery; it was a profound shift in my life's narrative, providing fertile ground for development and new experiences, much like the seasons that prepare the environment to flourish anew.

This evolution was both enriching and challenging. Embracing a new culture, learning a language, and adapting to a different lifestyle required more than just physical presence; it demanded resilience and openness. Living in Japan, each day was a lesson in adaptation—whether navigating the intricate transit system, engaging with students in the classroom, or connecting with the community through local traditions and cuisine. The dynamic interplay of learning and teaching brought unique insights. As I taught English, I also absorbed the subtleties of Japanese culture, which in turn, enriched my understanding of both myself and the world. This reciprocal relationship between teacher and learner underscored the transformative power of change. It wasn't merely about adjusting to a new environment; it was about thriving within it, allowing each new experience to mold me into a more rounded individual.

Furthermore, the challenges I faced, from initial cultural shocks to overcoming language barriers, illustrated the importance of flexibility and persistence. These challenges were not roadblocks but stepping stones that led to greater personal growth and professional fulfillment. They taught me the value of pushing beyond comfort zones, demonstrating that true growth often requires us to embrace the unfamiliar and the uncomfortable. In this way, my journey in Japan was a vivid illustration of life's seasons, each phase bringing its own set of lessons and opportunities for growth. Just as nature cycles through spring growth, summer abundance, autumn harvest, and winter rest, so too did my experiences cycle through phases of learning, challenge, abundance, and reflection. This seasonal rhythm helped frame my time in Japan, not just as a series of events, but as a cohesive narrative of personal evolution, driven by the inevitable and invaluable changes that each new season brought. This seasonal rhythm helped frame my time in Japan not just as a series of events, but as a cohesive narrative of personal evolution, driven by the inevitable and invaluable changes that each new season brought. Every challenge was met with a renewed perspective that fostered deeper connections and understanding, turning potential obstacles into avenues for innovation and growth.

5. IN CONCLUSION

The decisions you make, especially when faced with closed doors, can pivot your life in entirely new directions. Previously, I had a habit of faltering when unexpected obstacles arose, but this time was different. I approached each closed door not with resignation, but with the resolve to turn it into a gateway, using confidence and creativity. This proactive approach transformed potential setbacks into stepping stones, illustrating how our reactions to challenges can define our path forward. Embracing closed doors as opportunities, rather than barriers, enables us to thrive, evolve, and discover new horizons we might never have reached otherwise.

This shift in perspective is crucial for anyone on the brink of change or facing seemingly insurmountable barriers. By redefining closed doors as hidden opportunities, we not only find the strength to persevere, but also unlock the potential for growth that lies beyond the initial disappointment. Each closed door encountered is an invitation to innovate, to rethink our strategies, and to find new, often unexpected, ways to achieve our goals. In doing so, we learn not just to survive but to thrive amidst adversity, turning what could have been a dead end into a new beginning. This journey teaches us resilience, adaptability, and the invaluable skill of turning challenges into catalysts for personal and professional development.

Adopting this transformative approach demands a blend of resilience and creativity. It involves seeing beyond the immediate and often painful reality of a closed door, envisioning what could be, instead of what no longer is. This visionary mindset empowers us to harness the lessons learned from each setback and use them as stepping stones toward our next achievement. Instead of allowing defeat to define our paths, we learn to craft new paths, inspired by the possibilities that lie hidden beneath the surface of each challenge. This proactive engagement with life's inevitable hurdles not only fortifies our resolve, but also broadens our horizons, opening us up to new ideas, cultures, and experiences.

It teaches us the importance of adaptability—a key trait for anyone looking to navigate the complexities of modern living and achieve lasting success. By staying open to change and being willing to adjust our plans, we can better align with the ever-evolving landscape of our personal and professional lives. This adaptability ensures that when one door closes, we are already looking toward the next open door, ready to embrace whatever opportunities it may bring. With each closed door we encounter, we gather more knowledge, strength, and insight, which in turn equip us to handle future challenges with increased confidence and competence.

As we wrap up this chapter on navigating closed doors and discovering the roses hidden behind them, we carry forward the essential lessons of resilience, adaptability, and the transformative power of perspective. These lessons are not just theoretical but practical guides that equip us to face challenges with a renewed sense of purpose and possibility. As we transition into the next chapter, we will delve deeper into the personal and professional growth that arises from these experiences. We'll explore how continuous learning and adaptation can lead to profound self-discovery and fulfillment.

CHAPTER 3

CLOSED DOORS GIVE YOU TIME TO THINK

When I first ventured into the fishing industry, I had little idea what to expect. My mind conjured images from TV shows like *Deadliest Catch,* where rugged fishermen in vibrant orange suits braved icy waters to haul in Alaskan king crabs worth small fortunes. However, my journey began far from the cold seas of Alaska, in the warm, music-filled aisles of the Guitar Center in Orlando. At the time, I was studying for a Recording Arts degree at Full Sail University, immersing myself in the world of sound. It was there that I met Mike, a down-to-earth guy from New York with a strong Brooklyn accent. We connected over our shared passion for music equipment and talked about our dreams of acquiring gear to produce music. In one of our many conversations, Mike mentioned the idea of working in the fishing industry. He had a friend who had made good money working on a processing vessel, and the idea piqued my interest.

At 26, I was desperate for a financial breakthrough. I had just driven from Irving, Texas, to Orlando, Florida, to avoid having my car repossessed, and my life felt like a constant hustle. The chaos of that period was overwhelming—partying and drugs had become a regular part of my life, thanks to connections who made frequent trips to Miami, bringing substances back for free. The challenges were piling up: fights with friends, relationships falling apart, and the looming threat of eviction from my apartment due to unpaid rent. My only stable income was the GI Bill, which covered my education. Reflecting on it now, joining the military had been the best decision I ever made, even after my honorable discharge, but at that moment, I was drowning in financial struggles.

When Mike laid out the benefits of working on a fishing vessel—free meals and accommodations, and the opportunity to work on a ship in Alaskan waters for two months—it seemed like the lifeline I needed. I was in such a tight spot that I agreed to the idea, but only if Mike would join me in this venture. "Bro, the only way I'll do it is if we tag team and go together, knock out the B season, and make this money!" I told him. The plan energized us both, and we began preparing for the interview process with Trident Seafoods, one of the largest seafood companies in the world. They supply everything from the fish sandwiches at McDonald's to the fish sticks in Costco.

As we set out for the interview, which took place at a hotel along the East Coast, I was filled with a mix of anxiety and excitement. The contrast between the life I had envisioned for myself and the harsh realities I was facing couldn't have been more stark. This was a pivotal moment—a chance to step away from the chaos and into a new chapter that promised, not just an income, but perhaps a new direction in life. As the day of departure approached, the urgency of securing employment weighed heavily on me. I had to get hired. I had invested everything in this trip to D.C. for the interview, and it had to pay off. When we arrived at the Hilton Hotel and saw the long line of applicants—people who had traveled from various states, all hoping to secure a position with Trident Seafoods—I realized just how serious this was. It wasn't just a lifeline for me; it was the same for countless others, each with their own story of struggle and hope.

Standing in that line, I couldn't help but reflect on how life had led me here. The chaos, the desperation, the pivot toward an entirely new industry … it all seemed surreal. Yet, in that moment, it was clear—this was more than just a job opportunity—it was a chance to reclaim control over my life and possibly set a new course entirely. The stakes were high, but so was my determination. This was my shot at turning things around, and I was ready to give it everything I had. During the interview process, the reality of the situation set in. It was more than just an opportunity; it was a necessity.

Mike and I managed to learn more about the industry, further solidifying our understanding of its scope and impact. Discussing Trident Seafoods and the broader Alaskan fishing industry really opened my eyes. The staggering figures and the bustling activity it represented were akin to the Wall Street of the ocean—an ecosystem of high stakes and high rewards, driven by the relentless pursuit of marine riches.

OVERVIEW OF THE ALASKAN FISHING INDUSTRY

The Alaskan fishing industry is so vast and influential that capturing its full scope in a single book would be a monumental task. Renowned worldwide for its abundant waters, Alaska draws the attention of global stakeholders, from Japan to Europe, including bustling markets like London. These markets often face waitlists of a year or more for coveted catches like Alaskan king crab, sockeye salmon, and various types of cod. Alaska's fertile fishing grounds, supported by an extensive coastline rich in nutrients, significantly enhances the value of the fish harvested there. The commercial fishing sector serves as a major economic driver, generating billions in revenue annually and providing a significant source of employment.

The diversity of the catch is another cornerstone of this industry. Alaskan waters teem with multiple species of salmon: sockeye, known for its superior quality; king salmon; coho (also referred to as choho); and pink salmon, which is highly sought after by Japanese markets for sushi. Beyond salmon, the industry is known for pollock and an assortment of crabs, including snow crab, king crab, and Tanner crab. Salmon, beyond its culinary appeal, is a cultural icon, underpinning a highly profitable sector that extends to restaurants and food industries worldwide. The pollock fishery, one of the largest in the world, supports a broad range of products, from fish fillets and McDonald's fish sandwiches to Costco's fish sticks and surimi.

The high stakes of crab fishing, especially in the Bering Sea, are renowned for their profitability and the considerable risks involved. This aspect of the industry is famously depicted in the television show *The Deadliest Catch*, which highlights the perilous quest for Alaskan king crab. It's a sector marked by both high reward and high risk, suitable only for those with a strong resolve and readiness to face the demanding conditions of the sea. This rich tapestry of marine bounty, and the arduous labor required to harvest it, underscores the unique blend of danger and opportunity that defines the Alaskan fishing industry. Each season, fishermen and processors prepare for the rigorous demands of the sea, knowing well the physical and economic rewards at stake. These endeavors sustain local economies and contribute significantly to global seafood markets, highlighting Alaska's critical role in international food supply chains. The industry is a testament to human perseverance and the pursuit of economic gain while also playing a crucial role in maintaining ecological balance through sustainable practices.

THE CALL AND THE HIRING PROCESS

After the interview on the East Coast, I returned to Texas to await the results. Mike and I stayed in touch, keeping track of dates and times, anxiously waiting for the notification. We had asked the interviewer when we might hear back and were told to expect an email in two to three months. We were particularly interested in working on the *Aleutian Falcon*, a fishing processing vessel known for its high earnings.

After three months of waiting, I finally received the call from Trident Seafoods, and it couldn't have been more timely. Financially, I was strapped and desperately needed a break. This Seattle-based company, with its multiple branches, shore plants, vessels, catcher trawlers, and fishing vessels all over Alaska, employs around 20,000 people. Getting hired by such a large and reputable company was a huge opportunity. The email confirmed that I had been hired, and instructions were provided for onboarding, including the purchase of a one-way ticket to the specified location. I was instructed to bring my packing gear as detailed in the provided pack list.

As soon as I received the email, I called Mike, who had also received his confirmation. Despite being told there was no guarantee we'd be on the same vessel, the interviewer managed to arrange it for us. However, we still needed to get to Seattle. During the three-month wait, I worked various side hustles and nine-to-five jobs, saving every penny. So, when the time came, I had my gear packed and was ready to embark on my first journey into the fishing industry. As the day of departure approached, my anticipation grew. This opportunity with Trident Seafoods represented a lifeline out of my financial struggles. With my gear packed and a one-way ticket to Seattle in hand, I felt a mix of excitement and nervousness about the journey ahead.

Arriving in Seattle, the reality of my new venture began to sink in. The city buzzed with activity, and the docks were filled with massive vessels and bustling crews. Mike and I met up, and together we went through onboarding, orientations, safety briefings, and gear checks that marked the start of our journey. Trident Seafoods made it clear that this job would be demanding, both physically and mentally, but the potential rewards were substantial. We were assigned to the *Aleutian Falcon,* just as we had hoped. The vessel was impressive, with state-of-the-art processing equipment and a crew from diverse backgrounds, all seasoned and ready for the grueling work ahead. Our first day on the ship was spent familiarizing ourselves with the layout and meeting our fellow crew members. The camaraderie was immediate; everyone was there for the same reason—to work hard and make good money. This new chapter in my life was a stark contrast to the chaos I had left behind. The structure, the discipline, and the clear goals of the fishing industry provided a sense of purpose I had been missing. As I stood on the deck of the *Aleutian Falcon,* looking out at the vast ocean, I knew that this was the beginning of something entirely new. The journey ahead would be tough, but it was the opportunity I had been searching for—a chance to turn my life around and chart a new course.

*

FIVE PRINCIPLES ON THINKING AHEAD AS DOORS BEGIN TO OPEN

1. REFLECTION AND SELF-ASSESSMENT

During the waiting period for the hiring decision, it's crucial to reflect on your journey. Make sure that this path is genuinely what you want to pursue. Don't rush into something without a clear goal. Assess your past actions and financial struggles to decide if this opportunity aligns with your aspirations. Self-reflection helps you understand your willingness to take risks and identify your weaknesses as strengths in disguise. The waiting period allows you to see if you're prepared to take the necessary steps, and helps you ensure financial stability. Take this time to revisit your reasons for embarking on this path. Ask yourself why this opportunity is important to you and how it fits into your broader life goals. Consider the sacrifices you've made and whether they are justified by the potential outcomes. Reflecting on these aspects can provide clarity and reinforce your commitment, or it might reveal that a different path would better serve your long-term objectives.

Use this period to analyze past decisions and their outcomes. What lessons have you learned from your previous experiences—both successes and failures? Identifying patterns in your decision-making process can highlight areas for improvement and guide you toward more informed choices in the future. This introspection not only sharpens your decision-making skills but also builds confidence in your ability to navigate future challenges. Moreover, reflecting on your financial situation is essential. Ensure that you have a clear understanding of your financial health, and the steps needed to achieve stability. Consider creating a budget or financial plan that accounts for the potential income from this job, as well as any expenses you might incur. This financial planning can provide a sense of security and help you make informed decisions about your next steps.

During this period, take time to contemplate your personal strengths and weaknesses. Recognize the skills and qualities that have brought you this far and think about how you can leverage them in the future. Conversely, identify areas where you need to grow and develop. Viewing your weaknesses as opportunities for growth can transform them into strengths, enhancing your overall resilience and adaptability. Ultimately, this period of reflection is about aligning your actions with your goals and values. It's a chance to ensure that you're not just reacting to circumstances but making deliberate, thoughtful choices that move you closer to your desired future. By taking the time to reflect and assess yourself, you lay a solid foundation for making the most of the opportunities ahead, ensuring that when the door finally opens, you're ready to step through with confidence and purpose.

2. REEVALUATING PRIORITIES AND GOALS

When faced with closed doors, you are prompted to reassess your priorities and long-term goals. This pause can be crucial in realigning your actions with your true aspirations, ensuring that your future efforts are more focused and purposeful. It provides a chance to rethink your strategies and make more informed decisions about the direction you want to take in life. During these moments, take a step back and evaluate what truly matters to you. Are your current pursuits in line with your deepest values and long-term vision? This period of reflection can help you identify any discrepancies between your daily actions and your overarching goals. By doing so, you can adjust your path to better align with what you genuinely want to achieve.

Consider the bigger picture of your life. What are your ultimate aspirations, and how do your current activities contribute to or detract from these goals? This is an opportunity to prioritize the aspects of your life that bring you fulfillment and joy while minimizing or eliminating those that do not serve your best interests. This kind of reevaluation can lead to a more balanced and satisfying life. Reevaluating your priorities also involves practical planning. Look at the immediate and long-term steps required to reach your goals. Are there specific skills you need to acquire or improve? Do you need to change your approach or develop new strategies? Use this time to map out a clear, actionable plan that will guide your efforts moving forward.

Additionally, this pause allows you to consider the impact of your goals on other aspects of your life, such as your relationships, health, and personal well-being. Ensure that your ambitions are not pursued at the expense of these important areas. Strive for a holistic approach that supports overall harmony and well-being. Reevaluating priorities can also reveal new opportunities. Sometimes, a closed door can lead you to discover paths you hadn't previously considered. Be open to exploring these new directions, as they might align even more closely with your true desires and strengths. In essence, taking the time to reassess your priorities and goals is about making sure that every step you take is purposeful and aligned with your true self. It's a chance to ensure that you are not just busy, but productive in a way that brings you closer to your aspirations. By doing this, you create a roadmap that not only guides you but also inspires and motivates you to keep moving forward, even in the face of challenges.

3. DEVELOPING RESILIENCE AND ADAPTABILITY

Encountering closed doors and taking the time to think about your next move helps develop resilience and adaptability. These quiet moments allow you to plan for various outcomes and prepare for future challenges. By contemplating different scenarios, you build the mental flexibility needed to navigate unexpected obstacles and turn setbacks into opportunities for growth. Resilience is the ability to bounce back from difficulties and persevere despite challenges. During periods of waiting and reflection, you have the opportunity to strengthen this crucial trait. Reflect on past experiences where you faced adversity and emerged stronger. What strategies did you use? What lessons did you learn? By analyzing these experiences, you can identify patterns and techniques that will help you overcome future challenges.

Adaptability, on the other hand, is the capacity to adjust to new conditions. In today's fast-paced and ever-changing world, being adaptable is more important than ever. When you encounter closed doors, use the time to consider alternative paths and approaches. Think about how you can pivot your strategies to achieve your goals despite setbacks. This might involve learning new skills, embracing different perspectives, or finding innovative solutions to problems. By developing resilience and adaptability, you become more equipped to handle uncertainty. Life is unpredictable, and setbacks are inevitable. However, those who can remain flexible and resilient are better positioned to navigate these uncertainties successfully. They can see opportunities where others see only obstacles, and they can maintain a positive and proactive mindset even in the face of adversity.

Moreover, resilience and adaptability are interlinked. As you build your resilience, you become more adaptable because you are less likely to be discouraged by setbacks. Similarly, as you become more adaptable, your resilience is strengthened because you are more capable of handling change. This creates a virtuous cycle where each quality reinforces the other, leading to continuous personal growth. Developing these traits also involves practical steps. Engage in activities that challenge you and push you out of your comfort zone. Whether it's taking on a new project at work, learning a new hobby, or tackling a difficult problem, these experiences build your capacity to adapt and persevere. Additionally, practice mindfulness and stress-management techniques to maintain your mental and emotional well-being during challenging times. In summary, encountering closed doors provides valuable opportunities to develop resilience and adaptability. These periods of reflection allow you to prepare for future challenges, plan for various outcomes, and build the mental flexibility needed to turn setbacks into growth opportunities. By cultivating these traits, you enhance your ability to navigate life's uncertainties and emerge stronger and more capable than before.

4. STRATEGIC PLANNING AND INNOVATION

The time spent behind closed doors can be a golden opportunity for strategic planning and innovation. When you are not caught up in the hustle and bustle of daily life, you have the mental space to brainstorm new ideas, explore creative solutions, and develop detailed plans for achieving your objectives. This period of thoughtful reflection allows you to approach problems from different angles, leading to innovative approaches that can set you apart in your endeavors. Strategic planning involves setting clear, long-term goals, and identifying the steps needed to achieve them. During your quiet moments, take the time to map out your vision for the future. Consider where you want to be in the next five, ten, or even twenty years. What milestones do you need to reach along the way? Break down your goals into smaller, manageable tasks and create a timeline for completing them. This structured approach ensures that your efforts are focused and aligned with your overall aspirations.

Innovation, on the other hand, requires thinking outside the box and challenging the status quo. Use your time behind closed doors to let your mind wander and explore new possibilities. Think about the problems you face and consider unconventional solutions. Allow yourself to experiment with different ideas and don't be afraid to take risks. Innovation often comes from being willing to try something new, and learning from the outcomes, whether they are successes or failures. Brainstorming is a powerful tool during this period. Jot down all your ideas, no matter how far-fetched they may seem. Sometimes, the most creative solutions come from seemingly unrelated thoughts. Look for patterns and connections between your ideas and see how they can be integrated into your plans. This process not only sparks innovation but also helps you refine and improve your strategies.

Another key aspect of strategic planning and innovation is staying informed and educated. Use this time to research trends, technologies, and best practices in your field. Read books, attend webinars, and seek out thought leaders who can inspire and challenge your thinking. The more knowledge you acquire, the better equipped you are to develop innovative strategies that are grounded in current realities and future possibilities. Collaboration can also play a vital role in this process. While much of your planning may be done in solitude, don't hesitate to seek input from others. Discuss your ideas with trusted colleagues, mentors, or friends. Their feedback can provide new perspectives and help you refine your plans. Additionally, collaborative brainstorming sessions can lead to collective innovation, where the synergy of diverse minds generates solutions that you might not have conceived on your own.

Implementing your strategic plans and innovative ideas requires discipline and commitment. Set regular check-ins with yourself to assess your progress and adjust your plans as needed. Be flexible and willing to pivot when necessary but stay true to your overarching goals. This balance between adaptability and steadfastness is crucial for turning your vision into reality.

In conclusion, the time behind closed doors is invaluable for strategic planning and innovation. It allows you to set clear goals, develop detailed plans, and explore creative solutions. By using this period to think deeply and strategically, you can approach problems from new angles and develop innovative approaches that distinguish you in your pursuits. Embrace this time of reflection and planning as a foundation for future success and growth.

5. FINDING INNER PEACE AND FOCUS

Closed doors offer a sanctuary for finding inner peace and focus. Amid the chaos of daily life, these moments of solitude enable you to center yourself, reducing stress and mental clutter. This tranquility enhances your ability to think clearly and make decisions with a calm and composed mind. By fostering a peaceful state of being, you become more attuned to your intuition and better equipped to handle future challenges with confidence. In the quiet moments behind closed doors, you can engage in practices that cultivate inner peace. Meditation, for instance, is a powerful tool for calming the mind and achieving mental clarity. By focusing on your breath or a simple mantra, you can quiet the constant chatter of your thoughts, allowing a sense of peace to wash over you. Regular meditation practice can improve your ability to stay present and focused, even amid life's inevitable distractions and stresses.

Another way to find inner peace is through mindfulness. This practice involves being fully aware of the present moment, without judgment. By paying attention to your thoughts, feelings, and sensations as they arise, you can develop a greater understanding of your inner world. Mindfulness helps you recognize and release negative thought patterns, reducing their power over you. This heightened awareness fosters a sense of calm and equanimity, which is essential for clear and focused thinking. Journaling is also an effective method for achieving inner peace and focus. Writing down your thoughts and feelings can help you process and understand them more deeply. It provides a safe space to explore your emotions and gain insights into your experiences. Journaling can also serve as a tool for setting intentions and clarifying your goals, helping you stay aligned with your true aspirations.

Physical activity can further enhance your sense of peace and focus. Exercise, whether it's a brisk walk, yoga, or a workout at the gym, releases endorphins that boost your mood and reduce stress. It also provides an opportunity to step away from your daily concerns and connect with your body. Regular physical activity can improve your overall well-being, making it easier to maintain a calm and focused mind. Creating a peaceful environment is another crucial aspect of finding inner peace. Designate a quiet space in your home where you can retreat for reflection and relaxation. Fill this space with elements that promote tranquility, such as calming colors, soft lighting, and soothing sounds. By surrounding yourself with a serene atmosphere, you can enhance your ability to find peace and focus.

Finding inner peace also involves letting go of things that no longer serve you. This might mean releasing old grudges, forgiving yourself and others, or decluttering your physical space. Letting go of unnecessary baggage frees up mental and emotional energy, allowing you to focus on what truly matters. It creates room for new possibilities and positive experiences to enter your life. Spiritual practices, such as prayer or connecting with nature, can also help you find inner peace. These practices remind you of the larger picture and your place within it. They provide a sense of grounding and perspective, helping you navigate life's challenges with grace and confidence. Whether it's spending time in nature, engaging in spiritual study, or attending religious services, find what resonates with you and make it a regular part of your routine.

In conclusion, closed doors offer invaluable opportunities to find inner peace and focus. By engaging in practices like meditation, mindfulness, journaling, and physical activity, you can cultivate a tranquil state of mind. Creating a peaceful environment and letting go of *what no longer serves you* further enhance this process. By finding inner peace, you become more attuned to your intuition and better equipped to face future challenges with clarity and confidence. Embrace these moments of solitude as a sanctuary for your soul, allowing them to guide you toward a more centered and focused life.

*

TRIDENT SEAFOODS AND THE EXPERIENCE

Before I delve into my experience with Trident Seafoods, let me provide some background on the company. This information is essential to understand the context of my story and the significance of the opportunities I encountered. Trident Seafoods was founded in 1973 by Chuck Bundrant and two fishermen partners. Headquartered in Seattle, Washington, Trident Seafoods specializes in commercial fishing and fish processing, primarily in Alaska. Over the past 50 years, Trident has grown substantially, expanding the range of species it harvests and processes from king crab to virtually every commercial species of salmon, white fish, and other types of crab in Alaska. The company has also extended its global supply chain to include a network of trusted seafood producers worldwide.

An interesting fact about Trident Seafoods is its extensive workforce and infrastructure. The company employs over 9,000 people, including production crews, engineers, research and development teams, marketing and sales teams, operations staff, and support teams. Additionally, they collaborate with over 5,400 independent fishermen and crew members who work tirelessly to keep the industry thriving. Trident Seafoods operates more than 1,400 independent vessels each year and owns 33 vessels, including harvesting vessels, support vessels, and catcher-processors. The company also runs 15 shore plants, further solidifying its position as a leader in the seafood industry. Trident's commitment to sustainability and responsible fishing practices is another notable aspect of the company. They ensure that their operations adhere to strict environmental standards, maintaining the health and productivity of marine ecosystems. This dedication to sustainability not only supports the longevity of the fishing industry but also ensures that future generations can continue to enjoy the bounty of the seas. Understanding the scale and impact of Trident Seafoods helps illuminate why my journey with them was so pivotal. The company's vast network and robust infrastructure provided a backdrop for the unique experiences and challenges I faced. It also highlighted the importance of strategic planning and adaptability, essential skills that I had to develop to succeed in such a demanding environment. Now that you have a clearer picture of Trident Seafoods and its role in the fishing industry, I can share my personal journey with more context and depth. This knowledge will help you appreciate the significance of each step I took and the lessons I learned along the way.

WHAT REALLY HAPPENS ON THE FISHING VESSEL?

After on boarding and loading everything up, I quickly realized that the journey ahead would demand immense effort, drive, and passion. Boarding the vessel was one thing, but actually working alongside the people on the *Aleutian Falcon* was a completely different experience. Most of the management team were Hispanic and Mexican, a detail I found particularly interesting and admirable. I've always respected the hard work ethic of the Mexican and Hispanic communities and witnessing it firsthand on the vessel was impressive. They managed the *Aleutian Falcon* with skill and dedication. Mike and I were newbies, starting from the ground up on the butcher line. The living conditions were tight, with eight people per room in a bunk-bed style setup. The vessel could accommodate up to 80 people, including cooks, engineers, and quality control personnel. At times, it felt crowded, especially on certain days. However, on our off days, we would go to the top deck to take a breather and enjoy the view.

The international community on board was diverse, with people from Africa, the Philippines, Sudan, and other countries working as processors. They were involved in various tasks, including the butcher line, freezing, and maintenance. The process was intricate: after catching the fish, they would butcher and clean it, inspect it, and then store it in the freezer. The freezing area was located at the bottom of the boat, where it was naturally colder. This thorough processing was crucial for shipping large, prepaid orders to buyers who were often on waiting lists.

Working on the vessel involved long hours—sometimes 12 to 16 hours a day, with three to four breaks in between. Sleep was scarce, but we made the most of it when there was no fish to process. Interaction with the crew during these downtimes was essential. I read a lot of books and occasionally used the limited internet available on the two computers. There was only one phone on board for calling out, requiring a phone card. Cell phone service was non-existent until we were closer to the dock, so my phone was primarily used for reading and note-taking. This was our initial B season, and the experience was intense. The demanding work and unique living conditions were challenging, but they also provided a unique opportunity to learn and grow. There was more to come, but this was just the beginning of our journey on the *Aleutian Falcon.*

Despite the challenges, the camaraderie among the crew members made the hard work more bearable. We all shared the common goal of getting through the season and making the most of the opportunity. The long hours on the butcher line and the repetitive tasks could be mentally exhausting but knowing that we were all in it together helped keep our spirits up. One of the most fascinating aspects of the job was learning about the different stages of fish processing. From the initial catch to the final freezing stage, each step required precision and teamwork. The fish would first be cleaned and gutted, then inspected for quality. Any necessary adjustments or removals were made before the fish were weighed and stored. Seeing the entire process gave me a deep appreciation for the hard work and meticulous attention to detail required in the fishing industry. The physical demands of the job were intense. Handling heavy fish, working long shifts, and dealing with the cold and wet environment took a toll on our bodies. However, the intermittent breaks we had allowed us to rest and recharge. During these moments, I would often find a quiet spot to reflect on my journey and the decisions that led me to this point. It was during these times that I realized the value of perseverance and resilience. Closed doors gave me time to think about my past choices and future direction. The isolation on the vessel provided a unique opportunity to pause and evaluate where I was headed. With limited distractions, I could focus deeply on my thoughts, reflecting on what brought me to the *Aleutian Falcon* and what I wanted to achieve next. This introspection was invaluable, helping me understand the importance of each decision and its impact on my life.

One memorable night, we experienced a particularly rough sea. The vessel rocked violently, and many of us struggled to keep our balance. Despite the fear and discomfort, the crew's determination never wavered. We supported each other, ensuring everyone's safety and continuing with our tasks. It was a testament to the strength and solidarity that had developed among us. This experience underscored how adversity can sharpen our focus and build resilience, essential traits when facing closed doors in life. The lack of communication with the outside world was another challenge. With limited access to the internet and only one phone for calling out, staying connected with family and friends was difficult. However, this isolation also provided a unique opportunity for introspection. Without the constant distractions of modern life, I found clarity in my thoughts and a renewed sense of purpose. The quiet time allowed me to think deeply about my goals and how I planned to achieve them, turning the closed door of communication into a window of reflection.

As the days turned into weeks, I became more adept at my tasks and more comfortable with the demanding schedule. The initial feelings of uncertainty and anxiety gradually gave way to confidence and a sense of accomplishment. I began to see the closed doors I had encountered, as opportunities for growth and learning. Each challenge I faced helped me develop new skills and a better understanding of myself. Even on days when the work seemed endless and the conditions harsh, there was a sense of purpose that kept me going. The constant hum of activity on the vessel, the sound of the waves crashing against the hull, and the camaraderie among the crew all contributed to an environment where hard work and determination were valued and rewarded. This immersive experience taught me the importance of staying focused, and maintaining a positive attitude, even in the face of adversity. There were times when the monotony of the tasks and the isolation from the outside world felt overwhelming. On those days, I would remind myself of why I had chosen this path and the goals I wanted to achieve. This internal dialogue was crucial in maintaining my motivation and drive. It was a reminder that every step, no matter how small, was a move toward a better future.

In quieter moments, I would often stand on the deck, gazing out at the vast expanse of the ocean. The sheer magnitude of the sea and the isolation of our vessel provided a unique perspective on life. It was a humbling experience that made me appreciate the simplicity of our existence on the boat and the complexity of the world beyond it. These moments of reflection were a crucial part of my journey, allowing me to connect with my inner self and find peace amidst the chaos. As the B season continued, I found myself growing, not only in skills, but also in resilience and adaptability. The lessons learned on the *Aleutian Falcon* were invaluable, shaping my approach to challenges and opportunities both on and off the vessel. The experience reinforced the idea that closed doors, though daunting, can lead to significant personal growth and unexpected opportunities.

The journey on the *Aleutian Falcon* was far from over, and each day brought new challenges and learning experiences. Through it all, the support of my fellow crew members, the hard-earned skills, and the moments of introspection and self-reflection made the experience worthwhile. The closed doors I had faced before boarding this vessel had indeed given me the time to think, plan, and prepare for a journey that was as rewarding as it was challenging. As we sailed through the cold Alaskan waters, I knew that every obstacle overcome, and every lesson learned, was a step closer to a brighter, more fulfilling future.

As the season continued, I noticed that the ratio of men to women wasn't balanced. This was common knowledge among the workers and management who were familiar with the yearly seasons. Mike and I often talked with the veterans in the industry, learning a lot from their stories, which were filled with wisdom and discernment. One seasoned worker advised us, "Always observe. Be at the right place at the right time. Know what to do, and study the patterns of the people around you." He mentioned that those who joked around and laughed a lot usually got fired within the first three weeks of the B season. True to his words, we saw people getting fired, getting transferred to shore plants, and dropping out.

We learned that if you were fired, you had to pay your own way home. Whatever money you had from the fishing paycheck deposited into your bank account, was all you had. He also warned us not to let women distract us, as they could take us off our game. People on the boat were sneaking into different rooms, sleeping around, etc. The boat had coed sections for bathrooms and showers, with separate sleeping quarters for men and women. Human resources assigned bunks and rooms based on race, age, and group settings to ensure smooth operations. However, it wasn't always harmonious. Sometimes, they would mix Muslims with Christians, Asians with Blacks, Africans with people from the Philippines, and Sudanese with Ethiopians. Management, predominantly Mexican, had their own living quarters. Upper management, like the captain, electricians, and engineers, were usually white Americans each season; that was our experience.

The Quality Control (QC) specialists were mostly Hawaiian or Samoan and often connected to the transgender or LGBTQ+ community. The B season was a melting pot of diversity. As I continued to observe, I gradually got the hang of things day by day. I messed up a few times on the butcher line, particularly with the suction tube used to remove the guts from the salmon's cavity. The trainer showed me how to do it efficiently to avoid burnout and conserve physical energy since there were so many salmon to clean. To put it into perspective, we processed about 11 million pounds of salmon each season, earning roughly $8,000 to $10,000 for two months, not including bonuses for performance and attendance. It was an excellent way to save money without paying rent. However, not everyone's situation was the same. Some people had bills, mortgages, and child support payments. By the end of the season, they barely had 50 percent of their paycheck left. I heard many stories about different experiences on various fishing vessels. Beginners often started on vessels like the *Independence* and *Aleutian Falcon.* The goal was to move to share boats, which offered a percentage share for every package/catch. Two months on these boats could bring in $18,000 to $20,000.

After gaining three to four years of experience, I worked on share boats like the *Seattle Enterprise, Kodiak,* and *Island Enterprise.*

The diversity and dynamics aboard the vessels taught me a lot about resilience and adaptability. Working long hours under challenging conditions while managing interpersonal relationships and cultural differences required a high level of emotional intelligence. These experiences helped me grow both personally and professionally, reinforcing the importance of perseverance and the ability to adapt to ever-changing environments. As the days and years passed in the fishing industry, I experienced various levels of closed doors that gave me time to think. One of the reasons for writing this chapter is to inspire you to see "thinking" as an art. Your thoughts can literally shape every moment and factor in your life.

FIVE INTERESTING PERSPECTIVES ON THOUGHTS

1. THOUGHTS ARE POWERFUL

The way we think, speak, and conduct ourselves has a lot to do with how we think on a daily basis. Thoughts are incredibly powerful and can shape careers, grow businesses, find cures for major health problems, and much more. The thoughts you tell yourself are ultimately the thoughts you believe. Suicidal thoughts lead to death, lustful thoughts lead to teen pregnancy, and thoughts of revenge can lead to murder and life in prison. I think about every prisoner in the U.S. who sits in a cell every day, thinking about the things he could have avoided if he had been in the right environment. I know inmates have a lot of time to think, which is why it's important to stay positively active in something that can guide your thoughts and mind toward doing right. Positive thinking, negative thinking, and even numb, stagnant thinking still lead to a specific path where the thoughts can take you. Reflecting on my own experiences in the fishing industry, I realize how crucial it is to harness the power of thoughts constructively.

Your thoughts have a significant impact on your emotions and feelings. Negative thoughts can lead to negative emotions and actions, creating a cycle of negativity that can be challenging to break. This illustrates the profound influence our internal dialogue has on our overall well-being and decision-making processes. For instance, if you constantly tell yourself that you are not good enough, you may start to believe it, which can lead to a lack of motivation and a sense of defeat. Conversely, positive thoughts can elevate your mood and foster a more optimistic outlook on life. When you focus on positive affirmations and constructive thoughts, you build a foundation of self-belief and resilience. This can lead to greater confidence, improved mental health, and a proactive approach to problem-solving. By fostering positive thinking, we can enhance our emotional health and navigate life's challenges more effectively.

"The soul becomes dyed with the color of its thoughts."
— Marcus Aurelius

The power of thoughts extends to how we interact with others. Positive thinking can enhance our relationships by promoting empathy, patience, and understanding. When we think positively about others, we are more likely to treat them with kindness and respect, which in turn can lead to more meaningful and supportive connections. The mind-body connection also underscores the power of thoughts. Research has shown that positive thinking can improve physical health by reducing stress, lowering blood pressure, and boosting the immune system. This connection highlights how our thoughts not only shape our mental state but also influence our physical well-being. It's also important to recognize the role of self-talk in shaping our thoughts.

Self-talk is the running commentary that goes on in our minds, and it can be either positive or negative. By consciously directing our self-talk toward positive and affirming messages, we can reprogram our minds to focus on strengths and possibilities rather than limitations and failures. In essence, the power of thoughts lies in their ability to shape our reality. By choosing to cultivate a positive mindset, we empower ourselves to create a life that reflects our highest potential.

Our self-thought reflects our deepest beliefs and attitudes about ourselves and the world. If our internal dialogue is filled with negative messages, such as "I'm not good enough," "I'll never succeed," or "Why bother trying?" it can severely undermine our confidence and motivation. Over time, these negative thoughts can become self-fulfilling prophecies, leading us to avoid challenges and opportunities for growth. On the other hand, positive self-talk can reinforce our strengths and capabilities. Phrases like "I can handle this," "I am capable of achieving my goals," and "I am worthy of success," can bolster our self-esteem and encourage proactive behavior. This shift in perspective helps us view challenges as opportunities for learning and growth rather than insurmountable obstacles.

The power of self-talk lies in its ability to shape our reality. Our thoughts influence our emotions, which in turn affect our actions. For instance, if we believe we are capable and resilient, we are more likely to take on new challenges and persist in the face of setbacks. Conversely, if we constantly doubt ourselves, we may avoid taking risks and miss out on valuable experiences.

Reprogramming our self-talk requires conscious effort and practice. The first step in changing your self-talk is becoming aware of it. Pay attention to the messages you repeat to yourself throughout the day and reflect on whether these messages are helping or hindering your progress. Keeping a journal can be a useful tool for tracking and analyzing your thoughts. When you notice negative self-talk, challenge its validity. Ask yourself if there's evidence to support these thoughts or if they are based on irrational fears or past experiences. Reframe these thoughts by considering more balanced and realistic perspectives.

2. THOUGHTS PROCESS INFORMATION

The human brain is a remarkable organ, constantly processing information, even during sleep. This relentless mental activity is what allows us to learn, adapt, and respond to our environment. However, this continuous flow of thoughts can also lead to overthinking, worry, and stress if not managed properly. Understanding the mind's perpetual state of activity is crucial in developing strategies to quiet our thoughts and reduce stress through mindfulness and relaxation techniques.

Our brains are wired to be alert and engaged, always sifting through memories, analyzing current situations, and predicting future outcomes. This non-stop processing is beneficial for problem-solving and creativity but can become a double-edged sword. When left unchecked, the mind's incessant chatter can spiral into overthinking, where minor issues are blown out of proportion, leading to anxiety and stress. This is why it's essential to recognize when our minds are overactive and take steps to calm them. Mindfulness is one of the most effective techniques for managing an overactive mind. By focusing on the present moment and observing our thoughts without judgment, we can break the cycle of overthinking. Mindfulness meditation, in particular, has been shown to reduce stress and improve mental clarity. This practice involves sitting quietly, focusing on your breath, and gently bringing your attention back, whenever your mind starts to wander.

"The mind is its own place, and in itself can make
a heaven of hell, a hell of heaven."
— John Milton

Another useful strategy is practicing relaxation techniques. Deep breathing exercises, for instance, can activate the body's relaxation response, reducing the physical symptoms of stress and calming the mind. Progressive muscle relaxation, where you tense and then relax different muscle groups, can also help release tension stored in the body, leading to a more relaxed mental state. Journaling is another powerful tool to manage an overactive mind. Writing down your thoughts can help you organize and make sense of them, reducing the mental clutter. It allows you to reflect on your worries and anxieties in a structured way, often revealing patterns and triggers that can be addressed more directly. Engaging in physical activities is also beneficial. Exercise not only helps reduce stress hormones like cortisol but also increases endorphins, which are natural mood lifters. Activities like yoga combine physical movement with mindfulness, providing a dual benefit of physical and mental relaxation. Sleep is another critical factor in managing the mind's constant activity. Quality sleep helps reset the brain, process memories, and restore cognitive functions. Developing a good sleep routine, avoiding caffeine and screens before bedtime, and creating a relaxing pre-sleep ritual can significantly improve sleep quality, thereby reducing the mind's tendency to overthink.

Limiting exposure to information overload is another important strategy. In today's digital age, we are bombarded with information from various sources, which can contribute to mental fatigue. Setting boundaries for screen time, curating the content you consume, and taking regular breaks from digital devices can help manage the influx of information and give your mind the space it needs to rest.

In conclusion, while the mind's constant activity is a natural and necessary function, it's essential to manage it effectively to prevent overthinking and stress. By incorporating mindfulness, relaxation techniques, physical activity, journaling, and good sleep hygiene into our daily routines, we can create a balanced mental state. This balance allows us to harness the brain's power productively, enhancing our well-being and enabling us to face life's challenges with a calm and focused mind.

3. THOUGHTS CAN BE AUTOMATIC

Many of our thoughts can be automatic, and it's fascinating because our minds are incredible tools constantly in motion. They shape our past experiences, beliefs, and biases. While automatic thoughts can sometimes be helpful, guiding us through familiar situations and helping us make quick decisions, they can also be sources of distress and negativity. The key is to maintain a balanced and healthy mindset every day to understand and manage the power of automatic thoughts. Automatic thoughts are interesting because they can be spontaneous, unplanned, and pop up unexpectedly. They can be positive, neutral, or negative, and if unnoticed, they can be detrimental. When our automatic thoughts are predominantly negative, they can create cycles of distress, anxiety, and self-doubt. I know from experience that sometimes, even daily, I have to talk myself into waking up, saying, "Wake up! Get up!" because my body doesn't naturally do so. Sometimes we depend on alarm clocks or someone else to wake us up; but an automatic response based on an automatic thought is rooted in routine. Routine is powerful.

For example, imagine you're about to give a presentation at work. As you prepare, your mind might automatically generate thoughts like, "Oh, man, I'm going to mess up," or "Everyone will see me as a nervous person." These thoughts can intensify your anxiety and undermine your confidence, even if they're not based on reality.

Recognizing automatic thoughts is crucial. The first step is becoming aware of them. Pay attention to the thoughts that cross your mind, especially those related to stressful situations. Notice if your thoughts are mostly positive, negative, or neutral, and understand which one is dominant and how to handle it. Another helpful technique is to keep a thought journal. Write down your automatic thoughts as they occur, along with the situations that trigger them. This practice can help you identify patterns and triggers. Challenging automatic thoughts is the next step once you become aware of them. Ask yourself if these thoughts are based on facts or simply assumptions. For example, if an automatic thought is, "I'm not good enough for this job," challenge it by asking, "What evidence supports this?" and "What past successes prove my capability?"

After challenging your automatic thoughts, replace them with more balanced and realistic ones. Instead of accepting a negative thought at face value, reframe it positively. For instance, if you catch yourself thinking, "I'll never be able to learn this new skill," replace it with, "Learning a new skill takes time and practice. I'll focus on making progress each day." This shift in perspective can make a significant difference. In essence, the power of thoughts lies in their ability to shape our reality. By choosing to cultivate a positive mindset, we empower ourselves to create a life that reflects our highest potential. Remember, the mind is a powerful tool, and mastering it through awareness and positive reinforcement can lead to profound changes in our emotional and mental well-being.

This process of mastering our thoughts is not an overnight journey; it requires consistent effort and practice. The benefits, however, are immense. By becoming more attuned to our thoughts and consciously steering them toward positivity, we can significantly enhance our emotional resilience and mental fortitude. In the fishing industry, where closed doors are frequent and time for reflection is plentiful, this mental discipline can open up new opportunities.

Using affirmations is an effective method to foster positive thinking. Affirmations are positive statements that can help you overcome negative thoughts and self-sabotaging behaviors. When you repeat them often and believe in them, you can start to make positive changes. For example, affirming statements like, "I am capable and strong," or "I am worthy of success and happiness," can gradually replace the negative tapes playing in your mind. During my time waiting for the next fishing season or processing shift, I used affirmations to maintain focus and morale, helping me to see potential in every closed door.

Another powerful technique is mindfulness meditation. This practice involves focusing your mind on the present moment and observing your thoughts without judgment. It helps in slowing down the rush of thoughts and creating a space where you can discern the nature of your thoughts more clearly. Over time, mindfulness can help reduce the intensity and frequency of negative automatic thoughts. On the fishing vessel, this was particularly useful during long, grueling shifts. By staying mindful, I was able to manage stress better and remain open to new ideas and solutions. Likewise, surrounding yourself with positive influences can have a profound impact on your thought patterns. Engage with uplifting and supportive people, consume inspiring content, and immerse yourself in environments that encourage growth and positivity. These external influences can reinforce your internal efforts to maintain a positive mindset. On the ship, conversations with seasoned workers who had a positive outlook helped me stay motivated and focused on the bigger picture.

It's also beneficial to set aside time for self-reflection. Regularly evaluate your thoughts and feelings to understand how they influence your behavior and decisions. This practice can help you identify any recurring negative patterns and work on strategies to change them. Journaling is a useful tool for this purpose, allowing you to document your thoughts and track your progress over time. The solitary nature of fishing provided ample time for self-reflection, helping me to refine my goals and strategies continuously.

Incorporating gratitude into your daily routine can also shift your focus from negative to positive. By regularly acknowledging and appreciating the good things in your life, you train your brain to seek out and dwell on positive experiences rather than negative ones. This simple practice can have a transformative effect on your overall outlook and mental health. Even in the isolation of the sea, finding small things to be grateful for—like a beautiful sunrise or a successful catch—helped to maintain a positive spirit.

Lastly, don't hesitate to seek professional help if needed. Sometimes, negative thought patterns are deeply ingrained and require guidance from a mental health professional to navigate and overcome. Therapy can provide valuable insights and techniques tailored to your specific needs, helping you break free from the cycle of negative thinking. During your off-season, taking the time to seek professional advice can be incredibly beneficial, setting a stronger mental foundation for any challenges that may be ahead.

In conclusion, mastering the power of thoughts involves a multifaceted approach that includes awareness, positive reinforcement, mindfulness, supportive environments, self-reflection, gratitude, and professional support if necessary. By actively working on these aspects, you can harness the power of your thoughts to create a more positive, fulfilling, and successful life. Remember, the mind is incredibly powerful, and with the right tools and mindset, you can steer it toward achieving your highest potential. In the fishing industry, every closed door and every period of waiting is an opportunity to reflect, grow, and prepare for the next door that will open.

4. THOUGHTS SEEK PATTERNS AND CONNECTIONS

The ability to recognize patterns is not exclusive to humans; it is a fundamental skill that has evolved across the animal kingdom, playing a crucial role in the survival and success of various species. From insects to mammals, this cognitive ability helps animals navigate their environments, find food, avoid predators, and even communicate with each other. Let's delve into some fascinating examples from the animal kingdom that illustrate the importance of pattern recognition.

MIGRATION OF MONARCH BUTTERFLIES

One of the most remarkable examples of pattern recognition in the animal kingdom is the migration of monarch butterflies. These butterflies undertake an incredible journey, traveling thousands of miles from North America to Mexico each year. What's truly astounding is that young monarchs, who have never made the journey before, can navigate to the same overwintering sites as their ancestors. Researchers believe that monarch butterflies use a combination of environmental cues, such as the position of the sun and the Earth's magnetic field, to orient themselves during their migration. This innate ability to recognize and respond to these patterns is passed down through generations, showcasing the power of inherited cognitive skills.

SKILLED NAVIGATION OF RATS

Rats, often associated with less flattering characteristics, are actually highly-skilled navigators. They can find their way through complex environments, such as mazes, by creating cognitive maps—mental representations of their surroundings. These cognitive maps allow rats to plan routes and make decisions efficiently. To build these maps, rats recognize patterns in their environment, such as the layout of a maze or the location of food rewards. This pattern-recognition ability enables them to navigate their surroundings and make adaptive decisions, highlighting their impressive cognitive capabilities.

PATTERN RECOGNITION OF AFRICAN ELEPHANTS

African elephants are another example of animals that excel in pattern recognition, particularly in social contexts. These highly social animals live in complex societies and are capable of recognizing and remembering up to 100 individuals over a span of 10 to 20 years. This ability allows elephants to maintain social bonds and communicate over long distances.

Elephants recognize and remember other individuals by perceiving subtle patterns in sounds and behaviors associated with specific social contexts. This sophisticated level of social recognition is a key factor in the success and resilience of elephant societies. Pattern recognition is not only about navigation and social interactions; it also plays a crucial role in survival. For example, many animals can recognize patterns in their environment that indicate the presence of predators or food sources. This ability helps them make quick decisions that can mean the difference between life and death. The adaptability that comes from recognizing and responding to patterns is a significant evolutionary advantage, enabling species to thrive in diverse and changing environments.

In each of these examples, the ability to recognize and respond to patterns is closely tied to the survival and success of the species. Monarch butterflies can navigate to specific locations to survive and reproduce. Rats can efficiently find food and avoid predators, while African elephants maintain complex social structures that enhance their survival. These examples illustrate that pattern recognition is a vital cognitive skill shaped by natural selection for its survival and reproductive advantages. As Charles Darwin famously said, "It is not the strongest of the species that survives, nor the most intelligent. It is the one most adaptable to change." This quote underscores the importance of adaptability, which is often facilitated by the ability to recognize and respond to patterns. By honing our own pattern recognition skills and applying this cognitive flexibility to the challenges we face, we can find advantages and thrive in an ever-changing world.

Understanding and harnessing the power of pattern recognition can also apply to our personal and professional lives. By observing patterns in our behavior, relationships, and environments, we can make more informed decisions and navigate life's complexities more effectively. Whether it's recognizing a recurring theme in our thoughts, identifying trends in our industry, or understanding the dynamics in our social networks, the ability to see and interpret patterns can be a powerful tool for growth and success. In conclusion, pattern recognition is a fundamental cognitive ability that has evolved across the animal kingdom, enabling species to survive and thrive in their environments. By learning from these examples and applying similar skills in our own lives, we can enhance our ability to adapt, innovate, and succeed in an ever-changing world.

5. THOUGHTS ARE INFLUENCED BY EMOTIONS

It's mind-blowing how our thoughts are wired and deeply intertwined with the things we think about daily. Just as a skilled painter's brush-strokes are guided by his thoughts and the depth of his passion, so it is with our thoughts as they give color to the hue of our emotions. When we are gripped with thoughts of fear or anxiety, our minds begin to focus on threats and worst-case scenarios, such as the sudden terror of a gunshot or the devastating explosion of a bomb in a building. There's a quote that I love by Eckhart Tolle: "Awareness is the greatest agent of change." This powerful statement essentially says that the things we are aware of are usually the things that get our attention. The wrong awareness can lead to the wrong thoughts and typical emotions. It's important to recognize your emotions and thoughts based on how they relate to others. People can communicate with their eyes and reject you with subtle mannerisms, affecting your thoughts and feelings.

An interesting case study that fits the narrative of how closed doors give you time to think through the lens of thoughts and emotions is the Zeigarnik Effect. Dr. Bluma Zeigarnik, a Soviet psychologist, created this concept, which provides insight into how interruptions and unfinished tasks can impact our thoughts and memory.

In her research, Zeigarnik observed that waiters in a busy restaurant had a remarkable ability to remember complex orders but only until the orders were served. Once the meals were delivered, the waiters' memories of the orders quickly faded. Zeigarnik hypothesized that the human mind is more focused on incomplete tasks and that once a task is complete, the mind releases its hold on the related information.

This phenomenon can be applied to the idea that "closed doors give you time to think." When we are interrupted or faced with unfinished tasks, our minds continue to process the information related to those tasks, even when we are not actively engaged in them. By embracing the power of closed doors and solitude, we create a space for our minds to process unfinished thoughts, leading to breakthrough ideas and solutions. This concept is beautifully encapsulated by the renowned psychologist Carl Jung, who stated, "The creation of something new is not accomplished by the intellect, but by the play instinct acting from inner necessity. The creative mind plays with the objects it loves."

In summary, the Zeigarnik Effect demonstrates how unfinished tasks and interruptions can monopolize our thoughts, while the concept of "closed doors give you time to think" highlights the importance of solitude in allowing our minds to process these thoughts and generate new ideas. By embracing periods of isolation and uninterrupted reflection, we create the ideal conditions for creativity, problem-solving, and personal growth.

CONCLUSION

In the quiet solitude behind closed doors, we find a sacred space where our thoughts and emotions can dance freely, unencumbered by the distractions of the outside world. It is in these moments of isolation that we can truly explore the intricate relationship between our feelings and our thoughts, allowing us to gain a deeper understanding of ourselves and the world around us.

When we close the door and step away from the constant barrage of external stimuli, we create an opportunity for our minds to process the unfinished thoughts and emotions that we may have been carrying with us. This phenomenon, known as the Zeigarnik Effect, suggests that our brains are wired to focus on incomplete tasks, and that once a task is completed, our mental hold on the related information begins to fade. By giving ourselves the time and space to think, we allow our minds to work through these unresolved issues, leading to new insights, creative solutions, and a greater sense of clarity.

Behind closed doors, we can also practice the art of cognitive reappraisal, reframing negative emotions in a more positive light. In the absence of external influences, we have the freedom to explore our feelings without judgment, and to find new ways of interpreting and responding to them. As Carl Jung once said, "The creation of something new is not accomplished by the intellect, but by the play instinct acting from inner necessity. The creative mind plays with the objects it loves." By giving ourselves the time and space to play with our thoughts and emotions, we open the door to greater self-awareness, resilience, and personal growth.

In the solitude of a closed room, we can also tune into the physical sensations that accompany our emotions, using techniques like deep breathing or progressive muscle relaxation to better regulate our feelings and, in turn, our thoughts. By cultivating a deep sense of present-moment awareness, we can observe our inner world without getting caught up in it, allowing for greater clarity and perspective.

The power of closed doors extends beyond our personal lives and into the realm of creativity and innovation. Some of the world's greatest thinkers, artists, and innovators have relied on the solitude of closed doors to birth their most groundbreaking ideas. As Nikola Tesla once said, "The mind is sharper and keener in seclusion and uninterrupted solitude. Originality thrives in seclusion, free of outside influences beating upon us to cripple the creative mind. Be alone—that is the secret of invention: be alone, that is when ideas are born."

In a world that often demands constant connectivity and engagement, the act of closing the door and giving ourselves time to think can feel like a revolutionary act. Yet, it is in these moments of solitude that we can truly begin to understand and harness the power of our emotions in shaping our thoughts. As we navigate the ever-changing landscape of our inner world, may we find the courage to close the door, embrace the stillness, and allow ourselves the time and space to dance gracefully between thoughts and emotions, creating a life of purpose, resilience, and joy.

CHAPTER 4

THE URGENCY OF CLOSED DOORS

Reflecting on my own experience, when I lived in Irving, Texas, in 2004, I faced an urgent decision regarding my car payments. I was four months behind, and the repo man was urgently trying to tow my car. This situation forced me to act quickly and find a solution to avoid losing my vehicle. The urgency of the moment sharpened my focus and drove me to take the necessary steps to resolve the issue. In essence, adopting an urgent mindset for personal growth means treating your goals and aspirations with the same importance as emergencies. It involves recognizing the critical need for action and channeling your energy toward achieving meaningful results. By doing so, you can turn challenges into opportunities and ensure that you are continually moving forward on your path to success.

The life I lived when I was in the fishing industry was filled with many urgent moments that arose after closed doors. Working 12-hour days, I realized the wear and tear on my body was significant. It became discouraging because I wanted to continue the season, but my body was sending urgent signals to stop. This is a critical aspect of the urgency of a closed door—it tells you when to stop and how to maneuver to the next level. Often, the urgency doesn't appear until pain is involved. I'm not just talking about physical pain; I mean mental, spiritual, and emotional pain. These are usually the factors that take us under when we don't see the warning signs or the urgency of closed doors.

When this closed door happened for me in the fishing industry, I stopped caring about money and the usual things people worry about. When it's urgent, you need immediate care or a game plan to fix the situation. During the last season of my salmon run, we had both the B season and the pollock season because I was on a share boat. God blessed me with the opportunity to stay on the share boat for at least three seasons, but during my last season, my back gave out. I started having back spasms and couldn't lean over or sit down. This was a clear sign that it was time to move on, so I did. I left the fishing industry and decided to pursue ministry. I had been writing my book during this time, so I thought it was the right moment to shift my focus. However, I soon realized I needed additional income, so I began working in security. It was an urgent need, not only for income, but also for a job that required less physical strain. The security job provided stability and allowed me to stay in one place without much movement.

URGENCY OF UNEMPLOYMENT

One of the biggest urgencies that is common to most communities is the sudden-job-loss urgency. When that happens, having a game plan is crucial. Here's a case study about Sarah that fits this example well. Sarah was working as a marketing manager for a successful tech startup. Over the course of five years, she had been diligent, consistent, and passionate about her work, contributing significantly to the company's growth and success. However, one day she was suddenly called into her boss's office. For those familiar with such situations, being summoned usually indicates a significant issue, whether related to a project, a task or, unfortunately, job termination. Sarah was informed that due to a restructuring effort, her position was being eliminated, effective immediately.

This scenario exemplifies the urgency of a closed door. She needed a backup plan and had to quickly develop a budget to navigate this sudden change. She was shocked and devastated, having never been without a job before, and unsure of what to do next. After taking some time to process her emotions—an essential step that closed doors often force upon us—Sarah decided to view her sudden job loss as an opportunity for growth and reinvention. This sense of urgency can be a powerful motivator, prompting immediate action and strategic thinking.

Networking played a vital role in Sarah's strategy. She reached out to her professional network, informing them of her job loss and the types of opportunities she was seeking. Sarah attended industry events, joined relevant online communities, and set up informational interviews with people working in her field of interest. By leveraging her network, she increased her visibility and connected with potential employers who could offer new opportunities. Networking is not just about finding immediate job openings but also about gaining insights, advice, and support from peers and mentors in the industry.

SOLUTION: THE SIDE HUSTLE

While searching for a new full-time job, Sarah decided to leverage her skills and experience by taking on freelance marketing projects. This decision provided her with immediate income and kept her engaged in her field. Freelancing also allowed her to expand her professional portfolio and network further, which could lead to more permanent job opportunities. This approach highlights the importance of flexibility and openness to different forms of work, especially in times of urgency. Sarah began by reaching out to her existing network, letting them know that she was available for freelance work. She also created profiles on popular freelancing platforms, such as Upwork and Freelancer, to increase her visibility and connect with potential clients. To stand out in a competitive market, Sarah focused on showcasing her unique value proposition and the specific results she had achieved for previous clients. As she took on more freelance projects, Sarah realized that she enjoyed the autonomy and variety that came with this type of work. She began to consider the possibility of turning her freelance work into a full-fledged side hustle or even a permanent career path.

To build a sustainable freelance business, Sarah invested time in developing a strong personal brand and online presence. She created a professional website showcasing her services, testimonials, and case studies. She also started a blog where she shared industry insights and tips, establishing herself as a thought leader in her field. Additionally, Sarah focused on delivering exceptional work and building strong relationships with her clients. She prioritized clear communication, met deadlines, and went above and beyond to ensure client satisfaction. As a result, she began to receive referrals and repeat business, which helped her to grow her freelance income steadily.

Sarah's experience with freelancing and starting a side hustle taught her valuable lessons about adaptability, self-motivation, and entrepreneurship. She discovered new strengths and passions and developed a greater sense of confidence in her abilities. Even as she continued to search for a full-time job, Sarah realized that her freelance work had opened up new possibilities and career paths she had never considered before. In times of job loss or career transition, considering freelancing or starting a side hustle can be a powerful way to take control of your professional life and create new opportunities for growth and success. By leveraging your skills, building a strong personal brand, and delivering exceptional value to clients, you can turn a challenging situation into a catalyst for positive change and personal reinvention.

SOLUTION: REFLECT ON CAREER GOALS

A career is something that you do for a living to earn an income that you enjoy while sustaining your lifestyle effectively. Reflecting on career goals involves filtering out elements that add key value to your life. This reflection helps ensure that your professional path aligns with your personal values, aspirations, and overall well-being. Taking time to reflect on your career goals allows you to reassess your long-term aspirations. This means evaluating whether your current career path aligns with your personal values, passions, and future objectives. For example, Sarah's sudden job loss prompted her to reconsider her professional journey and explore roles that better matched her interests and skills. By regularly assessing long-term aspirations, you can ensure your career trajectory remains fulfilling and aligned with your true calling.

Reflection provides an opportunity to identify both strengths and areas for improvement. Understanding these aspects can guide your professional development efforts, helping you acquire new skills or enhance existing ones. In Sarah's case, she recognized the need to update her resume and tailor it to specific job opportunities, highlighting her strengths and addressing any skill gaps. This self-awareness and proactive approach can significantly enhance your career growth and adaptability. Reflecting on career goals also involves considering work-life balance. It's important to ensure that professional ambitions do not come at the expense of personal well-being and relationships. Sarah's period of unemployment gave her a chance to rethink her priorities, ultimately leading her to a role that offered, not only career advancement, but also a better balance between work and personal life. Striving for a healthy work-life balance is crucial for sustained career satisfaction and overall well-being.

By regularly reflecting on these aspects, you can make informed decisions about your career, ensuring it aligns with your goals and maintains a fulfilling professional journey. This process of filtering out what truly matters helps in focusing on career goals that add significant value to your life, leading to greater satisfaction and success.

URGENCY OF UNEXPECTED ILLNESS

I remember my first bout of seasickness in the fishing industry vividly. I couldn't eat, work, or escape the constant nausea. My body was struggling to acclimate to the rhythm of the sea. Life has its own rhythm, and when an unexpected illness strikes, it can disrupt your body, mind, and thoughts, shaking your ambition, drive, and passion. It can feel as though your game plan, routine, and sense of normalcy are compromised by the illness itself. One of the key lessons I've learned through these experiences is the importance of prioritizing self-care, especially when faced with an unexpected illness. This might sound simple, but it is profoundly powerful when applied. It's easy to neglect self-care when you're unwell, but it's crucial to listen to your body's needs. This means taking breaks from work or other obligations, practicing relaxation techniques, engaging in prayer or meditation, and seeking direct support from a therapist or counselor.

> *"It is not the load that breaks you down,*
> *it's the way you carry it."*
> *— Lou Holtz*

Over the years, I've also realized the importance of communicating with loved ones and friends during such times. When I was 26, I nearly overdosed on LSD. Struggling to breathe and fearing for my life, I called my mother for prayer. Despite having both parents as pastors, my prayer life wasn't particularly strong. I needed divine intervention. My mother's encouragement and prayer over the phone became a pivotal turning point in my life. From that moment, I knew I had to make significant changes. I adjusted my lifestyle, diet, exercise routine, sleep habits, and stress management. Embracing these changes not only helped me recover, but also laid a foundation for a healthier, more balanced life. Self-care isn't just about addressing physical health; it's about nurturing your mental and emotional well-being too.

By making self-care a priority, you can better handle the unexpected challenges life throws your way and continue to pursue your passions with renewed strength and resilience. The stress alone from job loss can provoke various forms of illness. Some illnesses can be complex and overwhelming. I just had a flashback of all the Red Bull, and Monster double-shot-espresso energy drinks I used to consume when I was younger. These habits significantly impacted my job performance. I was drained, out of breath, not physically fit, and constantly exhausted. The stress of sudden illness takes its toll on mental health as well. Not wanting to wake up in the morning due to congestion, muscle aches, spasms, blood pressure issues, strokes, and other ailments can be debilitating. What often hurts the most for people in these situations is the financial strain it brings on the family. Insurance is supposed to help, but what do you do when the medical bills are high and the insurance barely covers your needs? That's when life starts cutting the emotional veins and arteries of the inner heart. The burden can feel insurmountable, leading to further stress and exacerbating the cycle of illness.

URGENCY OF MENTAL HEALTH

Another key component to the urgency of closed doors is mental health and mental strain. Over the years, I've gone through various levels of mental health strain, and it created an urgency even after the door was closed. I've learned that counseling, therapy, and real family assistance, along with advice from trusted friends, goes a long way. Certain events that cause the urgency of closed doors can range from job loss, illness, or personal crisis, and these events can feel like doors are slamming in your face, leaving you trapped and feeling overwhelmed. The mental strain and health impact of a closed door can be significant, and it can affect every aspect of a person's life and well-being if it's not dealt with.

When faced with the urgency of closed doors, such as a sudden job loss or unexpected illness, people can tend to experience complex emotions like shock, disbelief, anger, grief, and anxiety. These are common initial reactions. However, the reality is that if it's not dealt with, it will sink you. The abrupt disruption to one's sense of stability, identity, and purpose can be unsettling and bring disorientation. The initial shock of it can be traumatizing.

"Closed doors demand we redefine our worth
beyond circumstance."

Even when the initial shock wears off, some people may grapple with feelings of depression, helplessness, despair, loss of control, or loss of certainty about the future, causing things to boil up due to self-esteem issues and negative self-talk. Sometimes, you can talk yourself into defeat with words that are traumatizing to yourself, such as "I'm a failure," "I'll never overcome this," or "I'm alone in this struggle. Nobody's helping me." This can literally exacerbate mental strain and make it even more difficult to maintain perspective. The practical challenges and limitations imposed by the closed door can create additional stress and barriers to mental well-being. Financial strain, difficulty accessing health care or supportive services, or social isolation can also contribute to the sense of being trapped and overwhelmed.

The key is having solutions and a way to tackle this effectively. Some people might choose therapy, counseling, spiritual guidance at a church, or a program that deals with meditation. Whatever your preference is, make sure it's useful and productive, and that it has value. The journey can be difficult at times, but *not* acknowledging it can really damage your inner core. You never want your inner core to be damaged, especially when it could have been dealt with by addressing your mental health and mental strain. These are things that I've gone through when it comes to mental strain, both in the fishing industry, and in ministry. I went through moments of feeling neglected, and unsupported when starting out in ministry. Then there was the pandemic which caused a huge mental strain, although there were moments when I managed to get through it. There were also times when I could have been better at what I did. These are just some of the mental health and mental strain challenges that can arise from the urgency of closed doors.

THREE THINGS TO REMEMBER ABOUT MENTAL HEALTH AND MENTAL STRAIN

1. VULNERABILITY IS STRENGTH, NOT WEAKNESS.

Admitting that you're struggling with mental strain and hurt, especially in the midst of closed doors, takes immense courage. It's a sign of strength, not weakness. Do not let society's stigma around mental health issues prevent you from seeking the support you need and deserve. It doesn't matter what title you hold, your position, or your level of education. We all experience mental health and mental strain scenarios, and we all need mentors, coaches, and trainers. Vulnerability is the birthplace of healing and growth.

2. DON'T TALK YOURSELF INTO DEFEAT.

Negative self-talk and self-criticism will only exacerbate the mental strain you are already experiencing. These negative thoughts fuel the problem, making it worse. Treat yourself with the same compassion you would show a loved one going through a similar struggle. Remember, you are not defined by your circumstances, and your worth is not determined by the closed doors you face.

3. PROGRESS, NOT PERFECTION.

Third, focus on progress, not perfection. Healing from the mental health impacts of closed doors is a journey, not a destination. There will always be setbacks and moments of struggle. However, don't let discouragement pull you back into the negative patterns of the past. Any progress, no matter how small, is still progress. Celebrate your wins, learn from your setbacks, and keep moving forward. Know that better days are ahead.

URGENCY TO REBUILD SELF-CONFIDENCE, SELF-ESTEEM, AND RESILIENCE

I love this category because when opportunities slip through your fingers and dreams are shattered, it's natural to feel incapable of moving forward as disappointment can eat away at your soul. It can literally make you feel crazy. My reason for including this is because of one of my favorite movies, *The Pursuit of Happyness* (2006), starring Will Smith. The movie follows the true story of Chris Gardner, a struggling salesman faced with numerous closed doors, including homelessness, while trying to create a better life for himself and his young son. Throughout the film, we witness Chris's relentless determination and unwavering belief in himself. Regardless of the impact on his esteem and confidence, he remained resilient. On a personal note, even after leaving the military, I continued to grow and develop, unlike many of my friends who lacked resilience and spiraled downward after leaving the service. It is crucial to ensure you are resilient and relentless on your way to achieving your goals.

Despite the harsh realities of poverty, rejection, and adversity, Chris refused to let his circumstances define him or diminish his self-worth. In one scene, overwhelmed by the weight of his struggles, Chris broke down in tears, but even in that moment of vulnerability, he found the strength to pick himself up and continue pushing forward. There's a heartbreaking scene where Chris and his son slept in a bathroom, using toilet paper as a blanket as he struggled with poverty in an effort to survive. Yet, Chris remained unwavering and determined, refusing to give up.

The cool part is that he eventually achieved his dream and became a successful stockbroker, proving that even when doors slam shut, the human spirit can prevail. *The Pursuit of Happyness* reminds us that the urgency to rebuild self-confidence and resilience is not just a personal journey but also a testament to the indomitable strength of the human spirit. It encourages us to look beyond our circumstances and see the limitless possibilities that await when we refuse to surrender to self-doubt. Don't surrender to self-doubt or ridicule because it can easily destroy you. There's an urgency that should come to mind whenever a door is closed, or something challenges your self-confidence. The urgency of self-confidence, resilience, and self-esteem can take you far when you truly understand who you are as a person. Your character, charisma, and clarity are interconnected with your esteem, resilience, and confidence.

Self-confidence is the unwavering belief in our abilities, our worth, and our potential. It is the fuel that propels us forward, even in the face of daunting obstacles and naysayers. With self-confidence, we approach challenges with a sense of assuredness, knowing that we possess the skills and determination to overcome them. Resilience is the capacity to adapt and bounce back from adversity. It is the quality that allows us to absorb life's blows and emerge stronger on the other side. Resilient individuals view setbacks, not as permanent conditions, but as temporary detours on the path to success. They possess the mental fortitude to learn from their failures, adapt their strategies, and forge ahead with renewed vigor.

Self-esteem, on the other hand, is the deep-rooted sense of self-worth and self-respect that serves as our anchor in turbulent times. It is the recognition that our value as individuals is inherent and not contingent upon external validation or accomplishments. With healthy self-esteem, we are better equipped to weather the storms of rejection, criticism, and disappointment without allowing them to erode our sense of identity.

Together, these three pillars form an unshakable foundation upon which we can build our dreams, pursue our passions, and navigate life's twists and turns with grace and resilience. By nurturing and strengthening each aspect, we cultivate a holistic sense of self that empowers us to embrace our authentic selves and unleash our full potential.

URGENCY OF HAVING A PLACE TO STAY

Throughout my life, the urgency to find a place to stay has always been significant, just as it was when I was younger. There were times when I had to sleep in my car, stay at my parents' house to get back on my feet, and constantly wonder where I would stay next. The fear of not knowing where my income or job would come from added to the urgency. However, as I grew older, I realized that finding the right environment and working with the right people makes all the difference.

The truth is, the urgency to find a home becomes most apparent when you're at your lowest point. Whether it's due to relationship challenges, natural disasters, or unexpected circumstances, securing a new place to call home can become an urgent priority. This urgency is often accompanied by the emotional weight of leaving behind a familiar environment and facing an uncertain future.

The search for a new home can be daunting, especially in competitive housing markets with limited availability. The pressure to act quickly can lead to hasty decisions and compromises. When I got my first home at the age of 43, I had to navigate the complex process of purchasing a home. This included signing a purchase agreement, securing mortgage loan approval, and building a relationship with the lender. Thankfully, as a veteran, I was able to use my VA home loan, which allowed me to bypass a down payment. The process also involved earnest money, closing costs, homeowner's insurance, title search insurance, property appraisal, home inspection, employment verification, tax records verification, and pest inspection reports. These steps are part of the journey that many people face when searching for a place to stay.

The key takeaway is to surround yourself with people who believe in you and speak life into your situation. Even when you don't have a place to stay, or find yourself *not* in the right environment, you can get closer to your goal by knowing you have what it takes. Persistence and consistency are crucial, even during slow seasons or when results aren't visible. The urgency of living expenses can be overwhelming, but it's important to use the resources you have—financial, emotional, and mental—to keep moving forward. Your story is an inspiration to many who face similar struggles. It emphasizes resilience, the importance of community, and the power of persistence. Thank you for sharing your journey.

URGENCY OF LOSING A FAMILY MEMBER

Losing a family member in any scenario, especially during COVID, can be daunting, frustrating, and create a sense of urgency that pushes you to become the best version of yourself. The sudden loss of a loved one is one of life's most profound and devastating experiences. Everyone has different ways of coping with such loss, but the reality is that grief is complex and deeply personal. There is no running away from it, and trying to cover it up is ineffective, especially when it involves a loved one you truly cared about.

COVID-19 took the lives of millions of people. When it first started, there was widespread nervousness and uncertainty. Churches closed and many people, including myself, lost friends and family members. I often asked, "Lord, have mercy, what do I do to cope with this?" Prayer and encouragement from family was helpful, but the truth is that grief is a multifaceted and deeply personal experience.

When you lose someone unexpectedly, the shock and trauma can be overwhelming. The immediate aftermath can be just as intense, filled with a whirlwind of emotions such as sadness, anger, disbelief, and even guilt. I'll never forget when my grandmother passed away between 2009 and 2010. I was devastated because she was a pivotal person in my life. When I was 16, I stayed with my grandmother in Texas, transitioning from Japan. Those two years taught me so much about appreciating life's simple joys, like gardening and living on a farm. She had cattle and grew vegetables, and living with her made me appreciate family and the natural world. When she passed away, I remembered all the lessons she had imparted: how to be kind, genuine, forward-thinking, and efficient. Her death grieved me deeply, especially because it happened while I was in Japan working as a teacher. That year was particularly tough, dealing with the aftermath of the stock market crash and trying to find a new job, all while mourning the loss of my grandmother.

It's crucial to seek emotional support from trusted friends, family members, and professionals. A strong support network can validate the range of emotions you're experiencing without judgment. Counseling or joining a grief support group can be incredibly beneficial. Additionally, self-care during such overwhelming periods is essential. Paying attention to how you eat, ensuring you get enough rest, and maintaining overall well-being are key factors. Establishing a daily routine can provide a sense of normalcy and stability during times of upheaval.

Engage in activities that you find comforting or that help you feel connected to the person you lost. Expressing your feelings is also important. Whether through journaling, talking with a friend, or participating in a support group, finding a way to articulate your grief can help process the loss.

Physical activity can be a powerful tool in managing grief. Exercise releases endorphins, which can help improve your mood and provide a healthy outlet for the stress and sadness associated with loss. Lastly, give yourself permission to grieve. Grief has no timeline, and it's important to allow yourself to feel and process the emotions as they come. There is no right or wrong way to grieve, and acknowledging your pain is a crucial step in healing.

If I could give an example, there's a movie called *Fatherhood* that was released in 2021 that powerfully illustrates the urgency of emotional support and coping mechanisms in the face of sudden, devastating loss. The death of Kevin Hart's character, Matthew's, wife shortly after giving birth to their daughter is what I'm referring to as an example. This tragic event thrusted an unprepared Matthew into single parenthood. He had to embrace single parenting and deal with profound grief while caring for his newborn by himself. The closed door of his wife's death created an acute urgency to find ways to process the emotional stress and adjust to his new reality. The film highlights how crucial it is to lean on one's support system during such a crisis. Matthew's family and friends rallied around him, offering a listening ear, childcare help, comic relief, and most importantly, reassurance that he didn't have to shoulder the burden alone.

Their emotional support brought them closer together, reinforcing the importance of maintaining a good mindset and a strong spirit. This act of keeping a positive outlook became a powerful coping mechanism as Matthew navigated life as a newly-single father. The film also depicted the urgency of self-care in the midst of grief and turmoil, demonstrating Matthew's vulnerability, exhaustion, and inner battles as he strived to be a great dad. How many times have we seen a scenario where a spouse dies during childbirth, leaving the other parent to take on all responsibilities? What if that happened to you? What if you were in a situation where you lost a spouse due to complications during childbirth and then had to shoulder the burden alone? These are the examples that highlight the urgency of losing a family member and how to cope with such a loss. It's crucial to consider, assess, and take time to heal in this world. The unimaginable pain of losing a partner during what should be one of life's most joyous moments—bringing a new life into the world—is a devastation that can shatter one's core. The urgency of emotional support becomes visceral and all-consuming. In that vacuum of grief, reaching out to loved ones, joining support groups, or seeking professional counseling is not just recommended—it's imperative for survival.

Coping with such a monumental loss while simultaneously caring for a newborn tests the limits of human strength. The competing needs and responsibilities can feel overwhelming. Yet, the alternative of retreating into isolation and despair robs the opportunity to honor the lost loved one's memory through the life they helped create. This is where the urgency of self-care, self-compassion, and perseverance becomes paramount. Allowing oneself to fully experience the stages of grief, while still carving out pockets of respite and solace, is the gentle balance required. Finding meaning and purpose in keeping the lost partner's spirit alive can be a powerful antidote to the soul-shattering pain.

Undoubtedly, confronting the urgency of such a profound loss reshapes one's existence forever. However, in that reshaping, an opportunity arises to rebuild with tools like resilience, community support, and faith—whether spiritual or secular. The path forward demands almost superhuman persistence, but also a mortal vulnerability in asking for help when needed most.

THE PROCESS OF LOSS

Losing a family member is one of the most profound and challenging experiences we face in life. It's a journey that takes us through a whirlwind of emotions, from shock and disbelief to intense sadness, anger, guilt, and loneliness. We may feel numb at times because it can be emotionally exhausting. Struggling to concentrate and make decisions are common challenges that come with the urgency of losing a loved one. Our appetite and sleep patterns change, and we may experience physical symptoms like headaches and fatigue. Sometimes we grapple with the reality of loss. The reality of it may not fully sink in until after the fact; and we may even question our faith and spiritual beliefs.

I want to encourage you that when you lose a loved one, it doesn't stop there. I want to encourage you to be purposeful and have the direction in life that you've always wanted, based on using the motivational side of the loss and turning it into the treasure that's already within you. Daily routines and responsibilities can obviously feel overwhelming, but continue to be courageous and strong from the inside out. You may withdraw from social media activities and relationships, and you may deal with triggers and reminders of the loss, but I want to encourage you to keep going and keep moving forward. At times, these challenges can feel like closed doors initially, even in the midst of the pain and the process of healing. That's another point—sometimes it takes a lot longer to grieve and a lot longer to heal, but it's okay—continue to do so. Anytime you feel like you need encouragement, you can always read this chapter as well.

We may find comfort in the memories of certain pictures or messages that we received from the loved one who has passed away. It's important as you navigate through this new reality of change. After losing a family member, it's crucial to discuss the decisions you're making with friends as well, because that is a key factor in the healing process. Even in the darkest times, there's hope.

Losing a loved one can lead to a renewed appreciation for life. It can also lead to finding new friends and a supportive community, offering professional, spiritual, and emotional comfort within a community of your choosing. It's important to remember that healing is not a linear process, and there will be ups and downs. You may struggle with the idea of forming new relationships or finding joy and happiness again, but it's still possible as you allow yourself to feel the depths of real love, in spite of what has been lost. You understand the journey of true self-discovery.

URGENCY OF PRIORITIES, AND SENSE OF PURPOSE

The urgency to reassess life goals, priorities, and sense of purpose often arises in the aftermath of a significant setback or a door closing unexpectedly. When we face a major disruption in our lives, it can shake the very foundation upon which we've built our plans and aspirations, forcing us to reevaluate our trajectories. This urgency can stem from various sources, such as job loss, relationship dissolution, health issues, or any other life-altering event that prompts us to question the path we're on. Suddenly, the goals that once seemed so clear and attainable may feel misaligned with our new realities or unfulfilling in the face of our changed circumstances.

In these moments, we're confronted with the opportunity to pause and reflect on what truly matters to us. The closed door, though initially painful, can serve as a catalyst for reassessing our priorities and realigning our goals with our deepest values and authentic selves. This process of reassessment can be both daunting and liberating. It requires a willingness to let go of preconceived notions and societal pressures, and instead, listen to the whispers of our hearts and souls. It demands courage to explore new paths, even if they diverge from the well-trodden roads we were once traveling on. For some, this reassessment may lead to a complete career shift or a radical change in lifestyle. For others, it may mean recalibrating their work-life balance, prioritizing relationships, or pursuing long-neglected passions. Regardless of the specific outcome, the urgency to reassess life goals and purpose can ultimately lead to a greater sense of authenticity, fulfillment, and alignment with one's true north.

However, this journey of reassessment is not without its challenges. It can be accompanied by feelings of uncertainty, fear, and even grief for the dreams and plans that must be left behind. Seeking support from loved ones, mentors, or professionals can provide invaluable guidance and encouragement during this transitional period. Ultimately, the urgency to reassess life goals, priorities, and purpose is a profound opportunity for growth and self-discovery. It invites us to shed the layers of expectations and societal norms that may have obscured our true callings, and instead, embrace a life path that is authentic, purposeful, and deeply resonant with our essence.

This journey of reassessment, though often challenging, holds the key to unlocking a life of genuine fulfillment and joy. It requires us to confront our fears, doubts, and insecurities head-on, and to cultivate the courage to step into the unknown, guided by the whispers of our hearts and the conviction of our values. In doing so, we not only liberate ourselves from the shackles of external expectations but also tap into a wellspring of self-knowledge and self-acceptance. We learn to trust our inner compass, to listen to the wisdom of our souls, and to chart a course that honors our unique gifts, passions, and purpose.

SOPHIA'S CLOSED DOOR THAT LED TO SCUBA DIVING

Sophia had always been a high achiever, excelling in her studies and landing a prestigious job at a top consulting firm straight out of college. For years, she worked tirelessly, putting in long hours and sacrificing her personal life in pursuit of career advancement and financial success. The allure of a six-figure salary, fancy office, and the respect that came with her position had been her driving force. However, during a much-needed vacation to a tropical island, Sophia's perspective shifted dramatically. On a whim, she decided to try scuba diving for the first time, and as she descended into the vibrant underwater world, she felt a profound sense of awe and connection she had never experienced before. The beauty of the coral reefs, the majesty of the marine life, and the tranquility of the underwater realm touched something deep within her soul.

In that moment, the urgency to reassess her life's goals and priorities became crystal clear. Sophia realized that her relentless pursuit of corporate success had come at the cost of neglecting her own sense of wonder, curiosity, and appreciation for the natural world around her. Upon returning from her vacation, Sophia made the bold decision to leave her high-powered consulting job and embark on a new path. She enrolled in a marine biology program, determined to turn her newfound passion for the ocean into a lifelong career. The transition was not without its challenges. Sophia had to adjust to a significant pay cut and navigate a completely different field. There were moments of self-doubt and criticism from those who questioned her decision to walk away from a prestigious career path.

However, Sophia's unwavering commitment to her newfound purpose propelled her forward. She became immersed in her studies, volunteered at local aquariums and conservation organizations, and built a network of like-minded individuals who shared her passion for preserving the health and beauty of the world's oceans. Today, Sophia works as a marine biologist, conducting research and leading conservation efforts to protect fragile coral reef ecosystems. Her work takes her to some of the most remote and breathtaking ocean environments, where she can share her love and knowledge of the underwater world with others.

Sophia's story serves as a powerful reminder that it is never too late to reassess our life's trajectory and realign ourselves with our deepest passions and values, even when it means venturing into uncharted territory. By courageously embracing the urgency of her calling, she discovered a profound sense of purpose and fulfillment that transcended the material trappings of her former life.

UNPACKING THE STORY

An interesting part of Sophia's story is that she was working a great job. She went to college. She had a six-figure income. However, her life took a dramatic turn based on just one vacation—one vacation changed her life. The first point that we could take away from this story is the trigger for change. Sophia's life-alternating experience of scuba diving during vacation exposed her to the beauty and wonder of the natural world, triggering a significant change in her perspective. Her unexpected, but profound connection with nature and water served as a catalyst for reassessing her life goals and questioning her corporate-driven priorities. The significance of this experience lies in how it prompted Sophia to pursue a more purposeful path, demonstrating the power of nature to inspire personal growth and transformation.

The second thing is the courage to pivot. I think a lot of us can relate to this because if you don't have the courage to pivot, that means you don't have the courage to change. The reason Sophia had the courage to pivot is because, in spite of the security, the prestigious job, and the financial success, Sophia recognized the urgency to align her life with her new profound passion. Then she resolved to courageously leave her high-powered consulting job to pursue a career in marine biology. That's important. Sophia's story teaches us the significance of real courage as the catalyst for change, and that leads us to the third key point … overcoming challenges.

Transitioning to a new career path was not without obstacles, including self-doubt and criticism from others; but Sophia's staunch commitment to her newfound purpose propelled her forward. She began to immerse in her studies, volunteering and building a supportive network and she was able to find purpose. Sophia's relentless pursuit of corporate success had caused her to neglect her sense of wonder and appreciation for the world around her. Recognizing this, she aligned her career with her passion for the ocean, and discovered a profound sense of purpose and fulfillment in protecting the marine ecosystem. Sophia's courage and journey serve as a powerful reminder that it's never too late to reassess your life trajectory and embrace authenticity. Her story illustrates the urgency of recognizing closed doors as opportunities for new beginnings and personal growth.

The last key point involves inspiring others. Sophia's story is a powerful reminder of how transformative moments can push us to re-evaluate our lives and priorities. Just like her life-changing scuba diving experience, we all encounter pivotal events that force us to reconsider our paths. These moments, whether joyous or painful, act as catalysts for personal growth and change. Imagine the splinter analogy—small yet capable of causing significant discomfort. Life's challenges, much like splinters, may seem minor at first but can have profound impacts if not addressed. They remind us to pay attention to the details and be mindful of our well-being. These transformative events, much like Sophia's scuba diving revelation, highlight the importance of staying open to change. They teach us resilience and the courage to pivot when necessary. Embracing these moments allows us to align our lives with our true passions and values, leading to greater fulfillment and purpose. In essence, the urgency of closed doors compels us to act, reflect, and grow. By navigating through these experiences with an open heart and mind, we can turn life's splinters into opportunities for healing and transformation. Much like Sophia's discovery of a new path in marine biology, we too can uncover new directions that bring us closer to our true selves.

URGENCY TO DEVELOP NEW SKILLS AND PURSUE EDUCATION

Education, in my personal opinion, holds the value that one assigns to it. Possessing a certificate or a degree does not necessarily equate to intelligence or an exceptional personality. The manner in which one studies, learns, and listens plays a pivotal role in the lifelong development of educational improvement. While some of the most successful individuals have dropped out of college to establish their own businesses, it is not a recommendation or provocation for everyone to follow suit.

Instead, the assertion is that if one possesses a well-formulated plan, a clear understanding of their objectives, and a defined trajectory, the guidance of a professor may not be essential to impart knowledge that one already possesses. Undoubtedly, formal education imparts valuable knowledge, but the true essence of what one makes of it manifests after the degree, when life's journey truly commences. The urgency of acquiring new skills and education can be self-taught, as well as learned through the general experience of living, encompassing failures, mistakes, and their consequent lessons.

THREE FUNDAMENTAL LIFE LESSONS TO REMEMBER ARE

1. BOOK KNOWLEDGE

While academic knowledge is invaluable, it is crucial to understand that mere theoretical comprehension is insufficient. The true value of book knowledge lies in its practical application and integration into one's daily life. Failing to transform theoretical concepts into tangible actions renders the knowledge redundant, and ultimately a waste of time and effort. Genuine wisdom emerges when one actively applies the lessons learned from books, continuously adapting and refining one's understanding through real-world experiences.

2. STREET KNOWLEDGE

Often overlooked in formal educational settings, street knowledge is the art of navigating the complexities of life. It encompasses situational awareness, the ability to read social cues, and a keen understanding of human behavior. Street knowledge entails recognizing potential threats, discerning ulterior motives, and protecting oneself from those who may seek to exploit or manipulate. In a world that can be unforgiving and isolating, street knowledge serves as a vital survival skill, enabling one to navigate challenges with resilience and resourcefulness.

3. HEART KNOWLEDGE

Perhaps the most profound form of knowledge, heart knowledge stems from emotional intelligence and the ability to connect with oneself and others on a deeper level. It is the wisdom that arises from lived experiences, empathy, and the capacity to heal from past traumas. Heart knowledge is the antidote to toxic relationships, generational curses, and the emotional baggage that can weigh heavily on one's psyche. By cultivating heart knowledge, one gains the power to break free from negative patterns, foster authentic connections, and ultimately live a life of greater fulfillment and emotional well-being.

In today's rapidly evolving digital landscape, formal education is no longer the sole avenue for skill acquisition. A wealth of online platforms, workshops, and self-guided learning materials are readily accessible, catering to diverse learning styles and schedules. The key lies in embracing a mindset of lifelong learning and seizing opportunities for growth whenever they present themselves. Developing new skills and pursuing additional education demands dedication, discipline, and a willingness to venture beyond one's comfort zone. It may necessitate sacrificing leisure time, embracing challenges head-on, and overcoming self-doubt or the fear of failure. However, the rewards of personal growth, increased competence, and expanded opportunities make the effort truly worthwhile. Ultimately, the urgency to develop new skills and pursue additional education is a testament to the innate human desire for growth and self-actualization. By embracing this urgency, individuals unlock their full potential, adapt to changing circumstances, and pave the way for a fulfilling and enriching life journey.

This urgency is not a one-time endeavor but rather a continuous cycle of learning and growth. As individuals progress through their careers and personal lives, new challenges and opportunities will inevitably arise, necessitating the acquisition of fresh knowledge and abilities. It is essential to cultivate a mindset of adaptability and embrace the ever-present need for skill development. Complacency and stagnation can be detrimental in a world that demands constant evolution and innovation. By remaining open to new experiences, seeking out mentors and experts in desired fields, and actively exploring emerging trends and technologies, individuals can stay ahead of the curve and position themselves for success. Within the professional realm, the urgency to acquire new skills and pursue additional education is a driving force that propels personal and professional growth. In our rapidly evolving world, complacency is a hindrance, and the embrace of lifelong learning becomes a necessity. This urgency can be fueled by career aspirations, personal interests, or a desire for intellectual stimulation, and it can be addressed through various avenues, including formal education, vocational training, self-directed study, and experiential learning.

Ultimately, true mastery lies in the synthesis of three fundamental forms of knowledge: book knowledge, street knowledge, and heart knowledge. Book knowledge imparts theoretical concepts, but its true value is realized through practical application and adaptation to real-world experiences. Street knowledge equips individuals with the situational awareness and resilience to navigate life's complexities; while heart knowledge fosters emotional intelligence, empathy, and the capacity to heal from past traumas, fostering authentic connections and personal fulfillment.

URGENCY TO DEVELOP ORGANIZATIONAL SKILLS FOR JUGGLING MULTIPLE PRIORITIES

By embracing the urgency to develop new skills, pursuing additional education, and cultivating a harmonious balance of these three forms of knowledge, individuals can unlock their full potential, adapt to changing circumstances, and contribute to the betterment of society as a whole. Education is not a finite destination but a lifelong journey of self-discovery, growth, and the relentless pursuit of wisdom in all its multifaceted forms. The following is an example of a celebrity who had to urgently develop new time management and organizational skills to juggle multiple priorities:

THE OPRAH WINFREY EFFECT

Oprah Winfrey is a media mogul, philanthropist, and one of the most influential figures in the entertainment industry. Throughout her illustrious career, she has worn many hats—talk show host, actress, producer, author, and entrepreneur—all of which required impeccable time management and organizational abilities. In the early years of her acclaimed talk show, *The Oprah Winfrey Show,* Oprah often found herself overwhelmed by the demands of her rapidly growing fame and responsibilities. As her show gained unprecedented popularity and her media empire began to expand, she realized the urgent need to develop robust time management strategies to maintain her productivity and sanity.

In an interview with Harvard Business Review, Oprah shared her approach to time management: "I had to start dealing with where I was putting my time and energy. I had to become productive to be able to get it all done." She began implementing strict schedules, prioritizing tasks, and delegating responsibilities to her team. One of Oprah's key strategies was to compartmentalize her day into specific time blocks dedicated to different aspects of her work. She would allocate specific hours for meetings, interviews, script reviews, and other essential tasks, ensuring that each area received her undivided attention without overlap or distractions.

Oprah also learned the importance of saying "no" to commitments that did not align with her priorities. As her fame grew, she was inundated with requests and opportunities, but she developed the discipline to decline anything that would stretch her too thin or compromise her ability to excel in her core areas of focus. Additionally, Oprah recognized the value of personal time and self-care in maintaining her productivity and overall well-being. She made it a priority to schedule dedicated time for exercise, meditation, and leisure activities, understanding that these practices would fuel her energy and creativity.

It's ok to say "no" to the commitments that
do not line up with your priority.

Oprah's commitment to time management and organization allowed her to navigate the demands of her multifaceted career while also pursuing philanthropic endeavors, such as the establishment of the Oprah Winfrey Leadership Academy for Girls in South Africa, and her involvement in various charitable initiatives. Through her relentless dedication and disciplined approach, Oprah Winfrey not only achieved unprecedented success, but also demonstrated the transformative power of effective time management and organization in enabling individuals to juggle multiple priorities and capitalize on their full potential.

UNPACKING OPRAH'S REAL-LIFE STORY

HUMBLE BEGINNINGS (1954-1964)

Some people might only know the Google quick search version of Oprah Winfrey. I'm going to give you an in-depth version of her life, broken down in layers. This will allow you to appreciate what she went through, how she did it, how she overcame it, how she strategized within it, and how she transformed what appeared to be a cycle of adversity and closed doors into purpose and power, using it to her advantage.

Oprah's humble beginnings started in Kosciusko, Mississippi, where she was born and raised by her unmarried teenage mother, Vernita Lee. She was born into poverty and started out in lack. The home in which she was raised had no running water or electricity. Her grandmother named her *Oprah* after the biblical phrase "Ruth, her visage cometh." During her early years, Oprah was raised on a farm by her grandmother, Hattie Mae Lee. She wore dresses that were made from potato sacks. At the young age of three, Oprah began attending a local church where she fine-tuned her skill and craft as a public speaker and performing artist.

When I began to study and research Oprah's life, I became fascinated by her ability to transform and adapt to the environments she was interested in. Always remember, "You adapt to the environments that you choose to adjust to, regardless of the obstacles and distractions around you." As Oprah continued to go to church, along with perfecting her speaking skills, her grandmother started teaching her how to read at a young age. She excelled at this skill rapidly. As she matured, Oprah endured prolonged sexual abuse and trauma from male relatives and acquaintances, starting when she was nine years old. This experience led to promiscuity and rebellious behavior in her teenage years.

MOVE TO MILWAUKEE (1964-1971)

The purpose for the move to Milwaukee was to help Oprah's mother, Vernita, and the family have a better life by looking for work as a housemaid. Despite living with her mother, Oprah faced constant instability, moving back-and-forth between relatives and experiencing homelessness. At age 13, while homeless, she gave birth to a premature baby who tragically died shortly after. In spite of negative downturns and setbacks, Oprah excelled academically. She became an honors student at Lincoln High School, re-dedicating herself to academics. This refocus and dedication earned her a full scholarship to Tennessee State University in 1971 to study communications.

MEDIA CAREER BEGINNINGS (1972-1976)

Oprah's foray into the media world was an unexpected and serendipitous turn of events. While working at a CBS affiliate station in Nashville to support herself through college, an opportunity arose that would set her on an extraordinary trajectory. In 1973, Oprah was asked to fill in as a reporter and subsequently as a news anchor, becoming the first Black female news anchor in the city. Her natural charisma and ability to connect with viewers were immediately evident, a harbinger of her future success in captivating audiences.

This initial taste of on-air work ignited a spark within Oprah, and in 1976, she relocated to Baltimore to join WJZ-TV as a reporter and co-anchor. It was during this pivotal period that Oprah had her first encounter with hosting a television show when she was reassigned to the locally produced talk show *People are Talking*.

BECOMING A MULTIMEDIA MOGUL (1987-2011)

As *The Oprah Winfrey Show* skyrocketed in popularity, Oprah's influence and ambition grew exponentially. In 1987, she made a pivotal move by launching her own production company, HARPO Productions, allowing her to gain ownership and creative control over her enormously successful show. With her newfound autonomy, Oprah expanded her reach into acting, starring in critically acclaimed films like *The Color Purple* and *Beloved*, adapted from the novels of literary giants. Her performances showcased her dramatic range and further solidified her as a multidimensional talent.

In the 1990s and 2000s, Oprah's media empire continued to diversify and dominate new platforms. Her launch of the influential "Oprah's Book Club" reignited national interest in literature and fostered a thriving community of readers. Her award-winning *O, The Oprah Magazine* became a beloved monthly touchstone for millions seeking inspiration and self-improvement. Oprah's Midas touch extended to television, where she produced and promoted numerous hit shows like *Dr. Phil*, *Rachael Ray*, and the Emmy-winning *Tuesdays with Morrie*. She even ventured into Broadway, producing hit musicals like *The Color Purple* and cementing her status as a multimedia visionary. In 2011, Oprah achieved another milestone by launching the Oprah Winfrey Network (OWN), a cable channel dedicated to uplifting and empowering viewers through inspirational programming.

PHILANTHROPIC WORK AND GLOBAL IMPACT

Throughout her meteoric rise to stardom, Oprah remained grounded in her commitment to using her platform to address social issues and uplift underserved communities. In 1998, she established the Oprah's Angel Network, a public charity that raised more than $80 million for humanitarian causes worldwide, including relief efforts for Hurricane

Katrina and the 2010 Haiti earthquake. Perhaps, her most enduring philanthropic legacy is the Oprah Winfrey Leadership Academy for Girls, founded in 2007. Located in Henley on Klip, South Africa, the boarding school provides a world-class education, leadership training, and mentorship to young women from disadvantaged backgrounds. To date, the academy has graduated over 600 students, empowering them to break cycles of poverty and become leaders in their communities.

ENDURING LEGACY

At 71 years old, Oprah Winfrey stands as one of the most influential and wealthy self-made women in the world, with a net worth estimated at over $3 billion. However, her true legacy extends far beyond financial success and accolades. Oprah's ability to overcome adversity, her authentic connection with audiences across all walks of life, and her unwavering commitment to using her platform for positive change have inspired millions worldwide. From her humble beginnings in rural Mississippi to becoming a cultural icon, Oprah's life story is a testament to the transformative power of resilience, hard work, and the relentless pursuit of one's dreams.

Even as she stepped away from her legendary talk show in 2011, Oprah's influence and impact have only continued to grow. Through her media ventures, public appearances, and philanthropic initiatives, she continues to shape narratives, challenge societal norms, and empower individuals to embrace their truth and reach for their highest potential. Oprah's journey serves as a powerful reminder that with determination, passion, and an unwavering belief in oneself, extraordinary achievements are possible—even in the face of seemingly insurmountable obstacles. Her life is a masterclass in using one's voice and platform to create meaningful change, while inspiring others to do the same. As she continues to evolve and leave an indelible mark on the world, Oprah Winfrey's legacy as a trailblazer, visionary, and catalyst for positive transformation will undoubtedly endure for generations to come.

The Urgency of Closed Doors and Life Lessons Oprah Winfrey's story is a profound testament to the power of resilience and the ability to transform adversity into opportunity. From her impoverished beginnings and traumatic childhood experiences, to the setbacks and rejections she faced throughout her career, Oprah encountered numerous "closed doors" that could have derailed her journey. However, her unwavering determination and refusal to surrender to circumstance allowed her to turn these obstacles into catalysts for growth and self-discovery. Her ability to adapt and thrive in challenging environments, harnessing the power of education and self-improvement, serves as a powerful lesson in the importance of embracing a growth mindset. Oprah's journey reminds us that closed doors are not permanent barriers but rather temporary detours on the path to realizing our full potential.

Moreover, Oprah's authentic connection with her audience and her commitment to using her platform for positive change underscore the profound impact that vulnerability and purpose can have. By courageously sharing her truth and amplifying the voices of others, she has inspired countless individuals to embrace their own stories and strive for a life of meaning and service. Ultimately, Oprah's legacy is a testament to the transformative power of perseverance, authenticity, and the relentless pursuit of one's dreams. Her life serves as a reminder that extraordinary achievements are possible when we refuse to be defined by our circumstances and instead choose to harness our inner strength, adaptability, and unwavering belief in ourselves.

Before we dive into the next chapter, I want you to remember that the urgency of a closed door can either make you or break you. It's what you do behind the closed door that makes the difference. All the examples that I have given you, along with the stories, are tools to equip, enhance, inspire, launch, and propel you to the next level of your goals, passions, and dreams all in one.

IN CONCLUSION

The urgency of a closed door is a pivotal moment that demands a choice—will you allow it to break your spirit, or will you use it as a catalyst to forge a new path? The decision you make in these moments of adversity can shape the trajectory of your life. The examples and stories shared serve as a powerful reminder that closed doors are not permanent barriers but rather opportunities for growth, adaptation, and the cultivation of resilience. They are the catalysts that ignite the fires of determination, pushing us to dig deeper, stretch beyond our perceived limitations, and unlock reservoirs of strength we never knew existed.

Embrace these tools as guideposts on your journey, for they are imbued with the wisdom and inspiration of those who have navigated their own closed doors and emerged triumphant. Let their stories equip you with the knowledge and courage to face your challenges head-on, to adapt and evolve, and to transform adversity into advantage. Remember, it is what you do behind the closed door that truly matters. Will you surrender to despair, or will you use this urgency as a launchpad to propel yourself toward your goals, passions, and dreams? The choice is yours, and the power to shape your destiny lies within.

Approach each closed door with the unwavering belief that it is not the end but merely a detour, a test of your resolve, and an opportunity to redefine your path. Embrace the urgency as a force that strips away complacency and ignites within you a hunger for growth, a thirst for knowledge, and an unshakable determination to reach for greatness. Let these examples and stories be the fuel that ignites your inner fire, inspiring you to rise above adversity, to adapt and conquer, and to emerge as the architect of your own destiny. For it is in these moments of urgency, when faced with the closed door, that the true mettle of your spirit is forged, and the boundaries of your potential are pushed ever outward.

Ultimately, the journey through life's closed doors is a test of character, a crucible that separates those who succumb to circumstance from those who refuse to be defined by it. Embrace the urgency, not as a burden, but as a sacred gift—a catalyst for personal transformation, a call to awaken the hero within, and a reminder that the greatest achievements often lie on the other side of the most formidable obstacles. With each closed door you encounter and overcome, you will emerge stronger, wiser, and more resilient, forging a legacy of perseverance and triumph that will inspire generations to come.

CHAPTER 5

THE TEACHER OF CLOSED DOORS

When most people think of teachers, the first image that comes to mind is someone who really knows what they're talking about, someone who is adept at instructing and imparting knowledge in a classroom. It's like a real-life architect formulating a game plan that students can walk through and apply before they build their own understanding. For a teacher to deliver a truly great lesson, students have to be willing to learn, be vulnerable, and adapt to the classroom environment. If I could be fully transparent, I owe every teacher an apology for not fully absorbing the lessons like I was supposed to. The reason for that is simple: I was caught up in my own world, wanting to rush the learning process, rather than submitting to the actual lesson and genuinely learning it. I would try to think ahead of the teacher, raising my hand five minutes before she even got started. Because of this, I had to learn the hard way. My comprehension level wasn't as strong as I thought it was growing up.

This realization made me understand that life itself is like a Teacher of Closed Doors. Life breaks down the definitions of what you're going through, how you perceive it, and how you cope with the outcomes of closed doors. Just as a teacher plans and prepares educational content to align with learning objectives and cater to different learning styles, life presents us with challenges and closed doors that align with our personal growth and learning needs.

When faced with closed doors, much like in a classroom, we must be willing to be vulnerable, to learn, and to adapt. Each closed door serves as a lesson, teaching us to set boundaries, recognize red flags, and value our time and effort. These lessons, whether learned in a classroom or through life's experiences, are crucial for personal growth and resilience. They remind us to approach challenges with the same dedication and openness that we would bring to any learning opportunity.

CLOSED DOORS WILL TEACH YOU LIFE LESSONS

Every closed door I encountered in life felt like a real-life case study, a lecture, and an introspective discussion with myself. Just as an effective teacher provides space for students to communicate their learnings through group discussions, my life offered me a parallel process of self-reflection and internal dialogue. One of the most significant challenges I faced with the Teacher of Closed Doors was my transition from the fishing industry to navigating the demands of everyday life. I felt a profound sense of real-life accountability that I knew I had to embrace to break free from any cycles of lack and disappointment that may have persisted in my past. In 2015, at the age of 35, I found myself dating again, accompanied by the desire to find a life partner with whom I could establish a covenant marriage blessed by God. However, the reality was that, despite being in my mid-thirties, the experience of navigating the modern dating world still felt like being a student, grappling with unfamiliar dynamics and lessons to be learned. My initial mistake of taking potential partners out for extravagant dinner dates on first encounters led me to realize that I was inadvertently setting the wrong expectations; some individuals were primarily motivated by the prospect of a free meal.

When it came to dating, the Teacher of Closed Doors taught me more than I ever imagined. To keep it all the way 100 with you, I was ticked off when I realized how many women just wanted a free meal and a lavish first date. The Teacher in that closed door taught me to start by going to coffee cafes, Starbucks, and not go over the top for women I didn't really know. They would say all the right things, smile, and use typical gestures to appear genuinely interested in me.

What did I learn from this? I realized that when you overdo things to impress people you don't really know, you not only run the risk of being broke, but you can also be taken advantage of. For instance, I remember a date with a young lady who seemed to have it all together—career, looks, kindness, no drama, and financial stability. The only problem was that she would always get a call in the middle of our dates, whether we were talking, eating, or just enjoying the moment.

> *"I realized that when you overdo things to impress people you don't really know, you not only run the risk of being broke, but you can also be taken advantage of."*

I was cool with it the first time, but when it happened repeatedly, it became irritating. I eventually mentioned to her that she should either turn her phone off, tell whoever was calling that she was busy on a date, or simply reschedule. This was during a time when my patience wasn't at its best, I'll admit. It was a challenge for me. I began to ask myself, "Why is she taking this third and fourth call? Does she even appreciate this moment? Apparently, this is something she often does with other guys. Am I just another guy?" As these questions began to flow, I realized this was the Teacher of Closed Doors in dating. I had to master taking time to heal from a lot of heavy pain and brokenness from the dates alone.

THE LESSONS WERE CLEAR

First, the importance of setting boundaries. When you set clear boundaries, you protect yourself from being taken advantage of and maintain your self-respect. Establishing boundaries helps you communicate your needs and expectations clearly. It creates a framework within which both parties can operate respectfully. Boundaries also serve as a litmus test for how much the other person respects you and your time.

Second, recognizing red flags early on. If someone is consistently distracted or unavailable, it's a sign they might not be fully invested in the relationship. Early recognition of red flags can save you a lot of heartache down the line. It's crucial to trust your instincts. If something feels off, it probably is. Red flags can be anything from lack of communication, inconsistency in actions, to always being too busy. Recognizing these signs early helps you avoid deeper emotional investment in someone who isn't right for you.

"If something feels off, it probably is. Red flags can be anything from lack of communication, inconsistency in actions, to always being too busy."

Third, valuing your time and effort. When you put a lot of effort into dating, it should be reciprocated. If it's not, it's better to move on and find someone who appreciates you. Your time and effort are valuable, and you deserve to be with someone who acknowledges and reciprocates them. Investing in a relationship should be a two-way street. If you're constantly giving and not receiving the same level of effort and commitment, it's a sign that the relationship is unbalanced. Moving on from such situations is not only wise but necessary for your self-respect and emotional health.

These experiences taught me to be more discerning and cautious. I learned to appreciate the value of genuine connection over superficial gestures. The Teacher of Closed Doors in dating helped me grow stronger, more self-aware, and better prepared for a meaningful relationship.

THE TOUGHEST CLASSES HAPPEN IN UNEXPECTED PLACES

In life, you don't always get easy options to choose from. Sometimes, the Teacher of the closed door is actually the classroom itself. For me, some of the toughest classes happened in the most unexpected places, like my early days of dating. I thought I knew the game, thought I had it all figured out. I would tell myself, "I'm not going to mess up again," but the Teacher of Closed Doors had different plans. After a series of failed attempts, I realized that I needed to take a break and focus on building a life with substance before diving back into dating.

Just as a teacher needs the right environment to educate students, I needed to be in the right environment to learn. I had to humble myself and adopt a student mindset. We all encounter different classroom settings in life, especially when facing closed doors. These experiences are not just classrooms; they come with homework too. Doing the homework of life means following through on what it takes to start fresh, get your own place, and get your credit in order.

Credit, for instance, is a classroom of its own. Maintaining good credit requires discipline and foresight. When I was in the fishing industry, I focused solely on making money, neglecting to establish and maintain good credit. That oversight made things harder when I wanted to make significant purchases like a car or a home. My credit was my biggest challenge, and I had to face it head-on.

The classroom taught by the Teacher of Closed Doors is uncomfortable. The instructor doesn't go easy on you, but the lessons toughen you up for life's real tests. You get practice handling disappointment much like lifting weights and gradually increasing the load to build muscle. This teacher equips you with the mindset, grit, and determination to kick down whatever doors stand in your way. Each closed door teaches you valuable lessons about resilience and perseverance. It's about gaining the strength to navigate life's challenges and emerging stronger on the other side. This process shapes you into someone who can handle setbacks with grace and use them as stepping stones to success. Embrace the lessons from these closed doors, as they prepare you for the open ones ahead.

THREE POINTS TO REMEMBER

1. SET CLEAR BOUNDARIES

Setting boundaries protects you from being taken advantage of and helps you maintain self-respect. This is crucial in all areas of life, whether it's dating, work, or personal relationships. Boundaries ensure that you prioritize your well-being and set the tone for how others should treat you.

2. RECOGNIZE RED FLAGS EARLY

Pay attention to the early signs that something might not be right. Whether it's someone being consistently distracted during a date or a job that feels off from the start, recognizing these red flags early can save you from bigger disappointments and heartaches down the line. It allows you to make informed decisions about whether to continue or move on.

3. VALUE YOUR TIME AND EFFORT

Your time and effort are precious. When you invest in something or someone, it should be reciprocated. If it's not, it's important to reassess and possibly move on to find situations where your contributions are valued. This principle ensures that you don't waste your resources on pursuits that don't offer meaningful returns. Remembering these points helps you navigate through closed doors more effectively. They teach you to be proactive, aware, and respectful of your own needs and efforts, which are key to building a fulfilling and balanced life.

2024 MOVIE: BAD BOYS (RIDE OR DIE)

The best way to break down the Teacher-of-Closed-Doors concept is through the lens of the movie *Bad Boys Ride or Die*. My wife and I watched it recently, and it's still fresh in my mind. In the movie, the city of Miami (FL) is under siege from a dangerous new cartel that uses cutting-edge technology to carry out sophisticated cybercrimes and precision heists. These criminals are next-level, pushing the city's police force to its limits as they find themselves outmatched and desperately in need of officers with unique skills to take down these tech-savvy criminals.

Enter Mike Lowry, played by Will Smith, and Marcus Burnett, played by Martin Lawrence. These legendary bad boys had retired from the force, living a quiet life. However, the new cartel's cyberattacks started to directly threaten the safety of their families, forcing Mike and Marcus out of retirement; but returning to the force wasn't as straightforward as before. Technology had advanced, and the old-school tactics they used to rely on were now useless against digitally-savvy criminals. This scenario teaches a vital lesson about the Teacher of Closed Doors. Sometimes, life presents challenges that require us to adapt and reinvent ourselves. Mike and Marcus face this head-on when their initial attempts to combat the cartel using outdated methods failed spectacularly. They realized that the closed door of their old ways of being the hero cops necessitated a different approach to survive a new kind of threat. They needed to master the digital landscape, just as they once mastered the streets.

By the movie's end, Mike and Marcus not only saved their families but also successfully navigated the digital world, showcasing the importance of reinvention. They learned that to overcome new challenges, they needed a team just as advanced as the enemy they were fighting. This is a fitting metaphor for the Teacher of Closed Doors in real life. When faced with a closed door, it's crucial to seek out new knowledge and skills, often relying on a team that complements your strengths and weaknesses.

LESSONS FROM THE MOVIE

1. ADAPT OR GET LEFT BEHIND

In the rapidly evolving world of 2024, Mike Lowrey and Marcus Burnett faced the harsh reality that their traditional police tactics and reputations as "Bad Boys" were no match for the sophisticated cybercrimes perpetrated by the new cartel threat. Rather than stubbornly clinging to the comfortable methods that had served them well in the past, they made the difficult choice to adapt by stepping out of their comfort zones.

By embracing the humbling process of learning coding, cybersecurity practices, digital surveillance and more from an unlikely mentor, they exemplified the core lesson: evolve with the changing landscape, or risk becoming obsolete. The Teacher of Closed Doors demands a constant willingness to let go of what's familiar and acquire new skills to remain relevant. Refusing to adapt is akin to accepting stagnation and irrelevance.

2. EMBRACE THE HUMBLING PROCESS

For two veteran cops like Mike and Marcus, icons who had solidified legendary reputations as the "Bad Boys" of the Miami streets, being forced to start over as novice students was an immense blow to their egos. However, their ability to humble themselves, set aside their pride, and eagerly learn digital warfare tactics from someone decades younger than them was a testament to the transformative power of the Teacher. This lesson reminds us that true growth and mastery often require a willingness to be humbled. The Teacher of Closed Doors shows no favoritism—everyone must go through the refining process of unlearning old habits, shedding arrogance, and embracing a beginner's mindset to obtain new levels of expertise.

3. NEVER STOP LEARNING

After decades of successful careers in law enforcement, Mike and Marcus could have easily chosen to remain complacent and enjoy their hard-earned retirement. However, when the new criminal threat emerged, the Teacher reminded them of the perils of stagnation through its tough love lessons. By inspiring them to constantly seek new skills and knowledge, even late in their careers, the Teacher exemplified that the moment we stop learning and evolving is the moment we start dying in relevance. The hunger to be lifelong students, always seeking to add new capabilities and understand emerging landscapes, is what allowed Mike and Marcus to remain vital assets instead of becoming obsolete relics. Complacency breeds atrophy—the Teacher's lessons urge us to continuously feed our hunger for growth.

4. FIND UNLIKELY MOTIVATORS

Just when Mike and Marcus had settled into the comfort of their retirement plans, an unexpected motivator—the threat to their families' safety—reignited their sense of purpose with an urgency they hadn't felt in years. This illustrates how the Teacher of Closed Doors can sometimes arrive through surprising sources of inspiration that shake us from complacency. The lessons remind us to remain open to new sources of motivation, which can emerge from unlikely places. What initially presents itself as an impediment may actually be a wakeup call prompting us to rediscover our drive and reassess our "why" for pushing forward with renewed vigor.

5. COMBINE NEW WITH PROVEN PRINCIPLES

While Mike and Marcus made the critical choice to evolve by adding digital skillsets and modern tactical approaches, they didn't completely abandon the core tenets and principles that had defined them as "Bad Boys" for so many years. Their experiences taught them to merge new knowledge and approaches with their proven fundamentals of loyalty, determination and commitment to justice. The Teacher's lessons show that true growth and longevity often lie in the wise combination of adopting new competencies while holding firm to timeless, undergirding values and principles that have been foundational sources of strength. Discarding the old, altogether, is rarely the wisest solution when evolving.

6. PAVE THE WAY FOR THE NEXT CLASS

With their success at defeating the criminal empire, Mike and Marcus didn't just save the day, they ended up pioneering the new prototype for law enforcement in the digital age. By becoming "cyber cops" who could deftly navigate both the physical and virtual spheres of threats, these two lovable relics created the blueprint to pass the torch to the next generation of crime fighters. This illustrates the Teacher's highest lesson—to use the closed doors we encounter as motivation to open new doors of opportunity for those who follow in our footsteps. The resilience we cultivate in facing our own setbacks is not just for personal gains—it's to pave more promising paths forward for the next wave of proteges coming behind us.

*

BORN INTO POVERTY

When poverty persists across multiple generations within a family, it creates a compounding effect, stacking hardships on top of each other. This makes it incredibly difficult to escape when you're born into the closed door of a setback or poverty. Children born into such circumstances often face numerous obstacles from the very start, like lack of access to quality education and resources. They attend underfunded schools with limited resources and support systems. Many cities in the U.S., including Chicago, still face this issue due to poverty and a lack of community investment. The community itself lacks resources, which can be seen as a closed door, but it teaches us unique ways to navigate through these limitations. Kids in these environments might find ways to access books, technology, and education by going to libraries or finding other creative solutions. Another significant challenge is limited exposure to activities and opportunities. Local and community activities that foster growth and education are often lacking in impoverished areas.

Inadequate nutrition and healthcare are also common in these environments, leading to high risks of malnutrition. Unstable housing and living conditions, including overcrowded areas and lack of basic amenities, further complicate life. While I was fortunate not to live in this type of environment, my heart goes out to those who do. They face chronic stress, violence, and other hardships that can seem insurmountable. Living in Brooklyn, New York, in 2007 and 2008, I witnessed firsthand how poverty and violence intersect. For example, Popeye's had a special deal offering a 10-piece chicken dinner for $4.99, which led to fights and even shootings in line. The lack of infrastructure and security made me constantly worry about my safety. These experiences taught me that there must be a better way to live.

HERE ARE SOME KEY TAKEAWAYS

The hardships associated with poverty can motivate you to think beyond your immediate circumstances. The drive to escape poverty can push you to think more strategically about your future, encouraging you to seek out education and opportunities that can help you rise above your situation. Education and personal talents are powerful tools for escaping poverty. Leveraging educational opportunities and honing your talents can provide a pathway to better opportunities. Use your gift(s) and talent(s) as a way out. Seek mentors and resources that can guide you. In today's world, technology offers unprecedented opportunities for personal growth and financial independence. Use your phone and the internet to create content, start a business, or connect with people who can help you. Platforms like YouTube, TikTok, and various social media can be powerful tools for building a brand and generating income. The Teacher of Closed Doors in poverty can be harsh, but it also offers valuable lessons in resilience, creativity, and the power of education. These lessons can help you navigate through life's challenges and find a path to a better future. Use these tips to inspire yourself and others to break the cycle of poverty and build a life of opportunity and success.

While the harsh realities of impoverished environments can instill a sense of hopelessness, it is crucial to reframe that mindset. The closed doors and limitations imposed by poverty should not be viewed as permanent barriers, but rather as catalysts for unleashing one's inner drive, resilience, and creative problem-solving abilities. A key lesson from the Teacher is the power of cultivating a growth mindset—the belief that abilities and circumstances are not fixed but can be developed and improved through dedicated effort. Those who embrace this mindset are more likely to view setbacks and challenges as opportunities for growth, rather than insurmountable obstacles.

Another powerful lesson lies in the importance of building a strong support system and seeking out positive role models. In communities affected by generational poverty, having access to mentors, community leaders, and peers who have successfully navigated similar challenges can provide invaluable guidance, inspiration, and a sense of possibility. Furthermore, the Teacher highlights the significance of developing a long-term vision and setting achievable goals. While immediate circumstances may seem dire, having a clear vision of the future you desire and breaking it down into actionable steps can help maintain motivation and a sense of direction amidst adversity.

Alongside this, the lesson of adaptability and resourcefulness cannot be overstated. Poverty often necessitates creative problem-solving and the ability to make the most of limited resources. Developing these skills can foster an entrepreneurial mindset, enabling individuals to identify opportunities and generate value in unexpected ways. Ultimately, the Teacher of Closed Doors, as exemplified through the challenges of poverty, imparts lessons that extend far beyond financial constraints. It instills resilience, determination, and understanding that one's circumstances do not define their potential for growth and achievement.

By embracing these lessons, individuals can transform the closed doors of poverty into open pathways for personal and professional development, breaking free from cycles of limitation and paving the way for a future of increased opportunity and fulfillment. The lessons imparted by the Teacher of Closed Doors, exemplified through the harsh realities of poverty, are not merely abstract concepts but rather a powerful blueprint for personal transformation and societal progress. While the challenges posed by impoverished circumstances are undeniably daunting, they also present a unique opportunity to cultivate a mindset of resilience, adaptability, and unwavering determination.

By embracing the growth mindset, seeking out positive support systems, and developing a long-term vision guided by achievable goals, individuals can transcend the limitations imposed by their current circumstances and unlock their true potential. The journey may be arduous, but the rewards of perseverance are immense—a life of increased opportunity, self-sufficiency, and the ability to inspire and empower others who find themselves facing similar closed doors.

Moreover, the lessons of the Teacher extend beyond individual growth, serving as a catalyst for broader societal change. As those who have navigated the harsh realities of poverty emerge empowered, they become agents of transformation, equipped with the knowledge, empathy, and drive to dismantle systemic barriers and create more equitable and inclusive communities.

In this way, the Teacher of Closed Doors serves as a reminder that adversity, when faced with courage and determination, can be transformed into a powerful force for positive change. The closed doors of poverty may be formidable, but they are not impenetrable—they are merely the starting point for a journey of personal growth, community empowerment, and the realization of a more just and prosperous world for all.

*

BETRAYAL CAN TEACH BEHIND CLOSED DOORS

The pain and devastation caused by betrayal have been some of life's harshest teachers for me, delivering brutal lessons through the closed doors of broken trust. When betrayal gets out of hand and real people get hurt, killed, bruised, frustrated, and overwhelmed all at once, it represents an agonizing crucible that few are prepared to endure. My personal definition of betrayal is a person who secretly goes behind your back to destroy your life, family, business, and well-being in the most treacherous way possible. This cuts to the core of why this experience is so traumatic. It's a violation of that fundamental human need for safety, security, and the ability to trust those closest to you.

The Teacher that emerges from such profound betrayal is as unforgiving as it is transformative, and I know that firsthand. It's lessons often come at an exorbitant emotional and psychological cost, but they possess the power to radically reshape your perspectives, priorities, and even your very identity, as they did for me. The words associated with betrayal that come to my mind—disloyalty, deception, double-crossing, fraud, treason, breach of allegiance, derailed devotion, and eroded dependability—all speak to the shattering of the social contracts and covenants that allow us to function and thrive as individuals and societies. I felt this intensely.

When those sacred bonds are violated, the Teacher arrives uninvited, forcing you to confront harsh truths about human nature, the fragility of trust, and the necessity of developing an almost impenetrable emotional fortitude. It's a closed door that can lead some to retreat into bitter cynicism and isolated self-preservation, as it initially did for me.

However, I was eventually willing to endure the painful process of healing and introspection, and the Teacher of Betrayal imparted invaluable wisdom. It cultivated in me a deeper sense of discernment, helping me identify toxic patterns and relationships before irrevocable harm was done again. It inspired a recalibration of my values and priorities, realigning me with my authentic self and the people who truly deserved my loyalty.

This Teacher also instilled in me a profound appreciation for the treasures of true friendship, love, and trust when they are hard-won and nurtured through life's tempests. The scars of betrayal, though permanent, became emblems of my resilience and reminders of the preciousness of genuine human connection. Ultimately, I chose not to succumb to the closed doors of bitterness and mistrust but rather to emerge from the ashes of betrayal as a more discerning, self-aware, and compassionate individual. The Teacher of Betrayal was merciless, but its lessons, absorbed with humility and courage, forged a character of remarkable depth, integrity, and wisdom in me.

WE ALL CAN RELATE TO SOME TYPE OF BETRAYAL

I think we can all relate to the subtleties of betrayal and the hardship that comes with it. The initial feelings of shock, disbelief, and devastation, when the reality of betrayal becomes clear, are often overwhelming and gut-wrenching. The truth is that it all hurts at once, especially when you have committed your time to trust a person who, behind closed doors, wasn't who you thought they were. Suffering at the hands of those we trusted and allowed close enough to deeply impact our lives shakes our core sense of self-worth, making even the strongest among us question our very fundamental sense of value and reason.

Betrayal can be so undercutting that it makes you say, "Wait a minute, they took advantage of me based on my kindness and my gullibility." Betrayal often feeds off gullibility, especially when reality kicks in. When reality sets in, emotions may run the gamut from rage and anger to confusion, fear, and profound sadness. Each sleepless night brings torment and the fear of being hurt again. "How could this happen?" is the question most people ask. "How did I miss the signs? How could I have been so blind? Was it me? Was it the environment? What was it? Will I ever be able to trust again?"

The key is to let betrayal teach you how to endure hardship even after the fact. Betrayal is its own teacher behind closed doors, and it's a psychological teacher as well. It can literally open doors for your mental health, teaching you how to maneuver when someone else betrays you, and helping you recognize the initial warning signs, or history signs that indicate something is wrong.

The restoration process takes time, but I have learned that the more time I take to heal, the more I see the bigger picture of that moment. I am at the age where I choose to be peaceful, kind, and genuine, but at the same time, direct and assertive. I do not assume that anyone can just run over me or see me as weak. It is crucial to ensure that the people around you—whether they are family, business associates, or influencers—see you as a trustworthy person.

Betrayal teaches us resilience, discernment, and the value of genuine connections. By embracing these lessons, we can rebuild our self-worth and navigate future relationships with greater wisdom and caution. In the end, the strength gained from overcoming betrayal can fortify us against future hardships, ensuring that we emerge stronger, wiser, and more self-aware.

BANKRUPTCY THAT MAKES YOU START FROM SCRATCH

I remember the time when I was so close to bankruptcy that I had to start from scratch, even at the age of 24. Bankruptcy is one of those unthinkable events that force you to rebuild from the ground up. It's as if your entire life is now a classroom, with a door that stubbornly refuses to open, teaching you lessons you never wanted to learn. This closed-door moment strips away the financial security and achievements you've worked tirelessly to build. Imagine all those years of saving and planning, only to face bankruptcy due to job loss or unforeseen circumstances.

Bankruptcy is a harsh teacher, and it demands that you confront the stark realities of what truly matters beyond material possessions and status symbols. It's like shedding the shackles of excessive materialism that only aggravate your wounds. Bankruptcy is a masterclass in humility and letting go of ego. We all can relate to this because our ego is intricately tied to our financial status. When your finances are disrupted, and you're left with no choice but to file for bankruptcy, it changes you fundamentally.

Over the years, I've heard countless stories from family members and friends who have faced bankruptcy. Some lived through the aftermath for five, six, or even seven years, unable to get approved for a home or a vehicle. They felt they had no choice but to file for bankruptcy, but I must stress that bankruptcy should never be your first resort. It's a long and arduous journey of lack and recovery.

The most important lesson bankruptcy teaches is resilience through adversity. Dusting yourself off and rebuilding from scratch requires an unflinching inventory of your true strengths, skills, and mindsets. You learn about diligence, sacrifice, and delayed gratification in the harshest ways possible, but these lessons are necessary for regaining your footing. Rebuilding requires mapping out new paths, making difficult choices, and staying committed to long-term goals over short-term desires. Highlighting long-term goals over short-term desires is crucial because if your goals are misaligned or unrealistic, it's vital to modify them. Be realistic with your aspirations.

The greatest gift from the Teacher of Bankruptcy is the opportunity for a radical fresh start when you've hit rock bottom. Financially, emotionally, and spiritually, you are forced to reexamine your purpose, passion, and priorities, free from the inertia of your previous path. Out of these ashes, a new you can emerge with a revised understanding of wealth. Hardship can revise and advise you, making you stronger and wiser. Confronting the closed door of bankruptcy head-on is incredibly challenging, but it is a doable process. By reframing your focus and balancing your grounded side, you can reinvent yourself in a new way and become your own teacher, even in the face of bankruptcy.

Bankruptcy doesn't just affect your finances; it affects your self-esteem, your sense of security, and your overall outlook on life. It's a harsh reminder that life doesn't always go as planned, and sometimes, no matter how hard you work or how careful you are, circumstances beyond your control can knock you down. As I navigated the aftermath of my near-bankruptcy experience, I discovered the true meaning of resilience. The process required me to dig deep and find strength I didn't know I had. It was a journey of self-discovery and growth, where I learned to value the intangible aspects of life—things like relationships, health, and personal integrity—over material possessions and financial success.

One of the most critical lessons from this period was the importance of a strong support system. Friends and family can be pillars of strength when you're going through tough times. Their encouragement and advice can provide the emotional and practical support needed to rebuild. Surrounding yourself with people who believe in you and your ability to overcome adversity is crucial. Moreover, the experience taught me the importance of financial literacy. Understanding how to manage money, budget effectively, and make wise financial decisions became a priority. I took the time to educate myself on personal finance, seeking out resources and learning from financial advisors. This newfound knowledge helped me make better choices and avoid the pitfalls that led to my near bankruptcy.

Another significant aspect of the recovery process was developing a healthy relationship with money. It's easy to become obsessed with accumulating wealth, especially when you're trying to recover from financial loss. However, I learned that true financial security comes from a balanced approach—one that prioritizes saving, investing, and spending wisely without letting money control your life. The journey through bankruptcy also highlighted the importance of mental health. The stress and anxiety associated with financial ruin can be overwhelming. Taking care of my mental well-being became just as important as rebuilding my financial stability. Practices like meditation, exercise, and seeking professional help, when needed, played a vital role in maintaining my mental health.

In retrospect, the experience of nearly going bankrupt was a pivotal moment in my life. It forced me to reevaluate my priorities, rebuild my life with a stronger foundation, and develop a deeper appreciation for the non-material aspects of life. The Teacher of Closed Doors, in this case, bankruptcy, imparted lessons that reshaped my character, fortified my resolve, and prepared me for future challenges.

Ultimately, these experiences serve as a testament to the human spirit's resilience. They remind us that even when faced with seemingly insurmountable obstacles, we have the capacity to rise, rebuild, and emerge stronger than before. By embracing the lessons from the Teacher of Closed Doors, we can navigate life's toughest challenges with grace, determination, and unwavering faith in our ability to overcome.

*

CHRIS TUCKER'S BANKRUPTCY STORY

Chris Tucker, the renowned actor and comedian best known for his roles in the *Rush Hour* series and *Friday,* faced a significant financial setback when he filed for bankruptcy in 2011. His story is a powerful illustration of how the Teacher of Closed Doors can impart hard but invaluable lessons.

Tucker's financial troubles stemmed from various factors, including excessive spending, unpaid taxes, and a lifestyle that outpaced his earnings. Despite his immense success in Hollywood, Tucker found himself owing the IRS over $14 million in back taxes. This closed-door moment stripped away the financial security and the achievements he had worked so hard to build, forcing him to confront the stark realities of his financial mismanagement.

The initial shock of bankruptcy for Tucker was overwhelming, much like it is for anyone else. The reality of losing financial stability can be gut-wrenching. For Tucker, who had reached the heights of fame and fortune, this fall from grace was a harsh reminder that success can be fleeting if not managed wisely. Bankruptcy taught Tucker humility and the importance of financial prudence. It's a lesson that resonates with many of us that no matter how much we earn, financial discipline is crucial. The Teacher of Closed Doors, in this case, was unforgiving but transformative. Tucker had to reassess his lifestyle, cut down on extravagant expenses, and make amends with the IRS.

One of the harsh truths that the Teacher of Closed Doors demands you confront is the realization that material possessions and status symbols are fleeting. Tucker's story reminds us that living beyond our means, regardless of our income level, can lead to devastating consequences. His journey through bankruptcy is a masterclass in humility and letting go of ego. It's about understanding that financial stability isn't just about how much you earn, but how well you manage it.

The lessons Tucker learned through his financial woes echo those that anyone facing bankruptcy must learn. It's about resilience through adversity. Picking up the pieces after financial ruin requires taking a hard look at one's strengths, skills, and mindsets. The Teacher of Closed Doors instills in you the necessity of diligence, sacrifice, and delayed gratification. For Tucker, this meant selling off luxury properties, downsizing his lifestyle, and focusing on rebuilding his career and financial health. Another critical lesson from Tucker's experience is the importance of setting realistic goals and managing expectations. Just like the rest of us, Tucker had to map out new paths, make tough decisions, and stay committed to long-term goals over short-term desires. This process highlights the need for practical financial planning and the importance of modifying goals when necessary.

The greatest gift from the Teacher of Bankruptcy is the opportunity for a fresh start. For Tucker, this meant reevaluating his purpose, passion, and priorities. He had to rethink his approach to money, fame, and life itself. Out of the ashes of financial ruin, a new Chris Tucker emerged, one who had learned from his past mistakes and was ready to build a more stable future. Tucker's journey is a testament to the fact that hitting rock bottom can be a turning point. It forces you to reexamine your values and what truly matters. Financial hardship can revise you and advise you, making you stronger and wiser.

In conclusion, Chris Tucker's bankruptcy serves as a poignant example of how the Teacher of Closed Doors operates. It teaches resilience, humility, and the importance of financial prudence. Whether you're a Hollywood star or an everyday person, the lessons are the same ... manage your finances wisely, set realistic goals, and learn from your mistakes. By facing the closed door of bankruptcy head-on, you can emerge stronger, more knowledgeable, and better prepared for the future.

*

FAT JOE'S STORY THAT LED TO BANKRUPTCY

As a long-time fan of Fat Joe, witnessing his journey through the highs of musical success to the lows of financial struggle has been both eye-opening and inspiring. Fat Joe, whose real name is Joseph Cartagena, isn't just a rapper; he's a legend in the hip-hop world with hits like "Lean Back" and "What's Luv?" that defined an era. Yet, behind the glitz and glamour, Joe faced a significant financial hurdle that many fans, including myself, were unaware of until it became headline news.

In 2012, Fat Joe was sentenced to prison for tax evasion after failing to pay taxes on more than $3 million in income over two years. This was a shocking revelation for many of us who admired his success and persona. Seeing someone you look up to face such public and legal humiliation is a reminder that financial mismanagement can happen to anyone, regardless of their level of success.

The Teacher of Closed Doors hit Joe hard, forcing him to confront the reality of his financial situation. For a fan, it's easy to get caught up in the persona that celebrities project, but Joe's bankruptcy was a sobering reminder that financial responsibility is crucial, no matter who you are. It was painful to see someone who had built such a successful career fall into financial ruin, but it also highlighted the importance of handling finances wisely.

One of the biggest lessons from Joe's experience is the need to prioritize financial management over a lavish lifestyle. As a fan, it's easy to get swept up in the glitz and assume that all celebrities have it together. Joe's bankruptcy taught us that excessive spending and neglecting financial obligations can lead to severe consequences. It's a powerful reminder that true financial success isn't about how much money you make, but how you manage it.

Joe's journey through bankruptcy also demonstrated incredible resilience and humility. Public figures often struggle with ego and maintaining their image, but Joe had to face his mistakes head-on and work to rebuild his life. For me, and probably many other fans, this was a lesson in humility and the importance of acknowledging and learning from our mistakes.

Rebuilding after such a significant setback requires strength and a commitment to change. Joe's experience showed us the importance of resilience and the need to develop diligence, sacrifice, and delayed gratification. These are essential qualities for anyone looking to recover from financial difficulties. As a fan, watching Joe navigate this path made me appreciate his strength even more.

Setting realistic financial goals and making informed decisions is another crucial lesson from Joe's story. As someone who grew up listening to his music, it was easy to see him as larger than life. However, his bankruptcy experience humanized him and underscored the importance of making smart financial choices, no matter your income level.

The greatest gift from the Teacher of Bankruptcy is the opportunity for a fresh start. For Joe, this meant reevaluating his financial habits and understanding the importance of paying taxes and managing income responsibly. His journey reminded us that out of adversity, we can emerge stronger and more financially savvy.

As a fan, Fat Joe's story serves as a powerful reminder that even our heroes face challenges, and that financial responsibility is vital. His resilience in the face of bankruptcy is inspiring, teaching us that with determination and the right mindset, we can overcome even the most daunting obstacles. The Teacher of Closed Doors, through Joe's experience, taught us valuable lessons in humility, resilience, and the importance of prudent financial planning. Watching him rebuild and come back stronger has been an inspiration, reminding us all that it's never too late to learn and grow from our experiences.

In closing, Fat Joe's journey through financial turmoil and his subsequent rise serves as a beacon of hope for anyone facing their own struggles. It's a testament to the fact that setbacks, no matter how severe, do not define our futures. Instead, they offer invaluable lessons and opportunities for growth. Joe's story illustrates that with courage, perseverance, and a willingness to learn, we can transform our greatest challenges into stepping stones toward a better and more secure future. As fans, we are not only entertained by his music, but also profoundly inspired by his resilience and ability to turn adversity into triumph.

*

WESLEY SNIPES' STORY THAT LED TO BANKRUPTCY

Growing up as a young teen, I would always get warnings from my parents, who were heavily involved with pastoring and church planting, not to ever get caught watching "New Jack City." It was forbidden due to the sex, drugs, and heavy violence depicted in the movie. When I got older, I realized why for many reasons. For every 80s and 90s baby out there, Wesley Snipes will always be remembered as Nino Brown.

In 2008, no one knew about his real tax issues, which were associated with bankruptcy. Legal fees and back taxes, combined with the impact on his career, created a perfect storm of financial turmoil. The story of Wesley Snipes is a powerful example of the Teacher of Closed Doors. When the doors closed on his financial security and personal freedom, Snipes was forced to confront some harsh truths about his life and choices. This period became a masterclass in humility and resilience for him. Despite the severe setbacks, Snipes did not let these closed doors define his legacy or future.

His journey highlights the critical need for financial literacy and responsibility. Snipes' failure to handle his taxes properly led to significant legal and financial repercussions, underscoring the importance of understanding and managing personal finances, no matter how successful one becomes. This experience taught Snipes the value of accountability. Facing the consequences of his actions head-on, Snipes accepted his mistakes, which is a powerful reminder that accountability is a crucial step in personal growth. After serving his prison sentence, Snipes didn't let his past mistakes dictate his future. He returned to acting, demonstrating remarkable resilience and the ability to reinvent himself. His comeback is a testament to the human spirit's capacity to recover and thrive even after significant adversity.

As fans, Snipes' story is a potent reminder that everyone, regardless of their fame and fortune, can face life-altering challenges. His journey through financial ruin and legal troubles taught us that setbacks are part of the human experience. The Teacher of Closed Doors, through Snipes' trials, showed us that these challenges could become powerful lessons in humility, responsibility, and resilience. Watching Wesley Snipes rebuild his life and career has been incredibly inspiring. It serves as a poignant reminder that it's never too late to learn from our mistakes, make amends, and chart a new path forward. The lessons from his experience encourage us to face our own closed doors with courage and determination, knowing that we, too, can emerge stronger and wiser.

Moreover, Wesley Snipes' story underscores the importance of perseverance and the will to fight back against adversity. His journey through financial and legal turmoil, and subsequent resurgence in the entertainment industry, teaches us that setbacks can be temporary if met with resolve and a willingness to learn. Snipes' ability to return to the big screen and regain his footing is a testament to his enduring talent and resilience. As we reflect on his experience, it becomes evident that the Teacher of Closed Doors is not merely about facing hardships but about emerging from them with renewed strength and wisdom.

MONEY DOESN'T SOLVE EVERYTHING

No matter how you look at it, the truth is money doesn't solve everything. The bright lights, the fast paychecks, the fame, and the fortune can blind many of us into a wrong reality. Yes, money can get you things, but that doesn't mean it's the solution for everything. Not all cures come from money. I've seen countless celebrities, business owners, and people in the news who earn so much, only to squander it through excessive spending, bad investments, being taken advantage of, or simply a lack of money management. The Teacher of Financial Irresponsibility doesn't discriminate based on tax brackets. Whether you're a minimum wage worker or an A-list movie star, the lessons around respecting money and managing it are prudent and should be applied by everyone. Money can help you find solutions, but it doesn't always solve everything. You can have everything and still have nothing at the same time.

This means that you could possess all the money in the world, achieve every detail of accomplishments and fulfillment, but if your heart, mind, and desires are all jacked up, or if you are missing something vital like love, health, or spiritual well-being, it won't matter how much money you have. Your well-being is far more important than the money you earn. We've seen countless stories of celebrity foreclosures, bankruptcies, asset seizures, and it's all over the tabloids and social media. Sometimes, these posts don't reflect reality. Celebrities often curate their public image to enhance their brand, but the behind-the-scenes reality can be surprisingly harsh, with some even living out of their cars. It's not always what it seems, and we can be quickly deceived by appearances.

> *"You can have everything and still have*
> *nothing at the same time."*

What can we learn from this? We learn the importance of surrounding ourselves with the right people, keeping an eye on our finances, and finding the right CPA to handle our money well. This prevents us from going through cycles of discouragement, guilt, and shame. The Teacher of Money Management is crucial because it can teach us more, behind closed doors, than any parent or teacher might be able to. Money can teach you valuable lessons about saving and spending, often through the pain of financial missteps.

Bankruptcy, Chapter 15, tax issues—all these examples highlight what it means to avoid becoming a statistic. Don't fall into the same traps over and over. You can avoid these pitfalls by doing the right thing the first time. So, remember, money doesn't solve everything, and true success comes from a balanced and well-managed life. In closing, it's essential to remember that money, while a powerful tool, is not the ultimate solution to life's challenges. The stories of celebrities and ordinary people alike who have faced financial ruin remind us that true wealth lies in wisdom, resilience, and the ability to learn from our mistakes. The Teacher of Closed Doors shows us that enduring financial hardship and coming out the other side is not just about recovery but about transformation. It's about learning the art of resilience, the importance of prudent financial planning, and the value of surrounding ourselves with the right people.

LEARN TO BOUNCE BACK

I've learned over the years that mastering the art of bouncing back is truly an essential skill. Despite the peaks, valleys, and ditches we encounter, there's always triumph on the other side if we're willing to go the distance for what we believe in. Don't let setbacks become stumbling blocks; let them serve as stepping stones. No matter how successful or talented you are, no one is immune to trauma or failure. We all face challenges, and sometimes these challenges can deliver gut-punching moments that knock us off our feet. However, the true measure of character lies in our ability to pick ourselves back up and continue moving forward.

Time and again, we see people in the news who hit rock bottom and experience subsequent trauma. The crazy part is that those quick to point fingers often struggle to overcome their own situations. It's important to encourage friends when they're going through tough times, hold them accountable, and remind them to keep pushing forward. This chapter teaches us how to bounce back. The stories and examples of celebrities caught up in tax problems aren't just tales of failure; they are illustrations of resilience, drive, and the refusal to let setbacks define them.

Consider the example of Robert Downey Jr. At the height of his career, his addictions and legal troubles threatened to destroy everything he had worked so hard to build. His journey back to success is a testament to the power of resilience and the human spirit's capacity to overcome adversity. We must be aware of how to bounce back to avoid being destroyed by challenges that threaten our hard-earned achievements.

We work too hard to give up now. We work too hard to let setbacks define our future. This chapter is designed to teach you the power of the closed door and the lessons it offers as the Teacher of Resilience. What better way to embrace these lessons than by learning how to bounce back effectively? By examining the stories of various celebrities and understanding their struggles, we gain insight into the universal nature of adversity and the incredible potential for recovery. These examples show that no matter the depth of our troubles, there's always a way forward. It's not just about paying the cost or going through tough times; it's about emerging stronger, wiser, and more determined.

So, remember, when you face a closed door, view it as an opportunity for growth. Let the setbacks teach you resilience. Let them remind you of your inner strength. Most importantly, let them propel you toward your next triumph. The power of the closed door lies not in its ability to stop you, but in its potential to teach you how to find another way forward.

We must remember that life's setbacks are not the end but rather the beginning of a new chapter. Each closed door we encounter offers a chance to learn, adapt, and grow. The stories of people like Robert Downey Jr. and other celebrities who faced tremendous challenges and bounced back serve as powerful reminders that resilience is a vital part of success. These individuals faced their adversities head-on, learned from their mistakes, and emerged stronger than ever. When we encounter our own closed doors, it's essential to take a moment to reflect on what these obstacles are teaching us. Often, these moments of hardship reveal our true strengths and capabilities. They force us to dig deep, reassess our goals, and find new ways to achieve them. It's during these times that we discover who we truly are and what we're capable of.

One key aspect of bouncing back is maintaining a positive mindset. It's easy to get bogged down by negative thoughts and self-doubt when faced with setbacks. However, adopting a growth mindset—believing that we can improve and learn from our experiences—can make all the difference. This mindset allows us to view challenges as opportunities rather than insurmountable obstacles. Another crucial element is seeking support. Just as we must encourage and support our friends in their times of need, we should also be willing to lean on others when we face our own challenges. Whether it's family, friends, or professional support, having a solid support system can provide the encouragement and perspective needed to navigate tough times.

Lastly, it's important to take proactive steps toward recovery. This might mean setting new goals, developing new skills, or simply taking better care of our physical and mental health. The journey to bouncing back is often gradual and requires patience and perseverance. However, every small step taken in the right direction brings us closer to overcoming our challenges and achieving our dreams.

Never despise the various levels of lessons that subtly and indirectly teach you about the bounce-back strategies you were born with organically. Life has a way of presenting these lessons through different experiences, each one a silent mentor guiding you toward resilience. There will be people in your life who will either discourage your bounce back or add optimal value to your comeback. These individuals, whether positive or negative, play crucial roles in your journey. The detractors teach you about your inner strength and the power of perseverance, while the supporters provide encouragement, perspective, and wisdom. Embrace these interactions and use them to fuel your determination. Recognize that every setback is a setup for a stronger return, and that the resilience within you is an inherent gift, waiting to be harnessed and honed through life's trials and triumphs.

In conclusion, the Teacher of Closed Doors offers invaluable lessons in resilience, determination, and personal growth. Embracing these lessons allows us to transform setbacks into stepping stones, turning adversity into opportunity. Remember, each closed door is not an end but a gateway to new possibilities. By learning to bounce back, we not only overcome our challenges but also unlock our true potential, paving the way for a brighter and more fulfilling future.

IN CLOSING THE BOTTOM LINE IS

In this journey called life, closed doors are inevitable. Whether it's a job rejection, a broken relationship, or a missed opportunity, these moments can feel like devastating setbacks that shake our confidence and challenge our dreams. However, the true masters of growth and personal evolution have learned to reframe these closed doors not as roadblocks, but as catalysts for self-discovery, transformation, and ultimately, a deeper fulfillment. Think back to a time when a door closed—perhaps a creative project was rejected, or a promotion you had your heart set on went to someone else. In that moment, it was natural to feel discouraged and even question your worth or abilities. Consider … what if that closed door was actually a redirection, a nudge from your inner soul to explore a new path that aligns more authentically with your true passion and purpose?

The annals of history are filled with stories of remarkable individuals who transformed life's setbacks into their greatest triumphs. J.K. Rowling's beloved *Harry Potter* series was rejected by numerous publishers before finding its way into the hearts of millions worldwide. Oprah Winfrey's resilience in the face of adversity, from enduring abuse to being fired from her first television job, paved the way for her to become a global icon of inspiration. Every closed door we encounter is an opportunity to cultivate self-love, establish healthy boundaries, and fortify our resilience. When a friendship ends, or a toxic relationship dissolves, we create space for more positive connections that nourish our souls. A financial setback can inspire us to develop better budgeting habits and financial literacy, setting the stage for long-term prosperity.

Embracing closed doors requires a willingness to lean into discomfort and trust the process of growth. A health issue may arise, prompting us to adopt a healthier lifestyle and prioritize our well-being. A dream home sale may fall through, only to lead us to an even more perfect sanctuary. A volunteer role may not work out, but it could guide us toward a more fulfilling way to give back and make a meaningful impact. Ultimately, the closed doors we encounter are not stumbling blocks but stepping stones, opportunities to refine our skills, recalibrate our priorities, and evolve into the best versions of ourselves.

By reframing our perspective and maintaining an unwavering belief in our potential, we can transform life's setbacks into catalysts for personal growth, self-discovery, and the realization of our deepest dreams. So, the next time a door closes, take a deep breath and embrace the uncertainty with open arms. Trust that this is not the end but the beginning of a new chapter, one that will challenge you to grow, adapt, and ultimately soar to greater heights. For every closed door is a gateway to a life lived with purpose, authenticity, and the unwavering pursuit of your highest potential.

CHAPTER 6

THE STRATEGY OF CLOSED DOORS

To be fully transparent, I wasn't the best student in school. I wasn't the smartest kid because I breezed through a lot of different things without paying close attention to the details. Good grades never came easy for me, and I often struggled with homework because I didn't take the right notes. It wasn't until I started facing real-life obstacles and closed doors that I realized the value of developing a keen intellectual mindset. When real-life challenges started coming my way, I learned quickly how essential it was to develop a strategic mindset. In school, while others were stuck facing the closed door of a difficult assignment or a failed test, I began to see these setbacks as opportunities to grow stronger and smarter. I had to adjust my approach, breaking things down piece by piece to avoid getting overwhelmed by frustration. Facing obstacles head-on and developing a strategic approach can turn setbacks into opportunities for growth.

When you're in keen mindset mode, you tune out distractions and begin to see roadblocks as challenges to overcome. This shift in perspective is crucial. Instead of seeing a closed door as the end, you see it as a detour—a chance to explore new strategies and solutions. I had to learn to adapt quickly and develop not just plans A and B, but also plans C, D, and E. Each detour along the way forced me to think more critically and creatively about my approach. A keen intellectual mindset involves being adaptable and ready with multiple strategies to overcome obstacles.

THE GENIUS BAR ANALOGY

Think of life's challenges like visiting the Genius Bar at Apple. People bring their devices to experts who know exactly how to fix them based on the specific model and issue. In life, we need to adopt a similar approach. We must understand the specific nature of each obstacle we face and develop tailored strategies to overcome them. It's about knowing which model, which device, and which method to use to fix the problem at hand. Tailored strategies based on a deep understanding of the problem are essential for overcoming obstacles.

The interesting thing about the Genius Bar is that the people helping you have to run a diagnostic test to see what the problem is. This diagnostic test acts as both a tester and evaluator, identifying what's missing, what needs to be removed, and what it will take to keep the device running correctly. Sometimes, the device is outdated compared to the new software changes and systems. In such cases, they often recommend that you get a new device and upgrade to stay current with the latest advancements since the last model was released.

This process at the Genius Bar is a great analogy for how we should approach life's challenges. Just like the diagnostic test, we need to evaluate our situation to understand what's missing, what's outdated, and what needs to be changed to move forward effectively. When we encounter closed doors, it's essential to run a "diagnostic test" on our strategies, our mindset, and our resources. Are our methods outdated? Do we need new skills or new approaches to tackle the challenges we face?

EMBRACING CHANGE AND UPGRADING

Sometimes, the obstacles we face require more than just a tweak or minor adjustment—they demand a complete upgrade in our approach. Just like outdated devices that can't keep up with new software, our old ways of thinking and doing things might not be sufficient for new challenges. Embracing change and being willing to "upgrade" ourselves is crucial. This might mean learning new skills, adopting new technologies, or even changing our mindset to stay relevant and effective in an ever-changing world. Upgrading ourselves might involve seeking out additional education or training to build new competencies. For example, if you're not finding it hard to keep up with technological advancements in your field, taking a course or earning a certification can provide you with the latest knowledge and tools. In a broader sense, it could also mean shifting your perspective—recognizing that the strategies and habits that served you well in the past may no longer be effective and being open to adopting new approaches.

Additionally, upgrading isn't just about adding new skills or knowledge; it's also about letting go of outdated practices that no longer serve you. Much like how we discard obsolete hardware, we need to identify and eliminate inefficient habits and mindsets. This could involve breaking free from negative thought patterns, changing unproductive routines, or distancing yourself from influences that hold you back. The Genius Bar approach also highlights the importance of persistence and adaptability. Diagnosing the problem and finding the right solution often requires multiple attempts and adjustments. Similarly, in life, we need to persist through challenges and be adaptable, continuously refining our strategies based on feedback and new information. This iterative process helps us navigate through closed doors and find new paths to success.

APPLYING THE GENIUS BAR STRATEGY TO LIFE

To wrap it up, the strategy of closed doors is packed with life lessons. Whether you're dealing with school, tech advancements, or real-life challenges, developing a strategic mindset is key. By breaking down problems, persisting through failures, and having multiple plans, we can turn setbacks into growth opportunities. Just like at the Genius Bar, understanding the specifics of each challenge allows us to craft the perfect strategy for success. So, embrace those closed doors, learn from every detour, and strategize your way to a brighter future. Remember, sometimes you need to run a diagnostic test on your life, upgrade your approach, and keep moving forward.

*

MY FIRST PRACTICE SERMON WAS A LEARNING STRATEGY

I'll never forget my first preaching class back in seminary. I had grown up admiring powerful ministers and their ability to captivate congregations with the Word. Now it was my turn to step into those big preaching shoes. I spent weeks meticulously preparing my first practice sermon, making sure I had crafted thoughtful insights and packaged them in an engaging, articulate way. The day arrived, and I stood in front of my classmates and professor, nerves buzzing but confident in my preparation. As I began to speak, I quickly realized that delivering a sermon was far different from simply writing one.

Despite my best efforts, I stumbled over my words, lost my train of thought, and struggled to connect with my audience. The feedback afterward was constructive but brutally honest. My delivery lacked passion, my points were muddled, and my message didn't land as powerfully as I had hoped. This experience felt like hitting a closed door at full speed. I had put in the work, prepared diligently, and yet, I failed to meet the mark. It was a humbling moment, but also a pivotal one. I realized that effective preaching, much like any other skill, required more than preparation—it demanded adaptability, presence, and the ability to connect deeply with an audience.

Taking the feedback to heart, I went back to the drawing board. I watched recordings of great preachers, not just for their content, but for their delivery, their body language, and their ability to connect emotionally. I practiced speaking with more passion, experimenting with different styles and tones. Just as I had learned to recognize patterns and adapt in video games, I began to see the patterns in effective preaching—how to build suspense, when to pause for impact, and how to bring personal stories into the message to make it more relatable.

Persistence was key. Each practice sermon became a little better than the last, each piece of feedback a stepping stone toward improvement. There were times I felt discouraged, but I kept pushing, kept refining my approach. I sought out additional resources, attended workshops, and even practiced in front of a mirror to get the nuances just right. This iterative process of trying, failing, learning, and trying again mirrored the persistence needed to master a difficult level in a game.

LEVERAGING SUPPORT AND MENTORSHIP

I also realized the importance of seeking help. Just like the support from fellow coaches can lead to breakthroughs, I reached out to experienced ministers and mentors who could provide guidance and feedback. Their insights were invaluable. They pointed out things I hadn't noticed, offered practical tips, and shared their own experiences of struggle and growth. This support system was crucial in helping me navigate through my closed doors and find new paths forward. Having a robust support network can make a world of difference when facing obstacles. Surrounding yourself with people who have been through similar challenges can provide, not only practical advice, but also emotional support. Knowing that others have successfully navigated the same or similar paths can be incredibly motivating. Their stories of perseverance and eventual success can inspire you to keep pushing forward, even when the going gets tough.

One of the most valuable aspects of mentorship is the practical guidance and constructive feedback that experienced individuals can offer. Mentors can help you identify blind spots and areas for improvement that you might not see on your own. They can provide specific, actionable advice that you can implement to overcome challenges more effectively. This feedback is often rooted in their own experiences, making it both relevant and practical. Mentors and supportive peers often share their own stories of struggle and growth, which can be incredibly enlightening. These stories provide real-world examples of how to handle setbacks and rejections. Learning about the obstacles they faced and how they overcame them can give you new perspectives and strategies to apply to your own situation. It also helps to normalize the experience of facing difficulties, reminding you that you're not alone in your struggles.

EMOTIONAL AND PSYCHOLOGICAL SUPPORT

Beyond practical advice, having mentors and a support network provides crucial emotional and psychological support. Facing closed doors and rejections can be disheartening, and it's easy to feel isolated. A supportive network offers encouragement and reassures you that setbacks are a natural part of the journey. This emotional backing can boost your resilience and help you maintain a positive mindset, which is essential for long-term success. Mentors and supportive peers can also help expand your network, opening up new opportunities that you might not have discovered on your own. They can introduce you to valuable contacts, recommend you for opportunities, and provide a platform for you to showcase your skills. Networking through your support system can lead to collaborations, partnerships, and new ventures that significantly enhance your career or personal growth.

Engaging with mentors and a supportive network encourages continuous learning and development. By regularly interacting with knowledgeable individuals, you're exposed to new ideas, perspectives, and best practices. This ongoing learning process helps you stay adaptable and prepared for future challenges. It also fosters a culture of lifelong learning, which is essential for personal and professional growth. Finally, having a strong support system can greatly boost your confidence. Knowing that experienced and successful individuals believe in your potential can reinforce your self-belief. This confidence is crucial when facing rejections and setbacks, as it helps you stay motivated and focused on your goals. Believing in yourself is often the first step to overcoming any obstacle.

Leveraging support and mentorship is a powerful strategy for navigating life's challenges. Whether you're dealing with career setbacks, personal struggles, or the pursuit of ambitious goals, having a strong support network can provide invaluable guidance, feedback, and emotional support. By seeking out mentors and engaging with a supportive community, you can gain new insights, learn from others' experiences, and find the strength to keep moving forward. Remember, you don't have to face your challenges alone—there's a wealth of wisdom and support out there waiting to help you turn closed doors into new opportunities.

UPGRADING MY APPROACH

This journey wasn't just about tweaking my sermons—it was about a complete upgrade in my approach to preaching. I had to embrace new techniques, let go of old habits that weren't serving me, and continuously innovate to stay relevant and effective. Much like the Genius Bar analogy, I had to diagnose what wasn't working and be willing to overhaul my methods to keep improving. To stay effective and engage my congregation, I needed to embrace new techniques in preaching. This meant stepping out of my comfort zone and exploring different ways to deliver my message. I began incorporating storytelling, using more relatable anecdotes to connect with my audience on a personal level. Visual aids became a staple, helping to illustrate complex ideas and keep the congregation's attention. I also experimented with varying my tone, pace, and volume to create a more dynamic and impactful delivery. These new techniques required practice and dedication, but the payoff was evident in the increased engagement and positive feedback from the congregation.

One of the hardest parts of upgrading my approach was letting go of old habits that were no longer effective. I realized that some of my traditional methods were not resonating with my modern audience. It was tough to admit that what had worked in the past was now holding me back. However, by critically evaluating my preaching style, I identified areas that needed change. This meant abandoning overly formal language in favor of a more conversational tone and shifting from rigid sermon structures to more fluid, interactive formats. Letting go of these old habits was liberating and allowed me to evolve and grow as a preacher.

CONTINUOUS INNOVATION

Innovation became a key pillar of my approach. I continuously sought out new ideas and methods to keep my sermons fresh and relevant. This involved staying updated with current events, cultural trends, and advancements in communication technology. I attended workshops, read books, and followed thought leaders in the field to gather new insights and inspiration. By constantly innovating, I ensured that my messages were timely and resonated deeply with my audience. This commitment to innovation kept my preaching dynamic and prevented it from becoming stagnant. Much like the Genius Bar analogy, I had to conduct regular diagnostics on my preaching methods. This involved seeking feedback from trusted peers and mentors, as well as being open to constructive criticism from the congregation. By diagnosing what wasn't working, I could make informed decisions about what needed to change.

Sometimes, this meant making minor adjustments, but other times it required a complete overhaul of my approach. Whether it was refining my preparation process, experimenting with different sermon structures, or incorporating new media, I was willing to do whatever it took to improve. Central to upgrading my approach was adopting a growth mindset. I embraced the belief that my abilities as a preacher could always be developed and improved. This mindset encouraged me to view challenges and setbacks as opportunities for growth rather than as failures. I remained curious and eager to learn, always looking for ways to enhance my skills and knowledge. This proactive attitude allowed me to continuously upgrade my approach and remain effective in my ministry.

LEVERAGING TECHNOLOGY

Leveraging technology played a significant role in my transformation. I began using multimedia presentations to complement my sermons, incorporating videos, slides, and graphics to make the message more engaging. Social media became a powerful tool for reaching a wider audience and maintaining a connection with the congregation throughout the week. I also explored podcasting and live streaming, allowing my sermons to reach people beyond the physical church walls. Embracing these technological advancements not only enhanced the delivery of my sermons but also expanded the reach of my ministry.

Feedback was crucial in my journey of continuous improvement. I regularly sought feedback from my congregation and peers, asking for honest opinions about what was working and what needed improvement. Reflecting on this feedback helped me identify areas for growth and adjust my approach accordingly. I learned to value constructive criticism and use it as a tool for refining my skills. This ongoing cycle of feedback and reflection ensured that I remained responsive to the needs of my audience and committed to my personal development.

Upgrading my approach to preaching was not a one-time event but a continuous journey of learning and adaptation. By embracing new techniques, letting go of old habits, and continuously innovating, I was able to stay relevant and effective in my ministry. Much like the Genius Bar, diagnosing what wasn't working and being willing to overhaul my methods was key to my growth. This journey required a growth mindset, the leverage of technology, and a commitment to seeking and acting on feedback. As I continue to evolve, I am confident that these strategies will help me navigate any challenges and keep moving forward with purpose and passion.

ANIMAL INSTINCT: SURVIVAL STRATEGIES IN NATURE

Let's begin by exploring one of nature's most ingeniously adaptive creatures—the mimic octopus. This remarkable cephalopod is a true master at confronting obstacles and emerging unscathed by deploying its mind-blowing impersonation abilities. When faced with a predator or environmental hazard blocking its path, the mimic octopus can shapeshift into an incredibly convincing visual and behavioral imitation of over 15 different marine species. From shrimp and lionfish to sea snakes and even other octopus varieties, it perfectly embodies the colors, movements, and defensive tactics of each disguise. This remarkable ability allows it to deftly navigate through situations that might otherwise leave it trapped or endangered.

ADAPTING THROUGH IMITATION

The mimic octopus's strategy is a brilliant example of adaptive thinking. By mimicking dangerous or unpalatable creatures, it can avoid predation and explore environments that might otherwise be too risky. This kind of adaptability is essential not just for survival in the wild, but also for thriving in our personal and professional lives. When we face closed doors or challenging situations, being able to adapt and change our approach can make the difference between failure and success.

THE POWER OF FLEXIBILITY

Flexibility is at the heart of the mimic octopus's survival strategy. It doesn't just stick to one form of disguise; it switches between many, depending on the threat it faces. This flexibility allows it to navigate complex environments and avoid dangers that a more rigid creature might not survive. In our own lives, being flexible and willing to change our tactics can help us overcome obstacles that might initially seem insurmountable. Whether it's a career setback, a personal challenge, or a new and unfamiliar situation, approaching it with a flexible mindset can open up new possibilities.

LEARNING FROM THE MIMIC OCTOPUS

The mimic octopus teaches us that adaptability and flexibility are crucial strategies for overcoming obstacles. It's not about being the strongest or the fastest; it's about being the smartest and the most adaptable. By learning to assess our environment and adjust our behavior accordingly, we can navigate through life's challenges more effectively. This might mean adopting new skills, changing our approach to problem-solving, or even taking on new roles to better fit the demands of our situation.

APPLYING ADAPTIVE STRATEGIES IN REAL LIFE

In our careers, for instance, we might face situations where our current skills and strategies are no longer effective. By taking a cue from the mimic octopus, we can look at these challenges as opportunities to develop new abilities and approaches. This could involve pursuing further education, seeking out new experiences, or even shifting to a different career path if that's what the situation calls for. The key is to remain open and adaptable, willing to change our approach as needed.

EMBRACING CHANGE AND INNOVATION

Just as the mimic octopus doesn't hesitate to transform itself in response to a threat, we too should embrace change and innovation. This means not just reacting to changes in our environment but anticipating them and preparing ourselves accordingly. By staying ahead of the curve and continuously updating our skills and knowledge, we can remain competitive and resilient in a rapidly changing world.

NATURE'S LESSONS FOR HUMAN RESILIENCE

The mimic octopus is a powerful reminder that adaptability, flexibility, and innovative thinking are essential for overcoming obstacles. Its ability to seamlessly transform and navigate through dangerous environments shows us that the key to success is not in brute strength, but in the capacity to change and adapt. As we face our own challenges, whether in our personal lives, careers, or broader societal changes, we can draw inspiration from this remarkable creature. By being flexible, learning new skills, and continuously adapting to our environment, we can turn closed doors into new opportunities and navigate life's challenges with grace and resilience. So, take a page from the mimic octopus's playbook. When faced with a closed door, don't see it as the end. See it as a call to adapt, innovate, and transform. Embrace the challenge, learn from it, and emerge stronger and more capable on the other side. Your journey is one of continuous growth and discovery, and with the right strategies, no obstacle is too great to overcome.

*

STRATEGY OF CLOSED DOORS IN GAMES

Growing up in the 80s, video games like Duck Hunt and Super Mario Bros were more than just a way to kill time—they were fascinating challenges that hooked me instantly. Sure, the 8-bit graphics look primitive nowadays, but back then, those simple games demanded real strategic thinking and perseverance from anyone who spent hours grinding away at them like I did. Every time I lost or couldn't beat a level, it was like a tease—I just knew there was some deeper strategy I was missing, some secret code waiting to be cracked if I could just figure it out. Those early struggles taught me that video games were more than just fun distractions; they were mental puzzles to analyze and master.

Overcoming in-game challenges got hardwired into my DNA from the jump, having cut my teeth mashing away on old Nintendo controllers. I'm talking those OG days of Duck Hunt, where I'd be zeroing in with that little light gun, trying to nail those quick-dodging, trash-talking duck laughs whenever I whiffed a shot. Or the insane focus required for perfectly using Mario through all those hazardous, enemy-stacked level gauntlets, jump after jump after jump. Even with those basic 8-bit graphics, I was unconsciously leveling up critical real-world tools—pattern recognition, perseverance, strategic thinking. Every time I failed, it wasn't just GAME OVER. It was feedback that I needed to adjust my timing, try new tactics, or just grind out the same sections relentlessly until I mastered them. Failure is feedback, not finality. The grind never stops if you keep observing, adapting your approach and persisting. When I finally graduated to more advanced systems like Sega Genesis, those rudimentary skills just got crazy augmented. Now I was navigating full 3D worlds, wrestling with wild combat mechanics, solving mind boggling environmental puzzles—the mental gymnastics went into overdrive even as my ability to analyze and dismantle any new obstacle skyrocketed.

"Failure is feedback, not finality."

*

ADVANCED GAMING SYSTEMS: A NEW FRONTIER OF CHALLENGES

The leap to more advanced gaming systems like the Sega Genesis was akin to stepping into a whole new dimension of complexity and challenge. The games were no longer confined to flat, two-dimensional spaces. Suddenly, I was plunged into immersive 3D environments that required a heightened level of spatial awareness and strategic planning. Every new game presented a fresh set of mechanics and intricacies to master.

Navigating these expansive worlds demanded not just quick reflexes but a deeper understanding of the game's logic and design. Whether it was battling formidable bosses with complex attack patterns or solving intricate puzzles that tested every ounce of my cognitive ability, each challenge honed my analytical skills. The thrill of overcoming these digital adversities mirrored real-life problem solving, where understanding the root of a problem and devising effective strategies to tackle it is essential.

One of the most valuable lessons from gaming was the importance of pattern recognition. Just as the mimic octopus learns to imitate various creatures to survive, I learned to recognize enemy patterns and level designs to progress. This skill is immensely transferable to real life, where identifying patterns can help in predicting outcomes and making informed decisions. Adaptability was another key takeaway. No two games were the same, and each required a unique approach. This constant need to adapt and evolve my strategies kept my mind flexible and prepared for any curveball that life might throw at me. It's about being open to change, experimenting with different approaches, and not being afraid to fail and learn from those failures.

Persistence, as emphasized earlier, is crucial. In gaming, as in life, the path to mastery is paved with numerous attempts and failures. Each setback is an opportunity to learn and improve. The games taught me to persist through challenges, to keep trying new tactics until I found what worked. This relentless pursuit of improvement is a mindset that has served me well in all areas of life. Continuous learning is a natural extension of this persistence. The gaming world is ever evolving, with new technologies and gameplay mechanics constantly emerging. Keeping up with these changes requires a commitment to learning and staying updated. Similarly, in our personal and professional lives, continuous learning and skill development are essential to stay relevant and effective.

LEVERAGING COMMUNITY AND COLLABORATION

Gaming also taught me the value of community and collaboration. While many hours were spent in solitary grinding, some of the most significant breakthroughs came from engaging with the gaming community. Forums, chat rooms, and now, social media platforms, are treasure troves of shared knowledge and collective problem-solving. Engaging with fellow gamers, exchanging tips and strategies, and collaborating on complex challenges highlighted the importance of leveraging collective wisdom. This principle applies equally well outside of gaming. Building a network of mentors, peers, and professionals who can offer guidance and support is invaluable. Collaboration not only broadens your perspective but also accelerates your growth by providing insights that you might not have discovered on your own.

The strategies and skills developed through gaming are incredibly applicable to real life. Pattern recognition helps in understanding and navigating complex situations. Adaptability ensures that we can adjust our approaches based on feedback and changing circumstances. Persistence and continuous learning keep us moving forward, even when faced with significant challenges. Leveraging community and collaboration enriches our experience and enhances our ability to overcome obstacles.

THE JOURNEY OF STRATEGIC GROWTH

The journey from mastering simple 8-bit games to conquering complex 3D worlds has been a testament to the power of strategic thinking, adaptability, and resilience. Each closed door, each GAME OVER screen, was not an end but a stepping stone toward greater mastery and understanding. These lessons extend far beyond the screen, shaping how we approach challenges in all areas of life. So, whether you're navigating the pixelated landscapes of early video games or the intricate complexities of modern life, remember to embrace each challenge with the same focus, adaptability, and persistence. Keep strategizing, keep learning, and keep moving forward. With the right mindset and strategies, no obstacle is too great to overcome. Your journey is one of continuous growth and discovery, and each closed door is just the beginning of a new adventure.

As we continue to advance in life, the challenges we face will inevitably become more complex, much like the progression from 8-bit games to expansive 3D worlds. However, with every new level comes new skills, new insights, and new opportunities for growth. The key is to remain undeterred by setbacks and to view each obstacle as an integral part of the learning process. The resilience built through countless retries, the adaptability honed through navigating diverse challenges, and the strategic thinking developed through overcoming in-game puzzles are all invaluable tools that equip us for life's journey.

In every failure, there's a lesson; in every rejection, a redirection; and in every closed door, an opportunity for innovation. This mindset transforms us from passive players into active participants in our own lives, capable of crafting our paths with intentionality and creativity. By consistently applying the principles of strategic thinking, adaptability, and resilience, we can turn every challenge into a launchpad for our next great achievement.

So, embrace your journey with the mindset of a gamer facing the ultimate quest. Treat each closed door as a puzzle to be solved, each failure as feedback, and each challenge as a new level to conquer. Your persistence, adaptability, and strategic thinking are the keys to unlocking endless potential. The skills you cultivate in overcoming these obstacles will harmonize into a symphony of success, creating a life rich with achievement, growth, and fulfillment. Remember, the game is never truly over—it's just the beginning of your next great adventure. Keep playing, keep striving, and keep believing in the boundless possibilities that lie ahead.

MUSICIANS AND REJECTION: CLOSED DOORS IN MUSIC

As a young teen, church involvement and volunteering were regular parts of my life. Growing up as a preacher's kid required much humility, understanding, discernment, and submission. My parents were deeply committed to serving God, preaching weekly, and teaching Bible study on Wednesdays. In Japan, where my parents were full-time pastors, church planters, visionaries, and missionaries, their dedication to reaching out to the local community for encouragement, guidance, and prayer was unwavering.

I vividly remember receiving a Casio keyboard from my mother as a birthday gift, sparking my journey into music. I taught myself to play the keyboard and quickly picked up other instruments available at the church. It became a passion, and I began playing for my father's church, located just outside the military base. The church was a haven for Navy sailors, government workers, and Japanese locals seeking a spiritual outlet. Despite my enthusiasm, I often felt like I wasn't giving my all. At times, I felt lazy about advancing my skills. When I didn't know how to read music and the worship leader changed keys, I'd hit the transpose button—a cheat code to play in a different key without learning the new chords.

Playing in all 12 keys, understanding scales and octaves, was a significant challenge for me. Even as I played at various events and settings, I felt like I was rejecting myself, closing the door on my own opportunities. Every real musician knows the importance of playing in every key, reading music, and following the music director's lead with song arrangements, melody patterns, and octave changes. I realized I was holding myself back by relying on shortcuts instead of pushing myself to learn and grow.

LEARNING FROM CRITICISM AND PERSEVERING

Rejection and criticism are common in the journey of any musician. For me, it was no different. I received feedback on my playing, my understanding of music theory, and my readiness to adapt during live performances. Instead of letting this criticism discourage me, I chose to see it as a learning opportunity. Each piece of feedback was a stepping stone toward becoming a better musician. To overcome my limitations, I adopted a growth mindset. I dedicated time to learning how to read music, practicing scales, and playing in all keys. I sought guidance from more experienced musicians, watched tutorials, and immersed myself in music theory. The process was challenging, but each small improvement was a victory that built my confidence. Persistence was crucial. There were days when progress felt slow, and the temptation to revert to old habits was strong. However, I kept pushing forward, knowing that mastery was a journey, not a destination. Each practice session, each performance, brought me closer to the musician I aspired to be. Playing music is not just about individual skill but also about collaboration. Being part of a church band taught me the importance of working with others, listening, and adapting. I learned to follow the music director's lead, to blend with other instruments, and to create a harmonious sound as a team. This sense of community and collaboration enriched my musical experience and pushed me to improve continuously.

TURNING REJECTION INTO OPPORTUNITY

Over time, I learned to view rejection and criticism as valuable feedback rather than obstacles. Each setback was an opportunity to refine my skills and deepen my understanding of music. By embracing this perspective, I was able to turn closed doors into new opportunities for growth and success. In conclusion, the journey of a musician is filled with challenges, rejection, and moments of self-doubt. However, it is through these experiences that we learn, grow, and create beautiful harmonies from discord. By embracing humility, developing a growth mindset, persisting through difficulties, and valuing collaboration, we can transform rejection into a powerful force for personal and artistic development. Just as I found my way through the challenges, every aspiring musician can learn to navigate the obstacles, create their own unique sound, and build a successful career.

ED SHEERAN: "SLEEPING ON SOFAS" TO STADIUM SUPERSTAR

It's only fitting to speak on an artist who embodies the journey of overcoming rejection and navigating closed doors to achieve global success. Ed Sheeran is the perfect example to illustrate this section of the chapter. His path to becoming a global musical icon in the past five years can indeed be encapsulated in the narrative "Sleeping on Sofas to Stadiums," reflecting his humble beginnings and meteoric rise.

EARLY DAYS (THE SOFA YEARS)

Ed Sheeran was born on February 17, 1991, in Halifax, West Yorkshire, England. He began writing songs at a young age and learned to play guitar, showcasing an early passion for music. At just 16, Sheeran moved to London to pursue his music career, embodying the resilience and determination needed to navigate through closed doors. During this time, he often found himself sleeping on friends' sofas and even spent some nights homeless, busking on the streets to make ends meet. Despite these hardships, Sheeran's passion for music never waned. He released his first EP, *The Orange Room,* in 2005, marking the beginning of his journey. Sheeran's relentless effort saw him continue to release independent EPs and perform at small gigs, gradually building a reputation. He harnessed the power of YouTube and online platforms to share his music, gaining a growing following. His big break came when he caught the attention of Jamie Foxx, who was impressed by Sheeran's talent and let him use his recording studio. This opportunity was a turning point, leading to Sheeran signing with Asylum Records in 2011. This phase of his life showcases the importance of leveraging support and mentorship, as the guidance and resources provided by Jamie Foxx were crucial in helping Sheeran break through initial barriers.

FROM SOFAS TO STAGES

With the release of his debut album '+' in 2011, featuring the hit single "The A Team," Sheeran's popularity skyrocketed. This rapid rise saw him transition from performing in small venues to headlining larger stages and festivals. His second album 'x' (2014) solidified his stardom, with tracks like "Thinking out Loud" becoming global hits. This period of his career highlights the power of persistence and continuous learning, as Sheeran refined his craft and adapted his approach to resonate with a broader audience.

By the time his third album '÷' was released in 2017, Sheeran had become a household name, headlining stadiums worldwide. The album's hit single "Shape of You" became one of the best-selling digital singles of all time. Sheeran's '÷' tour (2017-2019) broke touring records, becoming the highest-grossing tour of all time. This era of his career exemplifies how embracing innovation and upgrading one's approach can lead to monumental success. Sheeran's use of loop pedals and his unique blend of pop, folk, hip-hop, and rock influences set him apart and captivated audiences globally.

BEYOND THE STADIUM

Even after achieving monumental success, Sheeran continued to innovate and expand his horizons. He released *No.6 Collaborations Project* in

2019 and '=' in 2021, maintaining his presence at the top of the charts. Sheeran also ventured into acting, with appearances in *Game of Thrones* and *Yesterday,* showcasing his versatility. His journey underscores the importance of staying relevant and continuously seeking new opportunities, even after achieving significant success. Ed Sheeran's personal life also reflects his grounded nature despite his fame. He married his childhood friend Cherry Seaborn in 2018, and they are now parents to two daughters. Known for his philanthropy and support of various charities, Sheeran remains down-to-earth and committed to giving back to the community. His musical style, characterized by a blend of genres and the innovative use of loop pedals in live performances, continues to influence and inspire.

LESSONS FROM ED SHEERAN'S JOURNEY

Ed Sheeran's journey from "Sleeping on Sofas" to filling stadiums worldwide encapsulates the power of resilience, strategic thinking, and adaptability. His story highlights several key strategies:

Resilience: Sheeran never let rejection define him. Instead, he used it as motivation to keep improving and pushing forward. Ed Sheeran's journey to becoming a global musical icon is a powerful example of resilience in the face of rejection and setbacks. His story is a testament to how persistence, adaptability, and a relentless drive can lead to extraordinary success.

EARLY REJECTIONS: FUEL FOR IMPROVEMENT

Facing Numerous Rejections: Ed Sheeran's early career was marked by numerous rejections from record labels, with some even telling him he was "too chubby" and "too ginger" to make it in the music industry. Instead of letting these comments deter him, Sheeran used them as motivation to keep improving and pushing forward.

BRIT School Rejection: Despite the school's reputation for producing successful artists, Sheeran was rejected from the BRIT School for Performing Arts and Technology. Rather than being disheartened, he focused on honing his craft independently, demonstrating his commitment to his music.

PERSISTENCE IN LONDON: GRINDING THROUGH THE GIGS

Playing up to 300 Gigs a Year: When Sheeran moved to London at 16, he played up to 300 gigs a year, often to nearly-empty rooms. This relentless performance schedule allowed him to refine his skills and build resilience, even when immediate success seemed out of reach.

Overcoming Stuttering: As a child, Sheeran had a stutter. He credits rapping along to Eminem's music as a form of speech therapy that helped him overcome this challenge. This early experience with overcoming personal obstacles set the stage for his resilient approach to his career.

Handling Criticism: Even after achieving success, Sheeran faced criticism for his music and image. He consistently responded by focusing on his work and connecting with his fans, rather than letting negative comments affect him. This focus on his craft helped him maintain his trajectory.

Bouncing Back from Setbacks: In 2015, Sheeran took a year-long social media break to refocus on his music and personal life. He returned stronger, releasing his hugely successful album '÷' which featured hits like "Shape of You" and "Castle on the Hill." This break was a strategic move that allowed him to recharge and come back with renewed energy and creativity.

LEGAL CHALLENGES AND PERSONAL RESILIENCE

Facing Legal Challenges: Sheeran has faced several copyright infringement lawsuits. Rather than letting these legal battles derail his career, he defended his work and continued creating music. His ability to navigate these challenges while maintaining his creative output is a testament to his resilience.

Adapting to Fame: Despite the pressures of fame, Sheeran has maintained his down-to-earth personality and work ethic. He shows resilience in handling the challenges that come with stardom, staying grounded and focused on his music.

Mental Health Advocacy: Sheeran has been open about his struggles with anxiety and substance abuse, leveraging his platform to advocate for mental health awareness. By sharing his experiences, he demonstrates resilience and provides support for others facing similar challenges.

Ed Sheeran's journey from sleeping on sofas to selling out stadiums is a testament to his resilience. He has consistently used setbacks and criticisms as fuel to drive his ambition and improve his craft. Sheeran embodies the idea that persistence and hard work can overcome almost any obstacle. His story is an inspiring reminder that resilience, adaptability, and a relentless drive can transform rejection into success and lead to extraordinary achievements.

Leveraging Support and Mentorship: The support from Jamie Foxx and other mentors was instrumental in his early career.

1. **Jamie Foxx's Support:** In 2010, when Sheeran was still relatively unknown, he caught the attention of actor/musician Jamie Foxx while performing at an open mic night in Los Angeles. Foxx was so impressed that he offered Sheeran the use of his recording studio and even let him crash on his couch for a few

weeks. This support provided Sheeran with valuable resources and exposure at a crucial time in his career.

2. **Elton John's Mentorship:** Elton John has been a significant mentor to Sheeran since early in his career. John's management company, Rocket Music, took on Sheeran as a client in 2011. Beyond business support, John has offered personal advice and guidance, helping Sheeran navigate the music industry with a seasoned perspective.

3. **Support from Established Songwriters:** Early in his career, Sheeran collaborated with and learned from established songwriters like Steve Mac and Johnny McDaid. These collaborations helped him refine his craft, develop his unique style, and make important industry connections.

4. **Industry Mentors:** Atlantic Records executives Ben Cook and Ed Howard played crucial roles in Sheeran's development. They offered guidance on his musical direction and career decisions, ensuring he made strategic moves that aligned with his long-term goals.

5. **Peer Support:** Fellow British artists like Example and Passenger provided support and opportunities for Sheeran in his early days. Opening for these established acts helped him build his fanbase and gain credibility within the music scene.

6. **Stormzy and the Grime Scene:** Sheeran's collaborations with grime artists, particularly Stormzy, have been mutually beneficial. These relationships have allowed Sheeran to explore different musical styles and expand his audience, demonstrating his versatility and broad appeal.

7. **James Blunt Friendship:** Veteran singer-songwriter James Blunt has been both a friend and mentor to Sheeran. Blunt has

offered career advice and even co-written songs with Sheeran, contributing to his artistic development and success.

8. **Leveraging Social Media Support:** While not traditional mentorship, Sheeran effectively leveraged support from social media influencers and YouTube stars to gain exposure in his early career. This digital strategy helped him reach a wider audience and build a dedicated fanbase.

Ed Sheeran's ability to form genuine connections with established artists and industry figures, and his willingness to learn from their experiences, has been a key factor in his rise from "sleeping on sofas" to becoming a stadium-filling superstar. He's often spoken about the importance of those relationships in his career, highlighting how crucial it is for emerging artists to seek out and value mentorship opportunities.

Sheeran's journey illustrates the profound impact that support and mentorship can have on an artist's career. The guidance, resources, and opportunities provided by mentors like Jamie Foxx, Elton John, and Taylor Swift, among others, were instrumental in Sheeran's rise to fame. His story underscores the importance of building and leveraging a strong support network, staying open to learning from others, and using every opportunity to grow and develop. By forming meaningful connections and continuously seeking mentorship, Sheeran transformed his dreams into reality, demonstrating that resilience and strategic networking can overcome almost any obstacle.

Ed Sheeran's story is a testament to the fact that closed doors are not the end—they are simply opportunities to adapt, innovate, and emerge stronger. His journey from humble beginnings to global superstardom serves as an inspiration for anyone facing obstacles and seeking to turn their dreams into reality. Keep strategizing, keep learning, and keep moving forward. With the right mindset and strategies, no obstacle is too great to overcome.

In life, as in Sheeran's journey, persistence and resilience are key. When faced with rejection or setbacks, remember that these moments are not final—they are stepping stones to greater things. Use them to refine your skills, seek out mentorship, and continuously innovate your approach. Whether you're an aspiring artist, a professional aiming for the next level, or someone navigating personal challenges, let Sheeran's story remind you that with determination and the right support, you can turn any closed door into a gateway to success.

Each setback you encounter is a learning opportunity. When Sheeran faced rejection from record labels and even personal criticisms about his appearance, he didn't let these obstacles define him. Instead, he used them as fuel to refine his craft and prove his detractors wrong. His story shows that resilience involves more than just enduring hardships— it's about transforming those hardships into stepping stones. Seek out and value the support and mentorship from those who have walked similar paths. Just as Jamie Foxx and Elton John provided Sheeran with guidance and resources, look for mentors who can offer you wisdom, support, and opportunities. Building a network of supportive relation- ships can provide invaluable insights and encouragement as you navigate your own journey.

Innovation is also crucial. Sheeran's use of social media and online platforms to build his initial following exemplifies the importance of leveraging new tools and technologies to your advantage. In a constantly changing world, staying adaptable and open to new ideas can set you apart and help you overcome traditional barriers. Remember to main- tain a growth mindset. This means viewing challenges as opportunities to learn and grow rather than insurmountable obstacles. Each failure is not a reflection of your limitations but a chance to gain new insights and refine your strategies. Sheeran's willingness to embrace change, adapt his approach, and continuously improve is a model for anyone striving to achieve their goals.

Sheeran's love for music and his commitment to his craft drove him to keep going, even when the odds seemed stacked against him. Find what you are passionate about and let that passion drive you forward. Your dedication and hard work will pay off in ways you might not yet imagine. Finally, believe in yourself. Confidence in your abilities and your vision is crucial. Surround yourself with people who believe in you and your dreams, and let their support reinforce your self-belief. Sheeran's journey underscores the importance of self-belief and the impact it can have on your ability to persevere through difficult times. So, as you move forward in your journey, remember Ed Sheeran's story. Keep strategizing, keep learning, and keep moving forward. With the right mindset and strategies, no obstacle is too great to overcome. Your persistence, resilience, and willingness to adapt will turn every closed door into a new opportunity. The path to greatness is filled with challenges, but each one is a chance to grow stronger and more capable. Keep pushing forward, and let your journey be a testament to the power of resilience and the triumph of the human spirit.

IN CONCLUSION

It's important to understand that there's always an avenue and a strategy within the strategy. Just like the journey of Ed Sheeran, being stressed in one season propelled him to advance in the next season. Everything in life has an advantage as long as you're willing to go the distance for it. Think about all the times that the strategy was actually the advantage in disguise. Don't ever look at the closed door as the final closed door. See it as a strategy of opportunity, a strategy that opens even more doors. The essence of this chapter has been to illustrate that closed doors are not dead ends but gateways to new possibilities.

Each obstacle, each setback, is a chance to refine your approach, learn new skills, and grow stronger. Just like Ed Sheeran's resilience turned rejections into milestones on his path to success, you too can harness the power of persistence and strategic thinking to transform challenges into opportunities. Everything that we've covered in this chapter symbolizes the importance of seeing the bigger picture. Embrace it, run with it, and use it as you apply it to everyday life. The real power lies in understanding that each challenge is a piece of a larger puzzle, a step towards a more significant achievement.

Application doesn't go anywhere unless you understand the strategy of what you're doing. It's not enough to simply face a closed door; you must also analyze it, understand its nature, and devise a plan to either open it or find another path. This requires a keen mindset, a willingness to adapt, and the resilience to keep moving forward despite the setbacks. Many times, the strategy we develop in response to a closed door becomes the very advantage that propels us forward. Each rejection, each failure, teaches you something valuable about yourself and your journey. It refines your skills, sharpens your focus, and builds your resilience. The closed door is often the catalyst for innovation and growth.

The path to success is rarely a straight line, but a winding road filled with obstacles and closed doors. Yet, within those challenges lies an opportunity for growth, resilience, and the cultivation of a strategic mindset that can unlock your full potential. Embrace the lessons from the gaming world, where every failure was not a devastating end but feedback to adapt your approach, hone your skills, and persist until you mastered the level. Just as you leveled up by recognizing patterns, experimenting with new tactics, and grinding relentlessly until you overcame each in-game challenge, so too can you apply those principles to conquer real-life obstacles.

Draw inspiration from nature's most adaptive creatures like the mimic octopus, who deftly navigates threats by shapeshifting its very form and behavior. When facing closed doors, be willing to pivot, to challenge your assumptions, and to embrace new strategies that may initially feel uncomfortable but ultimately lead you to breakthrough solutions. Seek wisdom from mentors who have already traversed similar paths, and don't be afraid to leverage the collective knowledge of communities. Just as gaming forums and collaborative strategy-building propelled you through seemingly insurmountable levels, the guidance and support of others can provide invaluable insights and resources to help you overcome your own challenges.

In this chapter, I delved into how to develop a strategic mindset, emphasizing the importance of adopting such a mindset even when faced with obstacles. Breaking down problems into manageable parts is crucial. If you can't manage a problem in smaller, actionable steps, it's challenging to create a contingency plan. This is a key point we've explored. Learning from failures is another critical aspect we've covered. Failures are inevitable, but they shouldn't be seen as end points. Instead, use them to adapt, learn, and grow stronger. Don't let failures frustrate you to the point where you stop taking feedback or stop learning. Embrace them as opportunities for growth.

Adaptability and flexibility are essential qualities to cultivate. You must be flexible and adaptable to change and strategy, especially when confronted with closed doors. This chapter highlighted examples from the gaming industry, illustrating how to pivot strategies and find breakthrough solutions. The analogies and illustrations I provided demonstrate the importance of adaptability and flexibility. Pattern recognition is another crucial skill. I always tell those I mentor and coach to study, not just people, but their patterns. Understanding patterns is key to recognizing essential skills that might be lacking, even in the face of predictable outcomes. This chapter emphasizes the importance of pattern recognition.

Persistence and resilience are also vital. Drawing inspiration from Ed Sheeran's journey, this chapter showcases how persistence and resilience can lead to success. Ed Sheeran's life, along with the stories of other celebrities mentioned, exemplifies the power of resilience and determination. Continuous learning and innovation are indispensable. Always be willing to learn, innovate, and develop your skillset. It's like working a muscle—the more you exercise it, the more it expands, allowing you to handle greater challenges. This chapter underscores the importance of constant growth and development.

Leveraging support and mentorship is another key point. Ensure that your circle of mentors, coaches, and peers can offer you new insights and knowledge. If everyone knows the same things, there is no advantage. A true leader seeks out individuals who possess skills and knowledge they lack. Leveraging diverse support and mentorship enhances your ability to navigate complex situations. Finally, embrace change and upgrade. This chapter encourages adopting new technologies, shifting perspectives, evolving, and not being afraid to upgrade. The Genius Bar analogy illustrates the importance of specific, tailored strategies to overcome obstacles.

I hope this chapter has given you a deeper understanding of the strategy of closed doors and how to see the advantages they present. Embrace these strategies, apply them to your everyday life, and recognize that each challenge is an opportunity for growth. Keep strategizing, keep learning, and keep moving forward. Your journey is one of continuous growth and discovery, and each closed door is just the beginning of a new adventure.

As you strategize in life, you're going to encounter some of the most intriguing perspectives, even in the face of closed doors. The examples I shared about the gaming industry, the power of flexibility, and the leverage of technology weren't just idle talk. I truly believe that in the next decade, the advancement of technology will demand our absolute best. We must ensure that we are not only familiar with AI but also adept at integrating it into our business strategies. This is not about competing with AI, but instead collaborating with it. Many people view AI with apprehension, fearing job loss and uncertainty. However, we should see AI as a powerful ally, a strategic advantage that opens new doors when others close.

This perspective is crucial, especially for new developers and business owners. Embrace the potential of technology to transform challenges into opportunities. Remember, everything happens for a reason. This chapter aims to provide you with a profound insight into the strategy of navigating closed doors. Use this knowledge to position yourself advantageously in an ever-evolving landscape. Continuing this journey of embracing technology and turning obstacles into opportunities, we must understand the profound impact AI and other technological advancements can have on our lives and businesses. It's not just about keeping up; it's about staying ahead.

In this rapidly evolving world, flexibility and adaptability are your greatest assets. The gaming industry has shown us how quickly the landscape can change and how those who are nimble and innovative can thrive. Take this lesson to heart: be willing to pivot, to learn, and to embrace new technologies as they emerge. Consider how AI can enhance your business processes, streamline operations, and create new avenues for growth. It can analyze data more efficiently, predict trends more accurately, and automate routine tasks, freeing up your time to focus on strategic decisions and creative endeavors. This is not just about survival; it's about thriving in an era where technology is intertwined with every facet of life.

Think about the possibilities. Imagine using AI to understand your customers better, to anticipate their needs, and to deliver personalized experiences that exceed their expectations. Picture a future where you are not just keeping pace with change but leading it, where your business is not just another player in the market but a trailblazer setting new standards. This mindset shift is essential. Don't view closed doors as dead ends, but as opportunities to explore uncharted territories. When one path is blocked, technology can help you find a new route, often leading to unexpected and exciting destinations. For new developers and business owners, this chapter serves as a guide to harnessing the power of AI and technology. It's about understanding that every challenge is an opportunity in disguise, that every closed door can lead to a breakthrough if you have the right tools and mindset.

Stay curious, stay innovative, and most importantly, stay committed to leveraging technology to its fullest potential. This is your moment to redefine what's possible, to turn obstacles into opportunities, and to pave the way for a future where you and your business can thrive like never before. By adopting these principles, you can ensure that you remain on your A-game, ready to seize the opportunities that technology presents and turn them into lasting success.

In closing, remember that the future belongs to those who are willing to embrace change and harness the power of technology. With the right mindset and tools, you can transform challenges into opportunities and create a path to success that is both innovative and sustainable. Stay committed, stay adaptable, and most importantly, stay ahead. The journey is just beginning, and the possibilities are endless.

CHAPTER 7

TEARS BEHIND CLOSED DOORS

The tears we cry behind closed doors often reflect our deepest vulnerabilities. I can personally attest that the tears I've cried in private have been some of the most genuine. These were tears of disappointment, embarrassment, letdowns, setbacks, and insecurities. It felt like a collection of emotions bottled up until I was ready to share them. Tears carry the weight of our experiences, our triumphs, and the things we witness in life. In this chapter, I'm going to explore the various categories of tears, breaking them down piece by piece, both biologically and emotionally, to help you understand their roots. Biologically, tears are produced by the lacrimal gland to keep the eyes lubricated. Many people might not know this, but tears keep our eyes nourished and clear of dust and debris. This can be metaphorically applied to life—just as tears clear physical debris, they can also clear the emotional "dust" from our lives. Keeping our eyes protected with positive thinking can prevent the dust of drama, arrogance, or pride from clouding our vision.

There are several types of tears, each serving a specific purpose. Basal tears are constantly produced to keep our eyes moist under normal conditions. These silent guardians ensure our eyes remain hydrated and healthy. Have you ever sat under a fan or felt a breeze that made your eyes water? That's your body's natural response to keep your eyes hydrated. Then there are reflex tears, which respond to irritants like smoke, wind, or particles—much like the dust and debris scenario. Reflex tears act as a defense mechanism to flush out unwanted substances.

However, the focus here is on emotional tears. Over the years, I have shed many emotional tears behind closed doors. These tears were necessary for me to process what I was going through. I've also experienced reflex tears in response to the irritants of life—the figurative smoke from people's frustrations, jealousy, and conflicts. These reflex tears were my body's way of dealing with the emotional smoke that surrounded me.

There were times in my youth when I was so angry that I cried out of a desire for revenge. I cried because I was tired of being bullied. Many people don't know this, but I was bullied a lot growing up, and I would hold in my tears, making it hard to express myself. Those experiences taught me the importance of processing and expressing emotions. In this chapter, we'll delve into the different aspects of tears, discussing their biological and emotional significance. We'll explore how understanding the types of tears can give us a broader perspective on life and help us handle our emotions more effectively. This chapter aims to add value to your life and provide insights that will enrich your understanding of yourself and your experiences.

SINGLE PARENT TEARS

I know there may be a single parent reading this right now who has shed countless tears due to the immense pressures you have faced in the past 10 years. Being the sole income provider for a household brings a unique set of challenges and heartaches. When you alone are responsible for providing for your family, the weight of financial burdens can be over-whelming. The constant worry about how to stretch a limited budget to cover all expenses can bring tears to the eyes of a single parent. The struggle to afford basic necessities like food, housing, and childcare is a daily battle. Without a financial safety net for emergencies, the fear of an unexpected expense can be paralyzing. The uncertainty of not having a backup plan or safety net can make it difficult to move forward, leaving you feeling trapped and helpless.

Yet, in these moments of despair, it's crucial to persevere. Building a community of trusted friends and supporters can make a world of difference. These are the people you can turn to when you need to talk about your financial struggles, who can help you find solutions and offer support. It's not just about finding a job; it's about finding a career that upholds your dignity and provides for your family's needs. Single parent tears also stem from custody issues, the lack of resources, and the constant juggling of responsibilities. The limitations imposed by childcare needs can hinder job opportunities, while a lack of educational or institutional support further complicates matters. The absence of breaks or time off to manage personal and household affairs adds to the stress, bringing more tears. Coordinating schedules, transportation, and appointments is a relentless task that weighs heavily on single parents.

To every single parent reading this, I want to offer encouragement: you don't have to remain in this place of struggle. Building a sense of community, even if it takes time, is vital. Identify where the weaknesses lie, where the problems stem from, and work on yourself first. Avoid burning out by trying to do everything at once. Instead, cultivate a practice of self-care and tackle issues one by one. Align your dreams and goals with your strengths and passions. Remember, if you can nurture your children and teach them valuable lessons, despite the hardships, they will remember and appreciate your efforts. Never let your kids down, never give up on your parenting skills, and never let external issues or negative influences come between you and your children.

Life will throw challenges your way, but that doesn't mean you should stop striving for excellence. Pursue everything with a spirit of determination and resilience. You are not alone in this journey, and with perseverance, community support, and a focus on self-care, you can overcome these challenges and build a better future for yourself and your family.

Over the years, I've had countless one-on-one counseling sessions with clients who have shared their stories of the types of tears and obstacles they face. Those experiences have provided deep insights into the struggles of single parents. Here are three categories of tears that can bring valuable understanding to the experiences you or someone you know might be facing. These categories serve as tools for assessment to truly comprehend what's going on behind the tears of single parents.

1. EMOTIONAL TEARS

Emotional tears arise from the profound feelings of loneliness, frustration, and exhaustion that single parents often endure. These tears are a natural release, helping to alleviate the emotional burden that builds up over time. These tears arise from the depths of our psyche, carrying a torrent of overwhelming feelings that can no longer be contained. They are an outpouring of the soul, a release valve for the intense emotions that accumulate in the face of profound challenges and hardships. Despite being surrounded by people, single parents can feel isolated in their responsibilities. For single parents, emotional tears often stem from the relentless demands and sacrifices that come with raising children without a partner to share the load. The loneliness of facing life's challenges alone, without a shoulder to lean on or a listening ear to provide comfort, can be overwhelming. In those quiet moments, when the house is still and the children are asleep, the floodgates open, and emotional tears flow freely, offering a temporary respite from the constant pressure of being both nurturer and provider.

Frustration: Single parents carry the weight of a thousand responsibilities, from managing work and household duties to coordinating schedules and tending to their children's every need. The constant juggling act, coupled with the lack of support and the fear of letting anyone down, can lead to a buildup of frustration that eventually erupts in a cathartic release of emotional tears.

Exhaustion: Exhaustion also contributes to these tear-filled moments. The unrelenting nature of single parenthood, with its never-ending demands and lack of respite, can leave even the strongest individuals feeling depleted and drained. Emotional tears become a way to express the bone-deep weariness that seeps into every fiber of their being, a wordless plea for reprieve from the ceaseless grind.

2. FINANCIAL TEARS

The challenge of stretching a limited budget to cover all expenses is a daily battle that weighs heavily on single parents. It's a constant, looming presence that casts a shadow over their lives. With each passing month, they meticulously scrutinize every expense, desperately trying to make every hard-earned dollar stretch farther than seems humanly possible. The pressure of ensuring there's enough to cover essentials like rent, utilities, and groceries is a significant and unrelenting source of stress. The anxiety of knowing that a single misstep, one unexpected cost, could send their carefully constructed budget spiraling into disarray is a weight that never truly lifts from their shoulders.

For single parents, the struggle to make ends meet is not a temporary challenge but a persistent, ever-present reality. They live in a constant state of financial precariousness, where even the smallest deviation from the carefully planned budget could have catastrophic consequences for their family's well-being. Despite their best efforts to plan and budget meticulously, the weight of this financial burden never truly dissipates. The fear of the next unforeseen expense, the dread of falling behind on bills, and the constant need to make difficult choices between competing essentials can be emotionally and mentally exhausting. Yet, in the face of this relentless pressure, single parents display a remarkable resilience and determination to provide for their children, no matter the personal sacrifices required. They navigate this daily challenge with a steadfast resolve, stretching every dollar to its absolute limit and finding creative ways to make ends meet, all while shouldering the immense responsibility of raising their children alone.

Unexpected Expenses: Without a financial safety net, unexpected costs can be devastating. The fear and anxiety of not knowing how to handle these situations can lead to many sleepless nights and tearful moments. Perhaps one of the most significant sources of financial tears for single parents is the ever-present fear of unexpected expenses. Without a financial safety net or a partner's income to fall back on, even a minor car repair or medical bill can feel like a catastrophic event. The anxiety of not knowing how to handle these situations can be crippling, leading to many sleepless nights and tearful moments as they try to devise a plan to stay afloat.

In these moments, tears may flow from a place of sheer helplessness and despair. The realization that one unforeseen event could potentially unravel the carefully constructed life they've built for their family can be overwhelming. These tears represent the profound fear of not being able to provide for their children, of letting them down, and of potentially losing the stability they've worked so hard to create.

Long-Term Planning: The lack of financial stability can make planning for the future feel impossible. The uncertainty of being able to save for education, emergencies, or retirement can weigh heavily on a single parent's mind. Beyond the immediate struggles of making ends meet, single parents often shed tears over the long-term implications of their financial situation. The lack of financial stability can make planning for the future feel like an impossible task, with the uncertainty of being able to save for their children's education, emergencies, or even their own retirement weighing heavily on their minds.

These tears may stem from the fear of not being able to provide their children with the opportunities they deserve or the worry of becoming a burden on their loved ones in their later years. The inability to build a safety net or plan for the future can feel like a constant source of anxiety, leading to moments of hopelessness and despair.

In these instances, tears may flow as a release valve for the overwhelming sense of responsibility and the fear of not being able to secure a better future for their family. They represent the frustration of working tirelessly and still feeling like they are falling behind, unable to break the cycle of living paycheck to paycheck. Yet, even as these tears fall, they are a testament to the unwavering love and dedication that single parents possess. Each tear is a reminder of the sacrifices they make, the struggles they endure, and the resilience they must summon to keep pushing forward, all in the hopes of creating a better life for their children.

3. PRACTICAL TEARS

Practical tears are shed over the daily logistics and relentless tasks that come with single parenting. These tears often reflect the sheer physical and mental demands of managing a household alone.

Scheduling Conflicts: Juggling work, school, appointments, and activities can be overwhelming. The constant need to be in multiple places at once can lead to tears of frustration and exhaustion.

Household Management: Keeping up with the housework, cooking, cleaning, and maintenance can be daunting. The endless list of chores can feel like an insurmountable mountain when faced alone.

Lack of Time for Self: Single parents often have little to no time for themselves. The absence of personal time for rest and rejuvenation can lead to feelings of burnout and despair.

By understanding and addressing these three types of tears, single parents can better navigate their unique challenges. Remember, seeking support, prioritizing self-care, and setting realistic goals are essential steps toward building a fulfilling and resilient life for you and your children. These insights not only help in recognizing the struggles but also in finding ways to overcome them and move forward with strength and hope. In the face of overwhelming emotional, financial, and practical burdens, it's crucial for single parents to find solace in the knowledge that their tears are not only valid but also a powerful testament to their unwavering strength and resilience. These tears represent the depth of love, sacrifice, and commitment that fuels their journey, even in the darkest of moments.

While the path ahead may seem daunting, it's important to remember that single parents are not alone. Building a supportive network—whether through family, friends, or community organizations—can provide a much-needed lifeline and a source of encouragement. By sharing their experiences and leaning on others, single parents can find the strength to persevere and the wisdom to navigate even the most challenging circumstances.

Moreover, prioritizing self-care is not a luxury but a necessity. Single parents must find ways to replenish their physical, emotional, and mental reserves, whether through simple acts of kindness toward themselves or by seeking professional support when needed. Only by nurturing their own well-being can they truly show up as the best possible parent for their children. Finally, setting realistic goals and embracing a growth mindset can help single parents break free from the cycle of overwhelm and create a roadmap for a brighter future. By focusing on achievable milestones and celebrating small victories along the way, they can cultivate a sense of empowerment and hope, knowing that each step forward is a testament to their resilience and determination.

In the end, the tears shed by single parents are not a sign of weakness but rather a powerful affirmation of their strength, courage, and unconditional love. By acknowledging and embracing these tears, single parents can find the courage to continue their journey, secure in the knowledge that they are not alone and that their sacrifices are paving the way for a better tomorrow—for themselves and for their children. So, to all the single parents out there, let your tears flow freely, but never lose sight of the incredible strength that lies within you. Seek support, prioritize self-care, and set realistic goals that will guide you toward a more fulfilling and resilient life. Your tears may be a reflection of your struggles, but they are also a powerful reminder of the love that drives you forward, one step at a time, toward a brighter future.

PAYCHECK-TO-PAYCHECK TEARS

The relentless cycle of living from paycheck to paycheck can be traumatizing. It's a constant teeter-totter of financial ruin, where every dollar is stretched to its absolute limit. I think we can all relate to this. Personally, when I was younger, there were times when I had to live with my parents. I often struggled to navigate through paychecks to figure out why things weren't working. To make ends meet, I went into the fishing industry, and drove for Uber and Lyft, in addition to my regular job. Living from paycheck to paycheck is a precarious situation that can eat at your soul. It's like living on a tightrope, where one misstep could mean catastrophe, and the weight of responsibility feels like an ever-tightening noose. The tears that flow in these moments are born from a profound sense of helplessness and despair. They are the silent sobs that escape when the realization sets in, affecting your budget and perpetuating the cycle. It's a life lived in constant fear, where financial ruin looms every time you feel like you're making progress.

Every unexpected expense, whether a car repair, medical bill, or broken appliance, feels like a personal crisis that disrupts everything else. These tears are the manifestation of fear and uncertainty, not knowing how you'll weather the storm. However, the truth is that despite living paycheck to paycheck, there is a way to navigate through this with drive, perseverance, strategy, and support. I was fortunate to get out of my situation with the help of a supportive family. I understand that not everyone has a supportive family, a church to turn to, or a system in place; but I want to encourage you to see the bigger picture and navigate through it—despite living paycheck to paycheck. Remember, where there's a will, there's a way.

I've seen it time and time again with my clients. They shared their stories, and together, we found ways to help them financially. This topic is very sensitive to me because living from paycheck to paycheck is closely tied to the tears people shed behind closed doors.

CASE STUDY: THE JOURNEY OF JANE DOE—BREAKING THE CYCLE OF LIVING PAYCHECK TO PAYCHECK

Jane Doe is a single mother of two living in a small apartment in a suburban area. She works full-time as a cashier at a local grocery store, earning just above minimum wage. Despite her best efforts, Jane often finds herself living paycheck to paycheck, struggling to cover basic necessities like rent, utilities, food, and childcare. The constant financial stress leaves her feeling overwhelmed and anxious about her future and her children's well-being.

CHALLENGES

Jane's financial challenges are multifaceted. Her monthly income barely covers her essential expenses, leaving no room for savings or emergencies. Unexpected costs, such as car repairs or medical bills, often throw her budget into disarray. Jane has no financial safety net and relies heavily on credit cards to manage these unforeseen expenses, leading to accumulating debt and high-interest payments.

THE TURNING POINT

One particularly difficult month, Jane's car broke down, and the repair costs were beyond her immediate ability to pay. This incident was the tipping point that made her realize she needed to make significant changes to break free from the cycle of living paycheck to paycheck. Jane decided to seek help and enrolled in a financial counseling program offered by a local nonprofit organization. The breakdown of her car, a necessity for transportation and her daily commute, became a catalyst for Jane to take decisive action. She recognized that her financial situation was unsustainable, and continuing down the same path would only lead to further hardship. With a newfound sense of determination, Jane embarked on a journey of personal growth and financial empowerment, seeking guidance and embracing strategies that would help her regain control over her life.

STRATEGIES FOR CHANGE

1. **Financial Counseling and Education:** Through the financial counseling program, Jane learned how to create a realistic budget, track her expenses, and identify areas where she could

cut costs. She also gained knowledge about financial literacy, including managing debt and the importance of savings.

2. **Community Resources:** Jane discovered various community resources that could help alleviate her financial burden. She applied for assistance programs that provided subsidized childcare and food support, which significantly reduced her monthly expenses.

3. **Support Network:** Jane began attending support groups for single parents, where she met others facing similar challenges. This network provided her with emotional support, practical advice, and the reassurance that she was not alone in her struggles.

4. **Skill Development:** To improve her job prospects, Jane took advantage of free online courses and workshops. She learned new skills in customer service and basic accounting, which eventually helped her secure a better-paying job within the same company.

5. **Self-Care and Mental Health:** Recognizing the toll that financial stress was taking on her mental health, Jane started practicing self-care routines. She allocated time for exercise, meditation, and hobbies that she enjoyed, helping her maintain a more positive outlook and better handle stress.

Over time, Jane's efforts began to pay off. With a better-paying job and reduced expenses, she was able to start saving a small portion of her income each month. The financial counseling helped her create a plan to pay down her debt systematically. Her new support network provided ongoing encouragement and practical tips for managing her finances. Jane's journey is a testament to the power of resilience and the importance of seeking help. By taking proactive steps to address her financial situation, she was able to break the cycle of living paycheck to paycheck. Jane's story highlights that while the path to financial stability is challenging, it is achievable with the right resources, support, and determination.

Living paycheck to paycheck is a harsh reality for many individuals and families. Jane Doe's case study demonstrates that with strategic planning, community support, and personal perseverance, it is possible to overcome this cycle. Her experience serves as an inspiration to others facing similar challenges, proving that change is possible, and that financial freedom can be attained with effort and dedication.

Recommended books that can provide valuable insights to breaking free from the paycheck-to-paycheck cycle:

One book I highly recommend for understanding how to avoid the traps of living paycheck to paycheck is "The Total Money Makeover" by Dave Ramsey. Dave Ramsey is a well-known financial guru, recognized for his expertise in personal finance. This book is a comprehensive guide to getting out of debt and achieving financial freedom, and it outlines Ramsey's famous seven baby steps. These steps provide straightforward and actionable plans for taking control of your money, which is why I love this book so much.

1. The first baby step Ramsey discusses is to save $1,000 for a starter emergency fund. He emphasizes the importance of having a small emergency fund to cover unexpected expenses, preventing you from going further into debt when life happens.

2. The second baby step is to use the debt snowball method to pay off all debt except the house. This method involves listing all debts from smallest to largest and tackling them in that order, gaining momentum as each debt is paid off. This approach is powerful because it provides psychological wins along the way, keeping you motivated.

3. The third baby step is to save three to six months of expenses for a fully funded emergency fund. Once consumer debt is paid off, the focus shifts to building a more robust emergency fund to cover living expenses in case of job loss or other emergencies.

4. The fourth baby step is to invest 15% of household income for retirement. Ramsey stresses the importance of investing for retirement even while paying off debt. He recommends using employer-sponsored programs like 401(k)s and Roth IRAs to build your retirement savings.

5. The fifth baby step is to save for your children's college fund after securing your retirement. Ramsey advises saving for your children's education using tax-advantaged accounts like 529 plans.

6. The sixth baby step is to pay off your home mortgage early. Once other debts and savings goals are covered, Ramsey recommends focusing on paying off your mortgage to become truly debt-free.

7. The seventh and final baby step is to build wealth and give generously. This step is about building wealth through investing and then giving generously to causes you care about, which helps you flourish beyond financial stability. Throughout the book, Ramsey emphasizes the importance of living on a written monthly budget, avoiding new debt, and challenging common money mindsets. He provides practical tips for negotiating with creditors, selling possessions to raise cash, and making temporary sacrifices to achieve financial freedom faster.

The next recommended book is "You Need a Budget" by Jesse Mecham. This book provides a comprehensive look into the YNAB (You Need a Budget) narrative, a budgeting method designed to help individuals and families gain control over their finances and break free from the paycheck-to-paycheck cycle.

Jesse Mecham is the founder and CEO of YNAB, a personal financial software company that has helped hundreds of thousands of people worldwide manage their money more effectively. Mecham's journey toward financial literacy began when he found himself deeply in debt after college. This experience prompted him to develop the YNAB budgeting system to regain control over his finances. Today, YNAB is a well-regarded method for financial management.

THE YNAB METHOD IS BUILT AROUND FOUR SIMPLE RULES

1. **Give Every Dollar a Job:** This rule emphasizes the importance of assigning a specific purpose to every dollar you earn. By ensuring that your money is working toward your goals and priorities, you can avoid unnecessary spending and focus on meeting your financial obligations.

2. **Embrace Your True Expenses:** This rule encourages users to budget for irregular or non-monthly expenses, such as car repairs or annual subscriptions, by setting aside money each month to cover these costs when they arise. By planning for these expenses, you can avoid financial surprises and maintain a balanced budget.

3. **Roll with the Punches:** This rule acknowledges that life is unpredictable and that your budget will require adjustments. The key is to remain flexible and proactive in your budgeting approach, making tweaks as needed to stay on track.

4. **Age Your Money:** The ultimate goal of this method is to build a buffer of savings, allowing you to spend this month's income on next month's expenses. By aging your money, you create a

financial cushion that helps you break the cycle of living pay-check to paycheck.

One of the strengths of "You Need a Budget" is its emphasis on changing behaviors and mindsets around money. Mecham stresses the importance of proactive financial decision-making and taking owner-ship of one's financial situation rather than simply following a strict set of rules. This approach encourages readers to understand their financial habits and make informed choices that align with their long-term goals. The book provides practical steps on how to budget your money and manage your finances effectively. By following the YNAB method, you can develop a healthier relationship with money, reduce financial stress, and build a stable financial future.

*

TEEN TEARS

Teenage years are often portrayed as a carefree time of self-discovery in the transition from adolescence to adulthood, but there's way more to it than that. A lot of teens are already battling emotional storms due to toxic family environments and living situations. My personal tears as a teen came from being limited in doing things I really wanted to do, things that were not so religious and church oriented. Growing up as a preacher's kid, I was already a target. The church and congregation would always speak highly of both of my parents, who were in full-time ministry, and would keep a hawk-eye on my movements, to ensure I was on point with living up to the standards of a pastor's son growing up in church. From dating to personality and character, they wanted to know everything. I always felt that I had to live up to a certain standard and never felt that I could fully be myself. As long as I was living under my parents' roof, I had to abide by their rules, no questions asked.

Most of my teen years were spent in Japan on different military bases and also living off the base as well. I had my rebellion tears that would come up every time I wanted to do my thing on Saturday, going out with friends, drinking, and still having a fear of smelling like beer and liquor at the same time. There were times I had to repent and still get a spanking after I was caught. My dad would give spankings in a different way. To this day, my family still laughs at the humor that came from what my father used to do. If our report cards were low, with write-ups and school suspensions, he would always say, "Get on the edge of the bed, I'm on my way back home from work." When he would get home, he would take his time, get his Bible, give a mini sermon with specific Scriptures, and then give the spanking with the belt. The pain of hearing the sermon first, cut deep, knowing that the rod of correction was coming up next. I would put on layers of clothes to block the pain of spankings but it never worked because they had to be removed.

Bottom line, the lessons as a teen came with all types of tears. Peer pressure tears, sex tears of guilt, shame tears of knowing that it was wrong from the start, and lastly, the tears of disappointing God. There were times I was tired of feeling guilty over and over. I was like, "God, I know you're sick of me making these same typical excuses and broken, raggedy apologies that are not really sincere." I had to learn the hard way that God was not playing games with me. My tears had stories of consequences behind them. Tears behind car accidents, tears behind drug addictions, sex addictions, lust and manipulation addictions. My life was a daily rollercoaster when I wasn't in church. I would put on the mask over and over. I would even speak in tongues and have the Holy Ghost on Sunday and play cards with the devil on Monday. I would go to the bar on Tuesday, make love on Wednesday, get free drugs on Thursday, and pray that I wouldn't get arrested with a DUI on Friday.

I remember the tears of frustration that would well up when I couldn't hang out with my friends on Friday nights because of church commitments. The tears of anger when I had to miss out on school dances or parties due to my parents' strict rules. And the tears of loneliness when I felt like I didn't truly fit in anywhere—not with the church crowd, and not with the "worldly" kids either. It was a constant tug-of-war within my soul. The dichotomy of that double life was eating me up inside. I'd put on my best behavior at church, acting like the perfect, well-behaved son, while inside I was screaming for freedom, for a chance to find my own path without judgment or condemnation.

Weekends were the worst. Saturday nights were filled with tears of guilt and regret as I stumbled home, reeking of sin and feeling like a complete failure in the eyes of God, and my parents. Sundays were spent with a pit in my stomach, dreading the moment when I'd have to stand before the congregation, a fraud in their midst—but no matter how deep my struggles, I could never bring myself to open up about them. The fear of disappointing my family, of letting them down after all their sacrifices, was too great. So, I bottled it all up, letting the tears flow in secret, behind closed doors where no one could see the depths of my turmoil.

It was a vicious cycle that seemed never-ending—the rebellion, the guilt, the tears, and the endless cycle of repentance and promises to do better, only to fall back into the same patterns of sin and self-de-struction. Looking back now, I realize how much I was crying out for help, for guidance, for someone to see beyond the mask I wore and truly understand the storm raging within me. However, in those days, the stigma around mental health and emotional struggles, especially for a preacher's kid, was too great to overcome. So, I soldiered on, bottling up the tears, the pain, the confusion, until I thought I might burst. It wasn't until years later that I finally found the courage to confront my demons, to seek the healing and understanding I so desperately needed during those tumultuous teenage years.

Those early years of adulthood were a blur of trying to escape the chains of my past. I bounced from job to job, relationship to relationship, never staying in one place long enough to put down roots. The tears kept flowing, but now they were tinged with a bitterness and anger that I couldn't quite place. I was angry at my parents for the strict upbringing, angry at the church for the impossible standards, and angry at myself for never being able to measure up. But mostly, I was angry at God for allowing me to go through such turmoil and pain, for seemingly abandoning me in my darkest moments. The tears of anger and resentment would often flow into tears of self-pity and despair. I'd find myself in seedy bars, drowning my sorrows in cheap liquor and meaningless flings, trying to fill the void within me with fleeting pleasures that only left me feeling more empty and more alone than ever before.

It was a vicious cycle that seemed never-ending, a constant battle between the person I was raised to be, and the person I desperately wanted to become. The tears were my only constant companion, a salty reminder of the pain and confusion that consumed my every waking moment. Yet even in my darkest hours, there was a glimmer of hope, a tiny spark of resilience that refused to be extinguished. It was that spark that eventually led me to seek help, to confront the demons that had haunted me for so long. The road to healing was long and arduous, filled with more tears and setbacks than I care to recount; but slowly, painfully, I began to peel back the layers of hurt and resentment that had built up over the years.

Through therapy and self-reflection, I came to understand that my struggles weren't unique, that countless others had walked a similar path, carrying the same burdens of expectation and emotional turmoil. I learned to forgive—to forgive my parents for their shortcomings, to forgive the church for its rigid dogma, and most importantly, to forgive myself for the mistakes and missteps that had led me down such a painful road. With each tear shed, a little more of the weight lifted from my shoulders, until finally, I could breathe again, could look at myself in the mirror without feeling overwhelming shame and guilt. The tears didn't stop, but their nature changed. They became tears of healing, of growth, of a newfound appreciation for the journey that had brought me to where I was. As I stand here today, able to look back on those tumultuous teenage years with a sense of understanding, and even gratitude, I realize that the tears I shed behind closed doors were never a sign of weakness, but of strength—the strength to endure, to persevere, and ultimately, to emerge as a better, more compassionate, and more authentic version of myself.

FIVE THINGS TO REMEMBER

1. EMBRACING MY AUTHENTIC SELF UNLOCKED INNER STRENGTH

The tears I cried while struggling against the confines of being a "preacher's kid" illuminated the power of truly embracing my authentic self. Feeling trapped between living up to the church's rigid expectations and exploring my own desires beyond that constructed identity sparked an intense internal battle. However, each tear that streamed down my face became a symbolic unraveling of the tightly wound cocoon restricting my genuine self. With every anguished sob, another thread dissolved until finally, my true essence could emerge—radiant, unapologetic, and emboldened with an unshakable inner strength. As painful as that metamorphosis was, akin to a butterfly fighting its way out of the chrysalis, the resulting liberation—the ability to move through life in profound alignment rather than performative facades—instilled an invaluable resilience that would fortify me through future storms.

2. SELF-FORGIVENESS PAVED MY PATH TO HEALING

The overwhelming guilt from my moral missteps as a teen, coupled with the immense pressure of being raised in the scrutinizing "preacher's kid" spotlight, ensnared me in a vicious cycle of shame, repentance, and self-loathing. The constant stream of "broken, raggedy apologies" that never felt sincere only deepened the wounds, obstructing true healing. However, it was through the act of extending compassion and self-forgiveness that I ultimately discovered the key to breaking free. By consciously choosing to release the death-grip of unrelenting self-judgment and embracing the reality that mistakes are human, the path toward personal growth and inner restoration finally became clear. This pivotal self-acceptance—that flaws do not define my worth—catalyzed profound healing.

3. VULNERABILITY CULTIVATED DEEP CONNECTIONS

Keeping my emotional struggles buried, due to the stigma surrounding mental health and the burdens of a preacher's offspring, created an overwhelming sense of loneliness and isolation. Fearing judgment while upholding an indomitable facade prevented me from seeking solace and understanding from those around me. However, it was through the courageous act of vulnerability—stripping away the masks and openly expressing my inner battles—that I discovered the power to cultivate deep, meaningful connections. By boldly sharing my truth, I learned that others could, not only empathize, but often revealed parallel journeys, fostering a profound shared experience transcending individual circumstances. It was in these tender moments of raw vulnerability that the fertile ground for human connection took root.

4. PERSEVERANCE FORGED MY RESILIENCE

The perpetual cycle of rebellion, indulgence, and guilt-ridden repentance that defined my tumultuous teenage years could have cemented a self-perception of unwavering failure. However, it was my refusal to surrender to defeat—a tenacious perseverance through each anguished setback—that ultimately forged an unshakable resilience within me. Each tear-stained transgression became a crucible of sorts, tempering my spirit's fortitude until I could muster the resolve to confront my demons years later. The arduous path, scarred by missteps and self-doubt, ultimately revealed the resilience that had been incubating all along, awaiting its radiant emergence. This hard-won resilience became an indispensable well of strength and determination I could draw upon as future obstacles inevitable arose.

5. REFLECTION'S TEARS BLOSSOMED INTO PERSPECTIVE

While the tears of my turbulent youth seemed ceaseless, engulfing my every moment in anguish and confusion, it was through later reflection that those grief-drenched streams revealed profound perspective and even deepened gratitude. Those tears, which once felt like an inescapable deluge of suffering, unveiled their transformative role in shaping me into a wiser, more compassionate, and self-aware human being. Each salty droplet that striped my face in those tender years became, with hindsight's clarity, an instrument of personal evolution—carrying the seeds of wisdom, growth, and a renewed appreciation for life's complexities. It was through this reflective process that I came to honor those tears, not as burdens, but as sacred offerings nourishing my personal metamorphosis.

Reflecting on my journey through the turbulent years of adolescence, I realize that the tears I shed behind closed doors taught me invaluable lessons that have shaped who I am today. The struggle to balance the expectations of being a "preacher's kid" with my own desires revealed the power of embracing my true self. Each tear shed was a step toward unraveling the constraints that held me back, allowing my genuine, radiant self to emerge. This journey of self-discovery and acceptance instilled a resilience that fortified me through future storms. The cycle of guilt and self-loathing from my teenage mistakes was broken through self-forgiveness. By extending compassion to myself and acknowledging that mistakes are a part of being human, I was able to embark on a path of personal growth and healing. This pivotal act of self-acceptance catalyzed profound inner restoration.

The courage to strip away masks and openly express my struggles fostered deep, meaningful connections with others. Sharing my truth allowed me to discover empathy and parallel journeys, creating a sense of shared experience that transcended individual circumstances. Vulnerability became the foundation for genuine human connection. Refusing to surrender to the cycles of rebellion and guilt, I persevered through each setback, ultimately forging an unshakable resilience. The challenges I faced tempered my spirit, revealing a well of strength and determination that I continue to draw upon in the face of new obstacles. Reflecting on my past tears revealed their transformative power. What once felt like endless suffering became a source of wisdom, compassion, and self-awareness. Each tear carried seeds of growth, contributing to a deeper understanding and appreciation of life's complexities.

In closing, the lessons learned from these tears have shaped me into a stronger, more compassionate person. Embracing authenticity, practicing self-forgiveness, embracing vulnerability, fostering resilience, and reflecting on my experiences have all contributed to my personal growth. These lessons remind us that every tear shed in struggle can lead to profound transformation and strength. Stay resilient, stay true to yourself, and trust that each challenge faced has the potential to make you stronger and wiser. Your journey, with all its ups and downs, is a testament to your enduring spirit and capacity for growth. Keep moving forward with hope and determination, knowing that each tear has a purpose and every struggle a lesson.

TEARS OF REJECTION: A PERSONAL REFLECTION

There's something deeply impactful about the tears of rejection that can damage your inner soul. Take, for example, receiving a rejection letter from a dream college. It's a moment that can bring anyone to tears, especially if you've spent years working hard to maintain a high GPA, participating in numerous extracurricular activities, and preparing extensively for entrance exams. The pain of not getting that scholarship or acceptance letter after all your hard work can be overwhelming.

Rejection tears, or tears that come from rejection, are a unique form of emotional expression. They often arise when things get intense, turning into sadness and a sense of personal failure. This type of rejection can lead to embarrassment and self-doubt. However, it's important to remember that we all experience these moments. Personally, I've had my share of tears of rejection, often due to feeling hindered by my environment or circumstances.

Even athletes dealing with career-ending injuries can experience tears of rejection. The same goes for someone grieving the loss of a loved one or a pet. These tears can stem from a deep sense of loss and the feeling of being unsupported or misunderstood. It's especially hard when rejection comes from people who don't even know you or your capabilities. They judge you based on surface impressions, unaware of your true story and potential.

The tears of rejection can also appear in the workplace. Consider the employee laid off from a long-term job. This sudden change can bring about intense feelings of rejection and insecurity. These examples highlight the broad spectrum of situations that can trigger rejection tears.

As we navigate life, it's crucial to understand that these experiences are part of our journey. They test our resilience and our ability to overcome adversity. I want to encourage you, even before I close this chapter, to use these experiences as leverage for your forward movement. Recognize these challenging periods as tests of your strength and perseverance.

CONSIDER THE FOLLOWING EXAMPLES TO ILLUSTRATE THIS POINT

The Artist Facing Harsh Criticism: An artist receiving negative feedback on their work may feel a deep sense of rejection. Yet, this criticism can be used as a tool for growth and improvement.

Chronic Pain: Someone struggling with chronic pain may feel isolated and rejected by their own body. However, this battle can foster inner strength and resilience.

Natural Disasters: The aftermath of a natural disaster, such as a hurricane or earthquake, can leave individuals feeling abandoned and rejected by fate. Nonetheless, these experiences can lead to greater community solidarity and personal fortitude.

Career and Financial Strain: Abrupt career endings due to financial strain can cause tears of rejection. Yet, these setbacks often push individuals to explore new paths and opportunities.

Medical Diagnoses: Receiving a difficult medical diagnosis, like cancer, can be devastating. However, it also brings out the strength to fight and the importance of support systems.

Pre-Wedding Jitters: A bride or groom experiencing pre-wedding jitters or uncovering hidden truths about their partner can feel rejected and anxious. This period of doubt can ultimately strengthen their relationship through honesty and communication.

Immigration Challenges: An immigrant missing their home country or struggling to obtain a visa may feel a profound sense of rejection. Yet, these challenges can highlight their resilience and determination to build a better future.

These examples are reminders that the tests, trials, and adversities we face are meant to help us dig deeper and find our inner strength. When you encounter these situations, remember that you have the power to overcome them. Do not let the tears of rejection turn into depression or make you feel undervalued. Recognize your worth and understand that these experiences are shaping you into a stronger, more resilient person. You can master this. You can overcome this. You are valued, and you have worth.

*

PERSONAL REJECTION THAT TURNS INTO OPPORTUNITY

The best way to close out this chapter on rejection is to recognize its immense power and duality: it has the capacity to either make you or break you. Rejection can be one of the most transformative forces in your life, often ignited by just a single conversation or a single event. Looking back, the rejections that once broke my spirit and left me in tears became the very foundation upon which I built my dreams. Those painful moments were necessary—they pushed me beyond my comfort zone, forced me to confront my limitations, and ultimately propelled me toward the next level of growth. I needed those experiences to find myself, to discover the strength within, and to understand that rejection, though painful, is often a stepping stone to greater things.

When you're in the thick of rejection, it's hard to see beyond the hurt. It's easy to fall into the trap of self-defeat, to throw up your hands and say, "I give up. Rejection won. What I wanted didn't happen, so that must be the end of it." The truth is, this is where your mindset becomes critical. The words you speak over your life in these moments carry just as much weight as the rejection itself. If you allow yourself to speak defeat, discouragement, or negativity, you're giving that rejection even more power over you. It's important to catch yourself in those moments, to stop the spiral of negative self-talk, and to reframe your perspective.

Rejection has the potential to teach you some of life's most valuable lessons, but only if you allow it to. Instead of viewing it as a final verdict on your worth or abilities, see it as a challenge—an opportunity to grow, to learn, and to prove to yourself just how resilient you can be. Don't let the tears of rejection drown you in sorrow or self-pity. Those tears can easily become a pool that traps you, making you feel less valuable, unworthy, or incapable. If you're not careful, they can cripple your progress and stifle your potential.

In closing, I want to encourage you to view every rejection, every tear shed behind closed doors, as part of a greater journey. This chapter of your life can serve as a road map, guiding you through the rough patches and helping you navigate toward success. Let those tears and those moments of rejection become stepping stones, paving the way to the heights you're meant to reach. Everything we've discussed here—use it as leverage. Use it as a launchpad to catapult yourself to the next level. Let it fuel your dedication, sharpen your focus, and strengthen your commitment to your goals.

Remember, rejection is not the end of the road. It's often the beginning of a new path, one that you might not have seen without that push. Use it to propel you forward, to refine your purpose, and to build the resilience needed to persevere. The lessons of rejection are there to guide you, to fortify your spirit, and to prepare you for the success that lies ahead. Don't shy away from these moments; embrace them. Understand that each rejection is shaping you, molding you into the person you're meant to become. Let this chapter of your life be a testament to your strength, your perseverance, and your unwavering commitment to achieving your dreams.

CHAPTER 8

BROKEN BEHIND CLOSED DOORS

The word "broken" is incredibly multifaceted, weaving its way through various aspects of our lives, from language to culture. It's a term that carries with it a range of meanings and connotations, each depending on the context in which it's used. In Old English, "broken" comes from the past participle of "brecan," meaning "to break." The word's roots trace back to the Indo-European term "bhreg," which also means "to break." Grammatically, "broken" can be used as an adjective, such as in the phrase "a broken vase," or as a past participle, as in "the record has been broken." This duality of meaning is intriguing, particularly when you consider both the positive and negative implications of breaking something. On one hand, "breaking" can signify a triumphant moment, like breaking a record—a symbol of achievement and confidence. On the other hand, it can also embody something far more somber and painful, like a broken heart, a broken marriage, or a broken system. These are the moments that can lead to deep, personal sorrow, often hidden from the world. I think we can all relate to the word "broken" in one way or another, as it touches on the human experience in profound ways.

In this chapter, I want to focus specifically on the concept of being broken behind closed doors. This is a topic that resonates deeply with me because it's something that many people experience in silence. There are countless individuals who have been broken when no one was watching, yet they put on a mask, projecting an image that everything is fine. The truth is, every businessman, every teacher, every doctor, every parent has faced moments of being broken. It's a universal experience that cuts across all walks of life. For me, this is personal. I've gone through so many transitions in my life that left me feeling shattered. I had to pick up the pieces, piece by piece, trying to rebuild what had been broken. This process of picking up the pieces is something many can relate to, as it's a journey that requires resilience, patience, and a great deal of inner strength.

When we talk about "broken," we're not just referring to emotional or psychological states. The word can also be synonymous with terms like fractured, shattered, damaged, ruptured, malfunctioning, or violated. These synonyms expand the concept of brokenness to include a wide range of experiences, from breaking the law and facing the consequences to breaking rules and dealing with the aftermath. There's also the more literal side of brokenness, such as with physical objects—broken bones, broken glass, broken machinery. And then there are the systems and processes that can break, like broken supply chains or malfunctioning algorithms, which can have a massive impact on efficiency and effectiveness.

This idea of broken systems reminds me of an experience I had while traveling. Last year, I took my two daughters and my wife to Disney World. We were on vacation, and everything was going smoothly until suddenly, there was a system failure across the airline industry. A software update through CrowdStrike had caused a massive glitch, freezing operations across the U.S. Many flights were canceled, leaving people stranded, and we were worried that we might be stuck as well. I called Southwest Airlines to check the status of our flight, bracing myself for bad news. To my surprise, the representative told me that we didn't have to worry. Unlike other airlines, Southwest hadn't updated their software, so their system remained intact. While everyone else was dealing with a broken system, Southwest's original system kept things running smoothly.

This incident serves as a powerful metaphor for life. We all have our versions of being broken, and sometimes things break for reasons we can't immediately understand. Yet, in the midst of this brokenness, there can be moments of unexpected stability, resilience, and even blessing. Sometimes, the very things that break in our lives are what lead us to new insights, better systems, and ultimately, a stronger version of ourselves.

In the end, being broken isn't the end of the story—it's a part of the process. It's how we respond to the brokenness that defines us. Do we let it shatter us completely, or do we use it as an opportunity to rebuild, to upgrade, to become something new? Brokenness is not just about the pain or the loss; it's also about the potential for growth and transformation that comes afterward. We may all face moments where we feel fractured or shattered, but those are the moments that shape us, challenge us, and push us toward our next breakthrough.

BROKEN PROMISES

Broken promises are one of the most painful and common experiences we encounter in life. When someone breaks your heart or a promise they made, it feels like they've let you down in the most profound way. I've gone through seasons of broken promises—repeated instances that felt like they would shake me to the core and derail my entire life. The pain was real, and even though I made it through, the hurt lingered. Broken promises can be incredibly frustrating and misleading. They can weigh so heavily on you that they impact every aspect of your life. In some cases, broken promises can even lead to divorce. They're like a fungus, slowly eating away at your soul if you let them fester. It's like an internal parasite that gnaws at you from the inside, wearing you down bit by bit.

Broken promises come in many forms, and they often come from those closest to us. The people we trust the most often have the greatest power to hurt us with a broken promise. Imagine a promise that's been kept for years—10, 12, even 15 years—only to be shattered because of negligence, complacency, boredom, or a lack of discipline. It's devastating, especially when these broken promises lead to broken marriages, and ultimately, to divorce. I've personally been through a divorce, and it was one of the most difficult experiences of my life. It shook me to my core, leaving me questioning everything—why so much was happening at once, why I had made certain choices, and what my next move should be. I found myself asking why I even got into that situation in the first place. Why did I rush into a marriage at the courthouse, signing papers before really thinking it through, instead of starting out with a proper ceremony surrounded by family and friends? In hindsight, I realized I had done things backward, trying to cover up my actions and avoid feeling like I was "shacking up."

For those who grew up in the church, you know the stigma attached to shacking up, especially when you're striving to live a righteous life. I was trying to avoid that label, so I pushed forward with the marriage, thinking it would solve everything. However, in reality, I was forcing something based on my emotions and my flesh, thinking that if I did this ... then I would get that. The brokenness that followed was deep and personal, a result of trying to fill a void with something that wasn't right. Broken promises can also lead to brokenness in other forms of deep relational intimacy. For example, when a woman's hymen is broken prematurely, outside of the right context, it can cause a personal and emotional wound that lingers. The timing and circumstances of such an intimate act are crucial, and when it's done prematurely, it can leave a lasting impact on a woman's sense of self and her emotional well-being.

Broken promises cut deep, affecting us on emotional, spiritual, and relational levels. They challenge our trust in others, our faith in ourselves, and our hope for the future; but even in the midst of this pain, there's an opportunity for growth, for learning, and for healing. It's important to recognize the impact of broken promises, to understand how they affect us, and to take steps to heal from them. This might involve setting new boundaries, seeking support from loved ones or professionals, or simply giving yourself the time and space to process the hurt. While the pain of broken promises is real and significant, it doesn't have to define you. It can be a catalyst for change, for making better choices in the future, and for finding strength you didn't know you had.

In the end, broken promises are a part of life. They're painful, yes, but they're also opportunities for growth. They remind us of the importance of keeping our word, of valuing the trust others place in us, and of being mindful of the promises we make. While the brokenness they cause can be profound, it can also lead to a deeper understanding of ourselves, our relationships, and what truly matters in life. As we continue to explore the impact of broken promises, it's important to recognize that they can lead to a reevaluation of our values, relationships, and even our purpose in life. When someone breaks a promise, it forces us to confront the reality of human fallibility—the fact that even those we hold in high regard are capable of letting us down. This realization can be jarring, but it's also an opportunity to reassess our own expectations, both of others and of ourselves.

Broken promises often prompt us to question our own role in the situation. We might wonder if we were too trusting, too naïve, or too forgiving. These reflections can lead to a deeper understanding of our own boundaries and needs. Perhaps we need to be more discerning in whom we place our trust, or maybe we need to communicate our expectations more clearly. In some cases, the experience of a broken promise can lead to a newfound sense of empowerment, as we learn to advocate for ourselves and protect our emotional well-being. One of the most challenging aspects of dealing with broken promises is the sense of loss that accompanies them. When a promise is broken, it's not just the specific commitment that's lost—it's also the future that we had envisioned based on that promise. This loss can be profound, leading to feelings of grief, disappointment, and even despair. It's a mourning of what could have been, of the potential that was never realized.

For example, consider a couple that has spent years building a life together, only to have one partner break a promise that was fundamental to the relationship. Whether it's a promise of fidelity, of support, or of shared goals, the breaking of that promise can feel like the destruction of the life they had planned together. The dreams they had for the future, the plans they had made, and the trust they had built are all called into question. This kind of loss is deeply painful and can take a long time to heal. However, as difficult as it may be, it's important to recognize that broken promises can also be a turning point. They can serve as a wake-up call, prompting us to reevaluate our priorities and make changes that ultimately lead to a better, more fulfilling life. For some, this might mean ending a relationship that is no longer healthy or sustainable. For others, it might mean setting new goals and pursuing a different path that aligns more closely with their values and desires.

The process of healing from broken promises is not linear, and it's rarely easy. It requires patience, self-compassion, and a willingness to confront difficult emotions. Yet through this process, we can emerge stronger and more resilient. We learn to rebuild our trust—first in ourselves, and then in others. We develop a deeper understanding of what we need in our relationships and how to create boundaries that protect our well-being. In many ways, the experience of dealing with broken promises is a journey of self-discovery. It forces us to confront our vulnerabilities and insecurities, but it also provides an opportunity to cultivate strength and resilience. We learn that we are capable of surviving disappointment, of rebuilding after loss, and of finding new paths forward even when the road seems uncertain.

As we navigate the aftermath of broken promises, it's important to hold on to hope. While the pain may be intense and the healing process long, there is always the possibility of growth and transformation on the other side. Broken promises can teach us valuable lessons about ourselves and our relationships, helping us to become more discerning, more compassionate, and more committed to living authentically. Ultimately, broken promises are a part of the human experience. They remind us of the impermanence of life and the importance of being present in the moment. They challenge us to let go of the need for certainty and control, and to embrace the uncertainty and fluidity of life. In doing so, we open ourselves up to new possibilities, new connections, and new opportunities for growth.

So, while broken promises may leave scars, they do not have to define us. We can choose to see them as opportunities for learning and growth, as catalysts for change, and as reminders of the resilience and strength that lie within us. As we continue to move forward, we can carry with us the lessons we've learned, the strength we've gained, and the hope that no matter what, we have the power to create a life that is true to who we are and what we value.

Richard Paul Evans' quote, "Broken vows are like broken mirrors. They leave those who held to them bleeding and staring at fractured images of themselves," is indeed a powerful metaphor that captures the essence of brokenness and the deep emotional impact of broken promises. Let's break down this quote piece by piece to explore its meaning and how it relates to the experience of brokenness.

"Broken vows are like broken mirrors."

The comparison of broken vows to broken mirrors is striking. A vow, much like a mirror, is meant to reflect something whole and complete. When we make a vow—whether in marriage, friendship, or any other form of commitment—it's like creating a mirror that reflects our intentions, trust, and the promises we've made to another person. This mirror is supposed to be a clear, unblemished reflection of our relationship, one that we can both look into with confidence and assurance.

However, when a vow is broken, it's as if that mirror shatters. The clear, whole reflection is gone, replaced by jagged, fragmented pieces. The image that once represented something solid and dependable is now fractured, distorted, and difficult to piece back together. This comparison highlights the way in which a broken vow doesn't just affect the promise itself—it disrupts the entire perception of the relationship, and the individuals involved.

"They leave those who held to them bleeding …"

This part of the quote emphasizes the emotional pain caused by broken vows. Those who have held onto these vows—who have trusted in them, believed in them, and built their lives around them—are left bleeding when the promises are broken. This bleeding is both literal and metaphorical. It represents the deep wounds inflicted on the heart, the soul, and the psyche. The person who trusted in the vow is left vulnerable, hurt, and in pain, much like someone who has been physically wounded.

The image of bleeding also suggests that this pain is not easily healed. Just as a physical wound can take time to mend, so too do the emotional wounds caused by broken vows. The bleeding doesn't stop immediately; it continues, affecting the person's ability to trust, to love, and to see themselves as whole. This bleeding can represent the ongoing sorrow, anger, and despair that accompanies the realization that a promise has been broken, that something believed to be strong and enduring has been shattered.

"... and staring at fractured images of themselves."

This final part of the quote delves into the lasting impact of broken vows on one's self-perception. When a mirror breaks, the reflection it provides is no longer whole—it's fragmented. Each piece of the mirror reflects a different, disjointed image. Similarly, when a vow is broken, the person who held onto that promise is left staring at a fractured image of themselves. They may feel as though they've lost their sense of identity, their sense of self-worth, and their understanding of who they are within the relationship.

These fractured images represent the confusion and disorientation that often follows a broken promise. The person may question their own value, wondering what they did wrong or why they weren't enough to keep the vow intact. They might struggle to reconcile the person they thought they were, with the person they see reflected in the broken pieces. This can lead to a crisis of identity, where the individual no longer recognizes themselves in the same way, and where their sense of self has been fundamentally altered by the experience of betrayal and brokenness.

RELATING IT ALL TO BROKENNESS AND BROKEN PROMISES

When we consider this quote in the context of brokenness and broken promises, it becomes even more poignant. Broken promises, especially those as significant as vows, have the power to shatter not just relationships but the individuals within them. The pain of broken promises leaves emotional wounds that can bleed for a long time, affecting how we see ourselves and our place in the world. The metaphor of a broken mirror is particularly apt because it captures the idea that the damage caused by broken vows is not easily fixed.

Just as a shattered mirror can't simply be pieced back together to provide a clear reflection, the trust and confidence lost in a relationship can't easily be restored. The person who has been hurt by a broken promise is left to pick up the pieces, to try to understand what happened, and to figure out how to move forward with a sense of self that has been profoundly affected. In the aftermath of broken promises, it's common to feel like you're staring at a fractured version of yourself. The image you once had—of yourself, your relationship, and your future—is now fragmented. This can be incredibly disorienting and painful. It takes time and effort to start putting those pieces back together, and even then, the image may never be the same as it once was.

However, understanding this process can be the first step toward healing. Recognizing that it's normal to feel disoriented, to struggle with your self-image, and to feel the deep emotional wounds caused by broken promises can help you navigate the path to recovery. It's important to give yourself grace and time to heal, to slowly rebuild your sense of self, and to create a new, stronger image of who you are—one that incorporates the lessons learned from the pain and the resilience gained through the process.

In conclusion, Richard Paul Evans' quote beautifully encapsulates the devastating impact of broken vows and promises. It reminds us that the emotional wounds caused by these betrayals are deep and long-lasting, affecting not only our relationships but also our self-perception. It also offers a powerful insight: while the mirror may be broken, and the image fractured, there is still the possibility of healing, of finding a way to see ourselves anew, and of moving forward with a greater understanding of our strength and our capacity for resilience.

TYPES OF PRIVATE BROKEN PROMISES

The first category of private broken promises is the unfaithful spouse. This is a situation many have encountered, whether personally, through a friend, or in a painful divorce. Typically, it starts with a husband privately vowing fidelity to his wife on their anniversary. Yet, the breach occurs when he secretly engages in an affair with a co-worker. The consequences are devastating—when discovered, it can lead to divorce, tearing apart the family and damaging social circles. Infidelity often stems from dissatisfaction within the home, perhaps because something is missing or out of alignment. Actually, the real struggle lies in handling these private moments amidst the pain of a broken promise. There's a unique sting to a broken vow, especially when you've committed to a shared path, only to have it shattered by betrayal.

Another instance of a private broken promise involves the addicted friend. This friend promises their support group that they will stay sober. They may declare, "I won't drink; I've got this." Unfortunately, the breach happens when they relapse in secret, failing to confront their inner demons. We've all seen this scenario—where someone secretly falls back into old habits, whether it's a financial setback or an addiction. Secret relapses often lead to hiding the truth, and creating a web of deception that strains relationships and hinders the recovery process. The road to healing is long, and each breach only makes it harder to move forward.

Then there's the overcommitted employee. They assure their boss they can handle an important project alone. "No problem," they say, confident in their abilities. However, when pressure mounts, they falter, unable to complete the task because they didn't seek help. The result? The project fails, trust is broken, and the company suffers. This is why the discussion of private broken promises is so crucial—these breaches happen behind closed doors but have far-reaching consequences. The failure of a project disrupts future business and damages professional relationships.

The secret spender is another example. A partner agrees to stick to a budget to save for a house, but instead, they revert to old habits, making secret purchases and hiding bills. The breach here is clear—these actions derail the couple's financial goals, leading to trust issues and financial strain. When a budget falls apart, it impacts everything from filling the gas tank to buying groceries. The pressure of hidden spending can break a relationship, illustrating the profound impact of private broken promises.

Another example of a private broken promise involves the absent parent. A mother or father promises their child they'll attend a school play, a soccer game, or a recital, only to break that promise with a flimsy excuse. The breach isn't just about missing the event; it's about missing crucial moments in their child's life. The lie and the absence create a lasting wound, emphasizing the gravity of private broken promises.

Equally critical is the example of the plagiarizing student. They commit to academic honesty but then copy answers from online sources. This breach not only undermines their education but also jeopardizes their future. When caught, the consequences are severe—disciplinary action that can permanently affect their academic and professional life.

In situations where an elderly or ill person relies on a caregiver, a promise of care and attention is often made. When the caregiver neglects their duties, whether through indifference or being overwhelmed, it can lead to physical and emotional harm. The trust that is broken in this scenario is devastating, as the most vulnerable are left unprotected.

In business, partnerships are built on trust and mutual benefit. When one partner secretly engages in unethical practices, such as embezzling funds or sabotaging efforts for personal gain, it can destroy the business and the livelihoods of all involved. The breach is particularly damaging because it undermines the very foundation of the partnership.

A mentor promises to guide and support their mentee's professional growth. However, if the mentor becomes distracted or loses interest, they may neglect their responsibility, leaving the mentee adrift. The impact of this broken promise can be profound, stalling the mentee's progress and leaving them feeling abandoned.

Politicians often make promises to their constituents during campaigns, vowing to enact certain policies or improve conditions. When they fail to deliver on these promises, especially if done deliberately for personal or political gain, the betrayal can lead to widespread disillusionment and erode public trust in the system.

Then there's the unreliable friend. This is the person who promises to be there in times of need, offering a listening ear or a helping hand, but when you need them most, they're nowhere to be found. The breach of this promise can be deeply hurtful, as it leaves you feeling unsupported and alone during life's toughest moments.

A particularly concerning example involves the irresponsible parent. They may promise to set a good example for their children, to be a positive influence in their lives. Yet, when they engage in harmful behaviors like substance abuse or neglect, the promise is broken, causing long-term emotional and psychological damage to their children.

Finally, there's the disengaged spouse. They promise to nurture the marriage, to communicate and grow together, but over time, they become emotionally distant, failing to invest in the relationship. The breach here is subtle but damaging—without attention and care, the relationship withers, leading to feelings of loneliness and isolation.

Each of these scenarios underscores the heavy toll of private broken promises. The damage is done in secret, but its effects are public and long-lasting, reminding us of the profound responsibility we carry when we make commitments to others.

1. THE UNFAITHFUL SPOUSE

Infidelity is a word that carries a weight heavier than its letters. It's not just a simple broken promise; it's a betrayal that strikes at the heart of what it means to trust and be trusted. For many, this word brings back memories—some personal, others through the pain of a friend or family member. Maybe it's a story you've lived through, or perhaps it's one you've seen unfold from the sidelines. No matter how it touches you, the pain it causes is undeniable and real. Infidelity is a violation, plain and simple. It's a breach of the expectation that runs deep in any committed relationship—a betrayal of the trust and boundaries that both partners have agreed upon—but here's the truth: while infidelity can shatter lives, understanding its causes and addressing them can prevent devastation before it takes root.

Let's break it down because infidelity isn't just one thing—it's a spectrum of betrayals, each with its own kind of pain:

- **Physical infidelity** is often the first thing that comes to mind. This is the scenario where someone crosses the line with physical contact—whether it's a kiss or a full-blown affair—but it doesn't stop there.

- **Emotional infidelity** is just as real, just as damaging. It's when someone forms a deep emotional connection with someone outside their marriage, sharing intimate thoughts, feelings, and experiences. Often, this betrayal is hidden in secret texts, late-night conversations, or online chats. It might not involve physical touch, but the emotional scars it leaves are just as deep.

- **Then there's cyber infidelity,** which has become more common in our digital world. It's not just harmless flirting online—it's engaging in romantic or sexual interactions through sexting, virtual relationships, or even an addiction to online pornography. The anonymity of the internet makes these betrayals feel even more isolating, creating a virtual world where infidelity thrives. Then sometimes, it's a mix of everything—a combined infidelity that blurs the lines between physical, emotional, and cyber, multiplying the hurt.

- **But let's not forget about financial infidelity**—a betrayal that doesn't involve another person but can be just as destructive. This happens when one partner hides financial decisions, secret accounts, undisclosed debts, or makes major purchases without the other's knowledge. It's a betrayal that can wreak havoc on a relationship, creating a chasm of distrust that's hard to bridge. Here's the thing—I've seen it all. Friends, clients, and those who've walked through my office door have shared their stories of brokenness, of being shattered by a cheating spouse. Yet here's what I know—understanding the causes and consequences of infidelity is the first step toward healing and prevention. The pain is real, but it doesn't have to define you or your future.

So, what leads someone down this path of betrayal? What causes a person to break the most sacred promises? Let's shine a light on these factors and take away their power:

Betrayal is a path that no one sets out to walk, yet so many find themselves stumbling down it. The pain of breaking promises in private is compounded when it spills into the public eye, leaving both the betrayer and the betrayed grappling with the fallout. What leads someone to this dark road? It often starts with personal factors—those internal struggles that, left unchecked, can manifest in destructive ways. One of the most common personal factors is low self-esteem or a need for validation. When someone wrestles with their self-worth, they might seek validation outside their marriage, thinking that the attention of another will fill the void. However, here's the truth—your value isn't defined by someone else's attention. Your worth is rooted in the integrity of your actions, the commitments you honor, and the purpose you pursue—especially in marriage, where vows are sacred, remembering this can help guard against the temptations that prey on insecurity.

Unresolved childhood issues and past traumas are another significant factor. We all carry wounds from our past, but when those wounds are left untreated, they can drive us to seek comfort in all the wrong places. Many have thought that stepping outside their marriage would heal their hurt or fill their emptiness, only to find themselves more broken than before. True healing begins when you face these hurts head-on, refusing to let them dictate your future.

Then there are narcissistic personality traits—a major red flag when it comes to infidelity. Narcissists often feel entitled, prioritizing their own desires above the commitments they've made. They justify their actions by focusing solely on their needs, with little regard for the damage they cause. Here's the truth—true fulfillment comes from selflessness, not selfishness. Commitment begins with putting others before yourself, with choosing to love and honor even when it's difficult.

A history of infidelity in previous relationships is another critical factor. This often stems from scars and patterns picked up from observing parents or past experiences. While it's true that those who have cheated before are more likely to cheat again, it doesn't have to be that way. Patterns can be broken. Redemption is possible, but it requires real change, a commitment to honesty, and the courage to face the issues that led to betrayal in the first place. It's one thing to make a mistake, but it's another to learn from it, grow, and make sure it never happens again.

Think about the many divorces that could have been avoided if these personal factors were addressed before they led to betrayal. It's not just about avoiding infidelity; it's about building a relationship that can withstand the pressures of life by tackling these issues head-on. When we understand the personal context behind betrayal, we empower ourselves to prevent it, to heal from it, and to create relationships that are built on a foundation of trust, respect, and unwavering commitment.

When we dig into the factors that lead to betrayal, it's crucial to recognize that relationship dynamics play a significant role. The truth is, when betrayal happens behind closed doors, it's often the relationship factors that have quietly eroded the foundation long before the act of infidelity occurs. One of the most common relationship factors is a lack of emotional or physical intimacy. When the connection between partners begins to fade, it creates a void that temptation can easily fill. Whether it's an innocent scroll through Instagram or a casual encounter at the mall, if the relationship is already strained, these moments can spark the wrong kind of communication and attention. The absence of intimacy—both emotional and physical—opens the door for outside influences to creep in, leading to a path that neither partner intended to walk.

Poor communication and unresolved conflicts are another crucial factor that impacts relationships. When issues are allowed to fester, they will eventually cause damage. It's not enough to recognize the problem; you have to address it head-on. Strong relationships are built on open, honest communication, and that's not always easy. Being open requires vulnerability—being willing to share your deepest thoughts and fears without holding back. Being honest means telling the truth, even when it's uncomfortable. When you combine openness with honesty, you create a new level of communication that can resolve conflicts and strengthen the bond between you.

Mismatched sexual preferences are another common factor that can lead to frustration and, ultimately, infidelity; but here's the thing—frustration doesn't have to be the end of the story. Through understanding and compromise, you can find alignment in your relationship. It's about discovering what works for both of you together, adjusting to each other's needs, and finding a harmonious balance that satisfies both partners. Feeling unappreciated or neglected is a significant issue as well. When you feel like your efforts go unnoticed or your needs aren't being met, it's easy to start looking elsewhere for validation; but before letting those feelings push you toward betrayal, speak up. Let your partner know what you need, and be just as willing to listen to their needs. Love is a two-way street, built on mutual appreciation and care. Beyond these relationship factors, we also have situational factors. Life happens, and sometimes it throws us curveballs that we're not ready for. Major life changes, financial stress, or a death in the family can all strain a relationship, but these challenges don't have to knock you off course. Stay grounded, stay connected, and face these obstacles together. Whether it's debt piling up or substance abuse clouding your judgment, choosing clarity—both spiritually and naturally—is key. Choose the life you truly want and commit to facing these challenges hand in hand with your partner.

Equally important are the psychological factors—the desires for excitement or euphoria that can lead someone astray. The thrill of something new is intoxicating, but it's fleeting. The consequences, however, can last a lifetime. Instead of seeking that excitement outside, find it within the life you're building with your partner. Commit to finding joy in the everyday moments of your relationship. Overcoming fear of commitment or intimacy is another challenge. True commitment takes work, and it requires diving deep into the relationship, fully investing in your partner, and doing the hard work needed to keep the bond strong.

Unmet emotional needs are another common trigger for infidelity; but instead of looking outside your relationship to meet those needs, look within. Communicate with your partner, connect with them on a deeper level, and work together to rebuild what may have been lost. Curiosity or a desire for sexual experimentation can also be a factor, but it's essential to explore these desires within the boundaries of trust and mutual respect.

So, what's the takeaway here? Whether you're married, engaged, dating, or even single, these insights are vital. Use them as tools to understand the dynamics of relationships, the challenges that can arise, and the ways to navigate them with wisdom and grace. This isn't just for those who have already walked down the aisle; it's for anyone who wants to build a strong, faithful relationship. The key is to recognize these factors before they take root, to address them with courage, and to prioritize the love and commitment you've chosen. Whether you're on the brink of marriage or years into it, let these insights guide you toward a healthier, more resilient relationship, where trust is built, nurtured, and protected.

JAMES AND LISA'S STORY

James and Lisa had been married for eight years. They were the picture of a perfect couple—successful in their careers, active in their community, and seemingly content in their relationship. However, beneath the surface, their marriage had begun to show cracks. Over time, these cracks widened, eventually leading to an affair that threatened to destroy everything they had built together. The trouble began subtly, as it often does. After the birth of their second child, James and Lisa found themselves overwhelmed with responsibilities. Their once-regular date nights became infrequent, and their conversations, once filled with dreams and laughter, turned into logistical discussions about bills, chores, and the kids' schedules.

The emotional and physical intimacy that once defined their relationship started to fade. James began to feel unappreciated and neglected, while Lisa felt overwhelmed and disconnected. Neither of them addressed these feelings openly. They both assumed that the other was simply busy, that this was just a phase, but the reality was that they were drifting apart. James's feelings of neglect made him vulnerable. During a work trip, he reconnected with an old friend, Sarah. Sarah was attentive, empathetic, and willing to listen to his frustrations about his marriage. What started as innocent conversations quickly escalated into something more. The emotional connection James felt with Sarah filled the void that had grown in his marriage. Soon, this emotional infidelity evolved into a physical affair. For months, James lived a double life, hiding his infidelity from Lisa. The secrecy weighed heavily on him, but he rationalized his actions by blaming the distance in his marriage. He told himself that the affair was harmless, that it was just a way to cope with his unmet needs.

The affair came to light when Lisa accidentally discovered a series of text messages on James' phone. The messages were undeniable proof of his betrayal. The devastation Lisa felt was immediate and overwhelming. The man she thought she knew, the man she had trusted implicitly, had broken his vows. The betrayal wasn't just in the act of cheating; it was in the deception, the lies, and the violation of the trust they had built over the years. Lisa confronted James, and the truth came out. James admitted to the affair, but the damage was done. Lisa felt like her entire world had crumbled. She struggled with feelings of anger, betrayal, and deep sadness. The relationship she had invested in for so long now felt like a lie.

The impact of James' infidelity was profound. Lisa couldn't look at him without seeing the betrayal. Their home, once a place of comfort, now felt like a battleground. Their communication, already weakened, deteriorated further. Every conversation turned into an argument, and the tension in their home was palpable. Their children, though young, sensed that something was wrong. Financially, the affair also took its toll. James had spent money on gifts, dinners, and trips with Sarah—money that should have gone toward their family. The strain on their finances only added to the stress Lisa was already feeling. James, on the other hand, was filled with guilt and shame. He knew he had made a terrible mistake, but he didn't know how to fix it. The affair, which once seemed like an escape, had only led him into deeper despair.

Despite the overwhelming pain, Lisa and James made the difficult decision to try and salvage their marriage. They knew it would be a long and challenging process, but they weren't ready to give up on the life they had built together. They sought the help of a marriage counselor, who guided them through the painful but necessary conversations they had avoided for so long. In therapy, James confronted the personal factors that led him to infidelity—his low self-esteem, his need for validation, and his inability to communicate his feelings. He realized that he had been seeking comfort and attention outside his marriage instead of addressing the issues within it. For the first time, he understood that his actions weren't just a betrayal of Lisa; they were a betrayal of himself and the values he claimed to hold.

Lisa, too, had to confront her feelings. She learned to express her pain without letting it consume her. She realized that while James's actions were inexcusable, the lack of communication and intimacy in their marriage had created a space where infidelity could take root. Together, they worked on rebuilding trust, little by little. They established new boundaries, committed to open and honest communication, and made a conscious effort to reconnect emotionally and physically.

Healing from infidelity was not a linear process. There were setbacks, moments of doubt, and days when it seemed easier to walk away, but over time, James and Lisa began to see progress. The wounds slowly started to heal as they rebuilt their relationship from the ground up. They both understood that their marriage would never be the same, but they also realized that this could be an opportunity to create something stronger.

James cut all ties with Sarah and focused on regaining Lisa's trust. He became more involved in their family life, more attentive to Lisa's needs, and more committed to being the husband and father he had promised to be. Lisa, in turn, allowed herself to be vulnerable again, opening her heart to the possibility of forgiveness. The case of James and Lisa highlights the complex web of factors that lead to infidelity—personal, relational, and situational. It shows how easily a lack of communication and intimacy can create a fertile ground for betrayal. More importantly, it demonstrates that while infidelity can devastate a marriage, it doesn't have to end it. With a willingness to confront the issues, a commitment to change, and a lot of hard work, even the deepest wounds can begin to heal.

Their story is a reminder that prevention is key. By addressing the underlying issues early—whether they are personal insecurities, unresolved conflicts, or unmet needs—couples can safeguard their relationships against the temptations that lead to betrayal. For those who have already experienced infidelity, it's a testament to the power of forgiveness, the importance of communication, and the possibility of rebuilding trust. The road to healing is long and difficult, but with love, determination, and honesty, it is possible to create a stronger, more resilient relationship.

While James and Lisa's story illustrates the complexities of marital infidelity and the challenging path to reconciliation, it also touches on a broader theme that resonates across various types of relationships: the devastating impact of broken promises. This theme is particularly poignant when we consider another common scenario that tests the bonds of trust and loyalty—that of the addicted friend. Much like the betrayal in a marriage, addiction introduces a destructive cycle of promises and disappointments that can strain even the strongest of friendships. As we shift our focus to this equally challenging dynamic, we see how the themes of trust, secrecy, and the arduous journey of healing take on new dimensions yet remain fundamentally similar to what we observed in James and Lisa's story.

2. THE ADDICTED FRIEND

To fully embrace the concept of overcoming personal struggles, it's important to share my story from a personal perspective. In 2006, I was battling some serious addictions, particularly with drugs. Cocaine was my main vice, and because it was readily available to me, it quickly became a destructive habit. I also had a dangerous relationship with acid tabs, indulging in 12-hour highs that nearly cost me my life. I was the addicted friend who could never break free from the grip of these substances. My addiction wasn't just a habit—it was a complex web of dependencies rooted in a deep lack of willpower and a stubborn resistance to change. This period of my life was especially challenging because it coincided with my time in school in Orlando, Florida. I was supposed to be focused on building a future, but instead, I was spiraling further into addiction. The struggle was overwhelming, and the grip of these substances felt impossible to escape.

Understanding addiction is key to overcoming it. There are different levels and types of addictions that people face and recognizing them is the first step toward healing. The two main categories of addiction are substance addictions and behavioral addictions.

1. **Substance Addictions:** This category includes dependencies on alcohol, opioids, marijuana, nicotine, and other drugs. Substance addiction is characterized by the body's physical need for a substance, often leading to withdrawal symptoms when the substance is not available. My addiction to cocaine and acid fell squarely into this category, as I relied on these substances to escape reality, numb my emotions, and fill the void that I couldn't seem to address any other way.

2. **Behavioral Addictions:** While substance addictions involve chemicals, behavioral addictions revolve around compulsive behaviors that provide a similar "high." These can include gambling, shopping, eating, or even excessive use of the internet or social media. Although I was primarily dealing with substance addiction, the lack of control and compulsive nature of my actions mirrored the struggles faced by those with behavioral addictions.

Looking back, I can see how these addictions were symptoms of deeper issues that I hadn't confronted—pain, insecurity, and unresolved trauma. It took hitting rock bottom, facing the consequences of my choices, and a lot of hard work to begin climbing out of that dark place. The journey wasn't easy, and it required more than just willpower; it took a complete shift in mindset, lifestyle, and support from people who cared about me.

The experience taught me that addiction isn't just about the substances or behaviors themselves—it's about what drives us to them. Whether it's substance addiction or behavioral addiction, the common thread is often a search for escape, comfort, or control, but true freedom doesn't come from these temporary fixes. It comes from facing our struggles head-on, seeking help, and making the tough but necessary changes to reclaim our lives.

If you're reading this and can relate to the battle with addiction, know that you're not alone, and recovery is possible. It's a journey that requires patience, persistence, and the courage to confront the underlying issues. However, with the right support and a commitment to change, you can break free and build a life that's not defined by addiction, but by hope, healing, and strength.

THE CYCLES OF ADDICTION AND BROKEN PROMISES

The journey of someone trapped in addiction is often marked by a painful cycle of promises made and broken. This cycle doesn't just affect the addict; it deeply wounds those who care about them, leaving a trail of broken trust and shattered hopes. Understanding this cycle is crucial for anyone who has faced addiction or supported someone through it.

THE PROMISE PHASE

The Promise Phase is a moment that's deeply personal, a turning point where everything feels like it's either about to fall apart or finally come together. I've been there more times than I'd like to admit, standing at the edge of rock bottom, looking up at the wreckage of my life and realizing that something had to give. It's a moment of brutal honesty, where you're forced to confront the damage you've done—to yourself, to your relationships, to your future. The weight of all those choices and mistakes crashes down on you, leaving you no option but to face the truth head-on.

During this phase, there's a clarity that's hard to describe, a brief moment when the fog of addiction lifts just enough for you to see what you've been trying so hard to ignore. For me, it was the realization that I had pushed everyone away, that the people who cared about me were hanging on by a thread. I could see the hurt in their eyes, the disappointment, the fear—and in that moment, I couldn't lie to myself anymore. I knew I had to change.

The promises I made during the Promise Phase were always heartfelt. I remember the tears, the shaking hands, the way my voice would tremble as I vowed to stay sober, to get help, to finally turn things around. There's a desperation in those promises—a deep, sincere desire to make things right, to reclaim the life you've lost. You're not just making promises to others; you're making them to yourself. You tell yourself that this time will be different, that you have the strength to resist, that you can rebuild what's been broken.

For the addict, the Promise Phase is filled with hope. You start to imagine a future where you're free from the chains of addiction, where you can look in the mirror without shame, where you can rebuild the bridges you've burned. It's a powerful moment, one where you truly believe that you can turn things around. You start making plans—researching rehab centers, looking up support groups, maybe even talking about reconnecting with your faith. There's a sense of renewal, a feeling that you're finally taking the first steps toward the life you've been longing for.

While the Promise Phase is filled with genuine intention, it's also tinged with fear. You know deep down that you've been here before, that you've made these promises before, and that the path ahead is far from easy. You're not just battling the addiction itself; you're up against the memories of past failures, the guilt of broken promises, and the fear of letting everyone down again.

For the people who love you, the Promise Phase is a mix of hope and anxiety. They want to believe you—they really do. They see the sincerity in your eyes, hear the conviction in your voice, and they can't help but hope that this time will be different; but they've also been hurt before. They've watched you go through this cycle, seen you make promises that, despite your best efforts, you couldn't keep. They've been on the rollercoaster of hope and heartbreak, and while they're willing to support you, there's always that guarded skepticism. They want to believe, but they're afraid to get their hopes up too high.

This phase is marked by a fragile optimism. There's a cautious sense of possibility, both within you and among those who care about you. Everyone is walking on eggshells, hoping that this time, the change will stick. You might start taking tangible steps toward recovery, but there's always that nagging voice in the back of your mind reminding you of how hard this road is going to be.

The truth is: the Promise Phase, as powerful as it is, is just the beginning. Wanting to change isn't enough. You have to confront the tangled mess of physical cravings, emotional wounds, and psychological dependencies that have kept you trapped for so long. You have to be ready to fight, day in and day out, against the pull of addiction. The promises you make in this phase are real, but they need to be backed up with action, support, and a willingness to face the uncomfortable truths about yourself and your addiction.

For the promises made during this phase to lead to lasting recovery, they need to be more than words. They need to be the foundation for real, enduring change. That means holding yourself accountable, seeking out the help you need, and doing the hard work of rebuilding your life from the ground up. It's not easy, and it's not quick, but it's possible. The Promise Phase is a moment of potential, a turning point where change is within reach. However, to seize that potential, you have to be willing to walk the long, difficult road ahead, one step at a time, until those promises become your reality.

THE STRUGGLE PHASE

The Struggle Phase is the one that truly tests you. It's the internal battle that, if you've ever been caught in the grip of addiction, you know all too well. I remember it vividly, that relentless tug-of-war between the desire to keep the promises I made and the overpowering pull of the addiction that never really loosened its grip on me.

When you're in this phase, it feels like you're walking a tightrope, trying to maintain balance between the person you want to be and the person you're afraid you'll always be. There were days when I thought I had it all under control. I'd go for weeks, sometimes even months, without touching anything. Those periods of sobriety gave me hope. I started to believe that maybe this time I had finally beaten it, that the battle was behind me. I would cling to that hope, telling myself and those around me that I was done, that I was in control now.

The truth is: beneath that fragile confidence, the struggle was always there, lurking just beneath the surface. The temptation didn't just vanish because I wanted it to. It was always waiting for a weak moment, for the stress to build up, or for something to trigger that old, familiar craving. It's like living with a shadow that never quite goes away—no matter how bright the day gets, it's always just behind you, waiting for the right moment to catch up.

I can recall countless times when the pressure would start to mount. Maybe it was a fight with a loved one, stress at work, or just the emptiness that seemed to settle in when things got too quiet. Whatever the trigger, it would start as a whisper—"Just one more time. You've been doing so well, you can handle it." The rationalizations would begin to flow so easily, convincing me that I could indulge without falling back into the abyss. I'd tell myself that I deserved it, that I'd been strong for so long, and that I could keep it under control this time, but deep down, I knew better. I knew how easily that one time could turn into a hundred. The struggle wasn't just about resisting the substance—it was about resisting the overwhelming desire to escape, to numb out, to find a way to fill that void that always seemed to be there. It was about fighting the urge to reach for the thing that had brought me comfort for so long, even though I knew it was the very thing that had torn my life apart.

The hardest part of the Struggle Phase, at least for me, was the isolation. Even when I was surrounded by people who cared, I felt so alone in the fight. It was hard to admit that the cravings were still there, that the thoughts of relapse were still a daily battle. I didn't want to let anyone down, so I kept a lot of it to myself. The shame and guilt of even thinking about "using" again made me feel like I was already failing, even if I hadn't slipped yet. That isolation only made the temptation stronger because it felt like no one really understood what I was going through.

As the days passed, the stress of holding it all together would start to wear me down. I'd get tired of fighting, tired of pretending that everything was fine. The weight of the struggle would grow heavier, and there were moments when it seemed like giving in would be easier than continuing to resist. I knew that if I did, the cycle would start all over again, but in those moments, the immediate relief seemed worth the long-term cost.

The truth is, the Struggle Phase isn't just about resisting the substance—it's about dealing with everything that comes with it: the emotions, the triggers, the memories, and the loneliness. It's a constant fight against the part of you that's been conditioned to seek comfort in the very thing that's destroying you—and it's exhausting. Every day feels like a battle, and every victory, no matter how small, feels like it could slip away at any moment.

Here's the thing: pushing through the Struggle Phase is where real change starts to happen. Every day that you say no, every time you choose to reach out for help instead of giving in, you're building strength. You're proving to yourself that you can fight this, that you don't have to be a prisoner to your addiction. The struggle is where you find out what you're really made of, and where you start to reclaim the life you thought you'd lost.

For me, it was in the Struggle Phase that I began to understand that recovery isn't just about quitting the substance—it's about learning to live without needing it. It's about finding new ways to cope, new ways to find joy, and new ways to connect with others. It's about breaking free from the patterns that kept me trapped for so long; and while the struggle is tough—probably the toughest part of the whole journey—it's also where the most growth happens. It's where you start to see that maybe, just maybe, you're stronger than the addiction that's been holding you down.

So, if you're in the Struggle Phase right now, I get it. I've been there. I know how hard it is, but I also know that every day you push through is a day closer to freedom. Keep fighting. Keep reaching out. Keep believing that you can make it through—because you can.

THE RELAPSE PHASE

The Relapse Phase—it's the part of the cycle that haunts you, even when you're doing well. Unfortunately, it's often where things can spiral back to square one. I know this phase intimately because I've been there more times than I'd like to admit. You try so hard to stay on track, to keep the promises you made to yourself and to others, but then something happens. Maybe it's stress, maybe it's loneliness, maybe it's just that persistent, nagging craving that never quite goes away. Whatever it is, you find yourself slipping back into those old habits … often in secret.

Relapse isn't just a setback—it's a crushing blow. It hits hard because you know how much you've let everyone down—yourself, most of all. You've made promises, sworn that this time would be different, and yet here you are, back in the same destructive behavior. The shame that comes with it is overwhelming. You're not just disappointed; you're disgusted with yourself. It's like watching everything you've worked for crumble in an instant, and the weight of that failure is almost unbearable.

When you relapse, you don't want anyone to know. The guilt is too much to face, so you go into hiding, both physically and emotionally. You start covering your tracks, making excuses, and telling lies to keep people from finding out. You might convince yourself that you can handle it, that you can stop again whenever you want, but deep down, you know the truth. You're back in the grip of your addiction, and it's got you tighter than before.

The secrecy of relapse is suffocating. You're already battling the addiction, but now you're also dealing with the constant fear of being found out. Every conversation feels like a test, every glance from a loved one feels like they can see right through you. The lies pile up, and with them, the distance between you and everyone who cares about you grows wider. The isolation is like a dark cloud that follows you everywhere, making you feel more alone than ever.

As you sink deeper into that isolation, the addiction tightens its grip. It's a vicious cycle—one that feeds on your shame and guilt, driving you further into the behavior you're trying so desperately to escape. The more you try to hide it, the more control the addiction gains. Before long, it feels like there's no way out, and the promises you made during the last phase feel like a distant memory, something you're not sure you'll ever be able to keep.

Relapse is a painful reminder of how hard this battle really is. It's not just about the substance or the behavior; it's about everything that comes with it—the shame, the guilt, the secrecy, the isolation. It's a dark place and getting out of it feels impossible at times, but even in the midst of it, there's a part of you that knows this isn't the end of the story. There's a part of you that still wants to fight, even if it feels like you're losing the battle right now.

The Relapse Phase is brutal, but it's also a wake-up call. It forces you to confront the reality of your addiction, to see just how deep its roots go. It's a reminder that recovery isn't a straight line—it's a journey filled with setbacks and struggles. It's also a journey worth continuing, no matter how many times you fall. The key is not to stay in the relapse, but to find a way to rise from it, to learn from it, and to keep moving forward, one step at a time.

THE CONSEQUENCES PHASE

The Consequences Phase is the moment when everything comes crashing down. It's when the truth, no matter how well you thought you hid it, finally comes to light. I've been through this phase more than once, and each time, the impact was devastating. The lies, the secrecy, the relapse—it all comes back to haunt you, and there's no escaping the fallout. When your relapse is discovered, the reactions from those you care about hit hard. The look of disappointment in their eyes, the anger, the hurt—it's all right there, laid bare. You see the trust you've shattered, the relationships you've strained, and sometimes even broken beyond repair. The people who stood by you, who believed in you, who hoped against hope that this time would be different—they're the ones who suffer the most, and knowing that you're the cause of their pain only deepens your own.

The fallout is brutal. You're not just dealing with your own guilt and shame anymore; now you have to face the anger and disappointment of those you've let down. Sometimes, the rejection is outright. People who once supported you might distance themselves, unable or unwilling to keep going through the cycle with you. The weight of that rejection is crushing, making you feel even more isolated and alone; but it's not just the emotional damage. The Consequences Phase often brings a host of other problems to the surface. Legal issues that you'd been avoiding can come back to bite you. Financial troubles that were masked by your addiction suddenly become glaringly obvious. Health problems that you ignored or downplayed are now front and center. It's as if everything you tried to keep at bay while feeding your addiction finally demands to be dealt with, all at once. The pain during this phase is profound. It's not just about the immediate consequences—it's about the long-term impact on your life and the lives of those around you. The trust that's been shattered isn't easily rebuilt, if it can be rebuilt at all. The relationships that have been damaged might never fully recover. The financial and legal issues can take years to resolve, and the toll on your health might be something you have to live with forever.

What makes the Consequences Phase so hard is that it forces you to face the reality of your actions head-on. There's no more hiding, no more pretending that everything is fine. The facade crumbles, and you're left standing in the wreckage of what your addiction has done. It's a moment of reckoning, where you have to decide whether to keep running from the truth or finally confront it. For me, this phase was always the hardest to bear. It's one thing to live with the consequences yourself, but it's another to see how your actions have hurt the people you care about. The guilt, the shame, the regret—it all comes flooding in, and there's no way to escape it. You have to sit with it, feel it, and try to find a way to move forward.

The Consequences Phase is a painful reminder that addiction doesn't just affect the addict—it ripples out, impacting everyone connected to them. It's a stark reality check that the choices you make don't exist in a vacuum. They have real, lasting consequences, and those consequences are often more far-reaching than you ever imagined. This phase is where the damage becomes undeniable, and where the hard work of repair and recovery must begin—if you're willing to face it.

THE RENEWAL PHASE

The Renewal Phase is a familiar place, one I've found myself in more times than I care to count. It's that point in the cycle where, after the dust has settled from the latest relapse and the consequences have been laid bare, you find yourself making promises all over again. There's a strange mix of hope and desperation in this phase. On one hand, you're determined—absolutely convinced—that this time will be different. On the other hand, there's a nagging fear that maybe it won't be. Yet still, you cling to that flicker of hope because without it, moving forward seems impossible.

In the Renewal Phase, the addict begins to rebuild from the rubble. You swear, once again, that you're done with the drugs, the alcohol, the destructive behavior. You tell yourself, and everyone around you, that this time you mean it. You promise to seek help, whether that's through therapy, rehab, or a support group. You start talking about change as if it's already happening, as if just saying the words will somehow make it real, and for a moment, it feels like it might. There's a new energy, a fresh determination, and a belief that you can actually pull it off this time. Though deep down, if I'm being honest, there's always that underlying doubt. The Renewal Phase is filled with good intentions, but intentions alone aren't enough. I've learned that without something more, some-thing stronger than just the desire to change, the cycle tends to repeat itself. You can't just rely on willpower, because willpower eventually runs dry. You can't just make the same promises over and over again, hoping that this time they'll stick. Something has to shift, something fundamen-tal, or you risk falling back into the same patterns.

For me, I've found that significant intervention is what makes the Renewal Phase truly different. Whether it's professional treatment, a spiritual awakening, or even a complete change in environment, some-thing has to break the cycle. You have to dig deeper, to address the root causes of your addiction, to face the demons that keep pulling you back. It's not enough to just want to change—you have to be willing to do the hard work, to let go of whatever's been holding you back, and to embrace the uncomfortable, messy process of real transformation.

The Renewal Phase is also a test of endurance. It's easy to make promises when you're in the middle of the wreckage, but keeping those promises as time goes on, as the initial urgency fades, is where the real challenge lies. You have to stay committed, even when it gets tough, even when the temptation creeps back in, even when you start to doubt your-self again. You have to surround yourself with people who will hold you accountable, who won't let you slip back into old habits without a fight.

This phase is a new beginning, but it's also a crossroads. It's where you decide if you're truly ready to change or if you're just going through the motions. It's where you either break the cycle or get caught in it again and that choice—no matter how many times you've faced it before—is always in your hands.

The Renewal Phase gives you a chance to rewrite your story. It's a moment of possibility, where the past doesn't have to dictate the future, but it's up to you to make that possibility a reality. It's about more than just renewing your promises; it's about renewing your commitment to yourself, to your recovery, and to the people who believe in you. It's about finding the strength to keep moving forward, even when the path is uncertain, and trusting that this time, with the right support and the right mindset, you can finally make the change stick.

The Renewal Phase is a powerful reminder that no matter how many times you've fallen, there's always an opportunity to rise again. It's a chance to reclaim your life, to rebuild what's been broken, and to forge a path that leads to real, lasting change. However, this phase also demands honesty, humility, and an unwavering commitment to growth. It's not just about making promises—it's about taking action, learning from the past, and embracing the hard work of recovery. So, if you find yourself in the Renewal Phase, hold on to that flicker of hope. Let it guide you, but don't rely on it alone. Surround yourself with the support you need, dig deep, and trust in your ability to break the cycle once and for all. This time really can be different, but only if you're willing to fight for it, every single day.

BREAKING THE CYCLE

From my experience, breaking the cycle is not something that happens overnight. It takes time, patience, and a willingness to confront some hard truths about yourself, but trust me, once you start to break it down, it will all begin to make sense. When we talk about breaking the cycle, what we're really talking about is interrupting a recurring pattern— whether it's in behavior, thoughts, or circumstances—and replacing it with something healthier, something positive. However, to do that, we first have to understand the pattern itself. These recurring patterns often stem from old wounds—maybe a past trauma, a negative experience, or even a current situation that just won't seem to go away. For me, it took a lot of introspection, counseling, and self-examination to get to the root of my cycles. Yes, I leaned on my faith, attended church, and prayed for guidance, but I also knew that I had to take action. I had to dig deep, find the sore spot, the wound that kept reopening every time I tried to change. It's like a scar that you think has healed, only to find it's still tender, still capable of bringing you down if you're not careful.

When it comes to personal development, breaking the cycle often means overcoming negative thought patterns or self-defeating behaviors. It's about changing those unhealthy habits or addictions that drag you down, that keep you stuck in a place you don't want to be. It's about improving your self-esteem, boosting your confidence, and finally stepping into the person you're meant to be—but it's not just about personal growth. There are relationship factors, too. Maybe you're stuck in a cycle of toxic or abusive relationships, repeating the same destructive patterns over and over. Breaking that cycle might mean ending a relationship that's doing more harm than good. It could mean recognizing the signs of a toxic dynamic and choosing to walk away before it drags you down. It's hard, yes, but it's necessary.

Then there's the social side of breaking cycles. Take poverty, for example. Not everyone is born into wealth or has access to the resources they need to break free from a life of struggle. Many Americans, for instance, grow up without a steady father figure, dealing with the fallout of high divorce rates or being raised by a single parent trying to juggle everything on their own. These social cycles are tough to break, but they're not impossible. It takes effort, education, and sometimes a complete shift in mindset. We also can't forget the patterns of violence and discrimination that plague so many communities. Breaking those cycles requires courage, solidarity, and a commitment to change—both individually and collectively. Whether it's addressing inequality, standing up against violence, or simply refusing to perpetuate the hate that's been passed down, it's all part of the process.

Mental health is another critical area where breaking the cycle is vital. Whether it's managing symptoms of depression, developing healthier coping mechanisms, or learning to prioritize your mental well-being, these steps are crucial in creating a life that's not ruled by past pain or present struggles. Breaking these cycles is challenging, overwhelming, and often uncomfortable, but I'm here to tell you that you *can* get through it. That's why you're here, right? You're looking for ways to overcome, to break free, to finally live the life you know you're capable of living. Yes, addictions and other challenges may come and go, but they don't have to define you. They don't have to be your story forever. For some people, the struggles last only for a season; for others, they linger because they're never fully addressed, but you don't have to be one of those people.

You have the power to outsmart whatever is trying to hold you back—whether it's an addiction, a toxic relationship, or a negative thought pattern. Don't let it get the best of you. Keep pushing, keep fighting, and keep believing that you can break the cycle—because you can. You just have to take that first step, and then the next, and then the one after that. Before you know it, you'll be living a life that's not just free from the old cycles, but filled with new possibilities.

As you continue on this journey of breaking cycles, remember that it's not a one-time effort—it's a continuous process. There will be days when it feels like you're making real progress, and then there will be days when you feel like you're right back where you started. That's okay. What matters is that you don't give up. Keep moving forward, keep challenging those patterns, and keep seeking out the support and tools you need to create lasting change. Breaking the cycle is about reclaiming your power, your voice, and your life. It's about saying, "I refuse to let the past dictate my future. I refuse to be defined by the things that have held me back." It's about embracing your inner strength, even when everything around you seems to be urging you to stay the same. It's about knowing that you're worth the effort, worth the fight, and worth the change.

So, as you close this chapter, take a moment to reflect on where you've been and where you're headed. Know that every step you take toward breaking the cycle is a step toward a better, brighter future. It won't always be easy, but it will always be worth it. You have the power to change your story, to break free from the patterns that have held you down, and to build a life that reflects your true potential. Keep going. You've got this.

CHAPTER 9

REJECTION BEHIND CLOSED DOORS

Rejection is one of those experiences that most of us would rather avoid, but if we're honest, it's also one of the most transformative forces in our lives. If it wasn't for rejection, where would we be? It's a question worth pondering, because when you really think about it, many of the pivotal moments in our lives are born out of rejection. Personally, I know this all too well. If I hadn't faced rejection, even as a student, I wouldn't have found the drive to push through and eventually earn my degree in pastoral leadership. Rejection can be a cruel teacher, but it's also an effective one.

Rejection comes in many forms and touches every area of our lives. By definition, rejection is the act of refusing to accept, use, or consider someone or something. It's that stinging feeling when you're not chosen, not seen, not valued. The part that cuts the deepest is when people don't even see your potential or acknowledge your worth, even when you know, deep down, that you have so much to offer. It's that moment when you realize that your gifts, talents, and character just aren't enough for some people.

Here's the thing about rejection—it's not always the end of the story. In fact, it's often just the beginning of a new chapter, a redirection toward something greater. Take Walt Disney, for example. He was fired from a newspaper for "lacking imagination." Steve Jobs, the visionary behind Apple, was once forced out of the very company he founded. Madonna was dropped by record labels before she became a global icon. Michael Jordan, one of the greatest basketball players of all time, was cut from his high school basketball team. Marilyn Monroe was told by a modeling agency that she should consider becoming a secretary instead of pursuing a career in modeling. Then there's Steven Spielberg, who was rejected from film school, not once, not twice, but three times. Think about that—three times Spielberg was told he wasn't good enough. Yet, each of these individuals used their rejection as fuel to achieve greatness.

Rejection has layers, many layers, and it's worth breaking it down piece by piece. There's the public rejection that everyone sees, but then there's also the private rejection that happens behind closed doors, the kind that gnaws at your self-worth and makes you question your path. It's in these private moments that rejection can either break you or become the catalyst for your redirection. I've faced rejection behind closed doors more times than I can count, and each time, it forced me into what I call "figure-it-out mode." Have you ever been there? That place where you know you can't afford to stay still or stagnant … where you have to find a way to move forward or risk falling into a pit of despair? It's a tough place to be, but it's also where growth happens.

So why is rejection so hard to deal with, especially behind closed doors? One reason is the lack of closure and explanation. Sometimes you're left wondering why you weren't chosen, why you weren't enough, and that uncertainty can gnaw at you. Rejection can also strip away your dignity, leaving you feeling small and insignificant. Often, the pain of rejection is rooted in past wounds—experiences from childhood, adolescence, or even recent events that have left scars. Maybe it was a public humiliation, like stumbling during a speech at school, that still haunts you. Even if you managed to finish the speech, the memory of messing up lingers, making you feel inadequate long after the moment has passed. Rejection, in many ways, is mental. It's all in the mind, where those feelings of inadequacy and self-doubt take root and grow. That's why I chose to focus on this topic—to help you understand what it really means to be rejected behind closed doors and how to navigate it.

There's a psychological side to rejection that can't be ignored. The emotional impact is profound. Research shows that rejection activates the same brain regions as physical pain, which is why it hurts so much. There's also the fear that comes with rejection, leading to sensitivity and social anxiety. When your self-esteem takes a hit, it can leave you questioning your worth. The cognitive effects of rejection can distort your thinking, making you believe lies about yourself and your abilities. Then there are the social and professional aspects of rejection. On a relational level, romantic rejection can be particularly devastating. You might long for a deep, meaningful relationship, but find yourself stuck, unable to reach that goal. Maybe you've faced friendship rejection, where someone you cared about simply ghosted you, leaving you to wonder what went wrong. Rejection in any form can be isolating, especially when it happens repeatedly.

Socially, rejection can manifest in cycles of poverty, violence, and discrimination. Many people are born into situations where they lack the resources and opportunities to break free from these cycles. For example, the absence of a father figure in many American families, combined with the pressures of single parenthood, can perpetuate patterns of struggle and hardship. Breaking these cycles requires more than just willpower, it requires systemic change, support, and perseverance.

So, yes, rejection is challenging, overwhelming, and often uncomfortable, but you can get through it. That's why you're here, reading this, seeking answers and understanding. Rejection, when faced head-on, can become a tool for growth. It can push you out of your comfort zone, forcing you to confront your fears and rise above them. The things that come and go—like addictions, bad habits, and negative thought patterns—only stick around as long as you let them. Some struggles are temporary, lasting only a season, while others persist because they're never fully addressed. Know that you have the power to outsmart whatever is trying to bring you down, whether it's a situation, a person, or even your own doubts; don't let it defeat you. Remember, rejection is not the end; it's often just the beginning of something new. It's an opportunity to reassess, realign, and redirect your efforts toward something greater. So, the next time you face rejection, don't let it break you. Let it shape you, strengthen you, and push you closer to where you're meant to be. The path to greatness is often paved with obstacles, and rejection is just one of them. Embrace it, learn from it, and keep moving forward.

Rejection, as painful as it is, has a way of refining us. It strips away the unnecessary, the superficial, and the comfortable, leaving us with no choice but to dig deeper. It forces us to confront who we really are and what we're truly capable of. When everything else is taken away, when the doors close and the opportunities vanish, you're left standing alone with your resilience and determination. That's when the real work begins—the work of rebuilding, of reimagining, of recreating your path. One of the hardest things about rejection is that it feels so personal. Even when it's not, even when it's about factors beyond your control, it still cuts straight to the core. It's easy to start questioning your worth, to wonder if you're good enough, talented enough, or simply enough. Here's the truth … rejection doesn't define you. It doesn't measure your potential, your value, or your destiny. It's simply a part of the process, a stepping stone on the way to something better.

Think about all the times you've been rejected—each rejection was painful in its own way, but consider where you are now. Look at the strength you've gained, the wisdom you've accumulated, and the resilience you've developed. Rejection taught you to stand on your own two feet, to find a way forward when the path wasn't clear. It taught you to believe in yourself, even when others didn't. It taught you that no matter how many times you get knocked down, you can always get back up. This is the beauty of rejection—it's not just about what you lose, but what you gain in the process. You gain clarity about what truly matters to you. You gain insight into your strengths and weaknesses. You gain perspective on what you're willing to fight for and what you're willing to let go. Rejection can be a catalyst for growth, pushing you to evolve in ways you never would have if everything had gone smoothly.

However, let's not sugarcoat it. Rejection hurts. It's uncomfortable. It can make you feel like the world is closing in on you, like you're stuck in a cycle you can't escape. It can lead to sleepless nights, anxious thoughts, and a gnawing sense of inadequacy. The key is not to let it stop you. Feel the pain, acknowledge it, and then use it as fuel to move forward. Let it sharpen your focus and strengthen your resolve. Let it drive you to prove to yourself, not to anyone else, that you're capable of more than they ever imagined. There's a quote I often think about: "Rejection is merely redirection." It's a simple idea, but it holds so much truth. When one door closes, another opens—but only if you're willing to keep walking. Sometimes, the rejection you face is the very thing that pushes you toward your true calling, your true purpose. It's the universe's way of saying, "Not this way, but that way." And if you listen, if you're willing to trust the process, you'll find that where you end up is often far better than where you were trying to go in the first place.

So, what do you do when you're rejected? You reassess. You regroup. You remind yourself of who you are and what you're made of. You take a deep breath, and you take the next step forward. You don't let the rejection define your path; you let it refine it. You let it guide you toward new opportunities, new perspectives, and new strengths you didn't know you had.

In relationships, rejection can be particularly tough. Whether it's romantic, platonic, or professional, being told that you're not what someone is looking for can sting. Just remember, rejection in relationships often means that the person or opportunity wasn't right for you, not the other way around. It's better to be rejected for being yourself than to be accepted for being something you're not. Authenticity always wins in the long run, even if it means facing a few more closed doors along the way. In your career, rejection might mean you're aiming too low or that you're being redirected to a path that better aligns with your true talents. It might mean you're meant to create something of your own instead of fitting into someone else's mold. The greatest innovators, creators, and leaders didn't succeed because they avoided rejection—they succeeded because they learned from it, grew from it, and refused to let it stop them.

In life, rejection is inevitable, but it doesn't have to be the end of the story. It can be the beginning of a new chapter, one where you're stronger, wiser, and more determined than ever before. So, the next time you face rejection, embrace it. Lean into it. Let it teach you, mold you, and prepare you for what's next. Move forward knowing that what's next for you is often greater than you can imagine, and the only way to get there is to keep pressing forward, no matter how many times you face the word no.

5 POINTS TO REMEMBER

1. **Rejection is a teacher, not a judge:** It doesn't pass verdict on your worth; instead, it offers lessons in resilience, self-discovery, and adaptability. Each "no" is an opportunity to learn something new about yourself and the world around you. Embrace these lessons, for they are the building blocks of your future success.

2. **Your response to rejection defines you more than the rejection itself:** It's not about how many times you fall, but how many times you rise. The strength of your character is revealed not in moments of triumph, but in how you handle setbacks. Let your response to rejection showcase your determination, grace, and unwavering spirit.

3. **Rejection often protects you from paths that aren't meant for you:** Trust in the timing of your life. What feels like a devastating "no" today might be the very thing that steers you toward your true calling tomorrow. Have faith in the journey, even when the destination isn't clear.

4. **Never let rejection diminish your sense of value:** Your worth isn't determined by others' opinions or decisions. It's an inherent part of who you are, constant and unshakeable. Hold onto this truth, especially when rejection tries to make you doubt yourself.

5. **Rejection breeds innovation:** Some of the world's greatest ideas, inventions, and achievements were born from the ashes of rejection. When conventional paths are closed to you, you're forced to create your own. This is where true creativity flourishes. Let rejection be the spark that ignites your innovative spirit.

REJECTION IS A TEACHER IN ITS OWN CLASSROOM

It's easy to see rejection as the end of the road, as a harsh verdict on who we are or what we're capable of. Yet, I've come to realize that rejection, when viewed through the right lens, is a teacher in disguise. For me, rejection has been one of the most valuable teachers in my life. It taught me when to speak up and when to stay silent. It taught me how to navigate difficult situations with grace, and how to interact with people without letting their opinions shake my confidence. Rejection didn't just hand out lessons; it gave me the homework of learning how to manage my emotions and reactions, how to build resilience, and how to move forward without letting others see the impact it had on me.

Rejection wasn't just the teacher; it was also the exam and the classroom. It put me through tests I thought I could easily pass, only to show me that I had more to learn. It tested my humility, forcing me to confront my ego and realize that not everything was about me. It humbled me in ways that no other experience could, showing me the importance of grace, forgiveness, and patience, especially when dealing with people who might not understand or appreciate me.

So, why is rejection a teacher? Because it teaches you the lessons you never thought you needed to learn. It teaches you that life isn't always going to go your way, that not everyone will see your value or give you the chances you think you deserve. It teaches you to forgive—not just others, but also yourself. It teaches you humility, especially when people push your buttons or test your patience. Rejection forces you to dig deeper, to find strength in places you didn't know you had, and to keep going even when it feels like the world is against you.

Here's the thing—some people try to run from the Teacher of Rejection. They try to cover up their scars and bruises, pretending that the hurt didn't happen. They think that by ignoring it, they can move on unscathed, but the truth is, when we try to perform surgery on our own wounds without the proper tools, without the right surgeon, we often end up making things worse. Rejection can cut deep, and if we don't take the time to properly address those wounds, they can fester and leave us hurting, even more, down the line.

Rejection teaches you that you don't need to have all the answers, that it's okay to seek help, to rely on others when the burden feels too heavy. It teaches you that healing is a process, one that requires patience, self-compassion, and sometimes, the wisdom of others. The lessons rejection offers aren't always easy to swallow, but they're necessary for growth. They shape you into someone stronger, wiser, and more capable than you were before.

When you allow rejection to be your teacher, you start to see the world differently. You realize that every "no" isn't a dead-end; it's a redirection, a nudge toward a better path, a clearer purpose. Rejection has a way of stripping away the unnecessary, the distractions, and the things that aren't meant for you, leaving you with what truly matters. It forces you to confront your weaknesses, to refine your strengths, and to grow in ways you never thought possible.

I've learned that rejection can teach you the art of resilience—the ability to bounce back, to stand up after every fall, and to keep moving forward even when the road is rough. It teaches you that failure isn't fatal, that it's okay to stumble, and that each setback is a setup for a comeback. Rejection pushes you to dig deeper, to find that inner well of strength and determination that often lies dormant until it's tested. As you learn these lessons, you also begin to develop a thicker skin. Not in a way that makes you hard or bitter, but in a way that allows you to navigate life's challenges with grace and confidence. You start to understand that other people's opinions don't define you, that your worth isn't tied to their validation or approval. Rejection teaches you to stand firm in who you are, to believe in your abilities even when others don't, and to keep striving for your goals no matter how many doors close in your face. Perhaps, one of the most important lessons rejection teaches is humility. It reminds you that you're not invincible, that there are things you don't know and areas where you need to grow. It humbles you by showing you that you're not always going to get what you want, and that sometimes, the timing just isn't right. This humility, though difficult to embrace, is crucial because it keeps you grounded. It keeps you open to learning, to growing, and to becoming better.

Rejection also teaches you the value of perseverance. It's easy to give up when things don't go your way, but rejection challenges you to push through, to keep trying even when the odds seem stacked against you. It teaches you that success often requires persistence, that it's not always about how talented you are, but about how determined you are to keep going. The doors that close might just be leading you to the one that will open, but you'll never find it if you stop knocking. Rejection can teach you to appreciate the things you *do* have, the opportunities you've been given, and the people who stand by you no matter what. It reminds you that not every setback is a tragedy, that sometimes, the things we think we want aren't what we need at all. Rejection can make you more grateful for the journey, for the lessons learned along the way, and for the growth that comes from overcoming challenges. Ultimately, rejection teaches you that life is full of ups and downs, twists and turns; but it's in those moments of challenge that you find out what you're really made of. It's in those moments that you build character, develop resilience, and learn to navigate life with a sense of purpose and direction. Rejection isn't something to fear or avoid; it's something to embrace, to learn from, and to use as a stepping stone toward becoming the person you're meant to be.

So, as you continue on your journey, remember that rejection isn't the end. It's a part of the process, a crucial element in your growth and development. Let it teach you, guide you, and shape you. Let it be the force that drives you to be better, stronger, and more resilient, because in the end, it's not about avoiding rejection; it's about using it to propel you forward, to turn every "no" into a "yes," and to transform every setback into a step up.

HOW TO RESPOND TO REJECTION

Responding to rejection has been a transformative process for me, one that requires more than just enduring the pain—it's about actively re-shaping my mindset and reclaiming my power. One of the most pivotal ways I've learned to respond to rejection is through private time with God in prayer. That connection is where I find my grounding, where I pour out my frustrations and hurts, and where I listen for guidance and strength. However, prayer is just one piece of the puzzle. To truly over-come the sting of rejection, I've also developed confession techniques—affirmations, if you will—that help me rebuild my confidence, fortify my heart, and strengthen my mind against the negative thoughts that try to take root. These confessions are like armor for the soul, protecting me from letting rejection define who I am or dictate the direction of my life. They're a way of taking back control, of telling rejection, "You don't get the final say." Here are some examples that have helped me, and I hope they'll resonate with you, too:

- *"I've seen how this story goes, and I'm not going to let this issue write the rest of my chapter."*

    This confession is about reclaiming your narrative. Rejection might be a part of your story, but it doesn't get to decide how it ends. You have the power to choose what comes next, to write a new chapter that isn't defined by the setbacks you've faced. It's a reminder that the story isn't over and that you have the pen in your hand.

- *"I'm not letting you draft me into your game of going through the same cycles of defeat and rejection."*

    Rejection has a way of pulling you into a cycle—one that repeats the same patterns of defeat and self-doubt. This confession is a declaration that you're not playing that game anymore. You're not letting rejection trap you in a loop of negativity. Instead, you're breaking free, refusing to be a pawn in a game that doesn't serve you.

- *"Hey rejection, remember the time you made me feel embarrassed about my value and worth? Well, I've figured you out. I'm not letting you do that to me again because you messed up my financial situation."*

This is about confronting rejection head-on. It's a bold reminder that you've been through this before—you've seen how rejection tries to undermine your confidence, your self-worth, and even your financial stability, but now, you're wiser. You recognize the patterns, and you're not letting them repeat. It's a statement of empowerment, letting rejection know that its tactics won't work on you anymore.

These confessions are more than just words; they're tools for resilience. They help shift the focus from the pain of rejection to the power of your response. They remind you that rejection is just one moment in time, not the defining moment of your life. By speaking these truths over yourself, you're not just coping with rejection—you're actively overcoming it, one thought, one word, one day at a time.

Remember, rejection will come—it's a part of life—but how you respond to it is what truly matters. With prayer, positive confessions, and a steadfast focus on your goals, you can turn rejection into a stepping stone rather than a stumbling block. You have the power to redefine what rejection means in your life, to see it not as an ending, but as a necessary push toward something greater. Keep moving forward, stay grounded in your truth, and let these confessions be the fuel that drives you toward the success and fulfillment you're destined for.

As you continue on this journey of responding to rejection, it's important to remember that each instance of rejection is an opportunity—not just to prove others wrong, but to prove to yourself that you are stronger than any setback. The confessions you make aren't just about fighting off negative thoughts in the moment; they're about building a foundation of resilience that will carry you through the challenges ahead. They're about reinforcing your identity, reminding yourself daily of who you are, and what you're capable of, despite what anyone else might say or think.

One of the key aspects of this process is consistency. It's not enough to make these declarations once and move on. Just as rejection can be persistent, your response must be equally persistent. Each day presents new challenges, new opportunities for doubt to creep in, and that's why you have to be just as diligent in speaking life into your situation, in reaffirming your value, and in taking control of your narrative.

CONSIDER ADDING THESE ADDITIONAL CONFESSIONS TO YOUR DAILY PRACTICE

"I am more than enough, and I refuse to let rejection make me question my worth."

This is a powerful affirmation of self-worth. Rejection often tries to convince you that you're lacking in some way, that you don't measure up, but this confession is a declaration that you are complete as you are. Your worth isn't up for debate, and no rejection can diminish who you are at your core.

"Every 'no' I encounter is redirecting me to a better 'yes' that's waiting for me."

This confession helps reframe rejection as part of a larger plan. It's a reminder that every door that closes is leading you to a door that will open, one that's better suited to your gifts and purpose. It's about trusting that the path you're on is leading you somewhere meaningful, even if it's not the path you originally envisioned.

> *"I trust in the process, even when it's painful,*
> *because I know it's shaping me into the person*
> *I'm meant to become."*

This statement acknowledges that the journey isn't always easy. There will be pain, setbacks, and moments of doubt; but through it all, you trust that the process is refining you, preparing you for the greater things ahead. It's about having faith that the struggle is part of your story, not the whole story.

> *"I will rise stronger from every rejection,*
> *because I know it's not a reflection of my value,*
> *but a step toward my destiny."*

This is a powerful declaration of resilience. It's a commitment to not only survive rejection, but to thrive in spite of it. You're not just bouncing back—you're rising higher, becoming stronger, and moving closer to your destiny with every challenge you overcome.

These confessions are your tools for combatting the lies that rejection tries to tell you. They're reminders that you are capable, valuable, and destined for greatness, regardless of the obstacles in your way.

Another important aspect of responding to rejection is surrounding yourself with a community that uplifts you. While personal confessions and prayer are essential, having people in your corner who believe in you can make a world of difference. These are the people who will remind you of your worth when you forget, who will encourage you to keep going when the going gets tough, and who will celebrate your victories, no matter how small. Seek out those relationships and hold onto them tightly. They are part of your support system, your safety net, and your source of strength.

Also, don't be afraid to take rejection as a lesson. Each time you face it, ask yourself: What can I learn from this? How can I grow? How can this experience make me better, wiser, stronger? When you approach rejection with a mindset of growth, you transform it from a stumbling block into a stepping stone. It becomes less about what you lost and more about what you gained—a deeper understanding of yourself, a clearer vision of your path, and a renewed sense of purpose.

Ultimately, responding to rejection isn't just about defending yourself against negative thoughts—it's about actively building the life you want, and the life you deserve. It's about being intentional with your words, your thoughts, and your actions. It's about refusing to let anyone or anything dictate your worth and about stepping into the fullness of who you are meant to be.

So, the next time rejection comes knocking, don't shy away from it. Meet it head-on with the confidence that you are more than capable of overcoming it. Use your confessions, your prayers, and your community to rise above. Remember that rejection is not your enemy—it's your teacher, your motivator, your push toward the greatness that lies ahead. Keep pressing forward, keep believing in yourself, and watch as the doors that are *meant for you* begin to open, leading you into a future that is even brighter than you imagined.

HOW REJECTION PROTECTS YOU FROM THE PROBLEM

When most people think of rejection, they immediately associate it with pain, disappointment, and the setbacks that seem so obvious at first glance, but I want to challenge that perspective. What if we reframed rejection as protection? Rejection has the potential to act as a shield, like a soldier's armor on the battlefield. It protects you from the wrong paths, unnecessary heartache, and from wasting your time and energy in pursuits that won't bear the fruit you deserve. Think about it—rejection is like a guard standing firm, blocking you from distractions, dead-end pursuits, or situations that simply aren't meant for you. Sometimes, the very thing you want isn't aligned with what's best for you, and rejection steps in as your silent protector. The rejection had to happen, not to defeat you, but to save you from something that could have pulled you down even further.

One of the best examples of this kind of protection pertains to Steve Jobs. Sure, I've touched on his story briefly before, but let's dig deeper. In 1985, Jobs was fired from Apple—the very company he had built from the ground up. To most people, that kind of rejection would seem like the end of the road, a final failure—but what if that rejection wasn't the end? What if it was the protection Jobs needed? After being ousted from Apple, Jobs took the opportunity to explore new ventures. He founded NeXT and acquired Pixar, ventures that led to revolutionary success. His time away from Apple wasn't a failure—it was protection from stagnating, from becoming too comfortable in one place. This period of exploration prepared him for an epic return to Apple, where he revolutionized the tech world. Sometimes, rejection redirects us back to where we started—but this time, we return stronger, wiser, and more prepared for success.

Oprah Winfrey's story is another powerful reminder of rejection as protection. Early in her career, Oprah was demoted from her position as a news anchor because she was deemed "unfit for television." Can you imagine being told that you're not cut out for something, only to later become the face of an entire generation's talk show culture? This rejection protected her from a career that didn't suit her talents. Instead of sticking to news, Oprah was redirected to a space where her warmth, empathy, and presence could shine—becoming one of the most influential media moguls of all time. That rejection was not a failure; it was her protection from settling for less than her true potential.

And how about Walt Disney? He was fired from a newspaper job for "lacking imagination." Yes, the man who would later create some of the most imaginative and iconic animated films in history was told he wasn't creative enough. What if that rejection was the protection Disney needed? It shielded him from a career that would have confined him, keeping his brilliance locked in a box. That rejection pushed him toward animation and eventually led to the creation of the Disney empire. If he hadn't been rejected, who knows what the world would have missed out on?

These stories remind us that rejection is often the very thing that keeps us from settling for less than we're capable of. It's a powerful re-direction toward something greater. So, how do you navigate rejection and use it as protection in your own life? Here are some practical ways to approach it:

1. REFRAME YOUR PERSPECTIVE

Instead of seeing rejection as a failure, view it as redirection. Think of Steve Jobs—his firing wasn't the end; it was the beginning of a journey that brought him to new, groundbreaking ventures. Ask yourself, "What is this rejection protecting me from?" You might discover that the path you were on wasn't leading you where you truly wanted to go.

2. ANALYZE AND LEARN

Take a step back and reflect on what happened. Look at Oprah—her de-motion was not a reflection of her worth but an opportunity to reassess where her strengths truly lay. By examining your rejection objectively, you'll gain insights into how you can improve and grow.

3. CELEBRATE THE ATTEMPT

Walt Disney's first attempts weren't failures; they were steps toward his eventual success. Just because you were rejected doesn't mean you failed. Celebrate the fact that you put yourself out there. Every attempt, whether successful or not, is part of your growth.

4. SEEK FEEDBACK

If possible, ask for constructive feedback, just like many successful people do after a setback. Feedback helps you sharpen your skills and provides clarity on why the rejection happened. Sometimes, the feedback you get will give you the exact tools you need to pivot in the right direction.

5. PRACTICE SELF-COMPASSION

Rejection is a universal experience. Walt Disney, Oprah, Steve Jobs— they all experienced it, and so will you. Be kind to yourself in the process. Remember, rejection isn't a reflection of your worth. It's part of the process that refines you and realigns your path.

6. KEEP A REJECTION JOURNAL

Document your rejections, just as you would track your successes. Reflect on how each rejection helped you grow. Over time, you'll begin to see patterns of resilience and strength—proof that each rejection was actually setting you up for something better.

7. SET NEW GOALS

Use rejection as fuel to chase new dreams. After being rejected by the newspaper, Disney didn't give up—he went on to build an empire. Let rejection push you to aim higher and keep striving for what you truly deserve.

In the end, rejection isn't something to fear or avoid—it's a teacher, a guide, and, most importantly, a protector. It shields you from wasting your time, energy, and emotions on things that aren't meant for you. When you start to see rejection in this light, you'll begin to realize that it's not an obstacle; it's a redirection toward something far better. Each "no" is clearing the way for a bigger "yes."

So, the next time rejection comes knocking, don't see it as a roadblock. Think of Steve Jobs. Think of Oprah. Think of Disney. See rejection for what it truly is … protection. It's guarding your path, guiding your steps, and ensuring that you end up exactly where you're meant to be. Trust that rejection is working for your good—it's redirecting you to the place where you'll truly thrive.

When you embrace rejection as protection, your mindset shifts entirely. You no longer see rejection as a personal failure, but as a necessary part of the journey to something greater. This change in perspective not only strengthens your resilience but also liberates you from the constant fear of being told "no." Once you recognize that rejection is there to *guide* you, not defeat you, you can walk through life with a sense of peace and purpose, knowing that even the closed doors are serving your best interests.

Here's the truth: sometimes the very thing you're fighting to hold onto isn't meant for you. And rejection is the way life gently (or sometimes harshly) pushes you off that path and onto a better one. It's like that shield I mentioned earlier, deflecting the blows that could harm you and steering you toward safety, or better yet, success.

Think about it. How many times have you been rejected and looked back later, realizing how much better off you were *without* what you thought you wanted? That job you didn't get? It made space for a better opportunity. That relationship that fell apart? It allowed you to meet someone who truly values and complements you. That business deal that didn't go through? It pushed you to innovate in ways you wouldn't have if everything had gone according to your original plan. Rejection, in hindsight, often reveals itself as a disguised blessing, one that reroutes you to something greater than you could have imagined.

This brings us to another key point: rejection often comes to refine us. In the process of being turned away, we are often turned inward, forced to look at ourselves and reflect. It can bring out aspects of ourselves that need attention—whether it's our skills, our mindset, or even our emotional responses. Sometimes, rejection highlights the areas where we still need to grow, and that's where the real work begins. Growth doesn't happen without some discomfort. Rejection's protection doesn't always feel good in the moment. It can sting, leave you doubting yourself, and make you question if you're on the right path; but remember, the discomfort is part of the process. It's the catalyst that pushes you to grow, adapt, and become a better version of yourself.

One of the most powerful lessons rejection teaches is patience. It reminds you that things don't always happen on your timeline, and that's okay. Rejection often comes with the message: "Not yet." It's not necessarily a "never," but a reminder that you may need more time to prepare, more time to grow, or that the right opportunity hasn't presented itself yet. Patience isn't just about waiting; it's about *waiting well*—continuing to refine yourself, staying focused on your goals, and trusting that the right doors will open when the time is right.

Now, let's talk about relationships for a moment. Rejection in relationships can be one of the hardest forms of rejection to deal with because it feels personal. Whether it's a friendship, a romantic relationship, or even a professional connection, being told you're not the right fit can be deeply painful. Here's where protection comes into play: rejection in relationships often shields you from deeper heartache down the road.

Think about that friend who ghosted you, or that person who broke up with you, or the colleague who didn't see your value. In the moment, their rejection may have felt like the end of the world. However, as time passes, you realize that being rejected by them saved you from an even worse fate—one where you invested more of yourself into a relationship that wasn't aligned with your growth, your peace, or your future. Rejection in relationships clears the way for people who truly appreciate, respect, and love you to come into your life. It removes the distractions, the unhealthy connections, and the toxic dynamics that would have drained your energy and taken you further away from your purpose.

In the same vein, professional rejection protects you from settling for less than you're capable of. It's easy to get discouraged when you're passed over for a job or an opportunity, but sometimes that rejection is life's way of protecting your potential. It's saying, "You're made for more, and this isn't it." It's pushing you to hold out for the opportunity that will truly allow you to shine, where your gifts will be fully utilized and appreciated.

REJECTION SHOULD NEVER DIMINISH YOUR VALUE

The reason I chose to focus on rejection is because it's something we all experience, yet it's often misunderstood. Rejection is so relatable, and it's something that touches everyone's life at one point or another. The truth is, rejection should never diminish your value. I know we hear a lot these days about being a "high-value" person—whether it's a high-value man or a high-value woman. But what does that really mean? Does it mean that if someone rejects you or if you face failure, your value drops? Absolutely not. The danger lies in letting rejection convince you that your worth has decreased or that you are somehow "less than."

The nature of rejection can take many forms. It might be a "no" from an employer after a job interview, the end of a relationship, harsh criticism of your creative work, or not being chosen for a team or group. Here's what we need to remember—none of these forms of rejection define your value. They simply reflect that you weren't the right fit for that particular situation, and that's okay—because being the right fit isn't the same as being *good enough*. You can be an incredible person and still not be the right match for a specific opportunity.

Think about your intrinsic worth for a moment. Your value as a human being is not, and never will be, determined by external factors. It's not tied to the opinions of others. It's not based on your successes or failures. It's not defined by your relationship status, your job title, or your bank balance. Society might make it seem like income or status defines who you are, but what if all of that was stripped away? What if you lost everything? Would you still have value? Of course, you would—because your worth is inerrant, woven into your very existence. You are valuable simply because you are *you*. You're unique, irreplaceable, and that's what makes you special.

When you start to reframe rejection, it can be incredibly empowering. One of the key things to understand is that rejection is subjective. One person's "no" could very well be someone else's enthusiastic "yes." I've experienced countless rejections, but looking back, I realize that many of those people didn't recognize what I had to offer. Have you ever been in a season where you thought to yourself, "They just don't know what they're missing out on"? It's not about arrogance; it's about recognizing that sometimes, someone's rejection says more about their inability to see your potential than it does about your worth.

Here's something else to consider ... rejection is often temporary. Today's rejection could pave the way for tomorrow's success. I love this because it reminds me that just because a door closes today doesn't mean it's the end of the story. In fact, that closed door may be clearing the path for something far greater. Let me say it again: today's rejection *could be paving the way* for tomorrow's success. It's all about perspective. We've seen this happen time and time again with people who didn't give up after hearing "no." They kept pushing forward, and their persistence turned that temporary setback into long-term success.

Rejection is also a teacher. Each experience of rejection carries a lesson that can make you stronger and wiser. It challenges you to reflect on what happened, what you can learn from it, and how you can grow from it. Maybe it teaches you resilience. Maybe it helps you develop a thicker skin, or maybe it simply reminds you that failure isn't fatal—it's a part of the journey.

This leads me to the importance of nurturing your self-worth. It's so crucial to practice self-compassion. Be kind to yourself, just as you would be to a dear friend. It's easy to get caught up in negative self-talk when rejection happens, but that's exactly when you need to be your own best friend. Take care of yourself—mentally, emotionally, and physically. Make sure you're feeding your spirit with positivity, surrounding yourself with uplifting people, and maintaining your health.

Never forget the power of resilience. We all have our own version of value, but when we look at our worth, we need to see it as something deeply personal. It can't be defined by someone else's standards or categories. You are the only one who can truly understand the depth of your worth. So, when rejection tries to chip away at that value, remind yourself that rejection is an opinion, not a verdict. It doesn't get to define you. Only you get to do that.

So, the next time you face rejection, remember these truths: Your value is inherent. It's not based on what anyone else thinks or how many times you hear "no." Rejection is not a reflection of your worth, but a necessary part of growth. Most importantly, each rejection is either a redirection, a lesson, or a temporary obstacle that you will overcome. You are stronger, wiser, and more valuable than any rejection could ever make you feel. Keep moving forward, because your worth is undeniable, and the best is still ahead of you.

THE STORY OF MAGIC JOHNSON'S REJECTION AND REDIRECTION

Let's take a closer look at how rejection, when reframed, can become the catalyst for unexpected success by exploring the story of Magic Johnson. While we know Magic as one of the greatest basketball players of all time, his journey off the court tells a tale of resilience, rejection, and redefining success. Magic's life teaches us that rejection can act as protection, redirection, and a powerful motivator, pushing us toward our true purpose in ways we often don't foresee.

When Magic Johnson retired from basketball, he didn't just want to be remembered for his NBA achievements—he had a bigger vision. He wanted to transition into the business world and build an empire that would last far beyond his playing days. Yet despite his fame and monumental success on the basketball court, Magic quickly learned that the business world wasn't going to be easy. Rejection hit him hard in this new arena. Many major corporations and financial institutions turned him away. Despite his star power, they didn't believe Magic had what it took to be a businessman. To them, he was just another athlete trying to dabble in business—someone they assumed would fail.

Looking back, these early rejections served as protection. Although he was being turned down, those "no's" saved Magic from entering into partnerships with people who didn't respect his vision or see beyond his athlete persona. It protected him from deals that would have boxed him in, possibly molding him into someone else's idea of what he should be. That rejection was a blessing in disguise, allowing him to connect with the right people later down the line. Magic's ability to reframe rejection became his secret weapon. Instead of letting those early rejections make him feel inadequate, he used them as motivation. The doors that closed led him to focus his energy on finding people who truly believed in his vision.

One of his breakthrough moments came when he formed a partnership with Starbucks. Magic pitched the idea of opening Starbucks stores in urban communities—places where big corporations had often overlooked potential. Initially, even Starbucks CEO Howard Schultz hesitated, but Magic persisted, knowing that these neighborhoods were untapped markets full of potential. His idea wasn't just about business; it was about providing a high-quality experience to communities that deserved it. The partnership went on to be one of Starbucks' most successful expansions. The very rejections Magic faced early on had pushed him toward this innovative idea, showing him that the right opportunity just needed time to align.

What's remarkable about Magic's story is that, despite facing so much doubt, he never let rejection make him question his value. Many people saw him only as an athlete, someone who belonged on the court, not in boardrooms—but Magic knew better. His intrinsic worth wasn't defined by the opinions of others. He wasn't going to let their doubts diminish his belief in what he could accomplish. Even when countless business leaders dismissed him, Magic remained confident in his abilities, refusing to let those rejections tell him otherwise. This sense of self-worth is crucial because it reminds us that our value isn't tied to someone else's approval or recognition. Just because one person doesn't see your potential doesn't mean it isn't there.

As Magic navigated the business world, he understood the importance of persistence. Every time he was rejected, he celebrated the attempt, knowing that each effort was a step forward, even if it didn't produce immediate results. When one opportunity didn't pan out, he set his sights on another. This approach kept him moving forward at a time when many might have given up. Magic's belief in his vision and his ability to adapt meant that rejection was never a dead-end—it was a detour leading him to something better. Rejection became a teacher for Magic Johnson. Every "no" taught him something new about the business world, about pitching ideas, and about navigating partnerships. Those lessons helped him refine his strategies and become a smarter, more resilient entrepreneur. Instead of viewing rejection as failure,

Magic saw it as feedback—an opportunity to grow and improve. The setbacks he faced didn't discourage him; they sharpened him. Over time, those lessons turned into the foundation of his billion-dollar enterprise.

Magic's ability to set new goals after each rejection was another key to his success. When one deal fell through, he didn't stop. He kept moving, setting his sights on new opportunities, and tweaking his approach where necessary. Whether he was launching new ventures in real estate, owning movie theaters, or investing in sports teams, Magic continually evolved, expanding his empire with every step. His journey shows us that rejection isn't the end of the road; it's just part of the process that moves us closer to where we're meant to be.

Magic Johnson's transition from NBA legend to business mogul is a testament to resilience. The countless rejections he faced weren't barriers to his success—they were the very things that guided him toward his ultimate achievements. He used those early "no's" to fuel his desire to succeed, knowing that each closed door was bringing him closer to the right one. In the end, Magic's story reminds us that rejection is often the best kind of protection. It guards us from opportunities that aren't meant for us, forcing us to find the ones that are. His story shows us that just because someone doesn't believe in our potential doesn't mean we should stop believing in ourselves. Every setback is a chance to reframe rejection, to use it as redirection, and to stay confident in our own worth.

So, the next time you face rejection, think of Magic Johnson. Remember how every "no" led him to something bigger and better. Use rejection as a stepping stone, a chance to learn, and a reminder that the right opportunity is still out there waiting for you. The doors that close today are simply clearing the way for greater successes tomorrow. Rejection isn't the end of the road—it's just the beginning of your redirection toward greatness. Magic Johnson's story doesn't just end with overcoming rejection—it's about thriving despite it, and using each setback as fuel to push forward. What's incredible about his journey is how he didn't allow any rejection to halt his momentum. Instead, he used rejection as the key to unlock new doors that would have otherwise remained closed.

After finding success with Starbucks, Magic continued to expand his empire. He built Magic Johnson Theaters, a chain of movie theaters located in urban areas, which offered the same kind of high-quality entertainment experience that other communities took for granted. These theaters not only thrived financially but also served as cultural hubs for communities that had often been overlooked by mainstream corporations. Here again, rejection had directed Magic toward a purpose-driven project. By embracing the communities that others had rejected or overlooked, Magic proved that there was tremendous value in spaces that others failed to see.

This pattern continued when he became part of the ownership group that purchased the Los Angeles Dodgers. Many people questioned whether he could successfully transition into sports ownership, but Magic once again proved the doubters wrong. The Dodgers thrived under the leadership of the new ownership group, and Magic's involvement brought renewed energy and excitement to the team and its fans. His vision and leadership extended beyond the basketball court, beyond the boardrooms, and into the realm of professional sports ownership—an arena where few former athletes had succeeded before.

Magic's resilience also showed through his ability to face personal rejection. In 1991, when Magic announced that he had contracted HIV, the world was stunned. At the time, there was widespread ignorance and fear surrounding HIV and AIDS, and many people rejected Magic—not just professionally, but personally. He was asked to leave the NBA, and for a while, it seemed like his career and legacy were in jeopardy. Instead of allowing that diagnosis to define him, Magic once again reframed the situation.

He used his platform to become a powerful advocate for HIV awareness, educating the public and fighting the stigma surrounding the disease. What could have been the most devastating rejection of his life—being rejected by the sport he loved, and by society's fear and misunderstanding—became yet another opportunity for Magic to turn adversity into action. He started the Magic Johnson Foundation, dedicated to HIV/AIDS education, prevention, and treatment, making a lasting impact on global health.

The lesson here is that rejection, no matter how personal or profound, can become the foundation for something far greater. When Magic Johnson faced the public's rejection after his HIV diagnosis, he didn't let it diminish his sense of purpose. He turned the world's "no" into an opportunity to uplift others, to educate, and to lead in an area where he could truly make a difference. In doing so, Magic demonstrated once again that rejection isn't a dead end—it's a chance to redirect your energy toward something meaningful. One of the most striking things about Magic Johnson's story is his unwavering confidence in his own worth. He never let the opinions or rejections of others define who he was or what he could achieve. Even when he faced setbacks, Magic remained focused on the long game, knowing that his value wasn't contingent on whether or not others recognized it right away. His story serves as a reminder that our worth isn't determined by how others see us—it's determined by how we see ourselves, by how we rise after each rejection, and by the way we continue to pursue our vision, no matter the obstacles.

Magic's story also highlights the importance of adaptability. Each time he faced rejection, he didn't give up on his dreams. Instead, he pivoted, found a new way forward, and often achieved even greater success than before. Whether it was in business, sports ownership, or public health, Magic always found a way to turn rejection into an opportunity for growth and contribution.

There's a powerful message in Magic's ability to turn rejection into a launching pad for even greater success: rejection is not an indication of failure—it's an opportunity for redirection. It's not a reflection of your worth; it's a call to find your true path. Magic's story teaches us that resilience is born from rejection, and that each setback has the potential to propel us toward something better, something bigger, and something more aligned with who we truly are.

As you face your own rejections, remember Magic Johnson's journey. Understand that the setbacks you encounter today are not the end of your story; they are the beginning of a new chapter. Use rejection as fuel, as motivation to keep moving forward. Know that each "no" is clearing the way for the right "yes" that is waiting for you. Magic Johnson's legacy is not just about his success on the basketball court or his accomplishments in business—it's about his unyielding ability to rise above rejection, to turn adversity into advantage, and to stay grounded in his belief that his worth was never defined by anyone else. His story shows us that we are capable of overcoming anything, as long as we remain true to ourselves, embrace the lessons rejection has to offer, and keep our eyes on the bigger picture. Rejection isn't the end of the road—it's just another turn, leading you toward something greater. So when the world says "no," keep going. There's always a "yes" waiting around the corner, and when you find it, you'll look back and realize that every rejection along the way was just part of the path to your ultimate success.

HOW REJECTION FUELED THE CREATION OF AIRBNB

In 2007, two broke designers in San Francisco named Brian Chesky and Joe Gebbia were struggling to pay their rent. Now, before I go any further, this case study is about how rejection fueled the creation of Airbnb. Airbnb has become one of the most effective, efficient ways to find a place to stay when hotels are fully booked, offering a solution that changed the hospitality industry forever. The magic of their story isn't just in the platform itself—it's in how rejection became the spark that led to their innovation. Rejection often breeds innovation. That's a fact. So, as you read this, imagine me speaking directly to you—telling you how obstacles, setbacks, and closed doors can lead to breakthroughs. Brian Chesky and Joe Gebbia's story is a testament to that truth.

Both designers, Chesky and Gebbia, were struggling to make ends meet. With the annual industrial design conference approaching and hotels in San Francisco being fully booked, they saw an opportunity that no one else did. Here's where the genius lies: successful businesses solve difficult problems—sometimes, they solve problems no one realized were even there. Hotels were packed with conference attendees, leaving no space for anyone else. That's when Chesky and Gebbia had the idea to rent out air mattresses in their apartment to people attending the conference, calling it "Air Bed and Breakfast." Bet you didn't know that, huh? Yeah, Airbnb stands for Air, Bed, and Breakfast.

What started as a makeshift solution to their financial struggles became the foundation for something revolutionary. They wondered, "What if we created a platform for people to rent out spare rooms or homes to travelers?" It was a genius idea, but like all ideas, turning it into reality wasn't smooth sailing. Along with a tech-savvy friend, Nathan Blecharczyk, they began to develop this concept into something real. However, the journey was rocky from the start. Rejection became their constant companion. Investors were skeptical. They couldn't imagine people staying in strangers' homes or homeowners opening their doors to random travelers. It sounded risky, weird, and destined to fail.

One particularly brutal rejection came from Fred Wilson, a well-known venture capitalist. He flat-out rejected their pitch, stating that investing in Airbnb was a mistake. That's right, he believed putting any money into this idea was a surefire way to lose out. And there it was again—rejection. Time and time again, investors turned them down, and the doubt started piling up, but instead of giving up, Chesky, Gebbia, and Nathan doubled down. They used rejection as fuel. Every "no" they heard only strengthened their determination to prove people wrong. That's a lesson right there for you and me: When faced with rejection, turn it into a challenge. Prove the doubters wrong. Show them what you're really made of, and do it in a way that goes beyond their wildest expectations. So, the trio set to work refining their platform. They didn't just sit around feeling sorry for themselves—they innovated. First, they created detailed user profiles for both hosts and guests, complete with verification and reviews. They built trust—one of the key components missing in the initial idea. This was a solution to the skepticism investors had about people staying with strangers.

They also designed a secure payment system, ensuring that both hosts and guests were protected. It wasn't just about making money—it was about building a system where everyone felt safe. They even went as far as offering free professional photography services to make listings look more appealing and trustworthy. Customer support? They built that too, creating a robust system to handle any issue that might arise. All of these innovations were born from the feedback and rejection they faced. Rejection became the driving force behind their creativity. The features that set Airbnb apart from traditional hotel accommodations were the result of overcoming objections and addressing the very concerns that had led to rejection in the first place.

Think about that for a second: what started as air mattresses on a living room floor evolved into a global brand with thousands of listings across the world, offering everything from cozy apartments to luxury villas … and it all began with rejection. The beauty of this story is that every obstacle became an opportunity. Where others saw problems, Chesky, Gebbia, and Nathan saw solutions. They didn't let the rejections stop them; instead, they listened to the concerns, made adjustments, and created a platform that solved the very issues people thought would doom the idea.

Today, Airbnb is a household name. It redefined how people travel, created new ways for individuals to earn income by renting out their homes, and even helped cities deal with the overflow of tourists when hotels were at capacity. It's a perfect example of how rejection can be the gateway to innovation, if you're willing to push through and use that rejection to your advantage. So, what's the lesson here? Rejection doesn't have to be a stop sign. It can be the fuel that drives you to create something even greater. It can force you to refine your vision, strengthen your resolve, and build something that's truly unique. When Chesky, Gebbia, and Nathan were rejected, they didn't give up. They didn't see rejection as a dead end, but as a necessary part of the journey to success. The next time you're faced with rejection, whether it's in your career, personal life, or creative endeavors, remember this story. Rejection is only the beginning. Let it push you, let it challenge you, and let it become the driving force behind your greatest innovations.

HOW THEY RAISED THE MONEY

Let's dive into one of the most unconventional methods Brian Chesky, Joe Gebbia, and Nathan Blecharczyk used to keep their dream alive in the face of continuous rejection from investors. In 2008, during a time when their business was struggling to gain traction, they came up with a quirky, creative fundraising idea: cereal boxes. Yes, that's right—Obama O's and Cap'n McCain's cereal. With the 2008 presidential election in full swing, they designed and sold limited-edition cereal boxes inspired by Barack Obama and John McCain. The creativity behind this wasn't just in the design of the boxes but also in the timing and concept. The election was a hot topic, and they tapped into that enthusiasm, using the popularity of the candidates to sell a unique product. It was a bold move that showed just how far they were willing to go to keep their dream alive.

Here's the kicker—they actually raised $30,000 selling these cereal boxes. Think about that for a second. At a time when investors were slamming doors in their faces, these three entrepreneurs found a way to bring in much-needed funds in one of the most unexpected ways possible. It wasn't just about making ends meet. It was about proving their resourcefulness and commitment to their idea, no matter how unorthodox the path. This cereal box hustle was a defining moment for them. It showed that they weren't just dreamers waiting for a miracle; they were willing to roll up their sleeves, think outside the box (literally!), and do whatever it took to keep their startup alive. They weren't afraid to put their pride aside and get creative when they needed it most. It's one thing to say you're committed to an idea, but it's another to take such bold steps to prove it.

The persistence and creativity paid off. In 2009, Airbnb got accepted into Y Combinator, a renowned startup accelerator program that has helped launch major companies like DoorDash and Fanbase. This was a game-changing moment for them. Y Combinator provided not only funding but also mentorship and support from some of the brightest minds in Silicon Valley. The validation they received from being accepted into such a prestigious program gave them the boost they needed to push forward. Once Airbnb entered Y Combinator, its growth skyrocketed. What had started as a small, scrappy team of designers and tech enthusiasts quickly became a global platform. Today, Airbnb operates in over 220 countries and regions and is valued in the billions. What's more, the company has revolutionized the travel industry, creating economic opportunities for homeowners while offering travelers a new, more personal lodging experience. It turned the hospitality industry on its head.

The story of Airbnb shows us something incredibly powerful—rejection can be a catalyst for innovation. Every time Chesky, Gebbia, and Blecharczyk were told "no," it forced them to go back to the drawing board, refine their concept, and push the limits of their creativity. That's a huge lesson for anyone who's been knocked down by rejection. It's not the end—it's just another opportunity to try again, better and stronger.

Think about it. If they had been accepted by investors right away, they might never have had the pressure that led to the creation of those core features like secure payment systems, professional photography, or customer support. Those features became what set Airbnb apart, and they only came about because of the challenges the founders faced. In retrospect, all those rejections weren't roadblocks at all—they were stepping stones. They gave the team the resilience they needed to innovate, prove their concept, and build something far beyond what they initially envisioned. Without those challenges, Airbnb might never have become the revolutionary platform it is today. The lesson here is powerful: Rejection doesn't have to be the end of a dream. It can be the beginning of something even better than you originally planned. It's about how you respond, how you adapt, and how you innovate. Just like Chesky, Gebbia, and Blecharczyk, when faced with rejection, the question is: will you let it stop you, or will you let it propel you forward?

The story of Airbnb continues to serve as a powerful example of how resilience and creativity in the face of rejection can fuel success far beyond what was initially imagined. After they raised $30,000 from selling cereal boxes and were accepted into the Y Combinator startup accelerator, Airbnb's journey truly began to take off. However, their success didn't come overnight. Even after gaining some initial traction, the founders still faced significant challenges that tested their resolve and required them to dig even deeper into their well of persistence.

After being accepted into Y Combinator, they finally had the mentorship and funding to help bring their vision to life. Yet, despite this newfound support, the public was still hesitant. People were skeptical of staying in strangers' homes, and the trust issues that initially scared investors were still very much alive in the minds of potential customers, but this didn't stop Chesky, Gebbia, and Blecharczyk. If anything, the continued resistance made them push harder.

One of the most important things they did next was focus on building trust within their platform. They understood that without trust, Airbnb would never take off. This is where they truly showed their ability to turn rejection into innovation. From verified user profiles to reviews, secure payment systems, and professional photography for listings, the team addressed every concern people had. By facing the challenges head-on and adapting to meet their audience's needs, they built a system that made people feel comfortable inviting strangers into their homes and staying in unfamiliar places. This is another key lesson we can learn from Airbnb's journey: rejection forces you to evolve. If their concept had been accepted easily from the beginning, they might not have had to create these crucial features that ultimately made the platform what it is today. The skepticism they faced pushed them to go beyond a simple marketplace for spare rooms. It forced them to build a platform where trust, security, and reliability were at the forefront of the experience.

By 2010, Airbnb began to pick up steam. Hosts were making extra income, travelers were finding affordable and unique places to stay, and the platform was gaining attention. However, they still faced hurdles in terms of gaining widespread adoption. Many people still preferred the safety and familiarity of hotels, and cities began pushing back, raising concerns about regulation and the impact on local housing markets.

This is where resilience came into play once again. Instead of folding under pressure, the founders adapted. They worked with local governments to establish regulations that allowed them to operate legally while addressing the concerns of the communities they were operating in. They didn't shy away from the obstacles; they found ways to overcome them. And slowly but surely, Airbnb grew from being just a quirky alternative to hotels into a mainstream option that travelers around the world could rely on. Looking back, it's easy to see how the rejection and challenges Airbnb faced were essential to its eventual success. If Chesky, Gebbia, and Blecharczyk had given up after the first few investors turned them down or after their initial launch didn't take off, the platform wouldn't exist today. Instead of letting rejection defeat them, they used it to fuel their creativity and refine their vision. They turned every "no" into an opportunity to make their product better and stronger.

The cereal boxes, the initial skepticism, the struggles with trust and regulation—each one of those challenges was a stepping stone toward the global success Airbnb eventually achieved. Today, Airbnb operates in over 220 countries and regions, is valued in the billions, and has transformed how people think about travel and accommodation. The platform has created economic opportunities for millions of hosts, allowing them to generate income from their homes, while also offering travelers a more personal and often more affordable option than traditional hotels. The most significant takeaway from Airbnb's story isn't just about their eventual success—it's about how they got there. Rejection wasn't the end of the road for them; it was the beginning of a journey that required persistence, adaptation, and innovation. Every challenge they faced pushed them to think differently, to evolve their product, and to create something far greater than what they initially envisioned.

This case study reminds us that rejection isn't a barrier; it's an opportunity. When faced with obstacles, it's easy to feel discouraged, but if you keep pushing, keep innovating, and stay committed to your vision, those rejections can lead you to places you never thought possible. Chesky, Gebbia, and Blecharczyk's ability to pivot in the face of adversity, to get creative when the chips were down, and to believe in their idea even when others didn't, is what ultimately made Airbnb the giant it is today. In a world where we're often quick to view rejection as failure, Airbnb stands as a powerful reminder that rejection can be the fuel that drives us toward innovation and success. Each "no" isn't the end—it's just the beginning of a new chapter. The true mark of an entrepreneur, or anyone pursuing their dream, is how they respond when things don't go as planned. Will you give up? Or will you dig deeper, find new ways to solve the problems, and keep pushing forward? So, whether you're facing rejection in business, your career, or personal life, take a page from Airbnb's story. Use rejection as a stepping stone. See it as an opportunity to grow, to learn, and to come back even stronger. In the end, rejection might just be the very thing that sets you up for the success you've been dreaming of. As you move forward, remember that rejection is a part of the journey—not the end of it. Every successful entrepreneur, artist, or visionary has faced it, and what sets them apart is their ability to persevere, to see rejection as a moment of redirection, not failure. Each "no" is an invitation to sharpen your strategy, to dig deeper into your creative reserves, and to keep your eyes on the horizon of what's possible. Airbnb's story reminds us that success is often hidden behind multiple layers of challenges. It's not about how many times you get knocked down, but how many times you get back up with a renewed spirit and fresh perspective. Let rejection be your teacher, your motivator, and your catalyst for growth.

In the end, the road to success is not a straight line. It's winding, full of unexpected turns, and sometimes, dead-ends. But if you stay resilient, open to learning, and committed to your vision, you'll find that the very rejections you once feared were the building blocks of your greatest triumphs. Keep pushing, keep dreaming, and remember—sometimes, the "no's" are simply clearing the way for an even bigger "yes" that's waiting just around the corner.

CHAPTER 10

REST BEHIND CLOSED DOORS

Rest is one of the most overlooked components of success, but without it, even the most ambitious goals and dreams can feel impossible to reach. In this chapter, I want to dive deep into the true meaning of rest, especially the kind that takes place behind closed doors—the rest that no one sees but that fuels everything you do. It's the kind of rest that allows you to recalibrate your life, go to the next level, and most importantly, avoid burning out. Think about it. How many times have you found yourself chasing deadlines, chasing money, chasing goals, and constantly running from one task to another? It's easy to get caught up in that cycle, but that's exactly what turns life into a never-ending rat race. And trust me, you don't want that. What you want is something fulfilling—something that aligns with your purpose and talents. You want something that not only makes you feel accomplished but also refreshed.

Here's the truth: your talents and gifts should make room for you, but they can't carry you if you're running on empty. Just because your talent opens doors and keeps you moving forward doesn't mean you should ignore the importance of rest. Rest isn't just about sleeping, either. Sleep can be a quick fix, but real rest is about rejuvenation. It's about hitting the reset button on your mind, body, and spirit so you can show up with fresh energy and focus for the next challenge. I hear it all the time from clients who feel overwhelmed. They say, "I don't have time to rest because I'm juggling so much—work, bills, family." And while sacrifices are necessary at times for growth and success, nothing should come between you and your need for true rest. When you consistently sacrifice your rest, you sacrifice your ability to think clearly, to be creative, and to make sound decisions. It's one of the reasons people burn out, even while pursuing something they love.

> *"Here's the truth: your talents and gifts should make room for you, but they can't carry you if you're running on empty."*

Rest isn't a luxury—it's a necessity. It's part of the process that sustains you in the long run. It's how you maintain a balanced and fulfilling life. You can't pour from an empty cup, and you can't keep sprinting without ever slowing down to catch your breath. We all have moments where we push ourselves harder than we should, but the key is to never let that become a permanent way of life. Take a moment to ask yourself, when was the last time you truly rested? Not just slept for a few hours, but really gave yourself time to recharge, to step back, and to breathe deeply? Rest is what allows you to move from one season to the next with the strength and clarity you need. Without it, you're just going through the motions—grinding day in and day out without ever really enjoying the journey.

Make rest a priority. Honor the times when your body, mind, and spirit tell you they need a break. The world might constantly push the idea that hustle is everything, but the real joy happens when you find balance between working hard and knowing when to rest. So yes, go after your dreams, hustle, and grind, but always give yourself the space to rest, because in that rest, you find clarity, creativity, and the energy to keep moving forward with purpose.

Rest means something entirely different to me now. In my mid-40s, I'm in bed by 10 p.m. like clockwork, and I love it, but it wasn't always this way. When I was younger, I'd stay up all night, caught up in the party life, especially during 2006 and 2007. Back then, rest wasn't a priority, but now, I understand something I didn't then: real rest recalibrates you. You can sleep all night and still wake up feeling drained if you haven't experienced true rest. So, what is rest? It's more than just sleep. It's stepping away from the constant demands of life to restore your body, mind, and spirit. It involves both active practices like sleeping and passive ones like reflecting, sitting in silence, and yes—praying. I mention prayer because it has transformed my rest, taking it to another level. Rest isn't laziness, despite what many people think. It's vital. It even contributes to weight loss when you don't eat after 7 or 8 p.m.—your body burns fat as it rests!

Rest is essential for living a purposeful life. Without it, we become drained, stressed, and overwhelmed. The truth is, your body needs rest to function at its best. When your body is restored, it performs at its highest capacity. This means better health, improved productivity, and greater resilience to stress. Rest also clears mental fog. It gives your brain the space to rejuvenate, improving your focus, creativity, and even your ability to solve problems. Beyond that, rest brings emotional balance. It helps us release emotional burdens and regain perspective. There are different types of rest—physical, mental, emotional, and spiritual—and each one is necessary for a complete restoration of self.

Here's where I want to dive deeper—the kind of rest behind closed doors that leads to the breakthrough season you've been waiting for. If you rest at the right time, go to bed at a decent hour, and wake up refreshed, you'll notice how you start crushing your tasks. Deadlines? No problem. Productivity goes up; and all of it comes from simply prioritizing your seven to eight hours of rest. You need to establish a bedtime routine that signals to your body, "It's time to rest." This intentionality ensures you reap the benefits, but it's not just physical rest that matters. Mental rest is critical, too. Life's demands are relentless—work, traffic, deadlines—it can all pile up. That's why it's essential to take mental breaks throughout the day. Step outside, stretch, breathe deeply, and remind yourself, "I've got this."

Then there's emotional rest, which is the freedom to be authentic and let go of emotional weight. We've all been emotionally drained at some point. You have to recognize when you've hit that point and need to refuel. Scheduling alone time or journaling your thoughts can provide the emotional rest you need to continue showing up fully. So, as I unpack these levels of rest in this chapter, I hope you'll see that rest isn't just a luxury—it's a powerful tool for living a thriving, purpose-driven life. Rest is more than just hitting pause; it's about refueling for the journey ahead. When we prioritize it, we're investing in our future strength, clarity, and purpose. You see, the world often celebrates the hustle, the grind, the constant go, go, go—but what we fail to realize is that without rest, the grind eventually grinds us down. That's why the deeper levels of rest—physical, mental, emotional, and spiritual—are not just options, they are necessities.

Physical rest is the foundation. Your body is a temple, and like any temple, it needs maintenance and care. Sleep repairs the damage of the day and prepares you for what's next. Beyond sleep, physical rest allows your muscles to recover, your heart rate to slow, and your entire body to reset. Without it, we might find ourselves burning out long before we're able to fulfill the purpose set before us. Mental rest, on the other hand, is about stepping away from the noise of life. In this world of constant stimulation—emails, notifications, social media, demands—our brains are often on overload. True mental rest means unplugging. It's allowing space for clarity, creativity, and focus to rise up. It's in this mental quiet that some of our greatest ideas and revelations happen. The mind is like a field—it needs moments to lie fallow in order to grow fruitful again.

Emotional rest comes when we allow ourselves the freedom to feel without the pressure of pretending. We all carry emotional burdens, whether it's unresolved conflicts, unexpressed feelings, or unspoken stress. Emotional rest is the moment we stop holding it all together and let go of the weight. It's not a sign of weakness; it's a necessary release that brings balance and peace. Journaling, counseling, or even a deep conversation with a trusted friend can be part of this emotional reset.

Then there's spiritual rest, which I believe is the most powerful of all. Spiritual rest isn't just about taking time off; it's about reconnecting with the One who gives you strength. It's in prayer, in moments of reflection, where we tap into the divine peace that surpasses all understanding. When you're spiritually rested, you're not just rejuvenated—you're aligned. You're centered in God's purpose for your life, and that alignment fuels everything else.

However, what I really want you to grasp is this: rest isn't just something we do passively. We can actively create the conditions for rest. Just like you prepare for a big day, you need to prepare for rest. Establish a routine that primes your mind and body for sleep. Maybe it's dimming the lights, playing some soothing music, or reading a book. Maybe it's ending the day with a moment of prayer or reflection, thanking God for His provision and laying tomorrow's concerns at His feet.

The comeback season happens in the quiet spaces behind closed doors, where rest allows us to rise stronger. When you've taken time to restore, you find yourself more capable of handling stress, more equipped to take on challenges, and more attuned to opportunities. You start to see your productivity soar, not because you're working harder, but because you're working smarter, from a place of fullness instead of depletion.

Rest is the secret weapon in a world that glorifies busyness, and if you learn to rest well, you'll start to see how much more you can achieve. Rest is preparation for greatness, and when you honor it, you set yourself up for a season of victory. So, as I go deeper into this chapter, remember: the real power of rest isn't just in stepping away from life's demands—it's in coming back stronger, more focused, and ready to fulfill your God-given purpose.

REST WITH READING A BOOK

Over the years, I've come to realize that the act of reading a book behind closed doors is more than just a break from the world—it's a sacred moment of rest. In that solitude, you're not just finding time for yourself, you're creating a space where your mind can truly breathe. Imagine this: when you hold a book in your hands, it's not just paper and ink. It's a key—a key to countless worlds, limitless possibilities, and uncharted realms of imagination. Especially when the subject resonates deeply with your heart, soul, and mind. When you open a book in the quiet of your own space, you aren't merely flipping through pages. How often do we skim words, rushing through, without letting the meaning sink in? True rest comes when you allow yourself to fully engage with each sentence, to unlock the doors each chapter holds. In that moment, you're not just reading; you're stepping into portals of fascination and wonder. One second you're in your room, the next, you're walking the cobblestone streets of London, or perhaps you're piloting a spaceship across galaxies, your imagination painting the scene with every word.

Reading, at its best, is not an escape. It's an adventure for the mind—a journey for the soul. And in a world that constantly demands our attention, bombarding us with notifications, reading offers something invaluable: time. Time that costs you nothing but focus. That's why I've come to cherish the tangible experience of reading a physical book. The weight of it in your hands, the sound of each page turning, the sight of chapters waiting to be explored—it brings you fully into the moment. Even the simple act of placing a nightlight beside you creates a space for reflection, a place where the outside world falls away. Make no mistake: opening a book isn't just about the act of reading, or a purchase made with a click. It's about running toward something greater. Every page you turn strengthens your mind, expands your vocabulary, and challenges your perspective. Like a muscle, your imagination grows stronger with every mental rep. Reading, after all, is the gym of the mind, where your intellect and creativity get stronger with every story you consume. As you immerse yourself in new worlds and ideas, you're not just absorbing words; you're cultivating empathy by stepping into the lives of characters, gaining insights from all walks of life. You're fueling creativity, allowing your mind to transform words into vivid imagery. In the process, you unlock a treasure trove of knowledge, personal growth, and endless possibilities.

So here's my challenge to you: find that time behind closed doors to read with purpose. Choose a book that sparks your interest, and let it unlock new depths of thought and imagination. It's in these moments of rest that you may just uncover the keys to unlocking your own purpose, and as you embrace this quiet, transformative practice, you'll begin to see that reading is more than just a personal retreat; it's an invitation to discovery. Each chapter you immerse yourself in, each sentence you ponder, is shaping the contours of your mind. You're expanding not only your knowledge but also your capacity for critical thinking, creativity, and emotional intelligence.

Think of it this way: the world often pushes us into fast-paced, reactionary living, where everything is consumed in snippets—quick social media posts, rapid news flashes, endless notifications. In contrast, the time you spend with a book is a rebellion against that pace. It's a deliberate act of slowing down, of digging deeper, of savoring ideas that require more than a passing glance. In a world that's constantly demanding we move faster, reading invites you to slow down and truly engage.

There's something profound about choosing a book that speaks to you, that resonates with where you are or where you want to go. It's not just about the information on the pages—it's about the conversation you have with the text, the internal dialogue that shapes your own thoughts and beliefs. Reading becomes a mirror, reflecting parts of you that you didn't even know existed, illuminating pathways of growth and understanding that you hadn't considered before. This act of reading behind closed doors is a way of reclaiming your attention, of saying, "This is my time to invest in myself, in my ideas, in my own internal world," and that investment pays dividends. You'll find that as you read more, you start to think differently. You approach problems with more creativity, and your conversations take on a new depth because you've exposed yourself to new perspectives, new voices, new ways of seeing the world.

The beauty of this process is that it's entirely accessible. You don't need to travel across the world or spend exorbitant amounts of money. The only requirement is your time and willingness to explore. A book can take you anywhere, can introduce you to anyone, can help you understand anything. It's a portal, a teacher, a friend, a challenge—all in one. As you turn the final page of one book, don't see it as an ending. See it as the beginning of something new—a new journey, a new perspective, a new challenge for your mind to wrestle with. Let the insights you gain carry forward into your daily life, shaping how you see the world and your place within it. So, take that time. Close the door, shut out the distractions, and open yourself to the worlds waiting within the pages. You'll find that in doing so, you're not just reading—you're growing, expanding, becoming the person you were meant to be—and in that sacred space of rest, behind those closed doors, you might just discover that the most profound journeys are the ones you take within yourself.

KEY BENEFITS OF REST

1. ENHANCED COGNITIVE FUNCTION

The first benefit of rest is known as enhanced cognitive function, and I'm a living witness to this truth. After taking time to rest, I've noticed a remarkable increase in my attention span, memory, and problem-solving abilities. That's the beauty of cognitive restoration: it sharpens your creative thinking, improves mental flexibility, and enhances your ability to process information. But how exactly does rest improve cognitive function? Let's break it down. One of the most significant ways rest benefits the brain is through memory consolidation. For example, during sleep, your brain actively works to transfer information from short-term to long-term memory. This is crucial for learning and retaining new knowledge. So, when you rest, you're not just refreshing your body; you're solidifying the lessons and experiences you've gained.

Next, rest plays a major role in neural repair and growth. It actively contributes to the health and development of neurons—the very building blocks of the brain. This growth is a process known as neuroplasticity, and it's essential for learning and adapting. When we rest, the connections between neurons strengthen, allowing us to better adapt to new information, challenges, and environments. Another fascinating aspect of cognitive rest is toxin clearance. Many people are unaware that rest is essential for clearing toxins from the brain. During sleep, your brain clears out metabolic waste products, which helps maintain optimal neural function. It's like a cleansing process for your brain, ensuring everything functions smoothly and efficiently.

Then there's attention restoration. After adequate rest, particularly in natural environments, our ability to focus and concentrate improves significantly. Rest reduces stress hormones like cortisol and activates the body's parasympathetic nervous system, leading to lowered stress levels and improved function in the prefrontal cortex—the part of the brain responsible for complex decision-making and focus. Moreover, rest increases creativity and enhances emotional regulation. When you're well-rested, you're not only able to think more clearly but also manage your emotions better, which is critical in high-pressure situations.

Let me share a case study that illustrates how these components of rest work together in the life of a woman named Sarah Thompson. Sarah, 32, was a marketing executive in New York City. She prided herself on her relentless work ethic. Hustling became her mantra—she believed that working 70 hours a week and surviving on five hours of sleep would lead to success. She wore her exhaustion like a badge of honor and lived by the motto, "I'll sleep when I'm dead." Little did she realize that her lifestyle was slowly driving her toward that very outcome.

In March of 2022, Sarah hit her breaking point. During a critical client presentation, she suddenly felt lightheaded. Her vision blurred, and she collapsed right in front of her colleagues. Rushed to the hospital, doctors diagnosed her with severe burnout, chronic sleep deprivation, and dangerously elevated cortisol levels—a testament to the toll that a lack of rest had taken on her body and mind. Sarah's story is a stark reminder of how crucial rest is to our cognitive and emotional well-being. The very thing she avoided—rest—was the key to sustaining her productivity, creativity, and long-term success.

The lesson here is clear: Rest is not a luxury, it's a necessity. It's the foundation for enhanced cognitive function, emotional regulation, and overall health. Without it, we may find ourselves, like Sarah, on the brink of collapse. With proper rest, we can unlock our full potential, maintain our well-being, and live lives marked by clarity, creativity, and resilience.

Sarah's journey of recovery wasn't just a pause in her relentless pursuit of success; it was a radical shift in her entire way of living. After her collapse, her doctor, Dr. Emily Chen, recognized the severity of her burnout and devised a strict three-month rest restoration plan. It was a regimen designed, not only to heal Sarah's body, but to rewire her relationship with rest.

The plan was simple but powerful: Sarah was put on a strict eight-hour sleep schedule, with daily natural walks to reconnect her with the rhythm of nature. She had to undergo a complete digital detox, stepping away from the constant bombardment of social media. On top of that, she was introduced to cognitive behavioral therapy (CBT) for insomnia, which helped her break the cycle of sleepless nights. A carefully crafted nutrition plan focused on foods that promoted rest and recovery. Initially, Sarah was resistant, skeptical of whether these changes would truly make a difference. But deep down, she knew this intervention was exactly what she needed.

The first month was difficult. Sarah struggled with the idea of "wasting time" when she rested, her mind racing with thoughts of undone tasks and missed opportunities, but by the third week, something shifted. One morning, after a full, uninterrupted night's sleep, she woke up with clarity and solved a marketing problem that had blocked her progress for weeks. It was her first breakthrough, and it validated everything Dr. Chen had promised.

By the second month, Sarah was seeing even more profound changes. Her skin began to clear up, and her colleagues started noticing a distinct glow about her. She hadn't changed her diet significantly, yet she dropped 10 pounds—simply from resting and reducing stress. Her relationships improved, too. With her irritability gone, she found herself more present with her partner, and for the first time in years, she picked up a paintbrush, rediscovering her love for art. She felt calm, focused, and articulate—qualities that had been missing in her frenetic, sleep-deprived state.

By the time month three rolled around, Sarah had reached a new normal. She was working fewer hours, yet her productivity had skyrocketed. Her body was thriving—she hadn't caught a cold in months, an impressive feat considering her previously compromised immune system. Chronic back pain, which had plagued her for years, had almost completely vanished. She was overflowing with innovative ideas, feeling sharper and more creative than she had in years.

What Sarah experienced wasn't just a temporary recovery; it was the profound, long-term transformation that comes from prioritizing rest. Her story underscores a simple truth: When you embrace rest as part of your daily work life, the benefits are undeniable. Enhanced cognitive function, stress reduction, hormonal balance, and emotional regulation are just the beginning. Over time, you'll notice improved immune function and cardiovascular health, leading to a more resilient body and mind.

What Sarah learned—and what we can all learn—is that rest isn't a luxury. It's a necessity. It's not something to be earned after the work is done; it's the foundation that allows you to do your best work. The long-term impacts of rest compound over time, making you more effective, healthier, and happier. This isn't just about getting through the day. It's about thriving in the long term, building a life that's balanced, fulfilling, and sustainable.

2. STRESS REDUCTION

Stress reduction is incredibly important, and I've learned that firsthand. There was a time when I would go to bed at 9 p.m., but consistently find myself waking up at 2 or 3 a.m. These interruptions weren't just minor annoyances—they were tied to high blood pressure issues I was experiencing at the time. The strain that the high blood pressure put on my body had a direct impact on my sleep patterns, constantly waking me up throughout the night. It became clear to me that stress, even when it manifests physically, can have a profound effect on our ability to rest and recover. Stress reduction is, at its core, about decreasing psychological tension. It involves lowering the levels of stress hormones like cortisol, activating the parasympathetic nervous system—which is responsible for rest and digestion—and ultimately reducing mental strain. This process leads to an improvement in overall well-being, both physically and mentally.

The key components of stress reduction can be broken into several parts:

- **Psychological calming:** This is about finding ways to mentally unwind. Techniques like mindfulness, meditation, and deep breathing exercises are commonly used to calm the mind.

- **Behavioral changes:** These can include adjustments in daily routines, like incorporating more physical activity, improving sleep hygiene, or even cutting back on stimulants like caffeine that can exacerbate stress.

- **Social improvements:** Strengthening social connections and seeking support from friends, family, or a counselor can be crucial for managing stress. Sometimes, just having a network of people who listen can reduce the psychological burden we carry.

Now, let's look at the case study of Marcus Chin, which is an intriguing example of how stress reduction can impact someone's life. Marcus had always been a high performer, juggling multiple responsibilities in his career. At first, he prided himself on his ability to handle stress, often thinking that stress was what fueled his success. However, like many of us, Marcus reached a point where his stress levels began to catch up with him. He started to experience chronic headaches, poor sleep, and bouts of irritability that he couldn't shake. His productivity at work suffered, and so did his personal relationships. His body was sending clear signals that something needed to change.

Marcus, like many high achievers, initially ignored the signs his body was giving him. He assumed that pushing through the stress and relying on his usual routine of long hours and minimal rest would keep him on top. Instead, the headaches worsened, his sleep patterns became more erratic, and even his performance at work started to decline. It wasn't just that he was more irritable—his creativity and problem-solving abilities also took a hit. Eventually, Marcus sought help from a stress management specialist, much like Sarah did in her recovery journey. His doctor identified chronic stress as the root cause of many of his issues, including his headaches, sleep disturbances, and mood swings. The proposed intervention for Marcus involved a multi-faceted approach to reduce his stress levels and restore balance to his life.

The first step was creating a structured routine for relaxation and sleep. Marcus was encouraged to establish a bedtime ritual that allowed him to wind down properly before bed—this included turning off all screens an hour before sleep, engaging in calming activities like reading or listening to soft music, and practicing deep-breathing techniques to help activate his parasympathetic nervous system. Alongside the sleep routine, Marcus was introduced to regular mindfulness practices. At first, he was skeptical. The idea of sitting quietly and focusing on his breath seemed counterproductive to his fast-paced, action-oriented mindset; though, as with any new practice, Marcus gradually came to appreciate the mental clarity that mindfulness provided. It gave him a way to detach from the constant stream of work stress and anxieties that had been occupying his mind.

Within a month of making these changes, Marcus started to see results. His headaches began to subside, his mood improved, and his sleep became more consistent. Most notably, his focus and creativity at work rebounded. The very stress he had once believed was driving his success had, in reality, been hindering it. As his stress levels decreased, his productivity soared.

However, it wasn't just his professional life that benefited—Marcus's relationships also improved. He was less irritable and more present with his friends and family. The social connections he had been neglecting for the sake of work were rekindled, and he found new emotional support in the people around him. His overall well-being transformed as he learned to manage stress, rather than be controlled by it.

The case of Marcus demonstrates how vital stress reduction is to, not only our mental and emotional health, but to our physical health and productivity as well. When we allow stress to go unchecked, it affects every area of our lives, often in ways we don't immediately recognize. However, once we take steps to reduce stress—whether through mindfulness, relaxation routines, or social support—the benefits ripple outward. We regain our focus, creativity, and emotional balance. Our physical health improves, and we find ourselves more capable of handling life's demands with calm and resilience.

So, what can we learn from Marcus's experience? Stress reduction is essential to maintaining our cognitive and emotional well-being. By incorporating simple practices like better sleep hygiene, mindfulness, and social support into our lives, we can prevent the long-term damage that chronic stress can cause. When we actively reduce stress, we restore our energy, creativity, and overall health, enabling us to live more balanced and fulfilling lives.

3. DIGITAL DETOX

Let's talk about digital detox and how social media can consume so much of our time that it interferes with the rest we need. The truth is, the smartphone in your hand can be like the elephant in the room, subtly messing with your life. We live in an age of constant connectivity, where everyone feeds off the ability to reach anyone, anywhere, with just a tap. We carry it in our pockets, our data flows through it, and we even send humans to the moon with the technology in our devices. There's no denying that phones and computers are central to our daily lives. Social media promised to bring us closer together, but let's be honest—how many of us have found ourselves endlessly scrolling through feeds, comparing our everyday lives to someone else's highlight reel? How many of us have felt anxiety rise while reading posts, especially about tragedies, crimes, or the death of a celebrity we admired? And what about the random notification pop-ups that draw us in without warning? How often have we lost sleep, or even days, consumed by a single post?

When left unchecked, social media becomes a thief. It steals your time, your focus, your self-esteem, and even your sense of reality. It can make you feel like you're always missing out, triggering the fear of missing out (FOMO). It can also convince you that your life is lacking, that you're not measuring up to the curated perfection of others. Worse, it can drive a wedge between you and the people sitting right beside you. Here's the truth—life isn't meant to be lived through a six-inch screen. Your worth isn't defined by likes and followers. It's rooted in the purpose, the plan, and the design that God has given you. That's the real truth.

Reflect on the moments social media has stolen from you. Think about how you can reclaim that time and replace it with something meaningful—something that aligns with your values. It's not about rejecting technology altogether. It's about taking back control of your attention, your focus, and your life. It's about experiencing the joy of being fully present, undistracted by the noise of notifications and headlines. Imagine waking up without reaching for your phone. Picture yourself having a conversation without feeling the pull to check for updates. Think about completing tasks without the constant interruption of alerts. As we continue this chapter, consider how a digital detox could benefit you. Sometimes, we need to unplug to reconnect with the things that truly matter in life.

FOMO (FEAR OF MISSING OUT)

When I first came across the phrase FOMO, the fear of missing out, I immediately recognized how much of my life had been shaped by that very feeling. It's the fear of not being part of the moments you wish you could be, whether that's spending time with friends, being there for family gatherings, or just enjoying life's experiences as they unfold. FOMO can create a sense of urgency, making you feel that if you don't act at the right time, and in the right way, you'll miss out on something crucial, potentially leaving you unfulfilled.

What I've realized is that FOMO operates on so many different layers. Personally, when it came to my own journey with digital detox, FOMO was a huge part of what kept me tethered to my phone. I would think, "Let me just check real quick and see what my friends are up to." What started as a quick glance turned into an endless scroll—scrolling and scrolling—and before I knew it, two hours had slipped away. I hadn't accomplished anything, except feeding my worry about what others were doing while I wasn't.

Seeing friends at the beach, traveling, or on exciting newlywed vacations triggered that sense of longing. It wasn't as if I hadn't experienced those moments myself, but when time passes—especially after a busy year—you start thinking, "It's time to switch things up." Maybe this year we'll go on a cruise to the Bahamas or have a spontaneous weekend getaway. Yet, time has a way of slipping through your fingers, especially when you or your spouse have demanding jobs that make it hard to plan those moments of escape.

FOMO creates this relentless pressure, as if you're always rushing to catch up with the next big thing. It can make you feel like you need to constantly be in motion, constantly seeking out the next experience so you don't fall behind. What I've learned is that life doesn't have to be a race to keep up with others. It's about finding contentment in your own journey, recognizing that those experiences will come when they're meant to, and they don't lose their value just because they aren't happening on someone else's timeline. FOMO will always be there, lurking in the background, trying to make you feel like you're missing something, but the real challenge—and the real freedom—comes when you realize that you don't have to keep up with anyone else's story. Your journey is yours, and when you let go of the fear of missing out, you open yourself up to be fully present in the life you're living right now.

FOMO can be deceptive—it makes you feel like you're falling behind in life, missing out on crucial experiences others are constantly sharing on social media. It thrives on comparison, feeding that part of you that wonders, "Am I doing enough? Am I living fully?" That kind of thinking doesn't lead to joy. Instead, it leads to a cycle of dissatisfaction, always chasing the next moment instead of appreciating the ones right in front of you. As I continued my digital detox journey, I realized FOMO went deeper than vacations or the fun things my friends were doing. It made me feel like I was missing life's milestones—whether it was a friend starting a new business, someone else achieving a personal goal, or watching how fast others seemed to be moving through life compared to my own pace. That constant need to check in and see what everyone else was doing drained me, keeping me from being fully present in my own life.

The most eye-opening part of this process was recognizing how much time I was losing. Not just the hours spent scrolling through social media but how my mental energy was being siphoned away by comparison. Instead of planning things that actually mattered to me, I found myself stuck in a loop of watching other people live their lives—but life doesn't pause for you to catch up. While you're worrying about what you're missing, time is still ticking away. This led me to a simple but profound truth: I don't have to chase every moment. I don't have to measure my life by someone else's experiences. FOMO creates a false sense of urgency, a belief that if you're not doing everything right now, you're somehow behind. But life isn't a series of missed opportunities—it's a collection of moments, each valuable in its own way, even the quiet ones.

I started asking myself, "What am I truly missing out on?" It wasn't vacations or glamorous social media posts. What I was missing were the small, meaningful moments in my own life—time spent talking with my spouse, the satisfaction of completing a project, or the joy of unwinding without distraction. These moments bring fulfillment, not the constant pursuit of what others are doing.

As I embraced this new mindset, I let go of the fear of missing out. I started prioritizing what mattered most to me, focusing on my goals, my relationships, and my well-being. In doing so, FOMO began to lose its grip. The need to constantly check my phone and compare my life to others faded. I became more grounded in the present, appreciating the life I was building rather than longing for the life I thought I should have.

What I learned was this: FOMO is a thief of peace. It takes away the joy of being present by making you believe you need to be somewhere else, doing something else, to be happy; but true fulfillment comes when you stop chasing every experience and start embracing your own path. When you focus on your journey, you'll find that you're not missing out at all—you're exactly where you need to be.

MY JOURNEY WITH CHRONIC FATIGUE

I used to pride myself on being a high achiever. I'd always say, "I'll sleep later, I'm good. I'll just work through it." Sixty-hour workweeks were my norm, especially in the fishing industry. I made social commitments on top of that and kept up with my rigorous workouts and routines. I worked a demanding job in Alaska, and that relentless pace was throwing my life out of balance. I truly believed I was invincible, fueled by my own ambition, but the truth was, I was coping with caffeine just to keep myself going. Energy drinks became my go-to, something I relied on to keep up the pace. Little did I know, that lifestyle was sending me on a collision course with my health. My blood pressure began to spike. I developed hypertension, and in the course of five years, I nearly had a stroke—twice—due to the toll all that caffeine was taking on my body.

It started subtly. At first, I felt heaviness in my limbs. That turned into tension in my knees, and brain fog began to cloud my thinking. I couldn't sleep properly, and I blamed myself for not being able to keep up. In truth, what I was really dealing with was chronic fatigue, and I didn't fully understand how dangerous it was until one day, my body refused to move. The day I couldn't get out of bed was the day my world shifted. I had always been the first one to show up to work, ready to go as soon as my alarm went off, but that morning, my body finally said, "Stop!" I'd been running a race I couldn't win, covering my exhaustion with a smile and hiding behind my emotions. I'd call in sick, rest for a day, and then push myself back into the grind—only to repeat the cycle. Over time, one day turned into a week, a week into a month, and I found myself making more frequent trips to the doctor.

The doctors ran blood tests, trying to figure out what was going on. My blood pressure was so high that I remember thinking, I should have been dead a long time ago. Blood fatigue is dangerous. It can destroy your body if you don't take care of yourself. My therapist told me something that stuck with me: Your body is screaming at you. It's time to start listening. Those words marked the beginning of my healing journey. I had to learn to rest—from scratch. It might sound ridiculous, but it was true. I had to re-learn something as basic as rest. Who would've thought a grown man would need to learn how to do that? I used to glorify being busy. I was obsessed with productivity, and I took pride in my skills; but I didn't know how to rest. So, I started small. I would take five minutes just to be still, read something, and let myself slow down. Gradually, those moments began to add up. I realized that I could think through my pain instead of getting lost in it.

Recovery wasn't easy. It wasn't a straight path. Some days, fatigue would crash over me like a wave, leaving me gasping for air, but this time, I had the tools I needed. I knew how to listen to my body, how to honor what I needed. Today, my life is vastly different. I still have goals and ambitions, but they no longer come at the cost of my well-being. Chronic fatigue taught me a lesson I'll never forget—rest is not a luxury—it's a necessity. True strength doesn't come from pushing through exhaustion; it comes from knowing when to pause and recharge. If this sounds like your story, I urge you, not to wait for your body to force you to rest. Learn from these mistakes. Embrace rest as a vital part of your life. Your body, your mind, your soul, and your future will thank you for it.

Looking back, I realize that my pursuit of productivity at all costs came from a place of pride and a false sense of strength. I believed that to succeed, I had to keep moving, keep working, keep pushing through, no matter how tired I felt. Rest seemed like something I could only afford once I had "made it," but the truth is, without rest, you'll never get there. Your body will catch up to you eventually, and it will demand what it's been deprived of. What I didn't understand was that rest isn't a sign of weakness; it's a sign of wisdom. It's acknowledging that you can't pour from an empty cup. No matter how much you want to achieve, your mind and body need to be replenished. We often think that time spent resting is time wasted, but that couldn't be further from the truth. Rest is an investment. It's time that allows you to refuel so you can keep going, and more importantly, go further with more clarity and purpose.

The journey to recovery taught me the power of balance. I had to learn that ambition and rest can coexist. It's not about choosing one over the other but about finding a rhythm where both are honored. When I started giving myself permission to rest, everything began to change. My mind became sharper, my body stronger, and I gained a deeper sense of peace that allowed me to approach my goals with more intention and less urgency.

One of the biggest lessons I learned is that chronic fatigue is often a symptom of something deeper—something emotional, mental, or even spiritual. For me, it was the need to prove myself, to constantly push the limits and outwork everyone around me. I had equated busyness with worth, and that mindset nearly cost me my health. It took me a long time to see that my value isn't determined by how much I can get done in a day. My value is intrinsic, and yours is too.

As I began to heal, I found that I could actually enjoy the moments I used to rush through. I could savor conversations with loved ones, feel present in my body, and find joy in small things again. Life became less about the finish line and more about appreciating the journey. I stopped measuring myself by the endless to-do lists and started valuing the quality of my days, not just the quantity of work I could get done.

Now, I'm more mindful of how I spend my time. I still have big dreams and goals, but they no longer consume me. I've learned that the pursuit of success doesn't have to come at the expense of my health, my peace, or my relationships. I can work hard, but I can also rest well. I can strive for greatness, but I can also pause and reflect along the way.

The day I finally understood the value of rest was the day my life changed, and I hope, as you read this, you're encouraged to make that shift in your own life before your body forces you to. Don't let the world convince you that you have to be "on" all the time. You don't. Your worth, your impact, and your success will only grow as you honor the need for balance.

So, take the time to rest. Take the time to heal. Don't wait for burnout to be the thing that stops you. Choose to stop, choose to breathe, and choose to live in a way that nourishes both your ambition and your soul. Rest is where your strength is rebuilt, where your vision becomes clear, and where your future is shaped. Make rest a part of your journey, not just the place you go when you've reached your limit. You'll be amazed at how far it takes you.

MY BATTLE WITH DEPRESSION FROM SLEEP DISRUPTION

I never thought I'd be the type of person to struggle with depression. I was always the optimist, the one with the ready smile and the can-do attitude. Life wasn't always easy, but I prided myself on my ability to see the silver lining in any cloud. That was before sleep became my enemy.

It started innocently enough. A new job in a different time zone meant early morning conference calls. I'd wake up at 4 a.m., power through the day, and try to maintain some semblance of a social life in the evenings. "I'm just adjusting," I told myself. "I'll get used to it." But I didn't get used to it. Instead, my sleep schedule became increasingly erratic. Some nights I'd lie awake until the early hours, my mind racing with thoughts about work, relationships, and the endless to-do list that seemed to grow longer each day. Other nights, exhaustion would hit me like a truck at 7 p.m., only for me to wake up at 2 a.m., wide awake and unable to fall back asleep.

At first, the changes were subtle. I found myself more irritable, snapping at colleagues over minor issues. My usual enthusiasm for projects waned, replaced by a sense of overwhelming dread each time a new task landed on my desk. I chalked it up to stress, pushing myself harder in an attempt to regain my usual zest for life. As weeks of disrupted sleep turned into months, something more insidious began to take hold. The world seemed to lose its color, as if someone had dimmed the saturation on my life. Activities I once enjoyed now felt like monumental efforts. Meeting friends for dinner? Too exhausting.

The turning point came on a rainy Sunday afternoon. I found myself sitting on the couch, staring at the wall for hours, tears silently streaming down my face. I wasn't sad about anything in particular; I just felt ... empty ... hollow. As if the essence of who I was had been slowly draining away, leaving behind a shell that merely went through the motions of living. The doctor explained how lack of sleep can wreak havoc on the brain's neurotransmitters, particularly serotonin and dopamine—the very chemicals responsible for regulating our mood. My erratic sleep patterns had essentially thrown my brain chemistry into chaos, leaving me vulnerable to the creeping tendrils of depression. Recovery was a long and often frustrating journey. It involved a multi-pronged approach: therapy to address the negative thought patterns I'd developed, medication to help rebalance my brain chemistry, and most importantly, a complete overhaul of my sleep habits.

I had to relearn the art of sleeping. It sounds strange that something as natural as sleep would need to be relearned, doesn't it? However, years of neglect and disruption had left me with no idea how to achieve restful, restorative sleep. I started with the basics: a consistent sleep schedule, a relaxing bedtime routine, and a bedroom environment conducive to sleep. No more late-night work emails or scrolling through social media until the early hours. I learned about sleep hygiene, investing in blackout curtains and banishing electronic devices from my bedroom. The change wasn't overnight. There were setbacks—nights when anxiety would keep me awake, days when the depression felt so heavy I could barely get out of bed; but slowly, almost imperceptibly at first, things began to improve. As my sleep patterns stabilized, I started to feel glimpses of my old self emerging. The world began to regain its color. I found myself laughing—really laughing—for the first time in months. The fog of depression, while not completely dissipated, began to lift.

Today, I guard my sleep zealously. I've turned down job opportunities that would disrupt my sleep schedule, and I'm not afraid to leave parties early to maintain my bedtime routine. Some might call it boring; I call it self-preservation. I've learned that sleep isn't a luxury or a sign of laziness. It's a fundamental biological need, as crucial to our mental health as it is to our physical well-being. I've learned that pushing through exhaustion isn't a sign of strength, but a fast track to burnout and depression. To those reading this who see themselves in my story, please don't ignore the signs. Chronic sleep disruption isn't just about feeling tired; it can be the first step on a slippery slope to depression. Prioritize your sleep. Protect it fiercely. Your mental health depends on it.

Remember, in our fast-paced world that often glorifies hustle and grinds, choosing to prioritize sleep is a radical act of self-care. It's not always easy, but it's always, always worth it. Take it from someone who had to lose themselves to truly understand the value of a good night's sleep—your future self will thank you for it. Years have passed since I first confronted my sleep-induced depression, and the journey continues to unfold in ways I never expected. What began as a desperate attempt to reclaim my mental health has evolved into a profound transformation of my entire lifestyle. The most surprising change has been in my career trajectory. Once driven by ambition and the need to prove myself, I've shifted toward a path that aligns with my newfound respect for work-life balance. I transitioned from my high-stress corporate job to a role in health and wellness education, where I now help others understand the crucial link between sleep and mental health.

This career pivot wasn't without its challenges. There were moments of doubt, fears about financial stability, and the nagging voice of my old self questioning if I was "falling behind." Each time these doubts surfaced, I reminded myself of the dark place my previous lifestyle had led me. The peace of mind and vitality I now enjoy are worth far more than any corner office or impressive title. My relationships have deepened in ways I couldn't have imagined. With a well-rested mind and a more balanced emotional state, I'm able to be truly present for my loved ones. I listen more attentively, react less impulsively, and have the energy to nurture connections that I once neglected. My sister, who was instrumental in my recovery, often comments on how our relationship has blossomed. "It's like I got my sibling back," she says, "but an even better version."

Physically, the changes have been remarkable. The dark circles under my eyes have faded, replaced by a natural glow that no amount of makeup could replicate. My immune system, once weakened by chronic sleep deprivation, has strengthened. I rarely catch the colds that used to plague me several times a year. Even my digestive issues, which I had attributed to stress, have largely resolved—a benefit of good sleep I hadn't anticipated. My approach to exercise has transformed as well. Gone are the punishing 5 a.m. workouts I used to force myself through. Instead, I've embraced gentler forms of movement that complement my sleep schedule rather than competing with it. Yoga, nature walks, and swimming have become my go-to activities. I've found that this kinder approach to fitness, not only supports my sleep, but also brings a sense of joy and mindfulness to my day.

One of the most profound shifts has been in my perception of time. When I was constantly exhausted, days seemed to blur together in a haze of stress and obligation. Now, with a well-rested mind, I experience time more fully. I'm more efficient during work hours, which allows me to truly disconnect in my free time. Weekends feel longer and more rejuvenating. I've rediscovered hobbies I thought I'd lost forever—painting, reading for pleasure, even learning a new language. Of course, it hasn't all been smooth sailing. Life still throws curveballs, and there are times when my sleep suffers. A family emergency, a bout of illness, or even the excitement of a new project can disrupt my carefully cultivated routine. The difference now is in how I respond to these disruptions.

Instead of spiraling into anxiety about a few nights of poor sleep, I have tools and strategies to get back on track. I've learned to be compassionate with myself during these times, understanding that perfect sleep isn't always possible. The goal isn't perfection, but resilience—the ability to return to healthy patterns even after disruption. I've also become acutely aware of the societal pressures that led me to neglect my sleep in the first place. Our culture often equates busyness with importance, and rest with laziness. Challenging these norms isn't easy, but I've found it to be a crucial part of maintaining my health and advocating for others.

In professional settings, I'm now vocal about the importance of rest. I've turned down projects that would require unsustainable work hours, and I'm transparent about my need for adequate sleep. To my surprise, this honesty has often been met with respect and even admiration. I've had colleagues confide in me about their own struggles with sleep and mental health, leading to more open and supportive work environments. Looking back, I realize that my battle with sleep-induced depression, as painful as it was, gave me an invaluable gift: a deep, experiential understanding of the importance of sleep. This knowledge has become my compass, guiding my decisions in all areas of life. To those still struggling with sleep issues or facing the darkness of depression, I want you to know that there is hope. The journey to better sleep and mental health isn't always linear, and it requires patience and perseverance. However, the rewards—a clearer mind, a more balanced emotional life, improved physical health, and richer relationships—are immeasurable.

Remember, prioritizing your sleep isn't selfish; it's an essential act of self-care that ripples out to positively impact every aspect of your life and the lives of those around you. In a world that often seems to demand our constant attention and energy, choosing rest is a powerful statement. It's a declaration that your well-being matters, that you value the quality of your waking hours as much as the quantity. So tonight, as you prepare for sleep, know that you're not just resting—you're actively investing in your mental health, your relationships, your productivity, and your joy. Sweet dreams, and here's to the life-changing power of a good night's sleep.

CLOSING REFLECTION ON REST

As we come to the close of our exploration of "Rest Behind Closed Doors," I want you to take a moment to envision your own personal sanctuary of rest. This isn't just a physical space, but a state of being—a place where you can truly let go, recharge, and reconnect with your essence. Throughout this chapter, we've delved into the profound importance of carving out private moments of rest in our increasingly public and connected world. We've learned that rest isn't just about physical relaxation, but about mental, emotional, and spiritual renewal as well. Remember, behind closed doors, you have the freedom to rest without judgment, without the pressure to perform or present a certain image to the world. This is where you can be truly, authentically you. It's where you can let your guard down, where you can be vulnerable, where you can simply be.

In our personal lives, this private rest is where we rediscover ourselves. It's in these quiet moments that we can hear our inner voice, often drowned out by the noise of daily life. It's where we can process our experiences, reflect on our goals, and dream about our future. This isn't selfishness—it's self-preservation and self-discovery. From a cultural perspective, embracing rest behind closed doors is a radical act in a world that often demands constant connectivity and productivity. By prioritizing this private rest, we're challenging the notion that we must always be available, always be "on." We're reclaiming our right to privacy, to solitude, to quiet.

In our professional lives, this private rest is the incubator for our best ideas. It's where we can step back from the daily grind and see the bigger picture. Many of history's greatest insights and innovations came not in the hustle and bustle of active work, but in moments of quiet reflection. By allowing ourselves this rest, we're not falling behind—we're preparing to leap forward. For our families and relationships, the rest we take behind closed doors enables us to show up more fully when we step back out into the world. It allows us to recharge our emotional batteries, to process our feelings, to gather the patience and presence needed to nurture our connections with others. When we honor our need for private rest, we're better partners, better parents, better friends.

From a mental health perspective, this private rest is absolutely crucial. It's our first line of defense against stress, anxiety, and burnout. It's where we can practice mindfulness, engage in self-care rituals, or simply be still. In a world that can often feel overwhelming, these moments of private rest are like islands of calm in a stormy sea. As you leave this chapter, I challenge you to reevaluate your relationship with rest, particularly the rest you take behind closed doors. Are you giving yourself permission to truly rest, away from the gaze and expectations of others? Are you creating space in your life for these private moments of renewal? Remember, the rest you take behind closed doors isn't a luxury—it's a necessity. It's not selfish—it's essential. It's not wasted time—it's an investment in yourself, in your well-being, in your future.

So tonight, when you close your door to the world, see it as an act of self-love. When you draw the curtains, know that you're creating a cocoon for your own transformation. When you turn off your devices, recognize that you're turning on your connection to yourself. In these private moments of rest, you're not just recharging—you're rebirthing yourself. You're not just relaxing—you're realigning with your true self. You're not just resting—you're quietly revolutionizing your life. As you move forward, carry with you the knowledge that behind closed doors, in the quiet sanctuary of rest, lies the source of your strength, your creativity, your resilience. Honor it. Protect it. Cherish it. Remember, in a world that never seems to stop, your willingness to pause, to rest, to retreat behind closed doors—that is your superpower. Use it wisely, use it often, and watch as it transforms, not just your life, but your impact on the world around you. Rest well, rest deeply, and rest assured that in doing so, you're nurturing the very best version of yourself.

As you step into this space of rest, understand that you are giving yourself something more valuable than any external achievement could offer. You're giving yourself the opportunity to reset, to reflect, and to reconnect with what matters most. In these moments, you're not just pausing life—you're nurturing the life within you. You're building a foundation of strength that allows you to step back into the world with clarity and purpose. When the world tells you that success is measured by how much you do, how fast you move, or how many hours you put in, remember this: true success is found in balance. It's found in the quiet, the stillness, the moments when you choose to listen to your body, your mind, and your spirit. This is where you reclaim your power. This is where the seeds of greatness are planted and nourished, away from the noise, away from the constant demands.

Rest is not a retreat from life; it's a preparation for the next step in your journey. It's a conscious choice to prioritize yourself so that you can show up fully in all that you do. When you choose rest, you're not falling behind. You're positioning yourself to move forward with more energy, more focus, and more impact. So, as you move forward from this chapter, carry with you the understanding that rest is not a break from your purpose—it's an integral part of it. The time you take to recharge behind closed doors is the fuel that will propel you toward your dreams. It's the space where your vision sharpens, your heart strengthens, and your soul finds peace.

Remember, in a world that's always demanding more, your decision to pause is an act of defiance. It's a reminder to yourself that you are worthy of care, worthy of peace, and worthy of rest. You are deserving of moments that are yours alone, moments that restore your spirit and prepare you for the greatness that lies ahead. Rest well, rest deeply, and rest assured knowing that in these sacred, quiet moments, you are creating the best version of yourself—stronger, wiser, more resilient than ever before—and with that, you are not just changing your own life; you are changing the world around you.

As you continue to embrace the practice of rest, realize that every time you step away to recharge, you are making a powerful statement: you are choosing to honor your well-being over the demands of the world. This decision doesn't come easily in a society that often glorifies exhaustion, where burnout is worn like a badge of honor. But you know better now. You know that rest is not the enemy of progress—it is the foundation upon which true progress is built.

Think about the moments in your life when clarity struck—those insights that seemed to come out of nowhere. Chances are, they arrived not when you were running at full speed but when you gave yourself a moment to breathe. Rest creates the space for inspiration, for vision, for solutions to the challenges you face. It opens the door to creativity and allows your mind to wander freely, exploring possibilities you may have missed in the rush of daily life.

In this space of stillness, you also allow your body to heal. Rest repairs the wear and tear of the day, strengthens your immune system, and rejuvenates your energy stores. It's a process of restoration that goes beyond the physical—it seeps into your emotional and mental health, too. When you rest, you create room for emotional balance. You can reflect, release, and reset your internal compass, ensuring that you're moving in alignment with your true self. This isn't about stepping back forever; it's about learning the rhythm of life that includes both movement and stillness. Just like the tides, your energy ebbs and flows. In those moments of retreat, you are gathering the strength to rise again, stronger and more purposeful than before.

As you honor your need for rest, you'll notice something incredible begin to happen. The things that once felt overwhelming or insurmountable will start to seem more manageable. The tasks that used to drain you will no longer hold the same weight, because you'll be approaching them from a place of fullness rather than depletion. This is the beauty of rest: it doesn't slow you down; it prepares you to go further. So, I encourage you to make rest a regular part of your life—not as something you do when you're exhausted, but as a daily practice that sustains you. Find those moments behind closed doors where you can disconnect from the world and reconnect with yourself. Whether it's through quiet reflection, prayer, meditation, or simply sitting in stillness, let these moments be the fuel that powers your journey forward.

As you rest, trust in the process. Trust that you are exactly where you need to be. The world will always demand more, but you don't have to answer every call. You don't have to keep pace with anyone else's rhythm. Your journey is unique, and your path is yours alone. In rest, you will find the clarity, strength, and resilience to keep moving forward—not in a frenzy, but with calm, confident purpose. You will move from a place of wholeness, a place of alignment with who you truly are—and that, more than anything, will allow you to step fully into your calling, to fulfill the purpose that is uniquely yours.

Tonight, as you close the door on the world, know that you are stepping into something sacred. You are stepping into the quiet revolution of rest, a revolution that will transform your life in ways you can't yet imagine. Rest well, rest deeply, and know that in doing so, you are preparing yourself for the greatness that lies ahead.

CHAPTER 11

VULNERABILITY BEHIND CLOSED DOORS

Vulnerability is a word that carries a weight of complexity, and for me, it holds multiple layers of meaning. Before I dive into what it means to be vulnerable behind closed doors, I want to break down what vulnerability has meant to me personally. Growing up, I found myself vulnerable in various ways—vulnerable to the church, to life itself, and ultimately to God. In my younger years, I didn't have much of a choice. Vulnerability seemed like something that happened naturally in the presence of God, or in the structure of my daily life, but as I grew older, I realized that vulnerability wasn't something external—it was something I had to cultivate in myself. Life began to "life" in new ways once I turned 19 and started living on my own. The weight of decisions, responsibilities, and the reality of adulthood made me see vulnerability differently. I needed to be open to life itself, to the unpredictable journey it would take me on.

The first layer I want to unpack is the vulnerability of life itself. It's one thing to be open with others, but have you ever truly let your guard down when you're alone, behind closed doors, with no distractions? I'm not talking about a brief moment in between notifications or phone calls, but a real, uninterrupted time where you confront yourself. Maybe that's when the tears finally flow over the loss of a loved one or over unspoken frustrations about your career or your purpose. Maybe it's that moment when you realize you're not where you want to be, or perhaps, it's when you catch yourself smiling after realizing, "You know what? Despite everything, I've got this."

These moments of raw honesty, when you strip away the layers you present to the world, are powerful. They are signs of vulnerability—the kind that connects you to your deeper self. Your private emotions, the ones you experience in these moments, are like your internal compass. If there's one thing I want you to hold onto from this chapter, it's this: your private emotions are your internal compass. They guide you toward the truths you often bury beneath the surface. When you honor these emotions in solitude, it's not weakness—it's wisdom. There's a difference between being weak and being wise in your vulnerability. Weakness might feel like helplessness, a loss of direction, but wisdom comes from discernment. It comes from allowing yourself to be vulnerable so you can process, grow, and eventually move forward with strength.

Vulnerability shows up in various forms. There's practical vulnerability, the kind you experience in daily life. Then there's a deeper layer, something I call the truth zone. The truth zone is where you come face-to-face with the core of who you are. It's the place where you confront truths within yourself before you can share them with the world. It's the moment of honesty that forces you to reflect on the parts of yourself that need healing, realignment, or recognition. The truth zone is a mental, spiritual, and emotional space where you can capture lost moments and reclaim them by thinking through your experiences. Imagine someone like Sarah, a high-powered executive who takes 20 minutes at the end of each day to sit quietly in her home or office, processing her emotions before engaging with her family. That small but intentional act improves her stress management, sharpens her leadership skills, and enhances her well-being. That's what vulnerability behind closed doors can do—it can transform your mental and emotional space, preparing you to face the world more fully. It's in this private laboratory of growth, as I like to call it, where you build resilience, where healing takes place, and where your next breakthrough lies.

Now, let's look at the practical side of vulnerability. Start by designing a space that invites comfort and peace—a place where you can truly let your guard down. Establish boundaries around your private time. Don't allow anyone to infringe upon it. This space is for you, for your personal growth and for the nurturing of your soul. As we continue, we will dive deeper into this idea, piece by piece, because vulnerability isn't just a passing emotion—it's the foundation for true growth. It's in these moments of solitude that champions are made, and where you find the strength to rise again.

DO NOT DISTURB BUTTON

The truth is, we all need to embrace our own version of the *Do Not Disturb* button in life. This concept is powerful because it gives us permission to tune out the world and focus on what truly matters—the game plan you are meant to follow, the calling you are assigned to. It's about reclaiming your personal space, whether it's physical, mental, or emotional. Everyone's sanctuary looks different. Some might find it on their lunch break, sitting in their car, with headphones in, escaping through music. Others might retreat to the quiet of a garden shed, where the scent of wood and soil creates an invisible barrier, protecting them from the outside world. For some, it's as simple as sitting at a coffee table, the aroma of a fresh brew rising to meet them, signaling the start of their solitary, reflective time.

Here's the key—don't get caught up in everyone else's noise, forgetting to press your own *Do Not Disturb* button. It's not only okay—it's essential to say, "I need this time for myself." Vulnerability requires space. It requires the permission to heal, to recharge, and to reflect without interruption. Whether you're in the kitchen preparing a meal, in a workshop building something, or simply out walking your dog, these moments are crucial. Even in these seemingly ordinary activities, vulnerability and solitude can surface in profound ways. Cooking, for example, isn't just about feeding yourself or others—it can become a form of meditation, an opportunity to connect with yourself while creating something nourishing.

Everyone has their own way of finding that vulnerable space. For some, it's in the basement working on a project, for others it's at the gym where their body and mind can focus. Maybe it's a simple daily walk, a routine that allows you to reflect and breathe deeply. The method doesn't matter as much as the result: a space where you can be alone with your thoughts, emotions, and truths. Let me offer some practical steps for creating these moments of vulnerability. First, I encourage you to establish a daily honest hour. This is a sacred time where you check in with yourself. It's a moment of complete honesty, where you allow yourself to feel and process what's really going on in your heart and mind. Keep a private journal during this time—some of the most powerful realizations and breakthroughs happen when we write without filters, free from the expectations or judgments of others.

Next, find a designated truth zone in your home—a specific space that becomes your sanctuary. This could be a corner of a room, a chair by the window, or even a spot outside. Wherever it is, let it be a place where you feel safe to express yourself freely. This isn't just a physical space;

it's also about creating a mental, emotional, and spiritual sanctuary—a personal laboratory where you can grow, reflect, and realign.

Another essential element of vulnerability is building strength through these private moments. True strength doesn't come from avoiding vulnerability but from embracing it. Your most personal, vulnerable moments are where resilience is built. Consider these moments as a strength inventory. They prepare you for life's challenges, equipping you with the inner tools to overcome them. While you're in these moments, practice positive self-talk. Speak life over yourself, affirm your worth, and develop personal concepts that push you forward.

Consider a real-life example, like James, a military veteran who struggled with PTSD. James found solace in a daily routine that included journaling, being still, and creating space for his thoughts to breathe. Through this vulnerable practice, he began to heal and gain clarity. His moments of private reflection became the foundation for his resilience.

In today's world, there's also a digital side to this practice. While the digital world can often be a source of distraction, it can also be used as a tool for intentional vulnerability. For some, that might look like unplugging from social media or setting boundaries with technology. For others, it could be using mindfulness apps or digital journals to aid in their reflection time.

The point is this: Your *Do Not Disturb* button isn't just about escaping the chaos of the world— it's about creating intentional space for vulnerability, for truth, and for growth. You deserve that time—time to heal, time to dream, and time to rebuild from the inside out. Don't hesitate to press that button and prioritize yourself. Your growth, your resilience, and your strength depend on it.

Let's continue with this idea of the *Do Not Disturb* button in life because it's more than just about hitting pause—it's about reclaiming your power, your time, and your mental space in a world that constantly demands your attention. Every day, the noise of life grows louder: notifications pinging, emails pouring in, social media scrolling, and the pressure to keep up with everyone else's pace. Here's the truth: You can't move forward if you're always caught up in everyone else's rhythm. You need to create your own beat, your own flow, and that starts with knowing when to step back, tune out, and focus on your own path. The *Do Not Disturb* button isn't just for your phone—it's for your life. It's a signal to yourself and to others that you are making space for something sacred: your thoughts, your healing, your dreams. It's in those quiet, undisturbed moments where real progress happens. It's where you gain clarity, regain strength, and refocus on what really matters.

Think about it like this: You wouldn't expect a car to keep running without stopping for fuel, yet many of us do exactly that—we keep pushing without ever refueling our minds, our bodies, or our spirits. That's what the *Do Not Disturb* button allows you to do. It gives you permission to say, "I need to stop and refuel," without guilt or hesitation. Where do you find your *Do Not Disturb* moments? For some, it's the early mornings before the world wakes up—when the house is still, the air is crisp, and it's just you and your thoughts. For others, it's late at night, when the world finally quiets down, and you can let your guard down too. Maybe it's that sacred time during your commute, when you're alone in the car, and the only sound is the hum of the road beneath you. Or perhaps it's while tending to something as simple as a cup of tea or coffee—where each sip grounds you, reminds you that there's beauty in the small, quiet moments.

> *"You can't move forward if you're always caught up in everyone else's rhythm. You need to create your own beat, your own flow, and that starts with knowing when to step back, tune out, and focus on your own path."*

Here's the thing: wherever you find it, honor that space. Don't let anyone take it from you. Protect it fiercely because that's the time when you reconnect with your purpose. In a world that glorifies hustle and grind, taking time to be still is a radical act, but it's also necessary. It's in those moments of stillness that you find the mental clarity to make the right decisions, the emotional resilience to handle the challenges ahead, and the spiritual grounding to stay true to your path. I've seen it happen too many times—people who think they can push through without ever stopping, without ever hitting their own *Do Not Disturb* button. Eventually, the burnout comes. The exhaustion takes over. The joy of the journey gets lost because they've forgotten how to pause and reflect. Don't let that be you. Learn to embrace the power of stillness, the power of stepping back.

And it's not just about finding quiet moments for rest—it's also about finding spaces for creativity and deep work. Some of the most brilliant ideas, the most profound breakthroughs, happen in the spaces where you're not constantly reacting to life, but instead reflecting on it. When you press that *Do Not Disturb* button, you're telling the world, "I need this time to create, to think, to dream." Whether you're an artist, a writer, a business owner, or simply someone trying to find their next step, that time is vital. It's in those moments that you can hear your own voice again, free from the noise of the world.

Let's get practical for a moment. How do you cultivate this in your daily life? Start by setting boundaries. Boundaries aren't walls meant to shut others out; they're bridges that connect you to what truly matters. Create pockets of time where the only focus is on you—your mental health, your emotional well-being, your creative flow. Maybe it's an hour in the morning before anyone else wakes up, maybe it's a 15-minute break in the middle of your workday, or maybe it's a non-negotiable time in the evening when you decompress and reflect on your day.

Another essential step is curating your environment. Create a space that invites peace, focus, and vulnerability. It doesn't need to be elaborate—a cozy corner with a chair and a journal, a kitchen table with a warm cup of tea, a favorite spot in the park. The key is that it becomes your sanctuary, a place where you can press pause on the outside world and tune into your inner world. When you step into that space, you know that this is your time to process, to dream, to refuel. And remember, vulnerability is at the heart of this process. When you press that *Do Not Disturb* button, you're not just creating time for yourself—you're creating space for honesty. It's a time to ask yourself the tough questions: "What am I really feeling? What am I holding onto that's weighing me down? What do I need to let go of to move forward?" This is where the real work happens—behind closed doors, in the quiet moments, when no one else is watching. It's in these moments of vulnerability where you start to see the path forward with clarity and purpose.

Now, let's talk about the digital side of the *Do Not Disturb* button because we live in a world where it's easy to stay plugged in 24/7. Just because you *can* be connected at all times doesn't mean you should be. In fact, constant connectivity can rob you of your peace, your focus, and your creativity. So, take control of your digital life. Set boundaries with your devices. Turn off notifications when you're in your sacred space. Limit the time you spend scrolling through social media, and give yourself permission to unplug without guilt. There's a digital detox element to this that's incredibly powerful. When you step away from the screen, when you stop comparing yourself to everyone else's highlight reel, you start to see your own life with fresh eyes. You start to appreciate the moments that are happening right in front of you—the conversations, the quiet moments, the simple joys that get lost in the digital noise. Remember, pressing the *Do Not Disturb* button is about more than just disconnecting from distractions; it's about reconnecting with yourself. It's about honoring your need for rest, reflection, and renewal. It's about giving yourself the time and space to heal, to dream, and to grow. So, don't hesitate to press that button whenever you need it. It's not a sign of weakness—it's a sign of strength. It's the ultimate act of self-care and self-respect.

As you continue this journey, know this—the world will keep spinning. The emails will keep coming. The notifications will still be there when you're ready to return—but in those moments when you choose to press pause, when you decide to say, "I need this time for myself," you are making one of the most powerful decisions you can make. You are choosing your peace over the noise, your growth over the grind, your purpose over the pressures of the world. That is where true transformation begins. So, press the button, step back, and watch how your life begins to realign with who you truly are.

*

REHEARSING THE BIG SPEECH IN PRIVATE

When it comes to preparing for a big moment, like delivering a speech or presentation, there's a truth we often overlook: the most powerful work happens behind closed doors. It's easy to assume that the final performance—the moment you're standing in front of an audience, lights on you—is where the moment happens. It happens in those private moments when you're rehearsing, refining, and speaking your truth to an empty room. Rehearsing in private is where the real transformation takes place. It's where you can be vulnerable, where you can make mistakes, adjust, and try again without judgment. This is your space to confront your fears, overcome the self-doubt, and build confidence. Before you ever take that stage, the real work happens in solitude.

Think about it: every great speech, every legendary presentation, wasn't just born in the moment it was delivered. It was shaped, refined, and rehearsed long before anyone else ever saw it. Those private moments matter. They're the foundation on which you build something incredible. When you're alone, standing in front of a mirror or pacing around the room, you're not just going through the motions—you're creating the energy and momentum that will carry you through when it's time to face the crowd.

WHY IS REHEARSING IN PRIVATE SO POWERFUL?

For starters, practicing in private allows you to tap into a level of honesty that you might not be able to access in front of others. There's no one to impress, no one to critique, no pressure to get it perfect on the first try. It's just you, your voice, and your message. You can experiment with different tones, gestures, and phrasing without worrying about getting it wrong. This is your time to explore, to find what feels natural, and to refine your words until they resonate deeply. When you rehearse privately, you're also giving yourself the chance to mentally and emotionally connect with your material. A speech isn't just a collection of words—it's a message, a story, something that has to be delivered with passion and conviction. When you speak those words alone, away from the pressure of an audience, you can focus on their meaning. You can dive deeper into why you're saying them, how they make you feel, and what kind of impact you want to make.

It's not just about the words, either. When you rehearse, you're also practicing how to control your flow. Standing in front of a group of people can be overwhelming—their eyes on you, their reactions immediate, but when you've already gone through the motions in private, you've prepared your body and mind for that intensity. You've practiced how to breathe through the nerves, how to command the space with your presence, and how to manage the pacing of your words. That preparation is what sets you apart on the day of the speech.

BUILDING CONFIDENCE IN SOLITUDE

Here's another truth: confidence is built in the quiet moments. Confidence doesn't come from hoping you'll nail it when you walk on stage. It comes from knowing you've put in the time, the effort, and the repetition. Each private rehearsal is a brick laid in the foundation of your self-assurance.

The more you rehearse, the more those words become a part of you, so that when it's time to speak, you're not just delivering a script—you're sharing something real, something that comes from within. In private, you can make mistakes freely, without the fear of judgment. You can stumble, forget a line, or change your mind about how you want to express an idea. That's the beauty of rehearsing alone—you get to see those mistakes not as failures but as opportunities for growth. You can adjust, learn, and improve without anyone watching. By the time you're ready for the actual performance, you've already smoothed out the rough edges, and you step into the moment with a sense of ownership over your message.

THE ROLE OF VISUALIZATION IN PRIVATE REHEARSAL

As you rehearse in private, take it a step further—start visualizing the real thing. Picture yourself standing on that stage or in front of that audience. Feel the weight of the microphone in your hand or the podium beneath your fingers. Imagine the crowd in front of you—their energy, their reactions—and see yourself delivering your message with clarity and power. Visualization is a key part of rehearsal because it primes your mind for the actual event. When you rehearse privately and combine it with visualization, you're essentially walking yourself through the moment before it even happens. You're preparing your mind, body, and spirit for success. The more vividly you can imagine it, the more familiar the moment will feel when it finally arrives.

SILENCE: THE BEST SOUNDTRACK FOR REHEARSAL

Let's not forget one of the most underrated aspects of rehearsing in private: silence. In the quiet of your private space, there are no distractions, no interruptions. You can focus entirely on the sound of your own voice, the rhythm of your words, and the flow of your ideas. Silence is a powerful companion during rehearsals because it allows you to tune into the nuances of your speech. You can hear the places where your voice rises with passion and where it softens for impact. You can listen for the pauses that will give your audience time to absorb your words.

In this silence, you can find your authentic voice. This is the voice that you will bring to your audience—not the voice that is shaped by nerves or external pressures, but the voice that comes from a place of confidence, conviction, and clarity.

CREATING A ROUTINE FOR PRIVATE REHEARSAL

To really maximize the power of private rehearsal, create a routine around it. Set aside dedicated time each day or each week to work on your speech. Find a space where you feel comfortable, whether it's a room in your home, an empty office, or even outdoors. Make this time sacred. Turn off distractions, put your phone on *Do Not Disturb,* and give yourself the space to focus completely. As you rehearse, allow yourself to connect emotionally with your material. Speak the words aloud, listen to your voice, and feel the energy of your message. You're not just preparing to speak—you're preparing to own your moment.

Incorporate different layers into your rehearsal as well. Some days, focus on the content and flow of your speech. Other days, pay attention to your body language, your gestures, and how you move as you speak, and always remember to practice your breathing. Breath control is key to delivering your message with strength and calm.

PRIVATE REHEARSAL, PUBLIC POWER

The power of rehearsing in private is that it allows you to show up in public as your best self. By the time you stand before your audience, you've already done the work. You've made the mistakes, you've refined your message, and you've built the confidence that comes from deep, focused preparation. So, when you're preparing for that big speech, don't underestimate the value of those quiet, private moments. Behind closed doors, away from the pressures of the public eye, is where the real transformation happens. It's where you fine-tune your message, build your confidence, and step into your power, and when the day comes, when you finally take that stage, the work you've done in private will shine through. The audience will see someone who is not just prepared, but someone who owns the moment. You'll speak with confidence, clarity, and purpose—all because you took the time to rehearse, refine, and embrace the power of practicing in private.

MIRROR CONVERSATIONS: THE WORDS WE NEVER SAY

There's something profound that happens when you stand in front of a mirror, locked in a conversation with the one person you often overlook—yourself. Mirror conversations hold a power that goes beyond rehearsing for others or practicing what to say. It's where you confront the words and thoughts that never make it out into the world. The buried emotions, the truths you've tucked away, and the silent reflections that go unheard. In those quiet moments, there's no audience to impress, no distractions to divert your attention. It's just you, staring back at yourself with honesty.

These conversations are the ones we tend to avoid. Speaking to others is easy. We fill our days with external dialogue, sharing thoughts, opinions, and feelings; but when it comes to talking to ourselves, to truly reflect on what's going on within, it can feel uncomfortable. That's the beauty of mirror conversations—it's where real self-awareness begins to surface. You're not speaking to impress or persuade. You're speaking to reveal, to uncover the layers of who you are and what you're feeling.

When was the last time you really looked at yourself in the mirror and had an honest conversation? Not about the superficial details of appearance, but about what's happening beneath the surface. These moments of self-reflection can be some of the most transformative. They're opportunities to say the things we've been holding in, to acknowledge the thoughts that swirl in the background of our minds, and to confront the truths we've been avoiding.

FACING UNSPOKEN TRUTHS

Often, we avoid these conversations because we're not ready to face the truth. We avoid saying, "I'm struggling," or "I'm scared," or "I'm not happy," because it forces us to deal with those feelings; but when you look in the mirror and say those words out loud, something shifts. You give yourself permission to acknowledge what's real, even if it's uncomfortable, and in that acknowledgment, healing can begin.

Mirror conversations can be raw and unfiltered. They're the words you would never say out loud to anyone else—the thoughts you keep hidden. Maybe it's admitting you're feeling lost, or that you're disappointed in how things have turned out. Maybe it's acknowledging the fear of not measuring up, or the pressure of constantly trying to live up to other people's expectations. Whatever it is, these conversations create a space where you can let it all out without judgment.

THE POWER OF SPEAKING TO YOURSELF

When you speak to yourself in the mirror, it's more than just a mental exercise. It's a way to hold yourself accountable. You can't ignore the truth when it's staring back at you. You're forced to confront the reality of your feelings, your thoughts, and your actions. While it may be uncomfortable at first, there's a sense of relief that comes with finally speaking the words that have been stuck inside you. There's also a deeper connection that forms when you speak to yourself this way. You begin to hear your own voice differently. You start to recognize the tone you use when you talk to yourself. Are you compassionate? Are you harsh? Do you lift yourself up, or do you tear yourself down? Mirror conversations reveal not just the words you say, but how you say them. They're a reflection of your relationship with yourself.

HEALING THROUGH HONEST REFLECTION

It's in these moments of engaging in mirror conversations that we can begin to heal. By saying the things we've avoided, we release the weight of carrying them alone. We create space for new thoughts, for growth, and for self-compassion. Mirror conversations aren't about perfection. They're about presence: being present with yourself, no matter what you're feeling, and giving yourself the time and attention you deserve— and here's the thing: these conversations don't need to be long or complicated. They can be as simple as standing in front of the mirror for a few minutes each day and asking yourself, "How am I really doing?" Sometimes, you'll find the answers surprising. Sometimes, you won't have the answers right away; but the act of showing up for yourself, of speaking your truth, is what matters most.

THE IMPORTANCE OF VULNERABILITY

To engage in a mirror conversation is to be vulnerable. It's about being open with yourself, admitting your fears, your hopes, your disappointments, and your dreams. Vulnerability isn't easy, especially when it's directed at yourself; but it's essential for growth. These moments of raw honesty allow you to get to the heart of what you really need, what you're really feeling, and what you need to let go of. It's not uncommon to feel emotional during these conversations. After all, you're giving yourself permission to express things that may have been bottled up for a long time. Whether it's frustration, sadness, or even joy, these emotions need to be acknowledged, and the mirror is a safe place to do that. It's just you, standing in front of yourself, saying the words that need to be said.

PRACTICING SELF-COMPASSION

One of the most powerful outcomes of mirror conversations is the opportunity to practice self-compassion. As you stand there, facing your reflection, you're given the chance to speak kindly to yourself. To offer words of encouragement, understanding, and forgiveness. We're often our harshest critics, quick to point out our flaws and failures, but in these moments, you can choose to speak words of grace instead. Tell yourself, "It's okay to feel this way," or "I'm doing my best," or even, "I forgive myself." These small acts of kindness can go a long way in shifting how you see yourself and how you treat yourself in your everyday life. Mirror conversations remind you that you are worthy of compassion, that you deserve to be spoken to with kindness, and that you are enough—just as you are.

MOVING FORWARD

As you practice having these conversations, you'll find that the words you never say to others are often the most important words you need to hear. Mirror conversations aren't about fixing everything at once. They're about showing up for yourself, being honest about where you are, and taking the next step forward with clarity and purpose. So, the next time you find yourself standing in front of a mirror, don't just glance at your reflection and walk away. Take a moment. Speak the words you've been holding back. Ask yourself the questions you've been avoiding, and give yourself the space to be vulnerable, to be real, and to be heard. Because the most important conversation you'll ever have is the one you have with yourself.

THE EX-FILES: HOW WE REALLY HANDLE BREAKUPS IN PRIVATE

Breakups are one of those universal experiences that we all face at some point in life. Yet, despite how common they are, the way we handle them behind closed doors is often very different from the image we present to the world. Outwardly, we might appear strong, composed, and moving on; but in private, it's a different story—a more honest and raw one. Behind closed doors, breakups bring out a level of vulnerability and reflection that we rarely talk about. The emotions, the thoughts that swirl in our minds, and the quiet moments of self-doubt can be overwhelming. This is the side of breakups that doesn't get shared on social media, that we don't bring up in casual conversations with friends. It's the part of the journey we keep to ourselves—the ex-files that remain locked away in our own private archives.

THE REALITY OF EMOTIONS IN PRIVATE

The truth is, no matter how mutual or expected a breakup is, it still stirs up emotions that are often hard to process. The loss of a relationship, whether long-term or short-lived, feels like the rug has been pulled from under your feet. Instead of letting those emotions spill out in public, we often suppress them, trying to convince ourselves—and others—that we're fine. We say the right things: "I'm better off," or "It's for the best," but privately, there are tears, sleepless nights, and moments where we replay every conversation, trying to understand where it all went wrong. In private, breakups feel messy. There's no clean ending, even if you've parted on good terms. There's grief, anger, confusion, and a thousand "what-ifs." These are the moments when you sit alone, reliving memories, sorting through the emotional debris left behind. It's in these quiet moments that the real work of healing begins, though it doesn't feel like it at the time.

THE UNSPOKEN CONVERSATIONS

One of the most challenging aspects of a breakup is all the unspoken conversations you have with yourself once it's over. You replay everything—what was said, what wasn't said, what should have been said. In your mind, you have these imagined conversations with your ex, where you explain yourself better, or they finally understand what you were trying to say all along. These are the moments when you're talking to yourself in the mirror, or writing unsent letters, or drafting text messages you'll never actually send. In private, these conversations help us make sense of what happened. They allow us to process the pain, to explore the unresolved feelings, and to come to terms with the fact that not every question will get an answer. It's part of the healing process, even if it feels repetitive and exhausting at times. Eventually, these conversations begin to fade, but not before they've served their purpose.

THE BATTLE BETWEEN ANGER AND LONGING

Another hidden side of breakups is the inner battle between anger and longing. One minute, you're furious, thinking about everything your ex did wrong, the ways they hurt you, or how they failed to appreciate what you brought to the table. The next minute, you're hit with a wave of longing, remembering the good times, the laughter, the connection you once had. It's a push-pull dynamic that can leave you feeling emotionally drained. This private tug-of-war is natural. It's your heart and mind trying to reconcile two opposing truths—that the relationship had both beautiful moments and painful ones, and that it ended for a reason, even if part of you wishes it hadn't. It's easy to feel conflicted during this time, to go from deleting pictures and unfollowing them on social media, to staring at your phone wondering if they're thinking about you, too. These are the quiet battles we fight alone.

THE REBUILDING OF SELF-IDENTITY

What many don't realize is that after a breakup, we're not just grieving the loss of the other person. We're also mourning the loss of who we were in that relationship. Relationships often shape our identity, and when they end, we're left to figure out who we are outside of that connection. The *us* that once existed is gone, and now it's time to rediscover *me*.

This process can be painful and confusing. In private, we start asking ourselves questions like, "Who am I without this person?" "What do I want in life now?" and "What's next for me?" These are hard questions, and they don't come with easy answers. Honestly, it's in these private moments of reflection that we begin to rebuild. We slowly start to reclaim parts of ourselves that may have been overshadowed by the relationship. We remember what we used to love, what used to bring us joy, and we start nurturing those things again.

THE RITUALS OF LETTING GO

Letting go of an ex is often a gradual process, one that involves small, personal rituals. Maybe it's deleting their number from your phone or packing away the gifts they gave you. Maybe it's unfollowing them on social media or finally deciding to stop checking if they've seen your stories. These rituals might seem insignificant to others, but they hold great meaning for you. They're your way of taking steps toward closure. For some, these rituals might happen in an instant—an intense moment of cutting ties and walking away. For others, it's a slower, more deliberate process of gradually untangling yourself from the memories and emotions tied to the relationship. There's no right or wrong way to do it. What matters is that these rituals are done on your terms, in your own time.

HEALING IN SILENCE

Breakups force us to sit with ourselves in a way that few other experiences do. When the distractions are gone, and it's just you in the quiet of your own space, the healing begins. Healing doesn't happen overnight, and it certainly doesn't happen in public. It happens when you're alone with your thoughts, allowing yourself to grieve, to reflect, and eventually, to move on.

In private, you give yourself the time and space to heal without the pressure to have it all together. You don't have to pretend to be okay when you're not. You can allow yourself to feel every emotion, no matter how messy or inconvenient it seems. This is where true healing takes place—in the quiet moments when no one is watching.

MOVING FORWARD

As time passes, the intensity of the breakup fades. The hurt doesn't disappear entirely, but it becomes less sharp. You find yourself thinking about your ex less and less, and the pull of the past weakens. You start to focus more on yourself—your growth, your future, your dreams.

Eventually, you realize that while the breakup was painful, it also gave you an opportunity to rediscover yourself, to realign with who you are and what you truly want. It's a chance to step into the next chapter of your life, stronger and more self-aware. So, while the world may only see the public face of your breakup—the Instagram posts, the brave smiles, and the "I'm fine" responses—what matters most is how you handle it in private. It's in those private moments that you find the strength to heal, the courage to let go, and the wisdom to move forward.

THE COST OF NOT CHOOSING VULNERABILITY

When I look back at seasons of my life when I avoided vulnerability, I can clearly see how much it impacted my relationships, personal growth, and even my health. Not being vulnerable didn't just protect me—it kept me from fully experiencing life and connection. In those times, my relationships were like a house with all the lights turned off; the foundation was there, but you couldn't see what was inside.

The absence of vulnerability tends to leave relationships feeling shallow. Conversations stay at the surface level, like polite exchanges that don't truly reveal anything meaningful. I've been in that space—talking with people at church, at school, and on the job, but always keeping it general, never letting them into the deeper parts of who I was. Eventually, I realized they weren't going deeper either, so I followed suit. It's easy to fall into the trap of mirroring others and holding back, afraid to open up first. However, when we do this, people sense our emotional walls, and some begin to pull away. I've watched good connections deteriorate over time simply because neither side was willing to go beyond the pleasantries.

I noticed something else during those times: my relationships began to feel transactional, almost as if everything had to have a purpose, like a barter. While transactions are necessary in business, relationships thrive on connection. Not every conversation has to be an exchange; sometimes it's just about being there, sharing something meaningful, or supporting one another. Without vulnerability, it becomes easy to treat people as functions rather than friends.

THE EMOTIONAL BUILDUP

Choosing not to be vulnerable can have deeper emotional consequences as well. When we hide our true feelings, we don't release the pressure that builds within us. I'm a living testimony of that reality. There were times in my life when I bottled up so much emotion that it eventually came pouring out in anger and stress. During the pandemic, this was particularly challenging. With so many uncertainties, people suffering, businesses closing, and churches shutting down, it felt like the world was crumbling. The emotions I was suppressing were simmering under the surface, and without a healthy outlet, they were bound to spill over.

Holding onto unexpressed feelings is like carrying around a loaded pressure cooker. Eventually, it reaches a breaking point, and even the smallest spark can cause it to explode. When we hide our emotions, they don't simply go away; they fester and manifest in ways that we might not even notice at first. These triggers, like hairline fractures, can cause us to react in ways that seem out of proportion. A minor criticism, a small inconvenience—suddenly, these little things can become the tipping point for a cascade of emotion.

THE PHYSICAL TOLL

Suppressing emotions doesn't just affect our minds—it impacts our bodies too. When we hold everything inside, our bodies start to show signs of stress. I can recall times when tension would give me pounding headaches, my stomach felt like it was in knots, and I couldn't get a good night's sleep no matter how tired I was. Over time, I started noticing signs of elevated anxiety—my mind racing, my heart pounding. It's not something you can just think away; these physical reactions are your body's way of telling you that it's carrying a load it wasn't meant to bear alone.

I think about Sarah's story—a woman who prided herself on having it all together. On the outside, she was the definition of composure, but years of suppressed emotions led to a breakdown one day when a small work criticism tipped her over the edge. That minor event unleashed a flood of emotions that had been bottled up for years. It's a powerful reminder that we all have our limits and ignoring them doesn't make them go away.

STAGNANT PERSONAL GROWTH

Another consequence of avoiding vulnerability is that personal growth can hit a wall. When we're not open with ourselves, we become less open to change and learning. Vulnerability means admitting our weaknesses and being willing to face them. When we hide from our fears, we also avoid the risks that come with growth. I've seen how this fear of failure can prevent people, myself included, from taking new opportunities or embracing challenges that could lead to greater wisdom and understanding.

Growth happens when we're able to receive feedback without immediately putting up defenses. Without vulnerability, we often interpret feedback as criticism, rather than as an opportunity to learn. Looking back, I realize that at times I took things too personally, misinterpreting genuine advice for judgment. However, when we open ourselves to feedback, we can view it as a tool for growth instead of a threat.

THE BODY KEEPS SCORE

There's a reason people say that our bodies keep the score. Avoiding vulnerability takes a toll on physical health, too. Living with elevated stress hormones over time impacts everything from immune function to blood pressure. I saw this firsthand when I realized my tension and emotional suppression were manifesting as physical symptoms—chronic tension, headaches, and even fluctuations in my immune health.

It's a cycle that feeds into itself. Emotional walls lead to heightened stress, which in turn affects the body, which then impacts mental health. The cycle can become vicious unless we intervene. Vulnerability, as hard as it may be, is actually the key to breaking that cycle. It allows us to release some of the stress we're carrying, to open up and let our guard down in a way that frees us, even if just a little bit at a time.

BREAKING DOWN THE WALLS

The takeaway from all of this is simple: vulnerability isn't a weakness; it's a necessity. When we're not vulnerable, the cost is heavy—relationships stay shallow, emotional pressure builds, personal growth stalls, and physical health suffers. Learning to open up, even in small ways, is an investment in our well-being. It's a practice that can transform our lives in profound ways, helping us build real connections, grow as individuals, and preserve our mental and physical health.

If you find yourself holding back, if you're carrying the weight of hidden emotions, I encourage you to take the first step toward vulnerability. Start small—share a little more than you're used to with a friend, take a moment to acknowledge your feelings, or let yourself be honest about what you're going through. The world around you, and your own heart, will meet you with compassion; and the weight you've been carrying might just begin to lift.

CHOOSING TO OPEN UP

Choosing vulnerability is choosing freedom. It's a decision to live authentically and with depth, to break down the walls that keep you isolated and allow yourself to be known, seen, and understood. Letting go of the fear of judgment and embracing the courage to be real opens the door to genuine connection. Relationships become more than shared time; they become shared experiences where both people contribute their truths and receive the truths of others.

One of the greatest transformations that comes from embracing vulnerability is how it shifts your perspective on life's challenges. Failures and mistakes no longer have the power to crush you; instead, they become parts of your journey that make you stronger. Vulnerability allows you to admit when you're struggling, seek help when needed, and acknowledge that you don't have to have all the answers. It unlocks growth and support that stay inaccessible when we pretend everything is fine.

VULNERABILITY IN PRACTICE

Being vulnerable means more than emotional sharing—it's how you approach yourself and your life. Take moments to check in with yourself by asking, "What am I really feeling?" and "What do I need right now?" Journal without censoring your thoughts; let the pen reveal emotions you might not even be aware of. Breathe deeply and remind yourself, "It's okay to feel this way."

Give yourself grace when things don't go as planned. If you're accustomed to harsh self-talk, criticizing your every mistake, vulnerability encourages you to speak kindly to yourself: "I didn't get it right this time, but I'm learning." It's knowing that being human means faltering, but it doesn't mean failing.

Take James, a military veteran who struggled with PTSD. His healing began when he created daily private moments to process his emotions. Starting with short journaling sessions, he moved to meditation and spent quiet time reconnecting with himself. This practice helped him manage PTSD and transformed his life from one ruled by hidden pain to one of peace and resilience. Vulnerability was the door that moved him from surviving to truly living.

FINDING YOUR TRUTH ZONE

Everyone needs a space to be vulnerable—a truth zone where you can let your guard down. It could be a corner of your home, a chair for unwinding, or a spot in the park. Your truth zone is less about the physical space and more about the mental space you create when you step away from life's demands and allow yourself to reflect.

Your truth zone is where you say the words you've never said. It's where you admit you're tired, afraid, or hopeful for something you've never voiced aloud. It's where you celebrate wins, no matter how small, and remind yourself of how far you've come.

PRACTICAL STEPS TO EMBRACE VULNERABILITY

Daily Honest Hour: Dedicate an hour each day to be completely honest with yourself. Reflect on your feelings and what's been weighing on your mind.

Journaling: Maintain a private journal for unfiltered thoughts. Let your words flow freely, confronting emotions and building self-awareness.

Positive Self-Talk: Replace negative self-talk with positive affirmations. Remind yourself that vulnerability is strength.

Connect with Trusted People: Share with a few trusted individuals. Start small and experience the safety in openness.

Boundaries for Private Time: Guard your *Do Not Disturb* time. Let others know it's essential for your well-being.

THE REWARD OF BEING VULNERABLE

Opening up doesn't happen overnight. It's a process requiring practice, courage, and a willingness to face discomfort, but as you embrace vulnerability, it changes your life in profound ways. Relationships deepen, stress levels decrease, and you build resilience from being honest with yourself. Moments of vulnerability are where true growth begins—where you stop carrying the weight alone and find strength in embracing your full self.

Vulnerability moves you from guarded to grounded, from distant to deeply connected, from weary to wise. It's in those private moments, in your own truth zone, where the walls come down and your heart breathes. In those moments, you learn that being vulnerable is not the risk—it's the reward.

EXTENDING VULNERABILITY BEYOND YOURSELF

As you deepen your practice of vulnerability, consider how it impacts those around you. When you show up authentically, you invite others to do the same. You create an environment where openness is welcomed, where people feel safe to express themselves without fear of judgment. This ripple effect strengthens your connections and fosters a deeper understanding in your community. Take small steps to practice vulnerability in your interactions. Share a story of a time you overcame a struggle or admit when you need help. Let others see your humanity, and you'll often find they're ready to show theirs too. This mutual vulnerability enriches relationships, turning acquaintances into friends and deepening bonds with loved ones.

Remember, being vulnerable doesn't mean being exposed; it means being seen for who you truly are and allowing yourself to exist fully in that truth. As you continue on this path, may you embrace the beauty, strength, and growth that comes from choosing to open up, knowing that in every moment of authenticity, you are choosing a life of depth, connection, and real fulfillment.

CREATING AN ENVIRONMENT FOR OPENNESS

To deepen your practice of vulnerability, create an environment that fosters openness. Design your personal space to invite moments of reflection—a comfortable chair, soothing music, or a warm cup of tea can set the stage for self-discovery. Surround yourself with objects that inspire peace and safety, whether it's photos of loved ones, a cherished book, or calming scents. This environment reinforces that this space is yours—a place where you can show up as your true self. As you cultivate this space, recognize that being open with yourself isn't just beneficial— it's transformative. It's the foundation on which authentic living is built. It's where your past, present, and future can meet without judgment and where you can start piecing together your path forward with clarity and compassion.

The impact extends beyond your inner world. As you practice being vulnerable, those around you will feel the shift. Your openness invites others to be open too, fostering relationships built on trust and mutual understanding. It creates a ripple effect—as you show up authentically, you encourage others to do the same. Vulnerability, therefore, becomes not just a personal act but a communal one that strengthens connections and builds true support networks. Accepting imperfections doesn't mean settling for less or giving up on self-improvement; rather, it's understanding that who you are right now, with all your challenges and strengths, is enough. It allows you to be kinder to yourself when things don't go as planned. Life is full of twists and turns, and sometimes, despite your best efforts, setbacks will happen. Embracing these moments with grace instead of criticism reshapes how you see failure. It shifts it from being a dead end to becoming a stepping stone.

When you accept your imperfections, you allow yourself the freedom to learn without the constraints of shame. This newfound freedom creates space for growth that's authentic and resilient. You start to see challenges as opportunities for development rather than threats to your self-worth. It's in these moments of accepting imperfections where the deepest connections with others often form. When you show up with your whole self—flaws and all—you invite those around you to do the same. This shared authenticity deepens relationships, fostering an environment where everyone feels seen and valued. Think about the relationships in your life. The ones that mean the most are likely built on moments of raw honesty, where you've shared a fear, an insecurity, or a dream that felt too big. Those are the moments that strip away pretense and build true connection. When you show vulnerability, you open the door for others to meet you in that space, strengthening bonds that might otherwise remain superficial.

Now, let's not overlook the importance of patience in this process. Choosing to open up and embrace your imperfections is not an overnight transformation. It's a continuous journey of reminding yourself that it's okay to be a work in progress. There will be days when vulnerability feels empowering, and days when it feels too risky. On those harder days, take a step back and reflect on how far you've come. Celebrate the small victories—the times you spoke your truth, took a chance, or allowed yourself to *feel* deeply. Practical exercises can support this journey of acceptance. Start by looking at your reflection each morning and naming one thing you appreciate about yourself. It could be as simple as acknowledging your perseverance or the way you supported a friend. Pair that with recognizing one area where you're growing, like learning to communicate better or being more patient with yourself. These practices reinforce the idea that you are continually evolving and that it's okay to celebrate progress over perfection.

Another way to practice accepting imperfections is by reframing your self-talk. Instead of saying, "I failed," try saying, "I learned." Instead of saying "I'm not good enough," shift to, "I'm doing my best, and that's enough." These subtle changes reshape how you see yourself and your journey. They teach you to approach life with compassion, giving you the space to be vulnerable without self-judgment. Choosing to open up is not about changing who you are; it's about revealing who you are. It's about recognizing that you don't have to carry the weight of appearing perfect. You're allowed to be honest about your struggles and proud of your resilience. When you step into this mindset, you'll find that, not only do you grow, but you also inspire those around you to embrace their own journeys.

So, as you move forward, carry the knowledge that vulnerability is strength. It's the space where healing begins, where creativity flourishes, and where life feels most alive. Accept your imperfections, cherish the moments of honesty, and never forget that choosing to open up is choosing to live fully. Embrace the process, lean into the discomfort, and trust that each step is leading you toward a deeper, richer experience of life and connection. Remember, true strength lies not in never faltering, but in rising each time with greater understanding and compassion for yourself. Let your vulnerability be the bridge that connects your heart with those of others, and let it be the path that leads you to deeper self-awareness and fulfillment. Life is not about perfecting each moment but living fully in each moment—learning, loving, and embracing the beautiful imperfection that makes you human. So, open up, trust the process, and know that every step you take is a step toward a life that's more genuine, more connected, and more profoundly yours.

As you navigate the days ahead, hold onto the truth that vulnerability is not a sign of weakness but a testament to your courage. It's a reminder that you're choosing to show up authentically, with all that you are and all that you're becoming. Embracing vulnerability allows you to create deeper connections, not only with others but with yourself. It's in these moments that you find clarity, strength, and a sense of peace that comes from knowing you're living in alignment with your true self. Let vulnerability be your guide, helping you shed the masks that weigh you down and embrace the freedom that comes from being real. When challenges arise, lean into them with the knowledge that you don't have to face them perfectly—just honestly. Remember that every time you choose to open up, you're paving the way for transformation, healing, and growth; and when doubt creeps in, whisper to yourself, "I am enough, just as I am." Let this be the mantra that propels you forward and anchors you in moments of uncertainty. Trust that the journey of choosing to open up will lead you to a life marked by deeper relationships, greater fulfillment, and a profound understanding of who you are. Embrace each moment, celebrate each breakthrough, and know that your story is worthy of being seen, heard, and cherished.

CHAPTER 12

FINANCES BEHIND CLOSED DOORS

When people bring up finances and money in certain settings, the atmosphere can shift in an instant. It can get personal, intriguing, valuable, or downright uncomfortable. I'm writing about this now in the most honest way possible because I've been there—when my money was funny, and my change was strange. For those of you familiar with that saying, you know exactly what I mean. The worst feeling in the world is needing money for something essential and realizing you don't have it. It's that gut-wrenching moment when a bill deadline approaches, and you're counting pennies and hoping for a miracle. It's sitting at the table on a date and having that uneasy pause when the check comes, knowing you can't cover it fully. It's driving without car insurance and praying every time you get behind the wheel that today won't be the day something goes wrong. It's the anxiety of realizing there isn't enough money for groceries, gas, or even a simple night out with friends.

When money gets tight, life gets frustrating and deeply uncomfortable. There's an added weight that comes with financial struggles—a pressure that's hard to articulate unless you've been in the thick of it. You can't join friends for that concert or major event, and you find yourself constantly saying, "Maybe next time," while hoping they won't ask again too soon. You think twice before even the smallest purchases, calculating how long you can stretch each dollar, each dime. The moments behind closed doors are where the reality of financial stress hits the hardest. It's lying awake at night, staring at the ceiling and running the numbers over and over, trying to figure out what expenses can be cut and what can't be postponed any longer. It's those silent moments of panic when your bank account notification pops up, reminding you of how little you have left.

Here's the truth: facing financial difficulties isn't a sign of failure; it's part of life that many of us go through, often more than once. The key is how we handle those moments, the lessons we learn, and the resilience we build as we work through them. It's about getting real with ourselves and finding ways to improve, whether that means seeking financial advice, budgeting more effectively, or learning how to say "no" when it's necessary. Money behind closed doors is about more than just numbers. It's about the emotions, the pride, the fears, and the hopes that intertwine with every dollar earned and spent. It's about finding balance and discovering that, while money is important, it doesn't define your worth or the quality of your character. If you're in that space now—if your money's funny and your change is strange—know that you're not alone. Many have been there, fought through it, and come out stronger, and so can you.

ASKING MY PARENTS FOR MONEY IN MY THIRTIES

Living with my parents in my 30s after leaving the fishing industry was a humbling chapter in my life. Asking my parents for money at an age where I should have been financially independent was an experience that brought waves of shame, especially when it came to dating. The last thing a man wants to admit on a date is that he's still living at home. The unspoken reaction from women often felt like, "Oh no, this is a liability. I'm good and I'm out," or, "I'm not in a season where I choose to settle for someone who will drain me instead of adding to me." No woman dreams of a relationship where she has to shoulder the burden without seeing someone contributing to the table. That reality made me question my worth and challenged my confidence during that time.

Being in my 30s and living with my parents hit differently because society often expects people at that age to have their lives together—a steady job, a place of their own, and financial stability. In my case, life didn't go as planned. Coming out of the fishing industry, I had moments of financial abundance, but I squandered it on vacations, clothes, trips, and indulgences. It took six long months before I could contribute to the household and buy my own car, which I eventually used for Uber as a side hustle to make extra money. Yet, the biggest hurdle was the damage done to my credit score and the weight of debt that stalled any progress I tried to make.

The financial stress and the reality of my situation often left me in moments of raw vulnerability. There were times I would isolate myself, crying out and screaming prayers to God, hoping for relief from the burden I was carrying. I was trying to present an image of strength, preaching live online while standing in the beautiful home my parents had bought. What people didn't see behind those broadcasts was the reality of negative balances in my bank account, the constant anxiety about bills I couldn't pay, and the deep regret of failed financial decisions that haunted me.

One of the most painful memories was when I left the fishing industry with $8,000 in savings. I thought I was making a wise move by investing a significant portion of that money into a cryptocurrency scheme called "OneCoin," touted as the next big thing that would surpass Bitcoin. The hype around it was undeniable, and I fell for it without seeking divine guidance or using discernment. My trust and eagerness to secure a quick win led to devastating consequences. When news broke that the CEO of OneCoin was under investigation and possibly dead or imprisoned, half of my savings vanished overnight. The regret I felt was overwhelming; it was a bitter reminder of how easily ambition without wisdom could lead to downfall.

These experiences shaped me and taught me lessons that go beyond financial literacy. They taught me resilience, the importance of seeking wisdom, and the necessity of vulnerability in the face of hardship. Each setback reminded me that behind closed doors, where no one could see, the battles were real and relentless. Through it all, I learned that facing the truth of my circumstances and leaning into faith was the only way forward.

The aftermath of that failed investment left me shaken, embarrassed, and filled with regret. There's a particular type of silence that follows when you realize that the safety net, you thought you had, is gone. It's a silence that echoes with self-doubt and questions of, "Why didn't I see this coming?" and "How could I let this happen?" It's that moment behind closed doors when you're faced with the harsh reality of your choices and their consequences. I tried to keep a brave face in public. I kept going live, delivering messages, trying to maintain the persona of someone who had it together; but behind the screen, my world was falling apart. The bills were piling up, and I felt trapped in a cycle of disappointment. The shame was suffocating. The pride I once had in my independence was now a painful reminder of what I had lost.

Living with my parents in their beautiful new home only added salt to the wound. It was a constant reminder of my setbacks, and I couldn't escape the gnawing feeling of inadequacy. Each time I walked through the door, I felt like I was wearing a mask, pretending everything was fine when it was anything but. My parents were supportive and never made me feel lesser, but the disappointment I had in myself was loud enough for all of us. Dating during that time was another layer of difficulty. How do you explain that you're a grown man in his 30s, still trying to get back on his feet? I knew the stigma. I could see the judgment in people's eyes when I mentioned living at home or that my finances weren't stable. It wasn't just uncomfortable; it felt like a scarlet letter, branding me as someone who wasn't ready, wasn't capable. The fear of rejection kept me guarded, hesitant to be fully honest about my situation.

It wasn't until I started facing my situation head-on, without excuses or denial, that things began to shift. I had to confront my financial habits, my mindset, and most importantly, my relationship with money and security. The turning point wasn't glamorous. It was me, alone in my room, with nothing but a notepad and a pen, writing down every debt, every missed opportunity, and every financial misstep. The tears came freely as I laid it all out—my past mistakes and my determination to change them. I began to shift my focus from feeling sorry for myself to taking tangible steps forward. Driving for Uber became more than just a side hustle; it was a means to regain control. Each ride was a reminder that I was earning, contributing, rebuilding. I slowly started budgeting, making smarter financial choices, and learning from past mistakes. I stayed consistent, and little by little, I started to see progress.

The journey out of financial strain taught me lessons that no classroom ever could. I learned resilience, the importance of seeking wise counsel, and the value of humility. Behind closed doors, I found a version of myself that wasn't just defined by success or failure but by the willingness to get up after every fall. To anyone who finds themselves in a similar space, know this: the struggle may be real and raw, but it is not the end. Your worth is not tied to your bank account, your job title, or the opinions of others. There is a path forward, and while it might be slow and fraught with challenges, it's in those quiet, unseen moments behind closed doors where true transformation takes place.

THE REAL ISSUE WAS LACK OF FINANCIAL INDEPENDENCE

Financial independence is about reclaiming control and creating a life where you're not reliant on anyone else's help. When I was transitioning out of my parents' house, it wasn't just about having my own space—it was about standing on my own two feet financially. That journey had its challenges, and I know some of you reading this may be facing similar struggles. You might be scrolling through your bank account, frustrated with the lack of progress, wondering if true financial freedom is a dream only others get to live. Maybe you're dealing with debt privately, maintaining a brave face while you chip away at those balances. If this resonates, I see you, and I want you to know your private financial struggles are valid—and they're also the starting point for your financial transformation.

Every financial success story begins behind closed doors, in the small, often quiet decisions that set the foundation. Maybe it's choosing to save a little more this month or skipping that impulse coffee run. I used to have a problem with midweek spending, where I'd justify every little expense as harmless until I realized that, over time, those "harmless" purchases were holding me back. Learning to manage those choices, even small ones, was a powerful step toward independence.

The beauty of financial independence is that it doesn't need anyone's validation. You don't have to announce your financial wins on social media or get approval from friends or family. Real financial growth often happens privately, like the transformation of a caterpillar to a butterfly within a cocoon. Behind closed doors, you're free to confront your financial reality without judgment, make mistakes and learn from them, develop a personal relationship with money, and create strategies that fit your unique life.

When you build wealth privately, you can dream big without anyone telling you to be realistic or "just settle." This private journey is all about control—control over your choices, your future, and your freedom. While others might display wealth outwardly, you're quietly building something real and lasting. Not everything that glitters online is gold; often, the most sustainable wealth is built through quiet, consistent dedication. Financial independence requires discipline, dedication, and a commitment to your own goals. Every financial empire started with a simple decision to act, without waiting for permission or validation. Remember this when you're reviewing your budget, planning investments, and making the tough choices.

You're not just managing money—you're architecting your future freedom. Every dollar saved, every wise investment, and every debt paid off is a building block toward that independence. The journey to financial independence can feel lonely at times. I know firsthand the weight of feeling like you're starting from scratch, or the frustration of not feeling in control; but one thing I've learned is that you should never let money control you—you control it. Don't simply chase after money; build something real that will let it come to you. Financial independence isn't just a dream; it's a journey made up of small, consistent steps that, over time, lead to a life of control, choice, and true freedom.

As you continue on this path to financial independence, remember that every step forward, no matter how small, is progress. Building a solid foundation takes time, patience, and resilience. There will be moments when it feels like you're barely moving, or that every gain is followed by a setback. Trust that each decision you make toward managing your finances responsibly is contributing to something far greater than immediate gratification—it's laying the groundwork for a stable and fulfilling future. It's essential to celebrate your milestones, no matter how modest they may seem. Whether it's paying off a credit card balance, creating an emergency fund, or simply sticking to a budget for the month, these are wins worth recognizing. Financial independence is not about achieving perfection but about cultivating consistency and resilience. Every dollar you choose to save instead of spend, every debt you choose to tackle, and every small sacrifice you make contributes to your bigger vision.

This journey requires you to look at money in a new way. Instead of seeing it as something that controls you, view it as a tool you command. With that mindset, your financial decisions become acts of empowerment. Each conscious choice—whether to invest, save, or cut back on unnecessary spending—is an affirmation that you're building a life that aligns with your values and long-term goals. Remember, the path to financial freedom doesn't have to look like anyone else's. It's easy to feel pressured when others are posting about their lavish lifestyles or "quick" success stories, but those snapshots don't tell the full story. Financial independence built on authenticity and wisdom is often a slower process, one that grows quietly in the background until it blossoms into something meaningful and lasting.

Along the way, surround yourself with resources that reinforce your goals. Read books on personal finance, listen to podcasts about financial independence, or join online communities of like-minded individuals who are also on this journey. Every bit of knowledge you gain and every story you hear will reinforce the idea that financial freedom is attainable, even if it feels distant right now. Lastly, don't forget to nurture the mindset that will sustain you through this journey. Patience, discipline, and resilience are the qualities that will keep you moving forward even when progress feels slow. Financial independence isn't achieved overnight, but with each thoughtful decision and each wise investment, you're building a future where you're no longer defined or limited by financial constraints. So, keep going. Stay focused on your goals, protect your progress, and remember that this journey is as much about growth as it is about gaining financial freedom. Let every choice you make today bring you one step closer to a life defined by independence, control, and peace of mind.

MONEY BULLIED AND NUMBED ME AT THE SAME TIME

Writing this in all honesty and transparency, I used to see money as an enemy, a trap I couldn't escape. Every paycheck felt hollow, almost mocking me with its insignificance. Have you ever felt like money was more than just a necessity—that it held you in a vice, dictating your life with its limitations? Bills stacked up like autumn leaves, collecting faster than I could handle, each one a reminder of the cold financial winter I was trapped in. The truth is: money can get deeply emotional. It can push you to the edge, weighing down your spirit, yet still spark relief or excitement when a deposit finally hits. I'll never forget the pandemic, when everything turned upside down. Businesses closed, incomes dried up, and I found myself haunted by phone notifications that seemed relentless. Each buzz was a new reminder of obligations I couldn't shake, each ping a reminder of another bill waiting to be paid. Money didn't even feel like currency anymore; it felt like fear, anxiety, and shame all wrapped up in digital numbers. I remember lying awake in the early hours, 3 a.m. shadows creeping across my room, feeling crushed by the weight of every financial decision, every bill, every debt.

During those long nights, I began to realize something: my spending was reactive, not constructive. Car repairs, credit card payments, unexpected expenses—they were all fires I was constantly trying to put out. Instead of facing the issues, I was consumed by embarrassment, trying to avoid the shame of it all. Every financial crisis felt like another emergency, leaving me as a firefighter, scrambling to save what I could at the last second. When I finally did have some money, I spent it so fast that I could barely track where it went. It was less about planning and more about escaping, about soothing the discomfort and worry that had become constant companions. It was a trauma response, not a solution. I wasn't working toward stability; I was just trying to survive. Reflecting on this now, I see how reactive I'd become, always bracing for the next financial disaster, always feeling like I was just one step away from losing control. It took time and some hard truths to realize that handling money this way wasn't just unsustainable—it was hurting me. I needed to redefine my relationship with money, to move from a cycle of fear and reaction to one of intentionality and resilience. It was the first step in breaking free from those chains and building a foundation that wouldn't just get me through but would allow me to thrive.

As I began to untangle my relationship with money, I realized I had to step out of survival mode. I couldn't keep living as though I was trapped in a never-ending emergency, a cycle that drained not only my wallet but also my spirit. I needed a fresh approach, a mindset shift that would allow me to see money as a tool—not an enemy or a source of shame, but something I could work with to create a future I wanted. The first step was admitting that I needed help. I had to stop hiding behind pride and actually sit down with the numbers, really understand my finances in a way I'd avoided for years. I learned to face the reality of my expenses, even the ones that made my heart sink, like mounting credit card debt and overdue bills. It wasn't easy, but each step brought a sense of clarity that had been missing for so long. I could finally start asking myself what my financial goals were and, more importantly, how I wanted to feel about my money. I started by setting small, achievable goals. Things like saving $100 a month or cutting back on unnecessary expenses. I built a budget—not the kind that felt suffocating, but one that allowed for some breathing room and a little enjoyment. I learned that financial independence wasn't about cutting myself off from everything; it was about creating a structure that let me make intentional choices.

With each small goal I reached, I could feel the chains of financial fear loosening. I began to feel empowered rather than embarrassed. Instead of being reactive, I found myself becoming proactive. I was no longer that person panicking at 3 a.m. over unpaid bills. Now, I was taking control, building a future that felt stable and real, and with time, I learned to appreciate the beauty in financial growth. The process wasn't overnight; it was slow and steady, but it was worth it. I came to see every dollar saved, every debt paid off, as a victory. I was no longer fighting my money; I was building a life with it, one step at a time.

If I can offer any advice from this journey, it's this—facing your finances is like facing any other fear. It feels overwhelming at first, but once you're in it, once you see progress—even small progress—you start to feel a strength you didn't know you had. Financial independence isn't a one-time goal; it's a process, a shift that happens slowly and with intention. It's about honoring your future self enough to make decisions today that will give you peace, stability, and the freedom to dream. So, if you're in a place where money feels like a burden, know that there is a way forward. It starts behind closed doors, in those quiet moments when you decide to choose something different. Choose stability. Choose hope. With each choice, you'll find yourself moving closer to the life you've always wanted—one free from the fear and weight that money can bring. It's a journey worth taking.

As I continued on this path, I realized that financial independence was as much an inner journey as it was a practical one. I began to feel lighter, as though each decision I made to save or to plan lifted a weight off my shoulders. My relationship with money transformed from a reactive struggle to a proactive choice, a tool that worked for me rather than against me. Instead of fearing the next expense, I started looking forward to the future. I began envisioning the kind of life I wanted to live—one where financial security wasn't just a fleeting feeling but a lasting foundation. I started to recognize the power of small, consistent steps. Every time I resisted a purchase or made an extra payment toward a debt, it wasn't just about the money; it was about honoring my commitment to myself. There was a deep satisfaction in seeing my savings grow, however slowly, because each dollar saved was a reminder of my resilience. It reminded me that I was building something worthwhile, something that would give me peace for years to come.

One of the most profound shifts happened when I realized that financial independence wasn't about a specific number or income bracket. It was about creating stability, about knowing I could rely on myself to handle whatever came my way. It was about finding freedom—not the freedom to buy whatever I wanted, but the freedom from financial anxiety. It was about cultivating a mindset where I could face financial challenges with confidence, where I could trust myself to make wise decisions. As I gained more control over my finances, I noticed that the rest of my life started to change, too. My confidence grew in ways I hadn't anticipated. I was no longer defined by the money I made or the struggles I faced. I began to see myself as capable, resourceful, and resilient. The shame that had once filled me every time I looked at my bank account was replaced with pride for the progress I was making.

If there's one takeaway from this journey, it's that true financial freedom isn't just about money—it's about empowerment. It's about understanding that every choice you make, no matter how small, has the power to change your life. It's about knowing that while the journey may feel isolating at times, you're not alone. Many have walked this path and emerged stronger, wiser, and more fulfilled on the other side. So, if you find yourself in a place where financial independence feels out of reach, remember that each small step brings you closer. It's in the simple actions—the mindful decisions, the quiet sacrifices, the moments when you choose to believe in a better future. Keep in mind that financial independence isn't a finish line; it's a daily choice to invest in yourself, to bet on your own resilience, and to build a life that reflects not just your goals, but your true worth. Embrace the journey. Honor each step, and know that with each choice, you are creating a foundation of freedom and peace that will carry you forward, and stronger than ever before.

It's about much more than what's in the bank; it's about the mindset you cultivate and the intentionality you bring to every decision. I realized that financial freedom wasn't about a magical moment when I'd suddenly "arrive" at a certain dollar amount. It was in the quiet, deliberate choices I made each day, in how I treated each dollar with respect, and how I valued my own progress, no matter how small it seemed. Each payment I made toward my debt, each dollar I saved, felt like a small victory. Those moments began to build on each other, creating a momentum that kept me going, even on days when it felt slow or challenging. I started to understand that resilience isn't born from big leaps but from those steady, intentional steps forward. It's about building habits that empower you, even if the change feels incremental at first. Every time I prioritized saving over spending, I was choosing my future self, investing in my own peace of mind.

With time, I began setting new goals that reflected a greater vision for my life. Financial independence opened doors in my mind, and I started dreaming again. I realized that beyond the numbers, I was building something that could give me the freedom to make choices based on my values and passions rather than financial stress. I could finally imagine a life where money was a resource to support my dreams, not a chain that held me back. What's even more powerful is that this journey taught me to trust myself in ways I hadn't before. I learned that I am capable of handling challenges, that I have the power to create stability, and that I don't have to be defined by past mistakes. Financial independence allowed me to look forward without the shadow of shame or fear.

The road to financial freedom is ongoing, and I'm still walking it every day—but now, I carry with me a sense of purpose, a calmness, and a confidence that wasn't there before. I know that each decision, no matter how small, is building a future where I am in control, where I can thrive, and where I am truly free. If you're on this journey too, take heart. Remember that financial independence is not a destination you reach overnight but a path you carve with every thoughtful choice. It's not always easy, and there will be setbacks along the way, but keep going, keep choosing yourself, knowing that each step forward is leading you to a life defined not by limitations but by possibility. Financial freedom is within your reach, and as you move toward it, you're creating a life that reflects your strength, resilience, and deepest dreams.

STORIES OF PEOPLE AND MONEY BEHIND CLOSED DOORS

TIM'S $200K A YEAR EXECUTIVE STORY

The truth about many executives earning $200K a year is that their reality often doesn't match the polished image they project. Tim was one of them. His suit was always impeccable, and his office radiated success, lined with awards and framed recognitions. Yet, behind the sharp appearance was a man unraveling, weighed down by a financial reality he couldn't escape.

Tim's breaking point started with his divorce. At first, it felt like a manageable storm—papers filed, assets divided, joint custody of the kids settled, but as the months turned into years, the financial repercussions of that courtroom decision hit him harder than he'd ever imagined. Child support payments were relentless, consuming a significant chunk of his income. Every paycheck felt like a cruel joke, barely enough to cover the obligations that defined his new reality. What little he had left at the end of the month was too small to make a difference.

Taxes were another beast. Between federal, state, and city deductions, 30 to 35 percent of his six-figure salary disappeared before it ever hit his account. The frustration simmered inside him, spilling out in ways he barely recognized. Tim, once known for his composed demeanor, became short-tempered and impatient. Meetings that once inspired him now felt like battles he couldn't win. Every congratulatory handshake and "Great work, Tim" stung as a reminder of what he was pretending to be—a man who had it all together.

Tim's resentment began to seep into his personal life. His relationships with colleagues became strained; his friends noticed his irritability.

Even his children, during their weekends with him, picked up on the tension he tried so hard to mask. Tim wasn't just financially stretched; he was emotionally depleted. There were nights Tim sat alone in his small, rented apartment—a far cry from the suburban home he'd left behind—feeling like life was pressing down on him. The thought crossed his mind more than once: "What's the point of all this? Am I just working to survive, with nothing to show for it?" He stopped answering calls from old friends, skipped invitations to networking events, and avoided conversations about finances, at all costs. Every discussion about money felt like a spotlight on his failures. He hated the man he saw in the mirror—the one who, despite the titles and accolades, felt like he was drowning in a sea of expectations he could no longer meet.

A MOMENT OF RECKONING

One evening, after an especially difficult day, Tim found himself on the brink of despair. The weight of his financial burdens collided with the emptiness he felt inside. Sitting in his car in the office parking lot, he broke down. It was the first time he allowed himself to cry—not out of weakness, but out of sheer exhaustion. That moment became his turning point. Tim realized he couldn't keep pretending everything was fine. He didn't have all the answers, but he knew he couldn't face his struggles alone anymore. The next day, he made two calls: one to a therapist and another to a financial advisor. Both conversations were uncomfortable, but for the first time, Tim felt like he was taking control.

THE ROAD TO REBUILDING

With the help of his financial advisor, Tim began restructuring his life. He downsized further, letting go of unnecessary expenses and learning how to live on a tight budget. He worked with his therapist to address the anger and shame that had consumed him. Slowly but surely, Tim started to rebuild—not just his finances, but his self-worth. He learned to separate his identity from his bank account. He realized that his value wasn't tied to the numbers on his paycheck or the debt he was chipping away at. Through therapy, he unpacked the emotional weight he'd carried since his divorce, and through disciplined financial planning, he began to see progress, no matter how small.

THE LESSON IN TIM'S STORY

Tim's journey is a sobering reminder that income doesn't equal financial freedom, and success on paper doesn't guarantee peace of mind. Behind the clean suits and corner offices are often untold struggles, hidden in shame and fear of judgment. Tim's story also shows the power of vulnerability. By admitting he needed help, he opened the door to transformation. His road wasn't easy, but it was real, and it was his. For anyone reading this who feels trapped by financial burdens or emotional weight, remember: it's never too late to take the first step toward change. Tim's life began to heal the moment he chose to face the truth—and yours can too.

MICHELLE'S STORY AS A TEACHER

The life of a teacher is often painted as one of service and dedication, but for many, it's a balancing act on the edge of financial survival. For Michelle, a middle school English teacher, the facade of a comfortable middle-class lifestyle was meticulously curated—but it came at an overwhelming cost. By day, she was the picture of poise, standing in front of her classroom, inspiring students to find their voices through literature. By night, she was juggling three side hustles just to keep the lights on and maintain the life people assumed she had.

THE APPEARANCE OF STABILITY

On the surface, Michelle's life looked ideal. She had a modest but well-decorated home in the suburbs, drove a late-model car, and dressed in polished outfits that made her appear every bit the seasoned professional she was. Her colleagues often complimented her style, admiring her ability to "do it all." Parents at her school praised her commitment to their children's education, often asking how she managed to balance it all with such grace.

What they didn't see were the endless hours Michelle spent after school grading papers in her car before heading to her first side hustle: tutoring high school students in math—a subject she barely enjoyed but had mastered well enough to help struggling teens. After that, she would change into her work uniform in a gas station restroom and head to her second job as a server at a local restaurant. On weekends, she freelanced as a virtual assistant, scheduling social media posts and proofreading documents for a small business owner she'd never met in person.

Michelle didn't choose these jobs out of passion or extra ambition. She chose them because she had no other option.

THE REALITY BEHIND THE CURTAIN

Teaching, her main job, paid her just enough to scrape by, but not enough to truly live. The paycheck covered her mortgage and utilities, but not the rising costs of groceries, insurance, and the student loan payments she was still making years after earning her degree. She was terrified of falling behind, not only financially but in the eyes of those who looked up to her.

Maintaining the appearance of stability wasn't just about pride—it was about survival. In the world of education, reputation matters. Michelle knew that if parents or administrators got even a hint of her financial struggles, it could lead to whispers, assumptions, or even fewer opportunities for professional advancement. Teachers are expected to lead by example, to be pillars of the community, and Michelle was determined to uphold that expectation—even as it crushed her.

THE EMOTIONAL TOLL

Living this double life came at a steep emotional cost. Michelle was exhausted, constantly moving from one job to the next, with barely enough time to sleep, let alone recharge. Her weekends were consumed with side hustles and lesson planning, leaving little time for social connections. When friends invited her out, she often declined, citing "grading" as her excuse. In reality, she couldn't afford the dinners or the gas money to get there.

She avoided deeper conversations with colleagues about vacations, home upgrades, or hobbies, terrified that her financial reality might slip out. The isolation deepened, leaving Michelle feeling more alone with each passing day. The vibrant, hopeful teacher who once believed she could change the world was now running on fumes, questioning whether the sacrifices were worth it.

A MOMENT OF CLARITY

One night, after an exhausting double shift at the restaurant, Michelle came home and collapsed on her couch. She stared at the stack of unopened bills on the coffee table, the reminders of a financial burden she couldn't escape. Tears streamed down her face as she whispered, "How did I get here?"

That moment was a turning point. Michelle realized she couldn't keep living this way. She loved teaching, but the demands of maintaining her middle-class image were breaking her spirit. It was time to reevaluate her priorities.

THE JOURNEY TOWARD CHANGE

Michelle began by seeking financial counseling through a free community program. She created a budget that prioritized her essential needs while chipping away at her debt. She took a hard look at her side hustles and decided to quit the restaurant job, even though it scared her to lose the income. The time she gained back was spent building a tutoring network that eventually allowed her to work fewer hours for more pay. She also let go of the pressure to keep up appearances. Michelle started opening up to a trusted friend about her struggles, realizing that vulnerability didn't make her weak—it made her human. She stopped comparing her life to others, focusing instead on small, consistent steps toward stability.

THE LESSON IN MICHELLE'S STORY

Michelle's journey is a reminder that the image we present to the world is often just that—an image. Behind closed doors, even those who seem to have it all together may be fighting battles we can't see. Her story highlights the importance of acknowledging and addressing financial realities, no matter how uncomfortable they may be.

For those in similar situations, Michelle's story offers hope. It's a reminder that progress doesn't happen overnight, but it starts with one brave decision—to face the truth and take the first step toward change. Financial independence is not about maintaining appearances—it's about creating a life that aligns with your values and gives you the freedom to live authentically.

To anyone feeling trapped by financial pressures or overwhelmed by the weight of maintaining an image, know this: You are not alone. Your worth is not defined by your bank account, your possessions, or the lifestyle others think you should have. Real strength comes from owning your story and working toward a future that feels true to you.

PREACHING MY WAY INTO MY FIRST HOME: A TESTIMONY OF FAITH, CONSISTENCY, AND STRATEGY

During the pandemic, when the world seemed to pause, my journey took an unexpected turn that redefined my life and finances. I didn't set out to be a content creator, much less on TikTok. The idea of posting videos on a platform known for dancing and trends didn't appeal to me, but God had other plans. He spoke clearly, saying, "Go back to preaching one-minute messages. Keep them simple, practical, and applicable."

At first, I hesitated. How could such short messages make an impact? But obedience became my focus. I followed His lead, and what happened next was extraordinary. Within three months of launching my TikTok page, I went from zero followers to nearly 20,000. My strategy was clear and focused: each video followed a structured format—an introduction, scripture, illustration, main point, and closing statement. They were like mini-sermons, designed to meet people where they were.

THE VIRAL BREAKTHROUGH

Consistency became my greatest strength. I posted daily, stayed diligent, and trusted the process. Two of my videos went viral, each nearing a million views. The timing couldn't have been better. During the pandemic, people were at home searching for hope, encouragement, and meaningful content. My messages resonated deeply, not because they were perfect, but because they were authentic and rooted in God's word.

This experience wasn't only about gaining followers—it was about leveraging the opportunity to spread hope, build community, and create financial stability. TikTok became a platform for ministry, growth, and ultimately, a stepping stone toward owning my first home.

THE FINANCIAL SHIFT

Behind the scenes, my financial journey was transforming. The income I earned through TikTok live sessions and partnerships began to grow steadily, but what truly changed was my approach to finances. I learned that financial independence requires leveraging what you have to create opportunities for growth. However, the road wasn't without challenges. My initial investments in cryptocurrency were filled with missteps. I poured money into Dogecoin and other smaller cryptocurrencies, hoping for quick returns, only to lose a significant portion of my savings. Those experiences taught me the importance of research, patience, and discernment in financial decisions. Now, I make smarter investments, like Bitcoin, which has shown steady growth over time. For example, Bitcoin recently surged nearly 25%, reflecting its economic value. I believe its potential will only increase, and I've positioned myself to benefit from its rise. These lessons, though hard-earned, have become the foundation of my financial literacy.

BUILDING MY FIRST HOME

As my TikTok platform grew, I realized the power of leveraging influence for greater opportunities. The income I earned wasn't merely for consumption—it became a tool for transformation. I began saving intentionally, cutting unnecessary expenses, and reinvesting in areas that could grow my financial base. The process wasn't without moments of doubt or struggle, but I maintained the same mindset I had when creating content: consistency, persistence, and faith. Every dollar saved, every investment made, and every opportunity seized brought me closer to my dream of homeownership. Preaching my way into my first home was more than a financial journey—it was a spiritual one. It was about trusting God, taking calculated risks, and staying faithful to the calling He placed on my life. My testimony demonstrates that when you align your actions with God's instructions, doors open in ways you never imagined.

YOUR TURN

If you're starting from nothing, know that your journey can lead to incredible breakthroughs. Take what you have—no matter how small—and work with it. Use your talents, remain consistent, and stay open to opportunities. Whether it's starting a side hustle, creating content, or learning to invest wisely, the path to financial stability begins with one step of faith.

You don't have to know the whole plan; you just have to trust the process. When God is at the center, even your smallest efforts can yield extraordinary results. Keep going, keep building, and keep believing. Your story is still being written.

THE PATH FORWARD: LESSONS FROM MY JOURNEY

Reflecting on the journey that led me to owning my first home, I see a series of pivotal lessons woven into every step. These weren't just about money, platform growth, or strategy—they were about character, discipline, and the unshakable foundation of faith. I want to break down the lessons in a way that will empower you as you navigate your own financial and personal breakthroughs.

1. CONSISTENCY IS THE KEY TO BREAKTHROUGH

When I started posting one-minute messages on TikTok, there were days I felt invisible—days when the views didn't come, the engagement seemed low, and I questioned whether my efforts mattered. Then God reminded me that consistency isn't about instant results; it's about sowing seeds. Every message I recorded, every live session I hosted, every bit of effort I put in, added to something bigger than what I could see. Consistency isn't just about showing up; it's about showing up with faith and intention. Whether it's creating content, saving a small portion of your paycheck, or studying a new skill, the daily act of persistence builds something powerful. Over time, that compound effect can move mountains. The key is to not give up during the quiet seasons. When you feel unseen, when progress feels slow, that's often when the real growth is happening.

2. STEWARD WHAT YOU HAVE

I didn't start with a huge platform or endless resources. In fact, I started with very little—just my phone, my voice, and the desire to be obedient to what God was asking me to do. It would've been easy to say, "I don't have enough," but I realized that what's in your hand is enough when you give it to God. This applies directly to finances as well. Stewardship isn't about the size of your income; it's about how you manage it. I had to learn to make better decisions with what I had. Instead of spending impulsively, I started tracking every dollar. I set small, attainable savings goals. Even when the amount felt insignificant, I knew I was building habits that would sustain me in the future. Stewardship also means honoring the opportunities you're given. For me, that meant treating every TikTok post like a sermon in a packed church. Whether your current role feels big or small, give it your best. Excellence in small things sets the stage for greater opportunities.

3. INVEST IN LEARNING BEFORE INVESTING IN OPPORTUNITIES

One of the hardest lessons I learned was through my losses in cryptocurrency. When I jumped into investments without truly understanding the risks, I lost thousands of dollars. That loss wasn't just financial—it was emotional. It shook my confidence and made me question my decisions;

but looking back, it was one of the most valuable lessons of my life. Now, I approach every opportunity with preparation. I take the time to research, to ask questions, and to seek wise counsel. Investing in knowledge is just as important as investing in opportunities. Whether it's finances, a new business venture, or a personal decision, gaining knowledge *first* sets you up for long-term success. I also learned to surround myself with people who had the expertise I lacked. Don't be afraid to ask for help or to seek advice from those who've walked the path you're on. Pride can be expensive—humility can save you from costly mistakes.

4. LEVERAGE YOUR GIFTS FOR GROWTH

Your gifts are more valuable than you think. For me, preaching one-minute messages seemed small at first. I wondered if it would even make a difference, but God took that small act of obedience and turned it into something bigger than I ever imagined. Your gift might be cooking, writing, designing, teaching, or organizing. Whatever it is, it has the potential to open doors you never knew existed. The key is to use what you have. Don't wait for the perfect opportunity or the perfect timing. Start now. Leverage your gifts, not only to create income, but to create impact. When you use your talents to serve others, the rewards often come in ways you didn't expect. Whether it's financial stability, personal fulfillment, or deeper connections, your gifts are a tool for both growth and giving.

5. TRUST GOD'S TIMING

There were moments during this journey when I felt like nothing was working—moments when I wanted to quit—when the weight of financial pressure and personal doubt felt too heavy to bear; but God's timing proved to be perfect, even when I couldn't see it in the moment. Trusting God's timing means letting go of the need to control every detail. It's about surrendering your plans to His greater plan. It's about understanding that delays are not denials—they're often preparations. Every time I felt stuck, God was aligning the right audience, the right opportunities, and the right resources. This doesn't mean waiting passively. Trusting God's timing requires action. It's stepping out in faith, even when the outcome isn't clear. It's staying diligent, even when progress feels slow. And it's believing that the seeds you're planting now will bear fruit in the seasons to come.

WHAT I'VE LEARNED

Every breakthrough starts with a decision. Whether it's choosing to stay consistent, stewarding what you have, or trusting the process, it all begins with one step. My journey from posting one-minute messages to owning my first home wasn't easy, but it was worth every struggle, every lesson, and every act of faith. If you're in a season where the journey feels long, I want you to know this: you're closer than you think. Keep moving forward, keep trusting, and keep believing. The best chapters of your story are still being written, and when the breakthrough comes, you'll look back and see that every step mattered. Every sacrifice, every lesson, every moment of faith—it all led you to where you're meant to be.

CHASING MONEY VS. LETTING MONEY CHASE YOU

The older I get, the more I realize the importance of understanding the difference between chasing money and letting money chase you. It's not just about how much you work—it's about how effectively you work. The difference between endless hustle and strategic moves can determine whether your day is filled with exhaustion or true productivity.

Early on, I fell into the trap of chasing money. I worked tirelessly, trading hours for dollars, only to see my earnings barely cover the essentials. However, as time went on, I learned that working smarter—not harder—was the key to financial stability and freedom. One pivotal shift was leveraging my VA disability check. Instead of treating it as a single source of income, I used it as a foundation to build multiple streams of income. Currently, I have four streams of income, which has allowed me to navigate life's uncertainties, including taxes and unexpected expenses, with a sense of control and preparation.

The truth is, you can tell when someone is chasing money. They're constantly surrounded by scarcity—broke friends, mounting excuses, and the unending grind of giving their time to an underpaying job. The paycheck barely scratches the surface of their bills, leaving them stuck in a cycle of frustration.

EXAMPLES OF CHASING MONEY

1. THE DESPERATE NETWORKER

They jump at every MLM (multi-level marketing) scheme promising quick riches but delivering little value. They alienate friends and family with constant pitches to join their downline or buy overpriced products. Month after month, they end up spending more than they earn—losing an average of $500 monthly. The result? A strained social circle and deeper financial strain.

2. THE STATUS CHASER

They lease luxury cars they can't afford and max out credit cards on designer clothes to keep up appearances. On the surface, they seem successful, but their bank account tells a different story. Each month, debt piles up, eventually totaling a loss of $3,000 or more. The chase for status leaves them financially drained and emotionally exhausted.

3. THE OVERWORKED PROFESSIONAL

This person works 90 hours a week, sacrificing time with their family and their health. They make a respectable salary—$120K annually—but have no balance or quality of life. Gaining weight from stress and lack of exercise, they find themselves on a fast track to burnout. Despite the income, they feel like they're working to survive, not thrive.

4. THE SIDE HUSTLER JUGGLER

They take on every gig they can find, driving rideshares after work, delivering food on weekends, and selling items online late at night. While they admire their own grind, they're constantly drained and barely making progress. Their minimal gains don't justify the time and energy spent, leaving them stuck in an exhausting hamster wheel.

5. THE JOB HOPPER

Every six months, they're onto a new job, chasing higher paychecks but missing the opportunity to develop meaningful skills. While they may see temporary increases in income, their careers stagnate due to a lack of growth and consistency. Instead of climbing the ladder, they're stuck at the starting line of each new role.

FLIPPING THE SCRIPT: LETTING MONEY CHASE YOU

The key to letting money chase you is rooted in three principles: leverage, strategy, and intentionality.

1. **Leverage:** Use what you have to create more. For me, leveraging my VA disability check allowed me to create additional income streams, like investments and side hustles that didn't drain me.

2. **Strategy:** Stop working harder; start working smarter. Invest in skills and tools that multiply your efforts. This could mean learning about investments, developing a high-demand skill, or creating a scalable side hustle.

3. **Intentionality:** Focus on long-term growth over short-term wins. Instead of jumping at every opportunity, be intentional about the ones that align with your goals and values.

When you shift from chasing money to building wealth, everything changes. You begin to see time as your most valuable asset. You prioritize quality over quantity and start creating systems that allow your money to work for you. So ask yourself: Are you chasing money, or are you positioning yourself to let it chase you? Remember, every dollar you earn is a seed. Use it wisely, plant it strategically, and watch as it grows into the financial independence you deserve.

The journey from chasing money to letting money chase you starts with a mindset shift. It requires you to step back, evaluate your habits, and create a strategy for intentional growth. The hustle culture glamorizes constant movement, but without direction, all that effort leads to burnout instead of breakthroughs. Here's the reality: If you're always chasing, you'll never be in control. If you focus on building the right habits and systems, money will start chasing you.

BREAKING DOWN THE TRANSITION

1. KNOW YOUR "WHY"

Chasing money often comes from a place of survival or insecurity. The need to pay bills, keep up appearances, or avoid failure creates a frantic, unstructured approach. Letting money chase you begins when you identify your "why." Why do you want financial independence? Is it freedom, security, legacy, or the ability to give generously? Once your "why" becomes clear, it will guide your decisions and keep you grounded.

2. CREATE A FINANCIAL FOUNDATION

Letting money chase you doesn't happen overnight. It starts with building a stable foundation. For me, leveraging my VA disability check was a game-changer. That consistent stream of income gave me breathing room to explore investments, start side hustles, and set goals. Whether it's a part-time job, a pension, or savings, find your financial anchor and use it as a launchpad.

3. STOP TRADING TIME FOR MONEY

Chasing money often looks like trading time for dollars—working long hours, multiple jobs, and exhausting yourself. Instead, look for ways to make your money work for you. This could mean investing in stocks, real estate, or even starting a passive income stream like creating an online course. The key is to shift from reactive earning to proactive growth.

4. DIVERSIFY YOUR INCOME STREAMS

One income stream is rarely enough. Financial independence comes from having multiple streams that support you. For example, I currently have four streams of income. One is steady, one is long-term, and the other two allow me to take advantage of opportunities as they arise. Whether it's freelancing, investing, or building a small business, diversification protects you from unexpected financial challenges.

5. LEARN TO SAY NO

Chasing money often involves saying "yes" to everything—every gig, every opportunity, and every side hustle, no matter how draining. Letting money chase you means learning to say "no" to things that don't align with your goals. Focus your energy on high-value opportunities and trust that quality over quantity will pay off in the long run.

PRACTICAL STEPS TO LET MONEY CHASE YOU

1. AUTOMATE YOUR SAVINGS AND INVESTMENTS

Set up automatic transfers to savings accounts, retirement funds, or investment portfolios. When you remove the temptation to spend, your wealth grows consistently. Even small amounts add up over time.

2. DEVELOP A HIGH-INCOME SKILL

Instead of chasing small paychecks, invest in a skill that commands higher earnings. Whether it's coding, consulting, writing, or public speaking, mastering a marketable skill shifts the power dynamic in your favor.

3. TRACK AND OPTIMIZE YOUR SPENDING

It's easy to lose track of where your money is going. Start by analyzing your expenses. Identify the "leaks"—those small, unnecessary costs—and redirect that money toward savings or investments.

4. BUILD A NETWORK OF MENTORS AND ALLIES

Financial independence is rarely a solo journey. Surround yourself with people who inspire you, teach you, and challenge you to think bigger. Whether it's a financial advisor, a business mentor, or a supportive community, the right network can open doors you didn't even know existed.

5. FOCUS ON LEGACY, NOT LIFESTYLE

Chasing money is often tied to keeping up appearances. Letting money chase you is about creating a legacy. It's about building something that outlasts you—whether that's a business, investments, or a financial foundation for your family.

EXAMPLES OF TRANSITIONING FROM CHASING TO ATTRACTING MONEY

THE DESPERATE NETWORKER REIMAGINED

Instead of jumping into every MLM scheme, the networker invests in learning about affiliate marketing, a legitimate way to earn passive income online. They build a website, create valuable content, and earn through commissions—no pitches to friends required.

THE STATUS CHASER REDIRECTED

Rather than leasing luxury cars and buying designer clothes, the status chaser prioritizes financial education. They redirect their spending to assets like real estate or stocks, slowly building wealth that supports the lifestyle they truly want.

THE OVERWORKED PROFESSIONAL REFOCUSED

The professional scales back their hours and invests in productivity tools or software that streamlines their work. With better work-life balance, they pursue side projects that generate additional income and bring fulfillment.

THE SIDE-HUSTLE JUGGLER RESTRUCTURED

Instead of juggling multiple low-paying gigs, the side hustler identifies one or two high-value opportunities, such as freelance writing or consulting. By focusing their energy, they increase their hourly rate and free up time.

THE JOB HOPPER RECOMMITTED

The job hopper stops chasing short-term pay increases and invests in professional development. They take courses, gain certifications, and build a specialized skill set that commands a higher salary and long-term stability.

WHY THIS MATTERS

Chasing money leads to burnout, frustration, and often, financial instability. Letting money chase you requires discipline, strategy, and patience, but the rewards are immeasurable. It's about building a life where you're in control—not controlled by financial stress.

Remember, every decision you make today lays the foundation for your future. Whether you're saving a few dollars, learning a new skill, or investing in your network, each step brings you closer to financial independence. You don't have to chase money endlessly. Shift your mindset, put systems in place, and watch as the opportunities—and the money—begin to find you.

CHAPTER 13

RELATIONSHIPS BEHIND CLOSED DOORS

There's a truth I can no longer stay silent about. In my years of pastoral counseling, I've witnessed an epidemic that's quietly destroying relationships: the desperate need to maintain a perfect social media image. It's not just about the carefully curated photos or the meticulously planned anniversary posts—it's about the growing chasm between public perception and private reality. Behind every flawless vacation snapshot and heart-emoji-filled comment thread, countless couples are drowning in silence.

Just last week, a husband broke down in my office, his Instagram-perfect marriage crumbling. "Every 'like' felt like a lifeline," he confessed, his voice barely a whisper. "We thought if we could convince everyone else we were happy, maybe the happiness would become real." Here's the brutal truth: no amount of virtual applause can bridge the gulf between two hearts growing apart. Those fleeting dopamine hits from likes and comments are merely Band-Aids on bullet wounds, masking the deeper disconnection that festers behind closed doors.

The most insidious aspect of this digital masquerade is how it poisons authentic relationships through comparison. I've sat with too many couples who measure their private struggles against others' highlight reels, not realizing they're comparing their raw footage to someone else's final cut. The irony? Many of the seemingly perfect relationships they envied later ended in divorce. The polished posts were just that—a polish on a cracking foundation.

THE PRICE OF PERFORMANCE

The toll of maintaining this public facade is staggering. Recently, a wife realized she'd spent eight hours planning and executing the perfect anniversary photoshoot, but couldn't remember her last meaningful conversation with her husband. Another client described the gut-wrenching experience of watching his partner craft beautiful captions about their relationship moments after their worst arguments. "It felt like we were living two different marriages," he said, "… the real one and the Instagram one."

These performances, intended to protect their image, become the very thing that destroys their intimacy. Every moment spent filtering photos is a moment not spent nurturing real connection. Every carefully crafted caption represents an authentic conversation that never happened. In their desperate pursuit of external validation, these couples are trading their private bond for public approval.

THE FREEDOM OF AUTHENTICITY

Yet, there's hope. The couples who break free from this cycle all share one profound revelation: Freedom lies in authenticity. When they finally stop performing for an audience and start showing up for each other, something extraordinary happens. The fog of perfectionism lifts, and they rediscover what drew them together in the first place.

"I had forgotten what it felt like to *just be me* with her," one husband told me, his eyes bright with rediscovered joy. "No filters, no staging, no pressure. Just us." This is the transformative power of private authenticity—it creates a space where masks can fall away, and real love can take root. A thriving relationship isn't built on projecting perfection; it's built on creating a sanctuary where both partners can be fully themselves, vulnerabilities and all. The path won't always be smooth, but facing challenges together, without the pressure to perform, creates a bond that no amount of likes can match.

POSTING FROM A REAL PLACE VERSES POSTING FOR PEOPLE

What I want you to take away from this is simple: The strength of your relationship isn't determined by how it looks to others. It's determined by how it feels to you. Behind closed doors, in the quiet moments that no one else sees, is where the real work happens. That's where love is tested, nurtured, and grown. One couple I counseled shared a turning point in their marriage. They decided to step back from social media entirely for six months. During that time, they learned to communicate more openly, to prioritize time with each other, and to rebuild trust. When they finally returned online, their posts were less frequent but more meaningful. "We're not posting for anyone else now," the wife said. "We're just sharing what genuinely makes us happy." The testimony of love unseen is one that resonates deeply because it's rooted in what truly matters. It's not about how others perceive your relationship; it's about the bond you share when no one else is watching. When you invest in those unseen moments, you'll find a connection that can withstand the trials and temptations of the modern world.

As you reflect on your own relationships, ask yourself: Am I more focused on how we appear to others than how we truly feel together? If the answer is yes, don't despair. Every relationship has room to grow, to deepen, and to heal. It starts with choosing authenticity over appearances, connection over comparison. Behind closed doors is where the real story of your love is written. Make it one that's honest, one that's full of grace, and one that you're proud to live—even if no one else ever sees it.

RECLAIMING REAL CONNECTION IN A WORLD OBSESSED WITH ILLUSIONS

In a world where love is reduced to swipes and likes, where commitment has to compete with endless options, and where connecting often feels anything but real, we need to have an honest conversation about what it means to truly build and sustain relationships today. Relationships today are miles away from what they were in the 80s and 90s. For those of us who grew up in those decades, we remember a time when communication wasn't so instant but was far more intentional. We didn't have iPhones or notifications buzzing every second. Back then, connection required effort, patience, and presence—qualities that seem to have taken a backseat in today's swipe-right culture.

THE FAST-FOOD ROMANCE AND SHOPPING-MALL DATING

Look around you. What do you see? People hunched over their phones, scrolling endlessly through curated snapshots of other people's "perfect" lives—double-tapping on someone's proposal picture while ignoring the person sitting right across the table—planning the ideal Instagram post about a date while forgetting to actually enjoy it. This is what we've come to—a world where we appear connected but feel more alone than ever. We've developed what I call the "Fast-Food Romance." It's quick, convenient, and disposable. It requires no real commitment, just like pulling into a drive-thru to grab a quick bite. There's no substance, no nutritional value, and ultimately, no lasting satisfaction. Then there's the "Shopping-Mall Dating" mindset. These are the people always looking for the next best deal. Maybe she's not enough. Maybe he could be taller, richer, or more like some influencer. It's the constant search for perfection that leaves us disconnected and dissatisfied, blind to the beauty of the person already in front of us.

SOCIAL MEDIA PERFORMANCE AND INSTANT GRATIFICATION

Another modern trap is the "Social Media Performance." This is where people are more invested in showing love than actually living it. They're more focused on getting the perfect couple selfie than on fostering real connection. Their relationship becomes a performance, a highlight reel designed to impress others, while the real work of love is left undone. Then there's the demand for instant gratification—wanting the depth of a real relationship without putting in the work. They want the grand gestures, the emotional intimacy, and the steady commitment, but they're not willing to endure the mess, the misunderstandings, or the effort it takes to build something lasting. They want the harvest without planting the seeds or tending the soil.

WHAT REAL RELATIONSHIPS LOOK LIKE

Real relationships are not a highlight reel. They're not a perfectly filtered series of moments crafted for public consumption. They're messy. They're complicated. They're beautiful in ways that can't always be captured in a photo or post. A real relationship is when you choose to stay after the Instagram filters are gone, when you build something meaningful in a world obsessed with temporary fixes. It's about putting down your phone and truly seeing the person in front of you. It's choosing depth over half-baked moments. It's choosing to work through the hard conversations, the misunderstandings, and the struggles instead of walking away at the first sign of discomfort. Real love requires showing up—not just once, but consistently.

WHAT'S BEEN FORGOTTEN

Today, talking has replaced dating. Hanging out has replaced commitment. Keeping options open has replaced loyalty. Following someone on social media has replaced genuinely knowing them. But here's the truth: the human heart hasn't changed. We still crave real, genuine connection. We still want to be loved, understood, and valued for who we are—not for what we post or how many likes we get. Real relationships begin with presence, with choosing to see and value the person in front of you. They thrive in the quiet, unfiltered moments—when it's just the two of you, no audience, no performance. Love grows in the messy, the mundane, and the meaningful.

So, as you navigate relationships in this digital age, ask yourself: Are you building something real, or are you just playing a part for the crowd? Are you choosing convenience over connection, or are you willing to do the hard, beautiful work of love? Because in a world that's obsessed with the temporary, the true treasure is in what lasts—and what lasts is built behind closed doors, away from the filters and the applause.

THE QUIET WORK OF LOVE

Real relationships don't thrive on the applause of others—they thrive in the quiet work behind the scenes. It's in the moments no one else sees when love is tested and strengthened. It's the late-night conversations where you're honest about your fears and dreams. It's the forgiveness you offer when the other person doesn't deserve it but desperately needs it. It's showing up, even when it's inconvenient, even when it's hard. The truth is, relationships that stand the test of time aren't built on grand gestures; they're built on small, consistent acts of love. It's checking in with your partner during a busy day just to say, I'm thinking of you. It's choosing to listen without interrupting, to empathize even when you disagree. It's the effort you put into understanding their love language and speaking it, even when it doesn't come naturally. When we stop performing for the world and start investing in the person beside us, something beautiful happens. Trust begins to grow. Intimacy deepens. The walls come down. The relationship becomes a refuge, not a stage—and in that refuge, you discover the kind of connection that isn't fleeting but fulfilling.

RESISTING THE COMPARISON TRAP

One of the biggest threats to modern relationships is the comparison trap. Social media has turned us into spectators of everyone else's lives, constantly measuring ourselves against curated snapshots of perfection. But here's what we forget: We're comparing our behind-the-scenes to someone else's highlight reel. What we don't see are the arguments, the insecurities, the silent struggles they face when the camera is off. If we're not careful, comparison can creep into our own relationship and poison it from the inside out. Often, we start looking at what others have and questioning what we lack. "Why doesn't my partner plan romantic dates like that?" "Why don't we have vacations like them?" The truth is, their story is not your story. Your relationship is unique, and it will never look like anyone else's—and that's the beauty of it. The best way to resist the comparison trap is to focus inward. Rather than worrying about how your relationship appears to others, focus on how it feels to you. Are you both happy? Are you both growing? Are you building something that feels authentic and real? Because in the end, it's not the world's opinion that matters—it's the connection you share with each other.

NAVIGATING THE TOUGH SEASONS

Every relationship goes through tough seasons. There will be moments when you feel disconnected, when misunderstandings pile up, when life's pressures make you question everything. These are the moments that define your love—not the easy, carefree days, but the ones where you have to fight for each other. It's in these seasons that true commitment shows its value. Commitment says, "We're in this together, no matter what." It's the willingness to have the hard conversations, to own your mistakes, and to extend grace even when it feels undeserved. It's recognizing that love isn't always a feeling; sometimes, it's a choice—a daily decision to stay, to show up, to keep trying. Here's the truth: When you make it through those tough seasons, the connection on the other side is deeper, stronger, and more meaningful than you could have imagined. The struggles become part of your story, not as wounds but as reminders of what you've overcome together.

CHOOSING DEPTH OVER PERFORMANCE

In this world of fast love and fleeting connections, choosing depth is an act of rebellion. It's choosing to build something real in a culture that values surface-level interactions. It's choosing to put your energy into the relationship itself rather than how it looks to others. Depth means being vulnerable—sharing your fears, your insecurities, your dreams. It means allowing yourself to be fully seen, even when it's uncomfortable. It's about creating a safe space for your partner to do the same, without judgment or criticism. One couple I counseled shared a powerful moment of transformation. They had been arguing for weeks, each feeling unheard and misunderstood. One night, instead of another argument, they sat down and asked each other, "What's really going on? What do you need from me right now?" That simple act of vulnerability shifted everything. They stopped trying to win and started trying to understand. It wasn't a grand gesture—it was an honest one—and it changed the course of their relationship.

A NEW VISION FOR LOVE

The truth is, love in the digital age doesn't have to be shallow or performative. We have the power to redefine what relationships look like. We can choose connection over competition, presence over performance, and depth over distractions. When you think about your relationship, ask yourself: "Are we building something lasting, or are we chasing temporary validation? Are we investing in each other, or are we letting the noise of the world drown out our connection?"

Love isn't meant to be consumed like content. It's meant to be lived, shared, and nurtured in the quiet, unfiltered moments behind closed doors. It's meant to challenge you, grow you, and bring out the best in you. When you choose to approach it with honesty, vulnerability, and commitment, you'll discover a connection that no amount of likes or shares could ever replicate.

THE HEART OF THE MATTER

At its core, love is about showing up. It's about seeing each other—not through the lens of filters or expectations, but as you truly are. It's about choosing to stay, to listen, to care, even when it's hard; and it's about celebrating the beauty of the journey, not just the destination. In a world that's constantly telling you to look outward, to chase validation, to compare, remember this: The most important relationship is the one you're building with the person beside you. It doesn't have to be perfect. It just has to be real. And in that realness, you'll find a love that lasts.

THE QUIET REVOLUTION OF REAL LOVE

Real love doesn't scream for attention. It doesn't need a stage, applause, or approval. It works in the quiet, in the spaces where growth happens. It's in the moments when you're both too tired to talk but still reach for each other's hand. It's when you laugh at the same joke for the hundredth time or when you silently forgive because the relationship is worth more than the argument.

What the world sees will never matter as much as what you build behind closed doors. It's in the whispered reassurances, the unspoken understanding, the sacrifices that no one else will ever know about. Those are the building blocks of love that lasts—not the grand gestures, but the small, steady acts of care that say, I choose you, today and every day.

RELEARNING HOW TO BE PRESENT

One of the most radical things you can do in this fast-paced, hyperconnected world is to slow down and be fully present. It's harder than it sounds. Phones buzz, notifications demand attention, and the temptation to document everything pulls you away from the moment. Being present is a gift you give to your relationship. It's choosing to look into your partner's eyes instead of at your screen. It's hearing their words, not just listening to respond. It's taking time to sit in the silence together, letting the world fade away as you focus solely on each other.

A couple I worked with decided to implement a no-phone policy during dinner. It felt awkward at first, with no distractions to fill the gaps in conversation—but over time, they began to rediscover each other. They laughed more, shared more, and realized how much they had been missing while scrolling. That simple change reconnected them in a way they hadn't experienced in years. Presence matters, and it's worth fighting for.

LETTING GO OF THE PERFORMANCE

There's freedom in letting go of the need to perform, to impress, to curate a version of your relationship for the world to see. When you release the pressure to look perfect, you create space for something far more valuable: authenticity. Authenticity is messy. It means admitting when you're wrong, showing up with all your flaws, and being willing to work through the hard stuff. It's also deeply rewarding. It's where true connection lives. When you stop performing and start being, you'll find that your relationship becomes a safe haven—a place where you can be fully yourself without fear. A friend once told me, "The most beautiful thing about my marriage is that it's mine. No one else sees the way we care for each other in the small moments, and I wouldn't trade that for anything."

That kind of intimacy can't be captured in a photo or explained in a caption. It's built in the quiet, in the unglamorous, in the real.

RECLAIMING THE MEANING OF LOVE

In a world that often cheapens love, making it feel transactional or temporary, we have the power to reclaim its true meaning. Love isn't a commodity to be consumed or a status symbol to flaunt. It's a sacred bond, a mutual commitment, and an ever-evolving journey. To truly love someone is to see them—not who they pretend to be or who the world thinks they are, but who they are at their core. It's choosing to walk beside them, to share their burdens, and to celebrate their victories. It's a daily choice, not a one-time declaration—and here's the truth: Love isn't always glamorous. It's not always easy—but it's always worth it. When you pour into your relationship, when you prioritize connection over convenience, when you choose to love deeply rather than superficially, you'll find a joy that's far greater than anything the world can offer.

MOVING FORWARD TOGETHER

As you navigate this digital age, remember that the most meaningful parts of your relationship won't be found in a post, a like, or a comment. They'll be found in the everyday moments that only you and your partner share. They'll be found in the trust you build, the understanding you nurture, and the love you choose to give. So put down the phone. Look up. See the person in front of you, and know that what you create together is more valuable than any fleeting validation. Because when the world fades away, what remains is the connection you've built—the love that's yours, and yours alone.

WHAT REALLY HAPPENS BEHIND CLOSED DOORS IN RELATIONSHIPS?

Behind every filtered photo is an unfiltered story. Behind every perfect post is a private struggle. It's time we get real about what happens when the world isn't watching. You're not a human doing—you're a human being. The truth is, relationships thrive in that sacred, unfiltered space where two people meet each other as they really are, beyond the applause, beyond the image, beyond the pressure to perform.

Consider the executive power couple everyone envies. Their designer clothes are impeccable, their public presence flawless, but behind the scenes, they're spending nights holding each other through the heartbreak of fertility treatments. Those polished social media posts never show the therapy appointments they're attending together, because in today's culture, it's too candid to be cool. Their public success masks their private struggle, and the gap between what's seen and what's real grows wider every day.

Have you been there? Everything looks good on paper. Everything looks good in the post, but behind the doors of your home, when the cameras are off and the nights get long, the reality of strained communication or emotional distance becomes hard to ignore. Sleeping at opposite ends of the bed, exchanging cold silences—these moments never make it to anyone's feed, but they are the truths many live behind closed doors.

THE MASK OF PERFECTION

Then there's the perfect family in your neighborhood. Their vacation photos look like something out of a dream, but what those images don't show are the second jobs they're working to afford their children's private school education. They laugh for the camera, but the real conversations happen late at night during pillow talk, where they express their fears about making ends meet. The public front may be for the 'Gram,' but the private tears tell the real story. Let me be clear: this isn't about exposing the gap between perception and reality. This is about honoring the sacred space where real love grows—the space where the facades fade, and true connection begins.

WHERE REAL LOVE LIVES

Real love isn't in the highlight reel; it's in the unspoken moments that don't make it to social media. It's built in the trenches of life, where vulnerability, sacrifice, and persistence live. Here are a few places where love truly shows its strength:

- **In Silent Hospital Rooms Where Hands are Held:** It's when one partner sits quietly by the bedside, their presence saying more than words ever could.

- **During Midnight Conversations About Fears and Dreams:** It's when you're both too tired to talk but know that these late-night exchanges are the glue holding you together.

- **Through Quiet Acts of Daily Support:** It's in the coffee made without being asked, the small errands run to make the day easier, the unwavering show of care.

- **In Moments Never Captured by a Camera:** The little gestures—folding laundry together, laughing over inside jokes, a knowing glance in a crowded room—these are the pieces of a life shared, invisible to the world but deeply felt by the heart.

WHEN REAL LOVE HAPPENS

Real love happens when the influencer couple turns off their phones and has a real conversation. It's when newlyweds face family disapproval together, standing united despite external pressure. It's when long-term partners, even after the storm of betrayal, choose each other again, re-affirming their commitment to rebuild what was broken. These are the stories that aren't broadcasted but are the backbone of what it means to love and be loved. They are the quiet triumphs, the battles fought in private, and the choices made daily to nurture something meaningful.

THE UNSEEN BEAUTY OF LOVE

The most beautiful parts of a relationship are often the ones we never see. They're not in the grand proposals or the lavish gifts, but in the quiet strength of showing up for each other day after day. Real love doesn't require validation from the world. It only asks for the courage to be present, the humility to admit faults, and the grace to forgive. So, as you scroll through images of seemingly perfect relationships, remember that the real magic of love happens behind closed doors. It's not about the applause or the likes—it's about the unseen moments where two people choose each other, again and again, in spite of the mess, the challenges, and the imperfections.

Real love is messy, raw, and beautiful; and truthfully, it's far more powerful than any picture could ever capture.

Every solitary moment builds empathy. Private struggles, no matter how isolating, deepen the connection between two people. Every hidden battle fought creates a foundation of resilience that strengthens the core of a relationship. To every couple navigating challenges in the privacy of their shared lives: your struggle is not your failure. The obstacles you face are not a signal of defeat. The pain you carry in silence is not a sign of weakness, and the effort you pour into your relationship, even when no one else sees it, is never wasted.

Behind closed doors is where real love grows—not in perfection, but in persistence. It's where true strength is built, tested, and refined. It's where love becomes more than a feeling—it becomes a choice. A choice to stay, to try, and to fight for each other through the storms.

This season of struggle isn't just shaping your relationship—it's preparing it. The bond you forge in the fire of trials is the bond that propels you to the next level, one where authenticity, trust, and connection reign. You're not alone in this. The beauty of love is that its strength is revealed in its ability to endure, even in the shadows. Take heart, because what you're building behind those closed doors is far more powerful than anything the world could ever see. Behind closed doors, love takes on a deeper, quieter strength. It's not about grand gestures or perfectly curated moments for the world to admire. It's about the resilience built in the stillness. The moments when words fail, but presence remains. It's in the sacrifices you make for each other, the unspoken understanding that carries you through the hardest days, and the quiet faith that tomorrow will bring a new chance to grow together.

When you face the seasons of uncertainty, remember that the strongest trees grow their roots in the storms. What you're experiencing isn't the end of your story—it's a chapter that prepares you for the chapters yet to come. Each challenge is a lesson in patience, compassion, and compromise. Each small victory, like overcoming a disagreement or showing up when it's hard, is a testament to the love you're cultivating. True love doesn't need applause. It doesn't thrive on likes or followers. True love exists in the unseen acts of kindness, the words of encouragement whispered when the world feels heavy, and the commitment to keep showing up for each other, day after day. It's found in the courage to admit when you're wrong, to forgive, and to choose grace over pride.

For the couples working through the hidden challenges, know this: The effort you put into loving each other behind the scenes matters. It's the late-night talks that rebuild trust. It's the shared laughter that eases the weight of the day. It's the moments when you remind each other, "We're in this together." When the world sees only the polished surface, it's the depth of what you've built behind those closed doors that will sustain you. Your story may not be visible to others, but it's real … it's raw … and it's enough. Keep choosing each other, keep fighting for what matters, and trust that the love you nurture in private will shine brighter than anything public ever could.

THE STRENGTH BEHIND THE DOOR

Real relationships aren't defined by the carefully crafted highlights we share with the world but by the unfiltered, unscripted moments that unfold in private. It's behind those closed doors where love is truly tested and proven. The messy, complicated realities—the whispered apologies after a fight, the shared laughter in the midst of chaos, the quiet patience during a storm—these are the threads that weave a lasting bond.

Take, for instance, the young couple who just started their journey together. Outwardly, they seem like the perfect match, smiling in every photo, tagging each other in affectionate posts; but behind those snapshots is the quiet struggle of learning to navigate their differences—figuring out how to communicate through misunderstandings, how to balance their goals, and how to love each other in their imperfections. Those lessons won't trend online, but they're shaping a foundation that will carry them through.

WHEN STRUGGLES FORGE STRENGTH

The true strength of love emerges in the fire of challenges. Imagine the couple who just welcomed a child into their lives. Their social media shows the joy of new parenthood—tiny hands and sleepy smiles—but doesn't show the sleepless nights, the emotional toll of adjusting to a new normal, or the financial strain they're navigating together. Yet, it's in those sleepless nights that they become a team, in the whispered encouragement that their connection grows deeper, and in the shared sacrifices that their love solidifies.

Or consider the couple weathering a financial crisis. Publicly, they appear polished, confident, and in control, but privately, they're holding emergency meetings at their kitchen table, mapping out budgets, cutting back, and finding creative ways to stay afloat. The world sees their resilience as an outcome, but behind closed doors, that resilience is being forged in late-night conversations, mutual support, and the unshakable commitment to face life's challenges together.

THE POWER OF VULNERABILITY

Real relationships thrive on vulnerability—the ability to lay down the masks, to share your fears, your dreams, and even your insecurities. When two people are willing to be truly honest with each other, they create a bond that transcends surface-level connection. Vulnerability is what transforms conflicts into opportunities for growth, and misunderstandings into avenues for deeper understanding. Behind closed doors, love whispers: It's okay to not have it all together. It's okay to cry, to stumble, to admit when you're scared. It's okay to say, "I don't know how we'll get through this, but I'm glad I have you by my side." These moments are the quiet victories of love, the ones that don't get celebrated but deserve to be.

CHOOSING EACH OTHER EVERY DAY

True love is a choice—an everyday decision to show up for one another, even when it's hard, even when it feels inconvenient, even when the world feels like it's falling apart. It's in the small moments: holding hands in a hospital waiting room, preparing their favorite meal after a long day, or sending a simple text that says, "I'm thinking of you." This is where love finds its rhythm—in the mundane, the messy, the miraculous moments of shared life. It's in the arguments that end in understanding, the disappointments met with grace, and the joys magnified because they're shared. These moments may never make it to Instagram, but they're the ones that build a relationship strong enough to withstand the storms.

THE SACRED SPACE BEHIND THE SCENES

Behind closed doors is where the real magic of love happens—not the kind of magic that needs an audience, but the kind that transforms two imperfect people into partners for life. It's where the hard work of loving takes place, where forgiveness is offered, where sacrifices are made, and where the foundation for the future is built. So, as you admire the polished lives of others, remember that behind every filtered post is a story you'll never fully know… and that's okay. The beauty of love isn't in the spotlight—it's in the quiet moments, the whispered reassurances, the unspoken understanding, and the unwavering commitment that no audience will ever see.

In a world obsessed with appearances, cherish the unseen, because the most profound love stories aren't written for the public—they're lived behind closed doors.

THE UNSEEN WORK OF LOVE

Love behind closed doors isn't glamorous, and it rarely follows a script. It's the quiet determination to work through the tough days, the deliberate effort to communicate even when words are hard to find, and the unrelenting commitment to make each other better. This unseen work is the heart of a true relationship—it's what keeps two people moving forward, together.

Take the couple rebuilding trust after betrayal. They won't post about the late-night tears or the difficult conversations. They won't share the vulnerability it takes to admit, "I'm hurt, but I want us to heal." The world may only see their happy smiles months or years down the line, but the real story is in the daily choice to believe in their love again and to walk the long road of reconciliation.

THE SMALL GESTURES THAT SPEAK VOLUMES

Behind closed doors, love speaks in a language far more profound than grand gestures. It's in the quiet, unspoken acts of care that partners show for each other every day. A cup of coffee waiting on the counter. A favorite snack left on the table. A blanket pulled over someone who's fallen asleep on the couch. These acts, though seemingly small, carry the weight of love because they say, "I see you. I care for you. I'm here for you." These are the moments that won't trend, that won't be shared or celebrated publicly. Yet, they are the moments that make love real. They're the invisible threads that hold relationships together when everything else feels like it's falling apart.

THE STRENGTH IN PRIVATE STRUGGLES

Every couple has their own private struggles, and these challenges often become the crucible that forges unshakable bonds. The executive couple navigating fertility treatments, the family scraping together funds for tuition, the partners finding their way back to each other after a betrayal—all of them are facing battles the world will never see, but within these struggles lies the opportunity for profound growth. It's not the absence of difficulty that defines a strong relationship; it's the willingness to face those difficulties together. It's finding strength in shared vulnerability, turning pain into purpose, and refusing to give up on each other, no matter how hard it gets.

WHY LOVE THRIVES IN PRIVACY

The world doesn't need to see everything. In fact, the most enduring relationships are often the ones that prioritize privacy. Why? Because love doesn't need validation. It doesn't need an audience. It needs space to breathe, to grow, to stumble, and to recover. It needs room to exist free from judgment and comparison. Love thrives in privacy because it allows for authenticity. There's no pressure to perform, no need to live up to someone else's standard. Behind closed doors, couples can be their truest selves—flaws, fears, and all—and in that honesty, love finds its deepest roots.

BUILDING A LOVE THAT LASTS

If you're in a relationship, remember this: the real work of love happens when no one else is watching. It's in the moments of selflessness, the efforts to communicate, and the willingness to grow together. It's in the courage to be vulnerable, the grace to forgive, and the determination to keep choosing each other. For those not in a relationship, know this: love worth having is love worth waiting for. It won't be perfect, but it will be real, and when it comes, it will be built on a foundation of trust, understanding, and authenticity—things that are cultivated behind closed doors, not in front of an audience.

THE QUIET VICTORY OF TRUE LOVE

True love doesn't need to be shouted from the rooftops. It doesn't need to be polished for the public eye. Its beauty lies in the quiet victories: the problems solved together, the conflicts resolved with kindness, and the dreams built one day at a time. Behind every filtered photo, every perfectly framed post, remember there's an unfiltered story. It's in those unfiltered stories—those messy, raw, and beautiful realities—where the truest, most enduring love is found.

Cherish the love that grows behind closed doors, because that's where the real magic happens.

RELATIONSHIPS BEHIND CLOSED DOORS: FIVE REASONS FOR STRUGGLE, AND STRATEGIES FOR BREAKTHROUGH

Relationships are complex and nuanced. They often appear polished and perfect to the outside world but hide significant struggles behind closed doors. Over time, I've come to recognize the recurring patterns that cause relationships to falter, as well as the key strategies that help couples overcome those struggles. Drawing from personal experience and years of observation, let's explore five common reasons relationships face challenges and five strategies that lead to meaningful breakthroughs.

One of the most pervasive issues in relationships is communication breakdown. Have you ever been on a date where everything seemed perfect over the phone or in emails, but in person, the energy felt flat?

The conversation didn't flow, and the connection you were expecting just wasn't there. This kind of disconnection happens frequently because communication isn't only about words—it's about presence, energy, and understanding. Even more challenging are the unspoken expectations that often exist between partners. When one person harbors desires or needs they don't articulate, resentment begins to grow. Without clarity, both partners are left guessing, creating a cycle of frustration. Additionally, fear of vulnerability plays a significant role. Emotional walls can feel safer than honesty, but they create distance. In today's world, technology further complicates things. It replaces genuine connection with digital convenience. Text messages and social media often take the place of real conversations, and misunderstandings become the norm as tone and intent are lost in translation. Communication, which should serve as the bridge between two people, instead becomes the barrier that drives them apart.

Another critical challenge is the issue of trust. Trust is foundational to any healthy relationship, yet it's often fragile and difficult to rebuild once it's damaged. Past hurts frequently poison present moments, as unhealed wounds from previous relationships cast a shadow over new ones. Social media exacerbates this problem, feeding insecurities and doubts. A single post, a like, or a comment can raise questions, creating unnecessary tension. Financial secrets also erode trust, introducing a level of deception that leaves partners questioning what else might be hidden. Emotional walls grow higher over time, as past betrayals make it harder for individuals to open up. The fear of betrayal looms large, leaving many people hesitant to fully invest in their relationships. Trust is difficult to establish, and in today's hyper-connected world, where everyone's lives are on display, it feels more fragile than ever.

A third struggle that undermines relationships is identity loss. This occurs when individuals lose sight of who they are outside of the relationship. Often, personal dreams fade into the background as relational obligations take center stage. Instead of growing individually, both partners stagnate. The pressure to prioritize the relationship over personal growth can leave people feeling trapped, disconnected from their passions, and unsure of their sense of self. Over time, this loss of individuality leads to dissatisfaction, resentment, and a deep sense of longing for something more. In some cases, codependency creeps in, masquerading as love. This unhealthy dynamic can create the illusion of closeness while stifling true independence and self-worth. A strong relationship requires two whole individuals, not two people who have lost themselves in each other.

Emotional distance is another silent killer of relationships. Many couples find themselves in the same physical space but emotionally miles apart. They go through the motions of daily life, but the intimacy that once defined their connection has been replaced by routine. The demands of work, family, and other responsibilities create chaos, leaving little room for meaningful connection. Slowly, hearts grow cold, not because of a lack of love, but because of comfort and complacency. Over time, partners become strangers, sharing a life, but no longer sharing their hearts.

Financial stress is another significant burden, testing even the most committed couples. Money problems often lead to arguments, resentment, and feelings of inadequacy. Career demands steal time and energy, leaving little room for relationships to thrive. Society's unrealistic expectations only add to the pressure, making couples feel as though they're constantly falling short. These external factors challenge even the strongest bonds, forcing partners to navigate trials they often feel unprepared for.

Despite these challenges, breakthroughs are possible. Relationships can grow and thrive when both partners commit to doing the work. It starts with mastering communication. Genuine communication requires active listening—hearing what the other person is saying without judgment or interruption. It also means clearly articulating needs, desires, and boundaries. Unspoken expectations only lead to frustration, so clarity is essential. Creating a safe space for vulnerability is equally important. When partners feel seen and heard without fear of rejection, they're more likely to open up. It's also crucial to unplug from technology and be present. Eye contact, undistracted conversations, and shared moments foster connection in ways that no text message ever could. Finally, addressing misunderstandings quickly prevents small issues from festering and turning into larger conflicts.

Rebuilding trust is another key to breakthrough. This process takes time, consistency, and honesty. Addressing past hurts through open dialogue or professional counseling can bring healing. Transparency is vital—whether it's about finances, emotions, or intentions. Social media habits also play a role. Being mindful of what you post and how you engage online can prevent unnecessary misunderstandings. Trust is built through consistent actions, not just words. Over time, emotional walls can come down, creating space for deeper intimacy.

Maintaining personal identity within a relationship is equally important. Pursuing passions, hobbies, and individual goals ensures that both partners continue to grow. Supporting each other's dreams fosters a sense of partnership rather than sacrifice. It's essential to balance togetherness with independence, creating a dynamic where the relationship is a complement to each individual's life, not the entirety of it. True love doesn't erase individuality … it celebrates it.

Fostering emotional intimacy is another crucial step. Being emotionally present means engaging fully with your partner, not just physically but mentally and emotionally as well. Injecting spontaneity into the relationship can break the monotony of routines and reignite passion. Prioritizing quality time—whether through date nights, shared hobbies, or uninterrupted conversations—helps deepen connection. Small gestures, like thoughtful notes or acts of kindness, show your partner that they're valued and appreciated. When intimacy is nurtured, the relationship becomes a refuge rather than a source of stress.

Finally, external pressures weigh heavily on relationships. Family interference often strains partnerships, as loved ones—intentionally or not—create tension. Overcoming external pressures requires intentional effort. Setting boundaries with family members protects the sanctity of the relationship. Approaching financial challenges as a team creates unity and fosters problem-solving. Prioritizing the relationship over career demands ensures that your partner feels valued and seen. Ignoring societal expectations allows couples to focus on what works for them rather than chasing an unattainable ideal. External pressures don't have to break a relationship—they can strengthen it when both partners work together.

Ultimately, the strongest relationships aren't built on grand gestures or public displays. They're built in the quiet, unseen moments behind closed doors. They're forged in the late-night talks, the whispered reassurances, and the unwavering commitment to choose each other every day. True love is messy, raw, and beautiful. It thrives in authenticity, grows through vulnerability, and lasts because of persistence. Behind closed doors is where the real magic happens. Relationships may face struggles, but with intentional effort, they can emerge stronger, deeper, and more fulfilling than ever before.

When we talk about relationships thriving behind closed doors, it's important to emphasize that the true beauty of love lies in the small, consistent actions that build trust, connection, and intimacy over time. It's in the patience to understand, the courage to forgive, and the humility to admit when you're wrong. Love doesn't thrive on perfection—it thrives on persistence and genuine effort. Couples who find their breakthrough often realize that struggles are not the end of the story—they're the beginning of transformation. Each challenge, whether it's communication breakdown, trust issues, or external pressures, offers an opportunity for growth.

The process of overcoming obstacles strengthens the relationship, creating a bond that can withstand future storms. One of the most overlooked aspects of relationship success is self-awareness. Before you can fully commit to another person, you have to know yourself. This includes understanding your triggers, recognizing your strengths and weaknesses, and being honest about your needs. Self-awareness creates a solid foundation for any relationship because it allows you to approach challenges with clarity and maturity. It also prevents the projection of unresolved personal issues onto your partner. In the same vein, relationships flourish when both partners take responsibility for their own growth. It's not enough to expect your partner to fill in the gaps or compensate for your shortcomings. True partnership involves mutual support while still maintaining individual accountability. When each person is committed to becoming their best self, the relationship benefits as a whole.

The concept of seasons is another powerful truth about relationships. Every relationship goes through phases—times of joy, times of struggle, and everything in between. Recognizing these seasons helps couples navigate challenges with grace. The tough seasons, like financial strain or emotional disconnection, aren't permanent. They are opportunities to learn, adapt, and grow stronger together. Similarly, the joyful seasons should be cherished and celebrated. A balanced relationship acknowledges both the highs and the lows, understanding that both are essential for growth.

The role of forgiveness cannot be overstated in the process of rebuilding and strengthening a relationship. Holding onto past hurts only creates bitterness and resentment. Forgiveness doesn't mean forgetting—it means choosing to release the hold that pain has over you. It's a gift you give to yourself and your partner, allowing both of you to move forward without the weight of past mistakes. Forgiveness creates space for healing and paves the way for deeper trust and intimacy.

Equally important is the art of listening. Too often, communication becomes a competition where each person is more focused on being heard than on understanding the other. Active listening requires patience, empathy, and the willingness to set aside your own perspective to truly hear your partner. It's in these moments of attentive listening that breakthroughs often occur. When someone feels heard, they feel valued—and that sense of value can transform a relationship.

Another cornerstone of successful relationships is gratitude. In the busyness of life, it's easy to take your partner for granted. Yet expressing gratitude, even for the smallest gestures, can reignite appreciation and love. A simple "thank you" for making coffee in the morning or acknowledging their effort in planning a date can go a long way. Gratitude shifts the focus from what's lacking to what's present, fostering a culture of positivity and connection.

For couples dealing with external pressures like financial stress or family interference, teamwork is critical. Approaching these challenges as a united front strengthens the partnership and reinforces the idea that you're in this together. Instead of letting external factors divide you, use them as an opportunity to build resilience and problem-solving skills. When couples face challenges together, they create a bond that becomes a source of strength in future trials.

Finally, it's worth noting that love is not static—it's dynamic and ever-evolving. Relationships require continuous effort and intentionality. They demand that you show up every day, not just during the good times but also during the hard ones. Love is an active choice, a daily commitment to prioritize your partner, nurture the connection, and invest in the relationship. It's not about grand gestures or fleeting moments of romance—it's about the steady, unglamorous work of building something real and lasting. Behind closed doors, relationships are where life's most meaningful work happens. It's where vulnerability meets strength, where struggles are transformed into growth, and where love is refined through the challenges of life. When couples embrace this truth, they discover a deeper connection—one that goes beyond appearances and public displays. It's a connection rooted in authenticity, trust, and the quiet determination to choose each other every single day.

For those reading this, whether you're single, dating, or married, know that the effort you put into your relationships matters. Every conversation, every moment of forgiveness, every act of kindness adds to the foundation you're building. Love isn't easy, but it's always worth it. And the most beautiful relationships aren't the ones that look perfect from the outside—they're the ones that thrive in the unseen, messy, and raw realities of life behind closed doors. Relationships are not defined by the filtered highlight reels shared with the world; they are forged in the quiet, sacred spaces behind closed doors. They are not built on the applause of strangers or the illusion of perfection but on the raw, unfiltered truth of two people who choose each other every day, flaws and all. When we stop performing for others and start prioritizing what truly matters—authentic connection, trust, and commitment—we uncover the real beauty of love.

Think about the strongest relationships you admire. Chances are, their strength doesn't come from grand public gestures or social-media-worthy moments. It comes from the private sacrifices, the unseen forgiveness, the quiet laughter shared over life's simplest joys, and the ability to weather life's storms together. It comes from a mutual decision to keep showing up, even when the road gets rough, and to choose love over ego, connection over convenience. The work of love happens in the everyday moments—the late-night talks, the silent car rides after a disagreement, the small acts of service that say, "I see you. I'm here for you." These moments may never make it to Instagram, but they are the glue that holds relationships together. They are the foundation upon which real, enduring love is built.

For those who feel overwhelmed by the struggles behind closed doors, take heart. The challenges you face today are not the end of your story—they are the refining fire that will make your relationship stronger. With patience, humility, and a commitment to grow together, even the most broken places can be healed. It starts with small, intentional steps: listening more, forgiving freely, expressing gratitude, and choosing vulnerability over walls. Each step forward, no matter how small, strengthens the bond between you.

To the single person longing for a connection, remember this—the most important relationship you can nurture right now is the one with yourself. Learn who you are, embrace your worth, and grow into the kind of person you would want to be with. Love yourself enough to know that your value isn't determined by your relationship status but by the depth of your character. When you approach love from a place of wholeness, you'll attract a relationship rooted in mutual respect and authenticity.

To the couples who are thriving, never take for granted the gift of what you share. Keep investing in your relationship, even when things feel good. Keep communicating, keep growing, and keep choosing each other. The strength of your connection is a testament to the quiet, unseen work you've put in, and it will serve as a light for others navigating their own journeys. For those navigating the hardest seasons of love, let this be a reminder—struggles do not define your relationship—how you respond to them does. Choose to fight for what matters, to lean into the discomfort, and to trust that even in the hardest moments, growth and healing are possible.

Love is not a perfect picture; it's a dynamic, evolving journey. It's not always glamorous or easy, but it's always worth it. Behind closed doors is where the real story of love is written—a story of persistence, grace, and choosing to stay when it would be easier to walk away. It's where connection is nurtured, trust is rebuilt, and intimacy is rediscovered. So, as you reflect on your relationships, remember that the most important thing isn't how they appear to the world but how they feel to the two of you. Focus on what's real, what's true, and what matters. Invest in the small, daily acts of love that create a bond that no amount of external pressure can break.

At the end of the day, the quiet work of love behind closed doors is where life's greatest magic happens. It's not in the applause, the likes, or the perfection—it's in the messy, beautiful, and deeply human connection between two people who choose each other, time and time again.

CHAPTER 14

THE ADVANTAGE OF CLOSED DOORS

Imagine a caterpillar. To the outside world, it looks small, limited, even insignificant. Then, one day, it retreats into the solitude of a cocoon. From the outside, it appears as though nothing is happening—just stillness and silence—but inside that closed space, transformation is taking place. The caterpillar is shedding its old identity, preparing for a life it has never known. When it emerges, it's no longer bound to the earth. It soars. Have you ever faced a closed door and felt like it was the end of something? Maybe you've pounded on it in frustration, tried to force it open, or cried in despair. What if I told you that closed doors aren't barriers—they're opportunities? What if that door is not denying you, but preparing you? Behind closed doors, real transformation happens.

And this chapter is about understanding why those moments of privacy, struggle, and preparation are your greatest advantage.

THE POWER OF CLOSED DOORS: THE COCOON OF GROWTH

Closed doors are not prisons; they're laboratories. Think about it: a butterfly needs the privacy of its cocoon to develop its wings. Seeds must be buried in darkness before they can bloom. In the same way, the most meaningful transformations in life often happen behind the scenes, away from the applause of others. Serena Williams didn't become the greatest tennis player of her generation by chance. She spent countless hours on empty courts, perfecting her serve and working on her precision long before winning her first Grand Slam. Viola Davis didn't step into the spotlight as one of the most celebrated actors of our time without spending years honing her craft in small theater productions. What they both understood is this—the closed door isn't about hiding—it's about incubating. Behind closed doors, you can fall without an audience, fail without judgment, and refine without distraction. This is where weaknesses become strengths, ideas evolve into breakthroughs, and resilience is built brick by brick.

THE MISCONCEPTION OF CLOSED DOORS

Many people see closed doors as punishments or signs of rejection, but they're actually privileges. Behind those doors, you're free to experiment, to grow, and to heal. In public, mistakes can feel catastrophic. In private, they become lessons. Take the master chef in a bustling kitchen. Before serving a masterpiece to guests, they taste, tweak, and adjust their dishes in private. The audience only sees the final product, but the real value happens behind the scenes. This is your opportunity. Closed doors give you the time and space to refine your skills, confront your fears, and strengthen your foundation. When the world finally sees you, they'll witness the result of countless hours of unseen effort.

WOUNDS INTO WISDOM, FAILURES INTO FUEL

Closed doors are also spaces where pain turns into purpose. The wounds you face in private can become your greatest teachers. I've seen people cry over opportunities they thought were lost or relationships that didn't work out, but behind those tears, something powerful was growing. Every failure fertilizes the soil of future success. Every tear waters the seeds of resilience.

When I look at my own journey, I remember moments behind closed doors when I thought I was being punished. Over time, I realized those were the moments when I was being prepared. Behind those doors, I gained clarity, learned to trust the process, and developed a faith that could weather any storm.

THE DIFFERENCE BETWEEN HIDING AND INCUBATING

It's important to understand the distinction between hiding and incubating. Hiding is rooted in fear, avoidance, and shame. Incubating, on the other hand, is intentional. It's about preparation, focus, and transformation. Behind closed doors, you're not avoiding the world—you're getting ready for it. You're not retreating in fear—you're stepping back to grow. You're not hiding your flaws—you're sharpening your strengths.

PRACTICAL ADVANTAGES OF CLOSED DOORS

- **Privacy for Practice:** You can test your ideas, refine your skills, and make mistakes without the weight of external judgment.

- **Freedom to Fail:** Failure in public can feel humiliating; failure in private is just another step in the process.

- **Focus Without Distraction:** Closed doors allow you to block out the noise of the world and hone in on what truly matters.

- **Preparation for Greatness:** When the doors finally open, you'll emerge stronger, wiser, and ready to shine.

Closed doors are not your enemy; they're your ally. They're not obstacles; they're opportunities. Behind those doors, your story is being written—a story of resilience, transformation, and growth. So, what do you do when you face a closed door? You embrace it. Don't rush to open it; trust the process. Behind that door, every tear, every failure, and every moment of doubt is shaping you into the person you were meant to be. Here's your action step: the next time you encounter a closed door, pause. Reflect on what you can learn in this season. Use this time to strengthen your skills, deepen your character, and clarify your vision. Remember, every master chef was once a beginner experimenting in the kitchen. Every artist was once a novice practicing in solitude. Every success story has chapters written behind the scenes. So, bless the closed doors in your life. They're not keeping you out; they're inviting you in—to a deeper, richer process of becoming. Behind those doors, your future is being forged, and when the time comes for them to open, you'll be ready to soar. This is your cocoon. This is your laboratory. This is your advantage. Trust it. Use it. Let it transform you.

THE STRATEGIC ADVANTAGE OF SILENCE: THE LESSON FROM THE LION

Have you ever watched a lion hunt? Notice how it moves with deliberate patience, never announcing its presence, never rushing its moment. A lion understands a truth most humans have forgotten: the real advantage lies in strategic silence. Lions don't broadcast their strategy. They don't reveal their position. They move with precision because they know that success is often won behind the scenes, not in the spotlight. Now, think about your own life. How often have you felt pressured to show your progress before it was time? How often have you rushed into action without fully preparing? The lion teaches us that the key to winning—whether in life, business, or relationships—is knowing when to move and when to wait. This is the essence of advantage.

"Lions don't broadcast their strategy. They don't reveal their position. They move with precision because they know that success is often won behind the scenes, not in the spotlight."

The word "advantage" carries immense power. It means the ability to achieve something remarkable in spite of obstacles and through careful preparation. It's the comeback strategy that positions you for where you're going, not where you've been. Advantage requires patience, calculation, and the discipline to stay focused behind closed doors.

THE POWER OF STRATEGIC PATIENCE

Think of the lion again. Before it strikes, it observes. It studies its prey's patterns and mannerisms, conserving energy until the critical moment. This is not laziness—it's strategy. Lions don't waste time on uncertain attempts. They calculate every move, waiting for the exact moment to strike with precision and purpose. This principle applies to all areas of life. The entrepreneur who studies market trends before launching a business is practicing patience. The investor who waits for the perfect market conditions is demonstrating discipline. The negotiator who listens more than they speak is exercising strategic silence. In each case, success comes not from rushing but from preparing. Strategic patience also means resisting the urge to prove yourself prematurely. How often have you seen people announce their plans before they're ready, only to fall short because they lacked preparation? True advantage comes from knowing how to wait—not passively, but actively, by using the time to build strength, refine skills, and anticipate challenges.

> *"Strategic patience also means resisting the urge to prove yourself prematurely."*

THE SILENT APPROACH

Lions move in absolute silence. They stay downwind, remaining invisible until the last possible moment. They master the art of positioning, en-suring that every move aligns with their ultimate goal. In life, we can em-ulate this same principle by working quietly behind the scenes. Consider the entrepreneur who builds a business while keeping a day job. Or the artist who hones their craft in private before revealing it to the world. Or the leader who strengthens their skills quietly, away from the eyes of critics, before stepping into the spotlight. These individuals understand that true growth often requires working in the shadows. Silence is not weakness—it's a shield. It protects your ideas from unnecessary criti-cism and distraction, allowing you to focus fully on execution. When you master the silent approach, you can make moves that no one sees coming, giving you an edge over those who broadcast their intentions too soon.

REAL-WORLD APPLICATIONS OF ADVANTAGE

Strategic silence isn't just a principle reserved for lions or nature—it's a universal truth that applies to every facet of life. The power of advantage comes from preparation, foresight, and deliberate action, not merely reacting to what's thrown your way. Let's break this down into practical examples that highlight how strategic silence and preparation create the ultimate advantage.

THE CEO: CONTROLLING THE STAGE

The CEO who chooses the meeting location and sets the agenda understands the importance of framing the conversation. By choosing the environment, they ensure the setting aligns with their objectives—quiet, distraction-free, and conducive to focus. Setting the agenda allows them to guide the flow of discussion, placing their priorities at the forefront and subtly steering outcomes in their favor. This isn't manipulation—it's preparation. The CEO doesn't leave success to chance. They walk into every room knowing exactly what they want to accomplish and have already prepared for multiple outcomes. By shaping the environment, they transform a meeting into an opportunity to solidify their advantage.

THE INVESTOR: CREATING FAVORABLE TERMS

The savvy investor who negotiates favorable terms operates with clarity and patience. They've done their homework—studying market trends, analyzing risks, and identifying opportunities. When they sit at the negotiation table, they don't reveal all their cards. Instead, they listen intently, ask calculated questions, and wait for the perfect moment to make their move. In this case, strategic silence is a weapon. By speaking less and observing more, the investor gains insight into the other party's needs and motivations. This allows them to structure deals that align with their goals while creating win-win scenarios. Their strength lies in preparation, not in overpowering the other party.

THE LEADER: MASTERING THE SETUP

The leader who sets the stage for success understands the importance of groundwork. Before any team initiative, they invest time in understanding the dynamics of their team, anticipating potential roadblocks, and crafting a clear vision for the outcome. They don't jump into action without first ensuring that every resource is in place and every person knows their role. This preparation gives them the advantage. When challenges arise, they're not caught off guard because they've already considered the possibilities. Their calm demeanor in high-pressure situations is a direct result of their preparation behind the scenes. The leader isn't reactive—they're proactive, shaping the battlefield long before the first move is made.

THE ARTIST: PROTECTING THE CREATIVE PROCESS

The artist who works in solitude before unveiling their masterpiece understands the sanctity of closed doors. Creativity flourishes in environments free from unnecessary noise and external opinions. By guarding their creative process, the artist maintains focus and clarity, pouring their energy into refining their craft instead of defending their ideas prematurely. When the artist finally shares their work with the world, it's not the result of spontaneous inspiration—it's the product of countless hours of silent labor. Their advantage lies in the discipline of creation, not in seeking validation during the process.

"When the artist finally shares their work with the world, it's not the result of spontaneous inspiration—it's the product of countless hours of silent labor."

THE ATHLETE: BUILDING THE FOUNDATION

The athlete who trains behind closed doors embraces the power of preparation. Away from the crowds and cameras, they push themselves to the limit, mastering techniques and building endurance. They don't rely on natural talent alone—they refine their skills, correct their weaknesses, and prepare for every possible scenario. When game day arrives, their performance isn't an accident—it's the culmination of countless silent hours spent preparing. The advantage they hold is a direct result of their willingness to work in the shadows, away from the applause.

SHAPING CIRCUMSTANCES, NOT REACTING TO THEM

In all these cases, the advantage doesn't come from reacting to external circumstances—it comes from shaping them. Whether in business, art, leadership, or athletics, those who hold the advantage are the ones who control the narrative. They don't wait for opportunities to present themselves; they create the conditions for success. Strategic silence and deliberate preparation are the keys. They give you time to observe, to plan, and to ensure that when you act, your actions are purposeful and decisive. The real-world applications of advantage are endless, but they all share a common thread: those who embrace preparation, patience, and focus will always have the upper hand.

EXECUTION: THE CALCULATED STRIKE

Here's another critical lesson from the lion—when it moves, it commits fully. A lion doesn't waste energy on half-hearted attempts. Its strike is decisive, focused, and executed with precision. This level of commitment is essential when you're working behind closed doors. Imagine spending months preparing for a business pitch. You've done the research, rehearsed your delivery, and anticipated every possible question. When the day comes, you don't hesitate. You present your vision with confidence, knowing that you've prepared for this exact moment. This is what it means to execute with precision. Similarly, the strategist who shapes the battlefield before the fight begins is already halfway to victory. The lion doesn't just chase after its prey—it positions itself perfectly, ensuring that every move counts. This level of calculation is what separates those who achieve their goals from those who simply dream about them.

MASTERING THE ADVANTAGE OF CLOSED DOORS

In my 44 years of life, I've come to recognize the undeniable truth about the advantage of closed doors. It wasn't always obvious to me. There were times I found myself caught in cycles of frustration, asking, "Why am I putting myself through this?" Have you ever been there? Feeling like you're spinning your wheels, looking back and thinking, "If only I had done it this way," or "I should've known better." But here's what I've learned: Life becomes clearer when you strip away the coulda, shoulda, woulda's. The real advantage comes when you stop lamenting over the missed opportunities and start carving out a game plan for the ones ahead. I've seen this play out in my own journey, especially during my time as a veteran navigating the complexities of submitting VA claims. When I first started the process in 2015, I was determined to handle it on my own. I had my military experience, my documentation, and what I thought was enough knowledge to get through it. However, translating my service and struggles into a claim that would be approved? ... Now, that was a completely different story.

The denial letters kept coming—one after another. Each rejection felt like another closed door, and with every "no," my frustration grew. It wasn't until I found a team, people who truly believed in me and understood my struggle, that I began to see the light. With their guidance, those closed doors started to look less like failures and more like divine detours.

DIVINE DETOURS: THE HIDDEN ADVANTAGES

What I came to realize is that some of life's greatest blessings are disguised as setbacks. The canceled contract? It saved you from a toxic relationship. The delayed visa? It kept you out of harm's way. The lost opportunity? It created space for something better. I know this because I've lived it. What about you? Have you ever experienced a "no" that later turned out to be the best thing that could've happened?

Let's take it a step further:

- **The Denied Loan:** It saved you from a market crash you couldn't have predicted.

- **The Broken Contract:** It opened the door to an opportunity you didn't even know existed.

- **The Medical Scare:** It revealed a serious condition early enough to address it.

- **The Car Breakdown:** It kept you off a highway where tragedy could have struck.

These aren't just random events. They're the hidden advantages of closed doors.

TURNING PAIN INTO PERSPECTIVE

When we're in the middle of the struggle, it's hard to see the bigger picture. Closed doors can feel like personal attacks, but with time and reflection, they often reveal their purpose. I've watched people wrestle with heartbreak, rejection, and failure, only to emerge stronger, wiser, and more focused than before.

- **That broken friendship?** It protected you from betrayal.

- **That failed audition?** It led you to the role that would define your career.

- **That rejected patent?** It forced you to innovate something even better.

- **That failed business?** It taught you lessons no classroom ever could.

Every setback carries with it a seed of growth—if you're willing to look for it.

EMBRACING THE ADVANTAGE

The key to understanding the advantage of closed doors is shifting your mindset. It's not just about what you lost; it's about what you gained in the process. It's about realizing that every "no" is clearing the path for a better "yes." When my VA claims were denied, I could've given up. I could've stayed stuck in frustration and bitterness, but instead, I found a team who showed me how to turn those rejections into approvals. They gave me the tools, strategies, and encouragement I needed to move forward. Through that process, I gained something even greater than the approval—I gained clarity, confidence, and resilience.

THE LESSONS HIDDEN IN LOSS

The detours in life often lead to destinations we couldn't have planned for ourselves. The struggles refine us in ways success never could, and the closed doors, while painful in the moment, are often our greatest teachers.

So, the next time you face a rejection, a delay, or a failure, don't let it defeat you. Take a step back. Look for the lesson. Ask yourself, "What is this door protecting me from? What opportunity is it preparing me for?"

THE POWER OF PERSPECTIVE

I can't tell you how many times I've seen someone face a setback only to realize later that it was the best thing that could've happened. Whether it's a mistrade that connects you with your future mentor, a failed investment that protects your life savings, or a lost job that pushes you toward your dream career—there's always an advantage waiting to be discovered. Remember this: closed doors are not the end of the story. They're the plot twists that make the journey worthwhile. They're the moments that shape you, challenge you, and prepare you for the next chapter.

Embrace the advantage. Look beyond the disappointment. Trust that every "no" is setting the stage for a better "yes." When that door finally opens, walk through it with confidence, knowing that you're exactly where you're meant to be.

WHEN DENIAL BECOMES YOUR GREATEST PROTECTION

Let me take you back to a moment that defined an entire generation: 2008. Picture this: a loan application, crumpled and abandoned, held tightly in the trembling hands of someone whose world was falling apart. Their dreams were tied to that piece of paper. The tears came fast, and hope seemed to slip away just as quickly. If you lived through it, you know what I'm talking about. For me, it was a season of relentless rejection. Every loan I applied for, every credit card I tried to open—it felt like the world was conspiring to keep me in a rut.

At the time, it felt personal, almost cruel, but hindsight revealed a wisdom I couldn't see in the moment. Nine months later, the 2008 financial crisis hit hard. Markets crumbled, jobs vanished, and homes that were once sources of security became financial anchors dragging families under. As the chaos unfolded, those rejections that had stung so deeply began to look like shields.

THE SHIELD OF REJECTION

This is what most people don't realize—rejection isn't always punishment. Sometimes, it's protection. That denied loan wasn't a slap in the face; it was a hand pulling me back from a ledge I didn't even know I was standing on. Imagine taking on a mortgage right before the housing market collapse. Picture maxing out credit cards before interest rates skyrocketed. Those rejections didn't just stop transactions—they preserved futures. They redirected paths toward something better, something safer, even if it didn't feel like it at the time. This is the hidden truth about financial denial: it often protects us from outcomes we can't foresee. It's like driving in a dense fog. You can only see a few feet ahead, but rejection is the hand that keeps you from veering off the road entirely.

REDIRECTION IN DISGUISE

Every denied loan or failed application carries within it the seed of redirection. It forces you to pause, to rethink, to approach your goals from a different angle. At first, it feels like a dead end, but over time, you realize it's a detour that saved you from disaster. In 2008, as financial markets crashed, those denials spared me from overwhelming debt I couldn't have managed. They demanded that I become resourceful, creative, and resilient, and in that resilience, I discovered something I hadn't expected: the power of redirection. What felt like rejection in the moment turned into the very thing that safeguarded my future. That's the paradox of denial—it feels like loss, but it often prevents greater pain.

THE HIDDEN WISDOM OF "NO"

Denial teaches us patience, but it also demands that we see beyond the immediate "no." Think about this:

- A denied mortgage before a housing crash becomes a financial lifeline.

- A rejected business loan forces you to refine your plan and build a stronger foundation.

- A canceled credit card application keeps you from drowning in debt during a job loss.

THE DIVINE DETOUR

I call these rejections "divine detours." They might feel like roadblocks, but they're actually guardrails. They're there to keep you from stepping into something you're not ready for or something that's not ready for you. The timing of these detours is often miraculous. What looks like a setback is actually setting you up for something greater. What feels like rejection is actually protection from unseen storms. It's as if the world knows what's ahead of you better than you do and is guiding you toward safer ground.

STRENGTH THROUGH REJECTION

Each rejection you face builds something within you. Strength, resilience, patience—all of these are muscles that grow through the weight of denial. You begin to see patterns, understand timing, and learn how to pivot. In my own journey, every financial rejection forced me to dig deeper. It wasn't about giving up; it was about leveling up. I learned how to save, how to strategize, and how to prepare for opportunities that were truly meant for me.

BEYOND THE DOOR: WINDOWS OF OPPORTUNITY

The greatest opportunities often come not through the doors we're trying to force open, but through unexpected windows. A denial pushes you to look around, to consider paths you wouldn't have seen otherwise. For me, those closed doors in 2008 didn't end my journey. They reshaped it. They pushed me toward opportunities I wouldn't have considered—new ways of thinking, new ways of working, and ultimately, new ways of thriving.

REFRAMING REJECTION

So, the next time you're holding a rejection letter, pause. Take a deep breath. Instead of seeing it as the end of the road, ask yourself: "What is this protecting me from? What is this redirecting me toward?" Because rejection isn't the final chapter. It's the plot twist. It's the moment that shifts your story in ways you couldn't have imagined.

THE STRENGTH OF DENIAL

Remember, every "no" builds your character. Every closed door sharpens your focus. Every rejection carries within it the seed of protection and the possibility of something greater. So, don't curse the denied loan, the lost opportunity, or the closed door. Bless them. They're not obstacles—they're safeguards. They're not setbacks—they're setups for a future you haven't yet envisioned. When denial becomes protection, it's not just saving you from harm—it's preparing you for the better things to come. Trust the process—embrace the detours—and know that every "no" is leading you closer to your ultimate "yes."

THE WISDOM IN WAITING

Here's the thing about rejection—it forces us into a waiting room we didn't ask to be in. That waiting room can feel unbearable, but it's where some of the most profound lessons are learned. It's where we find patience we didn't think we had, strength we didn't know existed, and clarity we couldn't have seen otherwise. Waiting doesn't mean wasting time. It means preparing. The denial might have been a red light, but it doesn't mean the journey is over. It means you're being given time to recalibrate, to gather resources, to reimagine your path. Think about the farmer who plants seeds in the spring. There's no rushing the harvest. The rain has to fall, the sun has to shine, and time has to work its magic underground. The farmer isn't idle—he's tending the soil, ensuring the weeds don't choke out the growth, preparing for the abundance that's coming.

You're the farmer in this story. That closed door or denied opportunity is the seed. Know that just because you can't see growth yet, doesn't mean it's not happening.

EMBRACING THE LONG GAME

Rejection teaches you to think long-term. It's not about immediate gratification; it's about sustainable success. That denied loan or missed opportunity might feel like a loss today, but it could be the very thing that sets you up for a win tomorrow. In my own life, I've seen how stepping back and playing the long game has turned "no's" into powerful "yeses." The job I didn't get taught me skills that landed me the career I was meant for. The relationships that ended opened doors to deeper, more meaningful connections. The loans I was denied forced me to build a financial foundation that couldn't be shaken by future storms.

Playing the long game means trusting that the universe, or God, has a better view of the path ahead than you do. It means believing that the detour is leading somewhere worth going.

THE STRENGTH OF RESILIENCE

Every denial chips away at your ego, but it builds something far more valuable: resilience. Resilience isn't just bouncing back—it's bouncing forward. It's taking the hit, learning from it, and coming back stronger.

Rejection forces you to face your fears, confront your weaknesses, and sharpen your strategies. It's like forging steel—it's only through the fire that you become unbreakable.

SEEING REJECTION AS A GIFT

What if you could reframe rejection in your mind? What if, instead of seeing it as failure, you could see it as a gift? Consider the following:

- That denied loan taught you financial discipline.

- That broken relationship showed you what real love should feel like.

- That canceled contract saved you from a toxic environment.

- That delayed opportunity gave you time to grow into the person you needed to be.

In truth, the rejection isn't the end of the story—it's the beginning of a better chapter.

TRUSTING THE PROCESS

One of the hardest lessons I've learned is to trust the process, even when it doesn't make sense. Rejection feels unfair. It feels personal. Yet the truth is, it's often the most impersonal thing in the world. It's not about you—it's about timing, preparation, and protection.

When you trust the process, you stop fighting against the "no" and start looking for the "why." You start asking questions like: "What can I learn from this? What is this preparing me for? Where is this leading me?" When you start asking those questions, you begin to see rejection for what it really is: a stepping stone, not a stumbling block.

THE BEAUTY OF THE BIGGER PICTURE

If you zoom out and look at your life as a whole, you'll see that every rejection was part of a bigger picture. The missed opportunities, the closed doors, the unexpected detours—they all brought you to where you are today—and where you are today is exactly where you're supposed to be. When you look back, you'll see that the greatest blessings often came disguised as rejections. The moments that felt like the end were actually the beginning of something extraordinary.

MOVING FORWARD

So, what do you do now? You move forward. You take the rejection, the denial, the disappointment, and you use it as fuel. You let it refine you, not define you.

Here's your four-step action plan:

1. **Pause and Reflect:** Instead of reacting emotionally to rejection, step back and ask: "What is this trying to teach me?"

2. **Recalibrate and Strategize:** Use the time to build your skills, strengthen your foundation, and prepare for the next opportunity.

3. **Stay Open to New Paths:** The closed door might be pointing you to a better window. Be willing to pivot.

4. **Trust the Bigger Plan**: Even if you can't see it now, know that every rejection is shaping you for something greater.

Rejection isn't the enemy—it's the guide. It's the hand redirecting you from what wasn't meant for you to what is. It's the divine detour keeping you safe, keeping you prepared, and keeping you aligned with your purpose. Embrace it. Learn from it. Let it shape you into the person you're meant to become. Because the truth is, rejection isn't the end—it's just the beginning of a better story.

WHEN FEAR BECOMES YOUR LIFESAVER: THE GIFT OF EARLY WARNINGS

Imagine sitting in a sterile doctor's office, heart pounding, as the words you never expected hang in the air. It might have been a routine check-up, a follow-up to a symptom you shrugged off, or maybe something you'd avoided for far too long. In that frozen moment of panic, when fear grips your chest and time seems to stand still, it's impossible to imagine that hidden within this terror is a blessing—a silent protector you didn't realize was working in your favor.

We've all been there, or know someone who has. Perhaps it was the relative whose nagging cough turned out to be a symptom of something deeper, or a friend who ignored persistent fatigue until a routine test uncovered a hidden condition. These moments shake us to our core because they confront us with our vulnerability. Yet, they also reveal a powerful truth: sometimes, the very things we fear most are the ones that protect us.

This isn't just about medical scares; it's about life. Fear, when properly understood, can be a guide—a warning light urging us to pay attention to what's out of balance.

FEAR AS A SILENT GUARDIAN

Think about the timing of these medical revelations. A routine checkup that you nearly skipped catches something you couldn't see. An unexplained symptom turns out to be an early warning, not a death sentence. Persistent pain, once dismissed, leads to an intervention that changes the trajectory of your life.

These aren't random incidents; they are perfectly timed moments of protection. Early detection—whether it involves your health, your relationships, or your life choices—isn't an inconvenience— it's salvation wrapped in discomfort. The very things that alarm us—pain, fear, discomfort—are often the tools life uses to save us from something far worse.

Consider this: If you knew that your fear of going to the doctor could uncover a condition early enough to be treated, wouldn't you go? If you realized that the anxiety you feel about a particular situation is actually your intuition screaming for you to take action, wouldn't you listen? Fear isn't your enemy—it's your ally, urging you to act while there's still time.

THE ADVANTAGE OF EARLY INTERVENTION

I've often told my family, "Get a checkup every six months." Why? Because early detection isn't just about finding out what's wrong; it's about taking control of your future. It's about refusing to let silent threats grow unnoticed.

Here are some examples of fear working as a lifesaver:

1. THE ROUTINE CHECKUP THAT SAVES A LIFE

A colleague of mine once shared how a routine physical, something he almost skipped, revealed a heart condition he didn't know he had. The doctor told him, "If we hadn't caught this now, you'd be in serious trouble within a year." That routine checkup wasn't just a medical appointment—it was a divine intervention.

2. THE PERSISTENT PAIN THAT DEMANDS ATTENTION

Pain is the body's way of speaking to us. Ignoring it doesn't make it go away—it only delays the inevitable. A friend of mine had persistent headaches she kept dismissing as stress. When she finally saw a doctor, they found an underlying issue that required immediate care. Today, she's healthy because she listened to her body.

3. THE UNEXPLAINED SYMPTOMS THAT LEAD TO CLARITY

Sometimes, our bodies give us signals we can't explain—fatigue, discomfort, or a lingering feeling that something isn't right. These symptoms, though frightening, are gifts. They lead us to answers that could save our lives if we're willing to investigate.

LIVING PROACTIVELY, NOT REACTIVELY

The key to navigating life's fears, especially when it comes to health, is learning to act before crisis strikes. Here's how:

- **Prioritize Regular Checkups:** Don't wait for something to feel wrong. Make preventive care a habit. Catching issues early isn't about paranoia; it's about empowerment.

- **Listen to Your Body:** Pain, discomfort, and unusual symptoms are your body's way of communicating. Don't ignore them. Investigate, question, and act.

- **Adopt a Healthy Lifestyle:** Daily exercise, balanced nutrition, and stress management aren't just about looking good—they're about building resilience against the unexpected.

- **Face Fear Head-on:** Fear thrives in avoidance. The sooner you face it, the sooner you can turn it into a tool for growth and protection.

WHEN FEAR BECOMES A LIFELINE

Fear is often misunderstood. We think of it as something to run from, but in reality, it's something to run toward. Fear isn't here to paralyze you; it's here to prepare you. That sense of unease you feel about your health—it's a nudge to schedule that appointment. That worry about a recurring issue. It's a signal to dig deeper. I think about the times when fear saved me—not just in health, but in life. Whether it was a tough conversation I didn't want to have or a situation I couldn't ignore, fear was the catalyst that forced me to act. So, the next time fear grips you, pause. Ask yourself: "What is this trying to tell me? What action can I take to transform this fear into power?" The gift of early warning is one of life's greatest protections. Whether it's a routine checkup, a persistent symptom, or a gut feeling, these moments of fear are invitations to act—not out of panic, but out of wisdom. The next time you're tempted to ignore the signs, remember this: Fear isn't your enemy. It's your guide, your guardian, and sometimes, your lifesaver. Trust it. Use it. Let it lead you to the protection and power that lies on the other side.

TRANSFORMING FEAR INTO ACTION

Let's be honest: Fear rarely feels like a gift in the moment. It's unsettling, uncomfortable, and often overwhelming. Yet the truth is, fear has the power to shake us awake, forcing us to look closely at the areas of our lives that need our attention. The real challenge is not to let fear control you but to channel it into meaningful, purposeful action. Think back to a time when fear forced you to move. Maybe it was scheduling that overdue doctor's appointment. Perhaps it was a tough conversation you had been avoiding, or a leap of faith you finally decided to take. These moments weren't easy, but they became pivotal because you chose action over avoidance. Fear isn't here to paralyze you—it's here to push you forward. It's a signal, an alarm bell, reminding you that something significant is at stake. When you lean into that fear instead of running from it, you uncover clarity, courage, and ultimately, a sense of control.

THE WISDOM HIDDEN IN FEAR

Fear is rarely about what it seems on the surface. That nagging worry about a symptom isn't just about your physical health—it's about how much you value taking care of yourself. Anxiety over a financial setback isn't just about the money—it's about security, independence, and your future. Fear often points to deeper areas in your life that need your attention and growth.

When fear arises, it's an opportunity to ask yourself some honest questions:

- What exactly am I afraid of?

- What is this fear trying to teach me?

- What actions can I take right now to address it?

Fear is a teacher, even if it feels harsh. It shines a light on the cracks in your foundation, offering you a chance to strengthen them before they become bigger problems. Whether it's your health, finances, relationships, or career, fear's purpose is to guide you toward areas that need care and attention.

EMBRACING FEAR AS A LIFE STRATEGY

Instead of seeing fear as the enemy, start viewing it as part of your life strategy. Fear isn't a stop sign—it's a guidepost, a signal that something important is worth pursuing or protecting.

Consider someone who fears their job isn't fulfilling. That fear might be urging them to reevaluate their goals, seek new opportunities, or finally take a step toward their passion. Or think about a parent worrying about their child's behavior—that fear can lead to proactive steps, like seeking support, asking questions, and offering the guidance their child needs.

Fear, when approached with the right mindset, becomes a powerful tool for living intentionally. It keeps you sharp, focused, and aware of what truly matters.

WHEN FEAR BECOMES A TURNING POINT

The most profound shift happens when fear transitions into a moment of realization. It doesn't mean the fear disappears; it means you see its purpose. That doctor's visit you were afraid to schedule may catch an issue early enough to treat it. That leap of faith you hesitated to take might lead to opportunities you never imagined. Fear is often the spark that fuels resilience and transformation. Instead of letting it diminish you, you can use it to develop you. Instead of hiding from it, you can embrace it as a necessary part of growth. Fear doesn't have to be an obstacle—it can be the bridge to something greater. The next time fear shows up, don't run from it. Instead, recognize it for what it is: a messenger. Fear isn't here to stop you; it's here to alert you to the areas of your life that need attention, care, and action. Ask yourself, "What is this fear trying to show me?" and then take steps to address it. Whether it's finally addressing your health, making a bold career move, or having a difficult conversation, fear can be the push you need to take that next step. Fear, when harnessed, becomes a guide that directs you toward the actions that matter most. It's not the end of the road—it's a doorway. On the other side of fear lies a stronger, wiser, and more resilient version of you. So lean into it, take the step, and let fear become the force that propels you forward.

GETTING LOST FOUND ME

Back in the day, I used to question my advantage as though it were just another fleeting feeling, something with no real substance or weight. I didn't recognize it for what it was, but as I matured, as the years shaped my perspective, I came to realize that my advantage wasn't just some abstract idea. It was my ability to challenge the status quo, to resist the pull of doing things simply because "everyone else is doing it."

There was always a voice in the back of my mind, urging me toward the popular path: "Do this—it's trending. You'll get more views, more followers, more subscribers." However, deep down, I knew that chasing what everyone else was chasing wasn't my calling. I've seen brands crumble because they lacked the foresight to take their advantage wisely and strategically, quarter by quarter. They chased short-term gains while ignoring long-term growth. It was a lesson I couldn't afford to ignore.

When life slams a door in your face, that's when the real advantage begins to form. It's in those moments of rejection, failure, and frustration that hope, skill, and purpose start building the foundation for something greater. Even as you read these closing pages, remember you're not alone in this battle ... and yes, it is a battle. The battle isn't just external—it's internal. Sometimes the ideas and opportunities that define your advantage don't reveal themselves right away.

Let's get one thing straight: money isn't always the advantage. You can save up your life savings and still find yourself miserable, stuck in a cycle of discontent and failure. Real advantage isn't just about what you have in the bank; it's about what you carry within you. It's the ability to navigate, adapt, and grow in any circumstance.

A PERSONAL LESSON IN ADVANTAGE

I'll never forget the advantage I discovered while living in Japan. It wasn't handed to me—it was forged through struggle. Speaking the language became my lifeline, my way of getting from point A to point B on the intricate web of transportation trains, but truthfully, it didn't start that way. I had to get lost—many times—to find myself.

I rarely share this story, but during my 18 years in Japan, there were days when I was completely frustrated. I would stand on those crowded train platforms, exhausted, staring at maps I couldn't read, and feeling utterly lost. I was tired of the cycle—of getting on the wrong train, missing stops, and wasting hours trying to correct my mistakes; but in that frustration, a new skill was born. I started teaching myself how to ask the right questions:

"How do you get to Shibuya, sir?"

"Which station do I need to transfer to?"

"Which train is the fastest?"

"Which color represents the local, semi-express, or express train?"

These questions became my tools for survival. I remember one particular moment like it was yesterday. I took the express train instead of the local train because I was in such a rush to get to my destination, but instead of saving time, I missed all the key stops I needed. That mistake taught me something profound: rushing doesn't always get you where you need to go. Sometimes, slowing down and asking the right questions is the real advantage.

THE ADVANTAGE OF GETTING LOST

Looking back now, I see those moments of being lost as blessings in disguise. They forced me to grow in ways I wouldn't have otherwise. They taught me patience, humility, and the value of preparation. More importantly, they taught me to embrace the journey instead of fixating solely on the destination.

The advantage of getting lost is that it strips away the illusion of control and pushes you to rely on your resourcefulness. It's in those moments of uncertainty that you find your strength. You learn to navigate life not just by memorizing the map but by understanding the terrain.

THE POWER OF SELF-DISCOVERY

The truth is, we all have our own "train stories." Maybe yours isn't about transportation, but it's about a relationship, a career decision, or a personal setback. The details may vary, but the lesson remains the same: the advantage isn't always obvious at first. It often hides in the moments of frustration, in the detours and delays that force us to adapt and grow. The key is to recognize these moments for what they are—opportunities in disguise. When you take the time to reflect, to ask the right questions, and to adjust your approach, you'll begin to see the advantage unfolding.

So, the next time you feel lost—whether literally or figuratively—pause. Instead of panicking, ask yourself: "What can I learn from this? How can this moment shape me? What questions do I need to ask to get to where I need to go?"

SLOWING DOWN TO SPEED UP

As I've learned from my time in Japan, sometimes the fastest way forward is to slow down. To take the local train instead of the express. To pay attention to the stops along the way instead of rushing to the final destination. That's where growth happens. That's where transformation takes root. Your advantage isn't about avoiding mistakes—it's about learning from them. It's about turning moments of disorientation into opportunities for clarity. It's about finding strength in the process of getting lost and using that strength to forge a path forward.

So, don't underestimate the power of being lost. Don't dismiss the lessons hidden in your frustrations. Understand that those moments—however challenging they may feel—are the very things shaping you into who you're meant to be. Ultimately, when you finally arrive at your destination, you'll realize that the journey itself was the greatest advantage of all.

TRUSTING THE DETOURS

One of the hardest lessons to embrace is that detours are often part of the plan. When life doesn't go as expected, it's tempting to label those moments as failures or setbacks; but what if the detour is the route you were always meant to take? What if the stop you didn't plan for is where you're supposed to grow, recalibrate, and prepare for what's next?

Think about your own life. How many times have you faced what felt like an insurmountable roadblock, only to realize later it was steering you toward something better? That rejection letter for the job you thought you wanted led you to a role that actually fulfilled you. That relationship that ended unexpectedly freed you to meet someone who truly saw and valued you. That failed project taught you lessons that became the foundation for your next big success.

Detours have a way of revealing our resilience. They force us to think creatively, to adapt, and to find new ways forward. They also teach us patience—a virtue that is often overlooked in a world that celebrates instant results. The reality is, most lasting success isn't born in a straight line. It's forged in the twists and turns, the ups and downs, and the unexpected pauses along the way.

PREPARING IN THE SHADOWS

One of the greatest advantages of life's detours is the preparation that happens in the shadows. When the spotlight is off, and the world isn't watching, you have the freedom to experiment, to fail, and to grow without judgment. Think about the greatest artists, athletes, and leaders of our time. They didn't reach their peaks by accident. They spent countless hours practicing behind closed doors, honing their craft, and preparing for the moments when the world would see them.

J.K. Rowling didn't publish Harry Potter overnight. She wrote the manuscript while juggling single motherhood and financial struggles, enduring rejection after rejection before finding success. The point is, preparation is the silent advantage. It's the work you do when no one is clapping for you, the hours you invest when no one is looking, and the persistence you show when the odds seem stacked against you. Your current detour might feel like wasted time, but it's not. It's a season of preparation. It's a chapter of growth. Then, when your moment comes, you'll realize that every step, every stumble, and every pause was part of the process.

THE ADVANTAGE OF PERSPECTIVE

When you're in the middle of a detour, it's hard to see the bigger picture. The frustration, the uncertainty, and the doubt can cloud your vision, but perspective is the ultimate advantage.

Take a step back and ask yourself: "What is this moment teaching me? What skills am I developing right now that I'll need later? What opportunities can I create from where I am?"

Sometimes, we get so focused on the door that's closed in front of us that we miss the windows of opportunity opening all around us. Perspective allows you to shift your focus from what's lost to what's possible. It helps you see the detour, not as a dead end, but as a redirection.

EMBRACING THE JOURNEY

As I reflect on my time in Japan, the lesson that stands out most is this: the journey is the advantage. Every wrong train I took, every language barrier I encountered, and every moment of frustration added up to something greater. Those experiences taught me resilience, resourcefulness, and patience—qualities that have served me in every area of my life.

The same is true for you. Whatever detour you're facing right now, know that it's shaping you. It's equipping you with the tools, the wisdom, and the perspective you'll need for the road ahead.

So, embrace the journey. Trust the detours. Just remember that every twist, every turn, and every moment of uncertainty is part of the masterpiece you're creating. The advantage isn't in arriving—it's in becoming. When you finally reach your destination, you'll realize that the journey wasn't just a means to an end. It was the advantage that prepared you to thrive once you got there.

TWO CLOSING TIPS TO REMEMBER

1. EMBRACE THE PAIN OF THE PRESENT CLOSED DOOR

Let's be real—when life shuts a door in your face, it hurts. It's raw, it's heavy, and it can feel overwhelming. You might find yourself sitting in your car after a job rejection, tears streaming down your face, questioning your worth and wondering what's next. Maybe it's the end of a relationship you poured your soul into, or a business venture that collapsed after years of hard work. Whatever it is, the pain is undeniable, but here's the thing: pain is not the enemy—it's the beginning of something powerful.

When you face that closed door, don't run from the pain. Sit with it. Feel it. Let it sink in. Too often, we're tempted to numb the hurt—scrolling through social media, binge-watching shows, or jumping straight into the next thing to avoid the sting of rejection, but avoiding the pain only delays the lesson. Pain is a teacher, and when you embrace it, you allow it to do its work.

Take a moment to ask yourself: "Why does this closed door hurt so much?" Maybe it's because you tied your identity to it, or because it represented a dream you weren't ready to let go of. Whatever the reason, the pain is trying to reveal something deeper about you—your desires, your fears, your untapped potential. Think of pain as a compass. It points you toward growth, showing you the areas of your life that need attention and refinement. Without pain, we wouldn't know where to focus our energy. Without rejection, we wouldn't be forced to pivot and discover new paths. Sometimes, the very act of feeling the pain fully is what prepares you for the next chapter.

WHY PAIN IS NECESSARY

Hitting rock bottom is often where true transformation begins. When everything feels like it's crumbling, you're given the chance to rebuild from the ground up. Pain strips away the unnecessary and leaves you with the essentials. It forces you to confront the parts of yourself that you might have ignored.

For example, think about the athlete who trains tirelessly but doesn't make the team. The disappointment is crushing, but it also becomes the fuel for harder work, sharper focus, and renewed determination. That initial pain becomes the fire that forges their resilience. Similarly, when life closes a door, the pain you feel can become the catalyst for growth and reinvention.

STAYING IN THE MOMENT

It's uncomfortable to sit in pain, but it's also necessary. When you allow yourself to feel it fully, you gain clarity. You start to see the situation for what it truly is—not just a setback, but an opportunity to learn, to pivot, and to grow.

Staying in the moment doesn't mean wallowing in self-pity; it means acknowledging your emotions without judgment. Give yourself permission to grieve what you've lost but also remind yourself that this is not the end of the story. The pain you're feeling now is temporary, but the lessons it offers are permanent.

LEVERAGING THE PAIN

Here's where the shift happens: once you've embraced the pain, you can start to leverage it. Pain has a way of sharpening your focus and clarifying your priorities. When you're in the thick of it, you begin to see what truly matters. Maybe that closed door is forcing you to reevaluate your goals. Maybe it's pushing you to let go of something that wasn't serving you. Maybe it's showing you that you've been playing small and it's time to step into something bigger.

Instead of seeing pain as a barrier, start viewing it as a tool. What can this experience teach you? How can it shape you? How can you use it to fuel your next move?

THE POWER OF VULNERABILITY

There's strength in allowing yourself to be vulnerable with your pain. Talk to someone you trust. Write it out in a journal. Cry if you need to. Vulnerability isn't weakness; it's courage. It takes bravery to face your pain head-on and to admit that you're struggling. Yet in that vulnerability, you'll find connection, healing, and clarity.

FINAL THOUGHTS ON EMBRACING PAIN

Pain is a part of life, but it doesn't have to define you. When you embrace it, you take back control. You stop running, you stop avoiding, and you start growing. Every closed door comes with its own kind of pain, but it also comes with its own kind of promise—a promise that something greater is waiting on the other side. So the next time you're faced with a closed door, don't rush to move past it. Sit with the pain. Feel it fully. Learn from it. Then, when you're ready, use it as the foundation for your comeback because behind every moment of pain is the potential for growth, transformation, and a better version of you.

2. LET YOUR BROKEN DREAMS BIRTH BETTER ONES

When dreams shatter, it can feel like the end of the world. That failed business, the lost relationship, the opportunity that slipped through your fingers—it can be devastating—but here's a powerful truth … broken dreams aren't the end. They're the beginning of something better, something you couldn't have imagined while clinging to what you thought you needed.

Think about it—how many of the world's most transformative ideas and innovations came from the rubble of failure? Broken dreams are like seeds. When they fall apart, they plant themselves into the soil of your experience, growing into something stronger, something new.

THE BEAUTY IN BROKENNESS

There's a unique beauty in brokenness because it forces you to rebuild. When your original dream crumbles, you're left with two choices: you can either mourn what's lost, or you can use the broken pieces to construct something even greater. Let me tell you, the people who rise are the ones who choose the latter. Take, for example, the entrepreneur who loses everything in a failed startup. That loss doesn't have to be the final chapter. It can be the beginning of a more innovative business venture. Each mistake from the first attempt becomes a lesson, a building block for the next endeavor. Or think about a relationship that ends unexpectedly. It's easy to dwell on what went wrong, but what if that heartbreak is clearing the way for a partnership that aligns with your true values and aspirations? Sometimes, the love you lose teaches you exactly what you need to look for when love comes around again.

THE TRANSFORMATION PROCESS

When dreams break, they don't disappear—they transform. The key is allowing yourself to see the potential in the broken pieces. What can you salvage? What can you reimagine? What can you build anew?

Broken dreams often come with hidden lessons. They force you to ask tough questions:

- Was I chasing this dream for the right reasons?

- What did I learn from this experience that can guide me moving forward?

- How can I use this setback as a stepping stone to something greater?

These questions aren't easy, but they're necessary. They help you shift your perspective from one of loss to one of possibility.

BREAKING FREE FROM THE ORIGINAL PLAN

Sometimes, we hold so tightly to our original plan that we miss the better opportunities waiting for us. Broken dreams have a way of breaking us free from the constraints of our own expectations. Imagine someone who's been pursuing a specific career path for years, only to realize it's not fulfilling. Maybe they've poured time, money, and energy into climbing the corporate ladder, only to feel empty at the top. When that career collapses—whether through job loss, burnout, or a life change—it can feel like failure. Yet, in reality, it's an invitation to reevaluate, to pivot, and to pursue something that truly aligns with their purpose.

Broken dreams force you to ask, "What do I really want?" When you let go of the original plan, you create space for something better to emerge.

THE POWER OF RESILIENCE

The most successful people in life aren't the ones who never fail. They're the ones who bounce back from failure with determination and creativity. Broken dreams test your resilience, and in the process, they make you stronger. Think about a phoenix rising from the ashes. The fire may have consumed everything, but it also cleared the way for a new beginning. That's what resilience looks like. It's the ability to turn setbacks into setups for a comeback.

PRACTICAL STEPS TO REBUILD BETTER DREAMS

Here are some ways to let your broken dreams birth better ones:

1. **Reflect on the Lessons:** Take time to understand what went wrong and what you can learn from the experience. Maybe your business failed because you didn't understand your market, or your relationship ended because communication was lacking. Use these lessons as tools for growth.

2. **Reimagine Your Goals:** Broken dreams don't mean you have to abandon your aspirations altogether. Sometimes, they just need to be reimagined. If one path didn't work, think about other ways to achieve your goal.

3. **Take Action with Intention:** Start small. Take one step toward building something new. Whether it's writing down your next big idea, reaching out to a mentor, or learning a new skill, each step brings you closer to your next breakthrough.

4. **Surround Yourself with Support:** You don't have to rebuild alone. Seek out people who believe in you, who can encourage you and challenge you to see beyond your current circumstances.

5. **Embrace the Process:** Remember, rebuilding takes time. Don't rush it. Trust that each piece will fall into place as you continue to move forward.

EXAMPLES OF BROKEN DREAMS BECOMING BETTER ONES

- The artist who faced rejection after rejection, only to create a masterpiece inspired by their struggles.

- The athlete who was cut from the team and later discovered a talent for coaching and inspiring others.

- The student who failed out of their dream program, finding a different field that ignited their true passion.

CLOSING THOUGHTS ON BROKEN DREAMS

Letting your broken dreams birth better ones requires courage, vision, and the willingness to start again. Here's the beautiful truth: every shattered dream is a doorway to something greater. The very pieces that feel broken today can become the foundation for your next great success.

So, when life hands you a closed door, don't despair. Use it as an opportunity to reimagine, to rebuild, and to create a future that's even brighter than you ever dreamed possible. Sometimes, the dream that breaks is the dream that makes you.

The process may feel uncertain, even painful, but it is in this discomfort that transformation occurs. The beauty of broken dreams lies in their ability to force you to see beyond what is familiar and comfortable. They stretch your imagination, push your boundaries, and ignite creativity that might have otherwise stayed dormant. Think of the closed door as a canvas waiting for you to paint a new picture. It's a blank slate, inviting you to rewrite your story and reshape your vision for what's ahead. Every "no" carries within it the possibility of a better "yes." Every detour has the potential to lead you to a destination far greater than the one you originally planned.

The power of broken dreams is not just in what they take away but in what they give. They strip away illusions, distractions, and limitations, leaving room for authenticity, purpose, and growth. They teach you to trust the process, to persevere through challenges, and to find joy in the journey, even when the destination is unclear. So, let the pieces of your broken dream remind you of your resilience. Let them serve as evidence of your ability to withstand life's hardest blows and come out stronger. Let them inspire you to dream not just again, but bigger and bolder than before. Remember, every great success story began with a setback. Every remarkable achievement was born out of a challenge that seemed insurmountable at the time, and every person who has ever reached new heights started by looking up from the ground. You have what it takes to turn brokenness into brilliance, pain into purpose, and rejection into redirection. Let your closed doors become the advantage you never knew you needed, because the dream that breaks today might just be the dream that transforms your tomorrow.

CHAPTER 15

THE COMEBACK OF CLOSED DOORS

To do this chapter justice, I need to take my time with it, because this one is personal. I'm a living, breathing testament to what a comeback behind closed doors truly looks like. Actually, my life started with a comeback story in Hawaii. My very first breath was a miracle. Even now, I can't thank God enough for bringing me through and giving me a chance to be here, but I'll share more about that later in this chapter.

Comebacks aren't just parts of our stories ... they *are* the story. Every one of us has a comeback waiting to be written. There's something undeniably powerful about fighting for your life, your dreams, or your purpose when no one else is watching. The grit, the tears, and the relentless drive—they all happen behind closed doors—and when you emerge from that struggle, you're not just stronger ... you're unstoppable.

Picture Kobe Bryant when he dislocated his finger during a game. Everyone thought he was done, but instead of bowing out, he reset the injury right there on the court and jumped right back into the action, sinking his next shot (a 9-foot jumper) as if nothing happened. That moment captures the essence of a true comeback story: resetting what's broken, enduring the pain, and staying in the game.

Think about that—resetting what's broken. It's hard, it's raw, but it's necessary. Growth doesn't happen without pain, and transformation doesn't happen without discomfort. The willingness to face that discomfort is the foundation of every comeback. Take a moment to consider the storylines of the heroes we admire. When Black Panther was thrown off a cliff, he didn't give up. He came back, reclaimed his kingdom, and fulfilled his destiny. Superman steps into the phone booth not just to transform, but to rise above every setback. These iconic stories aren't just entertainment—they reflect our own lives. Every fall is an opportunity to rise.

Your own comeback story, even now, carries the same weight as the dreams you first dared to believe in. Don't give up on it. Don't give up on your assignment, your vision, or the fire burning inside you. Fighting for your purpose may require late nights, extra shifts, or moments of doubt, but let me assure you—it will all be worth it. When you truly value your time, you guard it like it's sacred. You don't allow distractions to bleed into the hours meant for building your legacy. Your comeback story is far too valuable to let temporary setbacks or unworthy priorities derail you. Time is your greatest resource. How you use it will determine the power of your comeback.

A true comeback is built on discipline, focus, and the courage to block out the noise. It's about managing time wisely, refusing to let setbacks define you, and resetting what's broken so you can rise again. This is your moment to take everything that tried to break you and use it to build something stronger. Trust me when I say: this is just the beginning of your comeback story, and the world hasn't seen anything like it.

This is the essence of the comeback behind closed doors: managing time wisely, staying focused, and refusing to let setbacks define you. It's about how you rise, how you change lives along the way, and how you bounce back like never before. For me, the real story of my comeback began in my mother's womb. I'll never forget the way she tells it—her voice always carrying both the fear and faith of that moment. She says the umbilical cord was wrapped tightly around my neck, cutting off my breath as I struggled to enter the world. My life began in a twist, in a literal chokehold, but here's the miracle—that chokehold became the very thing that set the stage for my comeback story. Somehow, by grace I can't fully comprehend, I wiggled and maneuvered my way free. My mother knew it was nothing short of divine intervention and a real miracle from God.

Isn't it interesting how life works? Sometimes it feels like circumstances are strangling the very breath out of us, but if we keep moving, keep pressing, we'll find a way through. That moment in the womb was just the beginning for me—a struggle, yes, but also a victory.

My mother wasn't even supposed to have me. Complications, doubts, and fears all pointed to the possibility that I wouldn't make it, but here I am. She calls me her "miracle baby," and every time I think about her words, I'm reminded of the power of grace in the midst of obstacles. Even when life feels like it's breaking apart, when uncertainty floods your path, there's still hope. That's when the comeback begins— not when it feels easy, but when something greater pulls you through.

From that first breath, my life has been a series of closed doors turned into comebacks. As the child of a military family, constant movement became my reality. From Hawaii to Japan and everywhere in between, I was always adjusting, adapting, and trying to fit in. Never having a place to truly call home left me feeling like I didn't belong. Each new state, and each new country brought its own challenges, but it also shaped me. Every transition became a lesson in resilience and adaptability.

Japan was another chapter, and it wasn't an easy one. As a young boy, I found myself in a Catholic school where I was the only African American student. My difference made me a target. I was bullied, teased, and often isolated—but looking back, I realize those painful moments were preparing me for something greater. Every cruel word, every sideways glance, every moment of brokenness was fuel. It wasn't comfortable, but it was necessary. The very people who thought they were breaking me were actually pushing me closer to my breakthrough.

It's funny how the battlefield of life starts in your mind. It's not about how many enemies you face—it's about how many victories you achieve. Each moment of pain, rejection, or hardship was planting seeds for a greater comeback. I didn't know it then, but I see it clearly now. The people who targeted me were giving me the ammunition I needed—indirectly fueling my growth, sharpening my focus, and building my strength.

So, what about you? Think of your own battles, your own struggles. What challenges have shaped your journey? Remember, the fight isn't over. Keep moving. Keep pushing. Every moment of resistance prepares you for a greater victory. Your comeback is closer than you think. When I think about those early days, I realize that life's chokeholds don't always mean defeat; sometimes, they're the very thing that forces you to find a new way forward, and every time you wiggle free, every time you rise again, you're writing a new chapter in your comeback story. So, if you're in the middle of your struggle, if life feels like it's got you in a chokehold, remember this: the fight isn't over. Keep moving. Keep pushing. You don't know it yet, but you're already making your way out. Your comeback is closer than you think.

THE COMEBACK OF FINANCIAL BREAKTHROUGH

A financial comeback isn't just about money it's about reclaiming your identity, your vision, and your power. The most powerful part of any comeback isn't the penthouse or the empire you'll one day build. It's the unfiltered moments, the nights when tears of frustration blur your vision, and the fire of determination that burns in your chest. It's the moment you decide to take your last resource, your last ounce of strength, and move forward.

THE LESSONS OF FINANCIAL COMEBACKS

1. RESOURCEFULNESS IN SCARCITY

Financial comebacks teach lessons no classroom ever could. When the world strips you bare, you discover resilience. When opportunities dry up, you learn to innovate, and when no one else believes in you … you learn to believe in yourself.

2. REJECTION AS REDIRECTION

The same "no" that knocks you down can propel you forward. Use every closed door as a reason to find your own entrance. Build something so undeniable that the people who overlooked you will one day knock on your door.

3. TEMPORARY PAIN, PERMANENT GROWTH

That car, that rejection, that pain—it's all temporary. However, the skills, the grit, and the vision you developed in those moments? … Those are permanent. Scarcity isn't the end of the story—it's the beginning of creativity and bold thinking.

YOUR NEXT MOVE

Now, think about what's ahead. That car is temporary. That rejection is temporary. Even the pain you're feeling now is temporary, but what you're building—the foundation of your empire—is permanent. One day, you'll look back and realize these moments of scarcity were your greatest teachers. When that day comes, you'll tell your story—the story of how you turned empty pockets into overflowing potential. The story of how you built something extraordinary from the ashes of loss. The story of how you became unstoppable, unshakable, and unbreakable.

So, take a deep breath. This is your moment. The world is waiting to see what you'll create next. Your comeback isn't just about reclaiming what you've lost—it's about discovering who you were always meant to be.

THE RESILIENCE THAT DEFINES YOU

Your comeback is more than a personal victory—it's a declaration of what's possible when courage and faith collide. It's proof that no setback, no loss, and no disappointment has the authority to define the rest of your life. Resilience is the invisible thread weaving your pain, perseverance, and purpose into a story that the world needs to see. Setbacks don't define your story; your response does. It's not the weight of your challenges that will shape your legacy—it's how you rise in spite of them. Each struggle, no matter how overwhelming, is quietly building a stronger, wiser, and more determined version of you. These challenges are the chisels, carving out a masterpiece that could only be revealed through fire and pressure.

Resilience isn't just about enduring the hardships—it's about transforming them. It's about looking at what tried to break you and choosing to build something unshakable in its place. It's the determination to see pain as the birthplace of growth and adversity as the soil where greatness takes root. Resilience allows you to take the bricks that life threw at you and use them to construct a fortress that no storm can destroy. Let's face it—life doesn't wait for perfect conditions. Resilience is about finding strength in the mess. It's the resolve to keep moving forward, even when the road is unclear and the weight feels unbearable. Every step forward, no matter how small, is an act of defiance against the voice of doubt. Each step proclaims, "I'm not done yet. My story is still unfolding."

Think about it: resilience is a declaration to yourself and the world that setbacks are not stop signs; they're stepping stones. It's not just about surviving the storm—it's about learning to dance in the rain. It's the decision to turn failure into fuel, obstacles into opportunities, and pain into purpose. Resilience isn't always loud. Sometimes, it's the quiet moments when you choose to rise again after falling, when you whisper to yourself, "One more step." It's in the tears you wipe away before facing the world again, in the strength it takes to show up even when you feel like giving up. These moments don't just prove your resilience—they define it.

Here's the beauty of resilience: it rewrites your story. It shifts the narrative from victim to victor, from broken to whole, from barely surviving to thriving. It transforms every wound into wisdom and every loss into leverage. It's not just a reaction—it's a strategy. It's the power to turn trials into triumphs and setbacks into setups for something greater—and with every step forward, you're not just surviving—you're rising. You're choosing to fight for a better tomorrow, even when today feels heavy. Resilience is the voice that says, "I will not let this moment defeat me. I will rise again." It's the fire inside you that refuses to be extinguished, the unshakable spirit that keeps going when the world says stop. So, when you think about resilience, remember this: it's not just about getting through—it's about coming out stronger, bolder, and better than before. Resilience doesn't just change your story—it transforms who you are—and every step you take, no matter how small, is proof that your story isn't over … it's just beginning.

THE BEAUTY IN THE STRUGGLE

There's an undeniable beauty in the struggle when you realize it's not a punishment but preparation. Struggles have a way of stripping away the unnecessary, forcing you to confront what truly matters. Every sleepless night, every tear that falls, and every moment of uncertainty is shaping you into someone stronger, wiser, and more resilient. These are not wasted moments; they are the furnace where your character is refined, your purpose is strengthened, and your faith is deepened. Struggles stretch you in ways comfort never could. They teach you to trust in your strength, lean into your faith, and push beyond limits you once thought were unbreakable. They demand that you dig deep, unearth hidden reserves of courage, and discover abilities you didn't know you had. The struggle isn't just something to endure—it's something to embrace. It's the process that prepares you for the breakthrough you've been praying for.

Take a moment to reflect on your current challenges. What lessons are hidden in the difficulties you're facing? What new skills are being forged in the fire of adversity? Perhaps you're learning patience when the answer doesn't come quickly, or resilience when life feels too heavy. Maybe you're discovering resourcefulness as you navigate limited resources, or courage as you take steps of faith into the unknown. These struggles are not just survival tools; they are the foundation of your breakthrough. Each challenge is a teacher, offering wisdom you couldn't gain any other way. Struggles sharpen your vision, clarify your priorities, and deepen your gratitude for what truly matters. They build the muscles of perseverance and strengthen the core of your character.

The beauty of the struggle is that it's not just shaping what you do—it's shaping who you are. It's preparing you for something greater than you could imagine. The weight you're carrying now is building the strength you'll need to rise to new heights. The tears you cry are watering the seeds of resilience and purpose within you, and while struggles may feel isolating, they connect you to a greater story. Every person who's achieved something extraordinary has faced struggles that tested their resolve. These challenges weren't the end of their story—they were the chapters that made their story worth telling. So, don't despise the struggle. See it for what it is: a gift wrapped in difficulty. It's the tool that chisels away what's holding you back and reveals the masterpiece within you. It's the journey that prepares you to walk boldly into your purpose.

Remember, the struggle is not permanent—but the strength it builds in you is. When you look back, you'll realize that these moments of hardship were not roadblocks—they were stepping stones, leading you toward the life you were created to live.

REWRITING YOUR NARRATIVE

Rewriting your story is a powerful act of ownership. It's not about how eloquently you can write it—it's about embracing your truth and using it to pave the way for your destiny. To rewrite your story means refusing to let circumstances define you and stepping into the role of the author of your life. It's about taking back control, turning pain into purpose, and shaping a narrative that propels you forward instead of holding you back.

For a long time, I was a victim of my own circumstances. Growing up, I tried to fit in everywhere, but deep down, I felt lost. I got tired of blending in, of being like everyone else. Even after joining the military—a place I believed had a purpose for me—I felt trapped. I felt like a machine, programmed to function, but not free to be myself. That's when I realized I needed to rewrite my story. I had to let go of the narrative that kept me stuck and create one that reflected my purpose, my authenticity, and my freedom.

Rewriting your story doesn't mean fabricating a new reality. It means reinterpreting your experiences in a way that empowers you. It means crafting a narrative compelling enough for you to believe in it, so it fuels you to take action and reach new levels of growth. Nobody knows your story like you do. Your story holds the keys to unlocking your future. Some of the most inspiring authors and leaders have achieved greatness because they had the courage to rewrite their life story, to tell the truth of what they've been through, and to embrace the lessons hidden in their pain.

That's why I welcome challenges. Challenges don't just test us—they shape us. Rewriting your story helps you appreciate the value of these challenges. It allows you to see the bigger picture instead of being consumed by the moment. When you're too close to the details, you can't see how everything comes together. It's like staring at a painting up close, unable to see the full image, but when you take a step back, suddenly the scattered dots become the sky, or the brushstrokes transform into a boat sailing across the ocean.

Life is like that. When you rewrite your narrative, you're stepping back to see how the pieces fit together. You start to recognize how far you've come and how much you've grown. Every challenge, every setback, every hardship becomes a brushstroke in the masterpiece of your story.

This chapter is about giving yourself permission to rewrite your narrative and take ownership of your journey. Your comeback is directly tied to how well you're able to do this. It's about shifting your mindset, embracing your truth, and letting go of the beliefs that limit you and keep you stuck.

So, take a step back. Look at your story with fresh eyes. See the moments that shaped you, the lessons that strengthened you, and the victories that brought you here. Your ability to rewrite your story will determine how far your comeback can take you. This isn't just about reflecting on the past—it's about creating the future you've always envisioned. The pen is in your hand, and the page is blank. Now is the time to write the next chapter.

THE RIPPLE EFFECT OF YOUR COMEBACK

Your comeback isn't just about you—it's a force of influence that ripples through the lives of those around you. What you overcome, how you rise, and how you persist in the face of adversity sends waves far beyond your personal circumstances. Whether you realize it or not, your journey is shaping, inspiring, and awakening something in the people quietly watching from the sidelines.

Every action you take to rise after a fall becomes a silent, yet powerful, message to others: "It's still possible." Your comeback story becomes a living testimony that no matter how hard life hits, there's always a way to stand back up. That's the ripple effect. It's powerful. It's real. It's happening every time you choose to keep going.

EVERY STEP YOU TAKE, SOMEONE NOTICES

Dragging yourself to the gym after months of feeling stuck might seem like a personal win, but there's someone in that same gym, silently watching. Maybe it's a beginner holding back, intimidated by the environment. When they see you showing up, struggling but pushing through, it plants a seed of hope: "If they can start again, so can I."

Going back to school at 45, juggling work, kids, and studies, seems like a personal achievement. But your children? They're absorbing every bit of that. They're learning firsthand that dreams don't have expiration dates. You're teaching them resilience, patience, and the power of lifelong learning without saying a word.

Rebuilding your business after failure isn't just about regaining financial stability—it's about proving that failure is neither fatal nor final. Your co-worker who feels trapped in their own setbacks watches you push forward, and suddenly, their own failures don't seem like dead ends—they seem like detours.

YOUR COMEBACK HAS FINGERPRINTS

Every comeback leaves fingerprints—imprints on the lives of others that you may never even meet.

- The colleague who notices your renewed energy and confidence begins to believe they can reinvent themselves too.

- The stranger who overhears your story in a coffee shop carries it with them, and it becomes the spark they needed to face their own fears.

- The family member who saw you broken now sees in you a powerful example of resilience. Your bounce-back becomes their blueprint.

That's the ripple effect. You may not realize how far your impact reaches, but trust me, it's moving through spaces and touching lives in ways you can't imagine.

A PERSONAL REFLECTION ON THE RIPPLE EFFECT

I experienced this firsthand. Just the other day at Planet Fitness, a man approached me out of nowhere and said, "I respect your consistency. I see you in here all the time, and it inspires me. Thank you." That moment humbled me. I wasn't working out for recognition. I was just staying committed to my own health journey. That's the beauty of it—you never know who's watching. You never know who's silently drawing strength from your effort, your discipline, and your refusal to quit. It made me think about all the times I felt invisible, wondering if anything I did even mattered, but that encounter reminded me that it all matters. Every small, consistent action matters. The ripple effect of my consistency was reaching someone, and it fueled them to show up for themselves.

YOUR STORY IS SOMEONE ELSE'S SURVIVAL GUIDE

When you rise, you create a pathway for others. Someone out there is struggling with something you've already overcome. Someone is waiting to see how you handle your setbacks to gain the courage to face their own.

Your comeback might be the exact evidence someone needs to believe they can overcome:

- That single parent who feels overwhelmed but watches you juggle work and family.

- That entrepreneur terrified to start again after failing once.

- That student who feels too behind to catch up.

YOUR VICTORY IS THEIR VISION

Your comeback is more than just a personal win—it's a beacon of possibility for others. It's a silent permission slip for others to dream bigger, fight harder, and rise stronger. So, when the journey feels too heavy, when you think no one understands or no one is paying attention, remember this: Your resilience creates ripples of courage in others. Keep pushing forward. Your story could be the reason someone else keeps fighting.

THE LEGACY OF YOUR COMEBACK

One day, you'll look back on this season of struggle and realize that your fight wasn't just for you; it was for every silent observer who needed to believe again. For every person who thought their story was over until they saw how you rewrote yours. That's the legacy of a comeback. It doesn't stop with you—it echoes. So, stand up. Keep moving. You're not just rising for yourself. You're rising for every life your story will touch.

THE MINDSET OF THE COMEBACK

There comes a pivotal moment in every comeback story when a decision must be made—a decision so firm, so unshakable, that it changes everything. This is the power of a made-up mind. It's a force stronger than circumstance, louder than doubt, and more powerful than any obstacle in your path. When you truly decide that you're going to rise, to reclaim what was lost, and to fight for what you deserve, the entire trajectory of your life shifts. It's no longer a question of *if* you'll succeed, but *how* you will make it happen.

A made-up mind doesn't wait for the perfect conditions. It doesn't need the bank account to be full, the circumstances to align, or the crowd to cheer. It starts when you say to yourself, "I'm doing this, and nothing is going to stop me." That's when the real comeback begins. It doesn't begin when life is easy or when opportunities are handed to you—it begins when you stand in the middle of your struggle and decide to move forward anyway.

This mindset is what separates those who talk about change from those who actually make it happen. When your mind is made up, obstacles transform into opportunities. Rejections are no longer setbacks; they become redirections to something better. Failure doesn't feel like the end; it becomes the foundation upon which you build something greater. Pain doesn't break you; it powers you forward. That's the incredible transformation that happens when you commit fully to your own success. A made-up mind doesn't waste time asking, "If I can do this?" It starts asking, "How will I do this?" It doesn't entertain the idea of maybe—it declares when. It doesn't see impossibility—it demands a way forward. That's the shift you must make in your thinking. Once you decide that you're going to rise, no bank account can define you, no rejection can stop you, no past can limit you, and no doubt can shake you. The most powerful part of this process isn't having the perfect plan. It's having the unwavering determination to move, even when the path is unclear. It's deciding to take the next step, even when you're unsure of where it will lead. Here's the truth: the most successful people didn't start with everything in place. They started with a made-up mind. They started in the middle of brokenness, confusion, and hardship, but they refused to let those things define them.

Transformation follows decision. When your mind is made up, something incredible happens—excuses begin to evaporate. The limitations you once believed in start to dissolve. Fear loses its grip, and purpose begins to rise. You don't wait for approval, validation, or permission. You simply move. You execute. You become. Look at yourself in the mirror and speak life over your situation. Declare, "My mind is made up. My decision is final. My comeback is inevitable. My victory is certain." Say it until you believe it. Say it until your actions align with it. Say it until you don't need anyone else to believe it because you already know it's true. That's how powerful a made-up mind is.

When your mind is made up, the mountains that once seemed insurmountable shrink to molehills. The walls that blocked your path turn into stepping stones. Delays are no longer disappointments but become moments of preparation. Setbacks are no longer defeats—they are setups for something greater. A made-up mind sees every challenge as an opportunity to rise, every failure as a lesson, and every obstacle as a chance to grow stronger.

This journey isn't just about getting through hard times; it's about creating a legacy. Every decision you make now is shaping the future not only for yourself but for those watching you. Your family, your friends, your community—they are all quietly watching how you navigate this season. Your fight, your resilience, your determination—it's all lighting the way for others. They may never say it out loud, but your comeback gives them permission to believe they can have one too. So, I need you to understand that this is not the time to break down. This is your time to break through. Nothing and no one can stop a person whose mind is made up. It's not just about this moment—it's about building something that lasts. This is not just about survival. This is about creating something so powerful, so unstoppable, that it becomes a monument to your determination and your destiny. Your comeback starts now. Your mind is made up. Your path forward is clear. Go after it with everything you've got.

When your mind is truly made up, you become unstoppable. It's not just a fleeting feeling or a burst of motivation that fades when things get tough. A made-up mind is a permanent shift—a deep, internal decision that no matter what happens, quitting is not an option. It's the moment when fear, doubt, and insecurity lose their power over you because you've already decided that success is your only outcome. You're not entertaining plan B because plan A is the only plan that matters. You've burned the ships, and now the only direction is forward. Let me tell you something real: life is going to test that decision. It's going to throw everything it has at you—delays, disappointments, distractions, and detours, but when your mind is made up, those obstacles become irrelevant. They don't disappear, but they lose their ability to stop you. That's the power of unwavering commitment. You stop negotiating with your goals. You stop making excuses. You stop waiting for perfect conditions. You act. You move. You execute.

Think about how many people talk themselves out of their own greatness. They start something, and when it gets hard, they quit. They blame the economy, their upbringing, their circumstances, or other people for why they can't move forward; but here's the truth—none of that matters when your mind is made up. You can come from nothing and still rise. You can have every reason to quit and still win, because success isn't about circumstances—it's about decisions. This is where resilience is born. A made-up mind builds endurance. It teaches you how to keep going when the progress is slow and the results aren't visible yet. It helps you push through sleepless nights, long hours, and silent sacrifices. It makes you realize that discomfort is temporary, but quitting lasts forever. The pain of discipline is nothing compared to the pain of regret. Once your mind is made up, regret is not an option.

Let's talk about the pain of starting over. Maybe you've lost it all. Maybe you're standing in the ruins of what used to be your business, your marriage, your career, or your dreams. Let me tell you this: starting over with experience is more powerful than starting for the first time. Now, you know what to avoid. You know what doesn't work. You've gained scars that have turned into wisdom, and when you combine that wisdom with a made-up mind, you are unstoppable. Don't fear starting over—fear staying stuck. Fear living a life where you know you could've done more, but didn't. Fear waking up one day realizing you let doubt talk you out of your destiny. A made-up mind doesn't dwell on the past—it's laser-focused on the future. It sees beyond current struggles and envisions the outcome. That vision becomes the fuel for every action you take.

Let me make this personal: I've lived through seasons where giving up seemed like the easiest option. Where it felt like everything I built was crumbling. Where support was scarce, and the pressure was overwhelming, but every single time, it was my decision to keep going that made the difference—not my resources, not my connections, not even my talent. Just the simple, stubborn decision that I wasn't going to let my story end in defeat. That's what you need right now—a made-up mind—not a half-hearted attempt—not a "Maybe if it works, I'll keep going." No.

A full, complete, no-turning-back decision. You have to decide that you're going to win—that you're going to rebuild—that you're going to create a future that honors everything you've been through. You owe it to yourself. You owe it to everyone who's silently watching you, hoping to find the courage in their own fight because of how you handle yours. Now, imagine the ripple effect of your made-up mind. Imagine how many lives you'll impact when you refuse to quit. Imagine your children seeing you rise after falling and learning that setbacks don't define them. Imagine strangers watching your journey from afar and finding the courage to fight their own battles. Your decision today has the power to inspire generations. That's the legacy of a made-up mind. So here's your challenge: Stop waiting. Stop hesitating. Stop doubting. Make up your mind right now that you are going to rise. You are going to fight. You are going to win. Once that decision is made, let no *thing* and no *one* deter you from it—not fear—not failure—not setbacks. You've already decided, and that's enough. Now move. Move with purpose. Move with clarity. Move with power. Once your mind is made up, nothing can stop you. This is your moment. Own it.

STRATEGIES FOR UNSTOPPABLE COMEBACKS

As we close out this chapter, it's important to recognize that an unstoppable comeback isn't a spontaneous event—it's a strategic, intentional process. The power of a comeback is rooted in how well you prepare, how well you execute, and how well you sustain momentum. The strategies I'm about to share aren't theoretical—they are real, practical, and designed to help you rise stronger, faster, and wiser than ever before.

THE PSYCHOLOGY OF AN UNSTOPPABLE COMEBACK

The first pillar of any great comeback is understanding the psychology behind it. Too many people equate setbacks with failure, but that's a dangerous mindset. Setbacks are not failures; they are data points. Let me say that again: setbacks are not failures, they are data points. They give you critical information about what went wrong, what needs to be corrected, and how you can pivot for success.

Consider Michael Jordan. When he was cut from his high school basketball team, he didn't decide he wasn't good enough. He used it as fuel. That moment wasn't a final verdict; it was feedback. The key is shifting from a fixed mindset—which says, "I failed"—to a growth mindset—which says, "I learned." That psychological shift is the foundation for every comeback.

PILLAR 1: RADICAL SELF-ASSESSMENT

Before you can rise, you need to confront where you are. This isn't about self-criticism; it's about gaining clarity. Radical self-assessment is about asking hard but necessary questions:

- **What specifically went wrong?** Break down the exact reasons for the setback. Be brutally honest.

- **Which factors were within my control?** Identify what was truly in your hands and what wasn't.

- **What patterns or behaviors contributed to this?** Recognize if certain habits or mindsets played a role.

- **What resources or strengths do I still have?** Don't focus on what you lost—focus on what you have left.

PILLAR 2: STRATEGIC RECONSTRUCTION

Now that you've gathered your intelligence, it's time to rebuild. This isn't about rushing to the next thing—it's about building smart and strong. Strategic reconstruction has two key components:

1. **Establish Your Non-Negotiables**

   Non-negotiables are the core habits and standards that you will not compromise on. For an injured athlete, it could be prioritizing sleep, nutrition, and physical therapy. For an entrepreneur, it could be daily learning, consistent networking, and refining your business model. These are your foundations.

2. **Create Incremental Milestones**

   Your comeback won't happen overnight. Break your goal into smaller, measurable steps. Every small victory compounds into momentum. These milestones are not just checkpoints—they are confidence builders.

PILLAR 3: THE PHOENIX PROTOCOL

This is the framework for transforming failure into your most powerful comeback. I call it the Phoenix Protocol because, like the mythical bird, you're going to rise from the ashes, stronger than before. This protocol unfolds in three distinct phases:

1. **Phase One: Recalibration**

   Accept your new reality without getting stuck in the past. Redirect your energy from "Why me?" to "What's next?" This phase is all about clarity. Recognize the hidden opportunities in your setback. There's always something to gain if you're willing to look for it.

2. **Phase Two: Reinvention**

   Use this setback as a chance to evolve. What wasn't working before? What systems, habits, or mindsets need to be discarded?
   Reinvent your approach. Learn new skills. Build new habits.
   Become the kind of person who is built to last, not just one who
   achieves a single victory.

3. **Phase Three: Resurgence**

   This is where you execute with discipline and consistency.
   Celebrate every small victory to keep your momentum alive.
   Document your progress, not just for yourself but to inspire
   others. Every step forward is proof that you are rising.

REAL-WORLD SUCCESS STORIES OF STRATEGIC COMEBACKS

Howard Schultz, the man behind Starbucks, was rejected by over 200
investors before someone believed in his vision for a coffee shop experience. Had he quit, the global brand we know today wouldn't exist. His
comeback wasn't about luck—it was about learning from every "no" and
refining his approach.

J.K. Rowling was a single mother living on welfare when her manuscript for Harry Potter was rejected by 12 publishers, but she didn't let
rejection define her. She used every rejection as a lesson, and today, her
books have sold over 500 million copies.

These aren't fairy tales—they're blueprints. Their success was en-
gineered through strategic comebacks, built on resilience, reinvention,
and relentless execution.

THE POWER OF MOMENTUM

Here's the truth: once you build momentum, it becomes a force of its own. Momentum isn't handed to you—it's created. It starts with the small wins. It's waking up earlier than you want to. It's making that uncomfortable call. It's showing up when no one's clapping for you. Each step forward builds the momentum that will eventually carry you to your breakthrough.

Momentum is fragile in the beginning, but once it builds, it becomes unstoppable. The hardest part is starting, but once you make that first move, the rest begins to align.

CLOSING CHALLENGE

Now it's time to turn strategy into action. Ask yourself:

- Where am I right now, and what caused this setback?

- What non-negotiable habits will I commit to today?

- What small, achievable milestone can I hit this week?

- How will I use my pain as fuel to rise?

It's not enough to read this and feel inspired. You need to move. The world doesn't wait for you to feel ready. It rewards action.

Let me leave you with this: Your comeback isn't waiting on better conditions. It's waiting on a better commitment. The moment you decide to fully commit, everything will begin to shift.

FINAL WORDS

As I wrap up with these final words, I want you to truly understand the weight of this moment. You are standing at the crossroads of your legacy—not just another chapter, not just another page—but the defining moment where everything you've endured, every setback, every heartbreak, every failure, becomes the foundation for your greatest victory. Behind you are the closed doors, the disappointments, the losses. Ahead of you stretches an infinite canvas, wide open, waiting for you to paint a masterpiece that only you can create.

Every legendary comeback started exactly where you are right now. That's the raw truth. I know because I've been there. I was standing in the very same place, staring down the path of giving up or pushing forward. I could've chosen to stay in the mud, to wallow in the weight of what life threw at me, but I didn't. I made a decision—a decision to fight, to rise, to own my comeback. And now, I'm challenging you to do the same. Think about everything that's tried to take you out, every moment that nearly broke you. Now, imagine flipping all of that pain, all of that loss, into power. You're about to witness the greatest version of yourself. You're about to step into opportunities that seemed impossible. You're about to breathe life into dreams that once felt dead.

Consider this: Walt Disney was fired from a newspaper for "lack of imagination." The same man went on to build an empire of imagination—an entire world where dreams come alive. I remember walking through Tokyo Disneyland, amazed that this experience, this magic, wasn't limited to one place. Walt's vision crossed oceans. His setback didn't define him—it refined him.

Think about Nelson Mandela. Locked away in prison for 27 years, yet he emerged with more power, more purpose, and more influence than ever before. His comeback wasn't just personal—it was global. His struggle gave birth to a movement that changed history.

Look at Apple. On the brink of bankruptcy, nearly forgotten, until it reinvented itself and revolutionized technology. Apple didn't just re-cover—it redefined innovation.

These comebacks weren't fueled by luck or perfect conditions. They were driven by one thing: the audacity to believe that a setback is not the end—it's a launchpad. Let me tell you this loud and clear: your setback is your setup for a stronger, smarter, and more resilient you.

You might be in a season right now where everything feels un-certain. Maybe your finances are wrecked. Maybe your relationships are strained. Maybe you've lost your sense of direction—but here's the truth—you still have what it takes. You still have the courage to move forward. You still have breath in your body, and as long as you're breath-ing, your story isn't over.

This isn't wishful thinking or empty motivation. This is the raw power of human resilience. Every great comeback was built by someone who simply refused to stay down. Someone who understood that even the smallest step forward breaks the gravity of defeat.

So, take that step. Send that email. Make that phone call. Write that first page. Apply for that job. Take that class. It may seem small now, but it's the spark that will ignite your transformation.

Let me be clear—this isn't about rebuilding the life you lost. This is about creating something new, something stronger, something more aligned with who you are meant to be. You're not here to patch up old dreams. You're here to design a life that's bolder, wiser, and more resilient.

Your comeback won't just affect you. It will ripple through the lives of others. When you rise, you become living proof that it's possible. Someone is watching your journey right now, silently hoping to find the strength to fight their own battles. You are the evidence they need that it can be done. The greatest truth about comebacks is this: they are born not from special talent, privilege, or luck—but from a decision. A decision to keep moving forward when everything in you wants to quit.

As you take that first step, I want you to remember something critical—this journey won't be easy. Comebacks never are. There will be moments when doubt screams louder than your dreams. Times when the weight feels unbearable, and you'll question if it's even worth it. Let me reassure you—it is. The pain you've endured, the losses you've suffered, the heartbreak you've carried—they weren't meaningless. They were the fire refining you, shaping you, strengthening you for what's coming next. Your pain has a purpose. Your scars are proof that you survived battles others never knew you were fighting, and those same scars will one day be someone else's roadmap to healing.

Here's the part most people miss: Your comeback requires consistency. Not perfection, not endless motivation—just consistent, intentional action. You don't have to sprint. You don't have to conquer the mountain in a day. You just have to keep moving—inch by inch, day by day. Some mornings, all you might manage is getting out of bed and facing the world … and that's okay. Other days, you'll feel unstoppable, ready to take bold steps toward your dreams. Both days matter. Both days count. Because every step forward, no matter how small, is progress.

Think of a seed buried in the ground. It doesn't sprout overnight. It battles through layers of dirt, through darkness, through the weight of the earth. It keeps growing, silently and steadily, until it breaks through and reaches the sun. That's you. You are breaking through, even when no one sees it yet. Your story isn't over, because you're still writing it. Now, let me tell you—the next chapter will be your most powerful one yet. One day, you'll look back on this moment and realize it was the turning point. The day you decided to rise. The day you stopped waiting for permission and started moving with purpose. The day you owned your story, your pain, your progress, and said, "This is mine … and I'm not done yet."

The world hasn't seen the best of you yet. Your family hasn't seen the strongest version of you. Your friends haven't witnessed the most determined version of you; and here's the truth—you haven't even met the most unstoppable version of yourself. That version of you is still in the making, forged through the fires of setbacks, refined through trials, and strengthened with every step you've taken forward, no matter how small. It's waiting for you to embrace the possibility of transformation, to claim the future that is already being prepared for you. Think about this for a moment: every closed door you've faced wasn't meant to *confine* you, but to *refine* you. Every rejection wasn't meant to discourage you but to redirect you. Every obstacle wasn't meant to stop you but to prepare you for the path that's uniquely yours. Let this truth settle deep in your spirit: Your best days are not behind you—they are still ahead of you. The world hasn't even begun to scratch the surface of what you are capable of becoming.

Now, let me leave you with this: refuse to quit. Refuse to settle for less than you deserve. Refuse to be defined by failure or bound by fear. No matter how difficult the path has been, no matter how steep the climb looks right now, you have more inside of you than you realize. Strength, resilience, courage, vision—it's all there, waiting for you to tap into it. Stand tall in the face of every closed door, every setback, and every doubt. When people count you out, let them watch you prove them wrong. Turn every "no" into a new opportunity. Turn every obstacle into a stepping stone. Turn every loss into a lesson that sharpens your edge and propels you forward. Let the very things that tried to break you become the foundation on which you build the rest of your life.

Your comeback is personal. No one else can do it for you, and no one else can understand the depths of what you've endured. Your comeback is powerful. It carries with it the strength of everything you've survived and the wisdom of everything you've learned. Most importantly, your comeback is necessary—not just for you, but for everyone watching you—those who need your story to ignite their own hope. Every victory you achieve, no matter how small, creates ripples that inspire others to rise up and fight for their own dreams. This moment, right now, is where you decide. This isn't just a story you're reading—it's a blueprint for the life you're about to create. It's the fuel for the transformation that's already in motion. This is your turning point. This is your chance to declare that you're not going to stop, no matter how hard the journey gets. You are going to rise. You are going to become everything you were meant to be.

Yes, the road ahead may still be difficult. You may still face moments of doubt, fear, and uncertainty, but here's what makes the difference: when your mind is made up, no obstacle can hold you back. When your spirit is unshakable, no setback can stop your progress. When your heart is committed, no failure can define your future. This is the moment where you stop asking, "What if I fail?" and start asking, "What if I succeed?" This is the moment where you stop waiting for conditions to be perfect and start creating your own opportunity.

Picture yourself at the crossroads of your legacy. Behind you is everything you've survived—the setbacks, the disappointments, the heartbreaks, the missed chances. Ahead of you is a blank canvas, a wide-open horizon waiting for you to paint the masterpiece of your life. You get to decide what happens next. You get to decide how this story ends.

Every legendary comeback started with the same ingredients you have right now: courage, determination, and a made-up mind. Walt Disney was fired for a "lack of imagination," but he went on to create magic that has inspired generations. Nelson Mandela spent 27 years in prison yet emerged to lead a nation into freedom. Apple was on the brink of bankruptcy before Steve Jobs returned and turned it into one of the most innovative companies in the world. These aren't just stories—they're proof that comebacks don't happen by chance. They happen by choice.

So, make the choice today. Decide that you won't be defined by what's behind you. Decide that you will take bold, intentional steps toward the future that's waiting for you. Decide that your setbacks are not the end of the story—they're just the beginning of your greatest chapter.

Take action. Send that email. Make that phone call. Write that plan. Take that first step, even if it feels small. What may seem insignificant now is actually the spark that will ignite the fire of your transformation. Success doesn't come all at once—it comes through consistent, intentional action. Every step forward is progress. Every moment of persistence is proof that you're not just surviving—you're thriving.

Here's the truth: This isn't just about achieving goals or reaching milestones. This is about becoming the person you were created to be. It's about discovering your resilience, unlocking your potential, and walking into your destiny with confidence and purpose. Your comeback isn't just about getting back to where you were—it's about breaking through to a whole new level.

So, go! Rise. Become. The world is waiting to see the best of you. Your family is waiting to see the strongest version of you. Your friends are waiting to see the most determined version of you. Best of all, you are about to meet the most unstoppable version of yourself. This is your time. This is your comeback … and it's going to be extraordinary.

www.ingramcontent.com/pod-product-compliance
Lightning Source LLC
Chambersburg PA
CBHW021657120626
46545CB00004B/1273